The

Perkin Warbeck Conspiracy 1491–1499

IAN ARTHURSON

SUTTON PUBLISHING

To Vicky – 'Oh it must be
rain on a night like this'

First published in the United Kingdom in 1994 by Alan Sutton Publishing Ltd, an imprint of
Sutton Publishing Limited · Phoenix Mill · Thrupp · Stroud · Gloucestershire · GL5 2BU

First published in this edition in 1997 by Sutton Publishing Limited.

British Library Cataloguing in Publication Data is available for this title.

ISBN 0-7509-1610-9

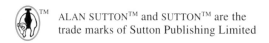
ALAN SUTTON™ and SUTTON™ are the
trade marks of Sutton Publishing Limited

Typeset in 9/10 Times.
Typesetting and origination by
Sutton Publishing Limited.
Printed in Great Britain by
WBC Limited, Bridgend.

Contents

List of Illustrations

Picture research by Vicky Arthurson and Amanda Davidge.

ACKNOWLEDGEMENTS

Thanks are due to the following for kind permission to reproduce illustrations: Archives Generals du Royaume (No. 29); Belgian Tourist Office (Nos 7, 8, 11, 51); the Board of Trustees of the Royal Armouries (Nos 41, 42); the British Library (Nos 15, 25, 35, 38, 44); Crown Copyright, Reproduced by Permission of the Controller of Her Majesty's Stationery Office (Nos 23, 26, 40); D.H. Davison (Nos 28, 43); Germanisches Nationalmuseum (No. 13); Giraudon (Nos 1, 37); Graphische Sammlung Albertina, Vienna (Nos 10, 21); Greater London Photographic Library (No. 3); Irish Tourist Board (No. 36); Kunsthistorisches Museum, Vienna (No. 27); Lauros-Giraudon (Nos 2, 16); the Mansell Collection (Nos 12, 19, 22, 24, 31, 34, 47); Mary Evans Picture Library (No. 20); Mechelen Archives (No. 18); National Gallery of Ireland (No. 6); Royal Collection. St. James's Palace. © HER MAJESTY THE QUEEN (No. 33); Royal Institution of Cornwall (No. 45); Scala (Nos 9, 49, 52) Society of Antiquaries of London (No. 17); Somerset Archaeological and Natural History Society (No. 46); Roger-Viollet (No. 4); Waterford Corporation (No. 14); Geoffrey Wheeler (Nos 39, 50).

    Thanks also to W.C. Sellar and R.J. Yeatman, and to the publisher, for permission to reproduce the extract on p. vii from *1066 and All That* (Methuen, 1930); to Mr and Mrs Harry Spiro of New York for permission to quote from their Manuscript Signet Letter of Henry VII, 16 September 1497; and to the Corporation of London for permission to reproduce Perkin Warbeck's Confession on pp. xi–xii.

Preface

In the summer of 1987 I was at a conference at Winchester. Going upstairs one afternoon I was suddenly aware of a conversation above me. A well-known historian was shaking with laughter and chortling, 'A book on Lambert Simnel! What next? One on Perkin Warbeck?' Too embarrassed to say anything I turned onto the corridor for my room. Every Monday during my PhD research I had put off the responsibility of a new week's research by working on the Warbeck problem, and I harboured the notion that there was an interesting story to be told. Nevertheless the conversation at Winchester is probably typical of attitudes to Warbeck. To most historians, as indeed to anyone who has heard of him, 'Perkin Warbeck is a bit of a joke.' The best joke about Warbeck is chapter 30 of *1066 and All That*, entitled 'Lambert Simnel and Perkin Warbeck'. Here it is in its entirety.

English History has always been subject to Waves of Pretenders. These have usually come in small waves of about two – an Old Pretender and a Young Pretender, their object being to sow dissension in the realm, and if possible to confuse the Royal issue by pretending to be heirs to the throne.

Two Pretenders who now arose were Lambert Simnel and Perkin Warbeck, and they succeeded in confusing the issue absolutely by being so similar that some historians suggest they were really the same person (i.e. the Earl of Warbeck).

Lambert Simnel (the Young Pretender) was really (probably) himself, but cleverly pretended to be the Earl of Warbeck. Henry VII therefore ordered him to be led through the streets of London to prove that he really was.

Perkin Warbeck (the Older and more confusing Pretender) insisted that he was himself, thus causing complete dissension till Henry VII had him led through the streets of London to prove that he was really Lambert Simnel.

The punishment of these memorable Pretenders was justly similar, since Perkin Warmnel was compelled to become a blot on the King's skitchen, while Perbeck was made an escullion. Wimneck, however, subsequently began pretending again. This time he pretended that he had been smothered in early youth and buried under a stair-rod while pretending to be one of the Little Princes in the Tower. In order to prove that he had not been murdered before, Henry was reluctantly compelled to have him really executed.

Even after his execution many people believed that he was only pretending to have been beheaded, while others declared that it was not Warmneck at all but Lamkin, and Permnel had been dead all the time really, like Queen Anne.[1]

1066 was published in 1930. Within five years G.W. had made the obvious connection, in *Notes and Queries* (1935). In an article called 'Richard, Duke of York, and Perkin Warbeck' he made a suggestion, for consideration by those who are interested in the matter; viz., Let us assume for the sake of argument that the 'strange youth' who appeared in Ireland and impersonated York's first cousin, Edward Earl of Warwick, was none other than Richard, Duke of York himself. Made prisoner on the field of Stoke, he was passed off as 'Lambert Simnel,' and became a scullion in the royal kitchen. By some means the scullion was exchanged for Perkin Warbeck, who thus took Simnel's place, and in due course became the King's falconer. It was this falconer, her son, who dictated to York the text of the letter written to Catherine Warbeck in October 1497, and attached his signature to it. He was 'the menial servant' who had persuaded the fugitive to come in from Beaulieu trusting in the King's mercy.

Extraordinary as the above suggestion may appear to be . . . [2]

Reading the article, it is difficult to know if it is derived directly from *1066* or if it is not a forerunner of the Penket Papers.[3] Alas G.W. was in earnest. He worked, nonetheless, in a tradition which flourishes. Historians still try to find in the events of 1487 the germ, if not the actual person, of the Perkin Warbeck conspiracy.[4] Working on Warbeck, or merely reading the chronicle sources it becomes quickly and sharply clear that in the 1490s no one in Henry VII's government considered his career amusing. He was, we know, the butt of many jokes, but the punishments meted out in 1495 alone clarify conclusively the threat he represented to Henry VII, whether we think this threat was real or the product of Henry's imagination.[5]

Two years after Winchester, in 1989, Tony Pollard introduced me to Alan Sutton. I agreed then to write a book on Warbeck. This, the resulting volume, has taken longer to finish than I anticipated when I first agreed to write it due to the usual commitments of life and work. I owe a great debt of gratitude to Tony and Alan for asking me to undertake this venture, thus extending my knowledge of things fifteenth century. Subsequently Jaqueline Mitchell must be thanked for the way she did her job of prising a manuscript from an unwilling author, the fate of all editors. Given the international nature of the Warbeck problem, I have to thank the Richard III and Yorkist History Trust who were kind enough to make me a grant to visit to the Archives Départementales du Nord, at Lille. In Lille I met Isabelle and Willy Maufroy. Willy is now archivist of Valenciennes. He has been unfailing in his help over Warbeck, which extended, at Easter 1992, to driving my wife and myself to Tournai. He also unearthed the strangest manifestation of the Warbeck phenomenon that I know: *Récits Historiques*, cautionary tales for children, by Mlle Carpentier, in which one Perkins (*sic*) Warbeck figures.[6] Latterly I have incurred a debt also to Janet Moore, a colleague at Nottingham High School for Girls whose proficiency in Latin has been a saving grace to my lack.

Beyond these practical debts there are three more. The first is to Margaret Condon. Over many years we have talked about Henry Tudor. I have always benefited from her immense knowledge of the reign, her knowledge of the Public Record Office, her tact, and her sense of humour. The second is to Cliff Davies who was kind enough to offer me hospitality at Wadham College just before Christmas 1992. Over the last few years we have developed a mutual interest in certain of the odder manifestations of fifteenth-century politics and I have benefited greatly from my conversations with him. Finally it is only right to thank Professor Michael Jones of Nottingham University. Michael has responded without stint to my uninformed questions about the social history of fifteenth-century France, and on occasion has lent me books on Brittany and France difficult to obtain elsewhere with ease.

There remains the greatest debt of all: to my wife who has sustained me over a testing period of writing. More than this: she has transcribed my handwritten first draft, at times almost impenetrable and indecipherable, and has talked over every aspect of Warbeck's career with me, many more times than I remember. There is little in this book which would be there if not for her.

Genealogical Table 1: The House of York

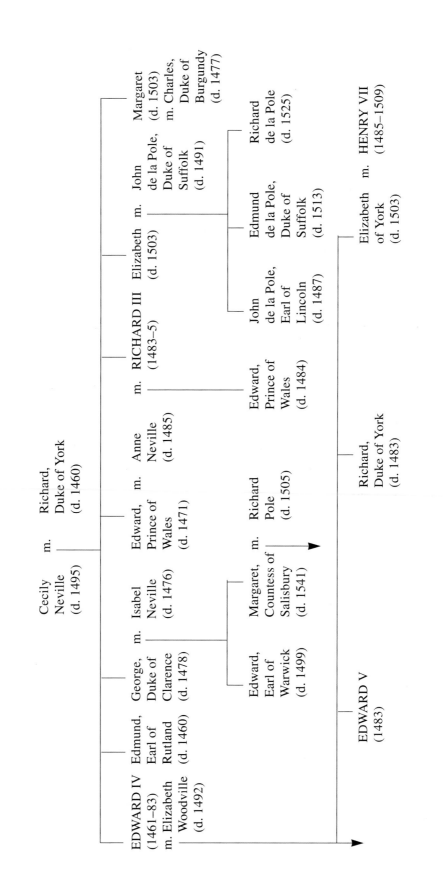

Genealogical Table 2: The Werbecques of Tournai

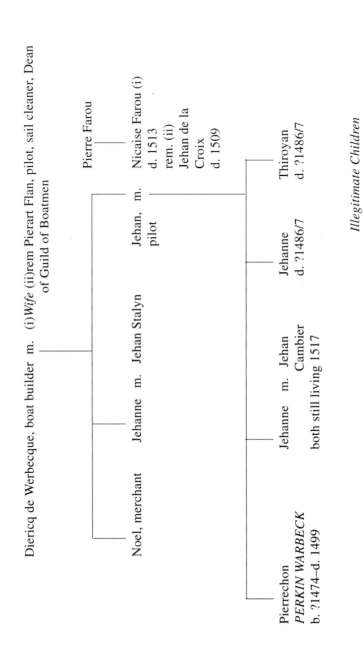

Diericq de Werbecque, boat builder m.   (i) *Wife* (ii)rem Pierart Flan, pilot, sail cleaner, Dean
                                                           of Guild of Boatmen

Pierre Farou

Noel, merchant   Jehanne m. Jehan Stalyn   Jehan, m.   Nicaise Farou (i)
                                                       pilot   d. 1513
                                                                      rem. (ii)
                                                                      Jehan de la
                                                                      Croix
                                                                      d. 1509

Pierrechon   Jehanne m. Jehan   Jehanne   Thiroyan
PERKIN WARBECK   Cambier   d. ?1486/7   d. ?1486/7
b. ?1474–d. 1499   both still living 1517

Illegitimate Children
Nicolas (dim. Colin) and
Innocent
both still living 1513

Perkin Warbeck's Confession

Perkin Warbeck as Richard, Duke of York

Fyrst is to be knowyn that I was born In the toun of Turney In Flaundyrs and my ffadyrs name is callid John Osbek, which said John Osbek was countroller of the said toun of Turnay, and my modyrs name is katharyn de Faro, and oon of my grauntsyris upon my ffadyrs side was namyd deryk Osbek which died, afftir whoos deth my Graunt modyr was maried unto the withynnamyd petyr Flamme that was Receyvour of the fforenamyd toun of Turnay & dean of the botemen that Row upon the watyr, or Ryver of leyscow, and my grantsyre upon my modir side was callid petir de Faro, The which had In his kepyng the keyes of the Gate of Seynt Johnis withyn the same town of Turnay, Alsoo I had an uncle namid mastir John Stalyn dwellyng In the parysh of seynt Pyas withyn the same toun, which had maried my ffadyrs systyr whoos name was Johan or Jane with whom I dwellid a certayn season, and afftirward I was lad by my modyr to andwarp for to lern Flemysh In an howse of a cousyn of myne & officer of the said toun callid John Styenbek with whom I was the space of half a yere, and aftir that I Retournyd agayn unto Turnay by Reason of the warris that were In Flaundyrs, And withyn a yere ffoluyng I was sent with a marchaunt of the said toun of Turney namyd Berlo & his mastyrs name Alexandyr to the mart of andwerp where as I fill syke, which sykenes contynuyd upon me v monythis, and the said Berlo sett me to bourd In a skynners hows that dwellid beside the hows of the Inglysh nacion, and by hym I was from thens caried to Barow mart & lodgid at the sign of the old man where I abode the space of ij monethis, and afftir thys the said Berlo sett me wyth a marchaunt In middylbourgth to service for to lern the langage whoos name was John Strewe with whom I dwellid from Crystemesse to Estyr, and then I went Into portyngale In the company of sir Edward Bramptonys wyfe In a shypp which was callid the Quenys Shypp And when I was comyn thidyr I was put In service to a knygth that dwellid In lushborn which was callid petyr Vacz de Cogna with whom I dwellid an hool yere, which said knygth had but oon Iye, and then becawse I desirid to see other Cuntrees I took lycence of hym, and then I put my sylf In servyce with a breton callid pregent meno, the which brought me with hym Into Irland, And when we were there arryvyd In the toun of Cork, They of the toun because I was ariad with soom clothis of sylk of my said mastyrs cam unto me and threpid upon me that I shuld be the duke of Clarence sone that was beffore tyme at develyn, and ffor as mwch as I denyed It, There was browgth unto me the holy Evangelyst & the Crosse by the mayer of the toun which was callid John le wellyn and there In the presence of hym & othyr I took myne oth as the trowth was that I was not the foresiad dukis sone nothir of noon of his blood, And afftyr this cam unto me an Inglish man whoos name was Sthephan poytron with oon John watir & said to me In sweryng grete othis that they knewe well I was kyng Richardis bastard sone, To whom I answerd with lyke othis that I was nott, and then they advysid me (not) to be afferd but that I shuld take It upon me boldly, and If I wold soo do they wold ayde & assyst me with all theyr powar agayn the kyng of Engeland, and not oonly they, But they were assuryd well that therlis of desmund & kyldare shuld do the same, ffor they forsid not what party they took soo that they mygth be Revengid upon the kyng of Engeland, And soo agayn my wyll made me lern Inglysh & tawgth me what I shuld doo & saye, and afftir this they callid me duke of york the secund sone of kyng Edward the iiijth, because kyng Richardis bastard sone was In the handis of the kyng of Engeland, And upon this the said John watyr, stephan poytron, John Tyler, hubert Burgth with many othir as the fforesaid Erlys, entrid Into this fals quarell, and withyn short tyme afftyr the Frensh kyng sent unto me an ambassade Into Ireland whoos namis was loyte lucas & mastir Stephan Fryon to advertize me to come Into Fraunce, and thens I went Into Fraunce, and from thens into Flaundirs, & ffrom Flaundyrs Into Ireland, & from Ireland Into Scotland, and soo Into Engeland.

from, *The Great Chronicle of London*,
ed. A.H. Thomas and I.D. Thornley (London, 1938)

Part One: To Cork

ONE

The Beginning and the End of the Problem

In December 1499 the curious traveller crossing London Bridge on his way to Kent could have seen displayed on poles the heads of two recently executed traitors. One only had been born a king's subject, John Atwater of Cork. The other was a subject by adoption, Perkin Warbeck, born in Tournai, originally a subject of the Duke of Burgundy. Their execution at Tyburn Tree had been watched by a huge crowd of people drawn by the fascination of Warbeck; to hear him rehearse once again that litany of his life: who he was, who his ancestors were, what places they had lived in, what masters he had served and that he, a Tournaisian, had called himself Richard, Duke of York, second son of Edward IV, only when forced to by John Atwater, sometime Mayor of Cork. Then, and not for the first time, he asked forgiveness of the King, and of anyone else he had offended. His confession and obligatory ritual obeisances to the Crown finished, he was hanged first and then came Atwater's turn.[1]

The chance meeting of these two was described by Warbeck in his confession; copies of which had circulated in every city in England, and every court in Europe, over the previous two years. Warbeck described how he and his master, a Breton merchant called Pregent Meno, had arrived in Cork. There Meno obliged Warbeck to wear some silks he was peddling. Instantly the men of Cork recognized him for who he was, Edward, Earl of Warwick, the Duke of Clarence's son, who they recognized because they had seen him in Dublin. Perkin vehemently denied all this and called for a crucifix and Gospel to swear an oath of denial. All this was witnessed by the Mayor of Cork, John Lewellen by name, and Warbeck swore not only that he was not the duke's son but that he was no blood relative either. However his trials were not over. He was approached by two Englishmen, of whom Atwater was one, who swore equally convincing oaths that he was in fact the bastard son of Richard III, John de Pontefract. Warbeck again countered with sincere oaths that he was not this person. But Atwater and the other man, Stephen Poytron, persisted and told Warbeck not to be afraid but to take it on him boldly, and that if he went along with them they would help him with the considerable power at their disposal, to overthrow the King of England. Help was guaranteed from the local Earls of Desmond and Kildare who like them wished for revenge on the king and so would make common cause with them. So, said Warbeck, against his will they made him learn English and taught him what to do and say; and finally, because John de Pontefract was in Henry VII's hands, they called him Duke of York. After this the conspirators – John Taylor, John Atwater, Stephen Poytron and Hubert Burke – aided and abetted by the earls began, what Warbeck called, this false quarrel. It was a quarrel which attracted immediate international support. The King of France sent a two-man embassy to Ireland, Louis Lucas and Stephen Frion, which recognized him as Duke of York, rightful heir to the throne of England and invited him to take up residence in France. Warbeck, or Duke Richard as he now was, was received in France as the true King of England. Thereafter the King of Scotland and Maximilian, the Holy Roman Emperor, also acknowledged him to be Richard Plantagenet.[2]

There is nothing in Warbeck's confession which should make us doubt its truthfulness. Whenever historians have pursued its detail, and they have done so to considerable extent, they have found evidence which substantiates it. And yet it remains tantalizingly unsatisfactory, a completely incomplete document. Why? Partisans of the House of York have suggested that it was produced under duress, a deliberately misleading document covering up the real story: Warbeck was Richard, Duke of York.[3] Historians aiming at objectivity have seen its reticence as proof of Henry VII's desire not to offend the guilty party. For, ten or so years after it had all begun, relations with the guilty had changed to such a degree that it was inadvisable to pin the blame too securely on any one person.[4] Yet this is to enter into a debate with a document which had a strictly limited purpose: to circulate sufficient personal and circumstantial material about Perkin Warbeck and so end the debate about whether he was Richard Plantagenet, Richard IV, true King of England or not. Warbeck's confession was not intended to tell the whole story, least of all to demonstrate in detail that every monarchy in Europe, bar one, had lent dignity to this conspiracy, and so pave the way for others. It was intended by Henry VII as a resolution of what was for him an unresolvable problem: that he could never completely translate his right as King of England by the victory at Bosworth, *de facto*, into a statement that he was rightfully, *de jure*, king. Henry VII's kingship rested ultimately on a transfer of allegiance by the greater part of the political community of Yorkist England from their master, Edward IV, and his murdered son, Edward V, to him. This transfer had been worked out in the two years before Bosworth and sealed with Henry's undertaking to marry the late king's daughter, Elizabeth of York. That Henry VII was a Yorkist king is now part of the consensus about him among late medieval historians. What is meant by this, that Henry used Yorkist methods of government, and that there was great continuity of service between Edward IV's government and his, is undeniable. But the ironic style of the statement and the overwhelming concentration on government and administration obliterates the motivating values of the chivalric élite who backed Henry before, and after, Bosworth.

It is the great Dutch historian Huizinga who draws our attention to the intensely personal nature of late medieval politics, so personal and so intense that the main driving force of politics in this period are loyalty to a lord and loyalty to his family, and blood; and what flowed therefrom: pursuit of his right, revenge, and the demand for justice.[5] Henry and his son Henry VIII always remained vulnerable to the claims in blood of surviving members of the Plantagenet family, such as the Courtenays and the de la Poles, because of the muddle and mystery surrounding the fate of Edward IV's sons. A sure signal of this vulnerability is given by Henry's own propagandist historian Polydore Vergil when he starts the history of Henry's reign with the transfer of the Duke of Clarence's surviving son, Edward, Earl of Warwick, from prison in Sheriff Hutton to the Tower of London. He was moved here, we are told, lest he stir up civil discord, sedition.[6] And indeed he had, all things considered, a better blood right to the throne than Henry.

On the continent the Burgundian historiographer Jean Molinet heard another story of the days after Bosworth; that Henry, taking the oath of allegiance in towns near to London before his coronation, proclaimed that if there were anyone of the line of King Edward who had a right to the throne, he should show himself and he, Henry, would help to crown him.[7]

However we read this story, at face value, or as part of a scheme to flush out immediate opposition to him in the London region, his initial vulnerability never far receeded. Not after 1499 when Henry attempted to free himself from the ghost of a Yorkist comeback by executing Edward, Earl of Warwick at the same time as Perkin Warbeck; nor later in 1504, when the story that the real Richard and his brother Edward V had been murdered by Sir James Tyrrell first appeared. Even on his deathbed, if one account is to be believed, he warned his eighteen-year-old son to execute the Yorkist claimant to the throne, Edmund de la Pole, rather than leave him alive in England if he was ever obliged to leave the kingdom to fight in France.[8] The people were not to be trusted as long as pretenders lived.

Had the Warbeck conspiracy never existed, or had it never taken on the strength which it did in 1493, it is possible that we would have been spared the awful final decade of Henry VII's reign; a decade of distrust, repression, imprisonment, and execution. It was, thought Sir Thomas More, a decade of perpetual winter; a decade which prompted some to begin moves against the monarchy under the Magna Carta.[9] That the Warbeck conspiracy developed well beyond its inauspicious beginnings was a tragedy for all whom it touched. But that it did so was due to its roots which ran long and deep into English and European politics. They began in the relationship beween the Wars of the Roses and European monarchs. They lay in the political method of the rising French state. They developed out of all proportion in 1492 and 1493 when Henry VII's obsessive reactions to the dynastic problems which confronted him converted a plot of small-time losers into a viable focus for discontent. And they already existed in the psyche of the late medieval Englishman who expected the imminent return of the dead leader.

TWO

A World of Displaced Men

The Europe into which Perkin Warbeck was projected as Richard IV was at a point of departure. Everywhere there was dislocation, the same strange mixture of old and new. In the east the Turks threatened the existence of Christendom. In the west methodical Portuguese sought for the route round Africa to Asia; but dreamers like Martin Behaim and Christopher Columbus dreamed of sailing to Japan across the Atlantic. All over Europe a religion compounded of philosophy, customary beliefs and magic satisfied the majority. Yet everywhere radicals, intellectuals and heretics called for renewal – psychological, spiritual and institutional. Scientists, mathematicians and geographers redefined the limits of the material world. Yet they coexisted with alchemists, fraudsters and astrologers. And as often as not they were the same people. All over Europe the old élite founded on rural wealth jostled for power with new urban and capitalist classes; confronting, adapting and exploiting them. All over Europe armies, based on Roman and medieval ideas and facts: archers, footsoldiers and knights, were giving way to the new technologies of gunpowder and cannon. Everywhere technology was in advance; from the Fenlands where the rich and prosperous, including the King of England's mother, drained land for profit, to the library where, in common with the upwardly mobile yeoman and gentleman, her son collected printed books rather than manuscripts.[1] If the sixteenth century saw the rebirth of Europe, then the hour of its conception was the fifteenth century, and the onset of labour was in 1492.[2] This was a rich, perhaps over-rich, culture waiting for that transforming event, the discovery of the new world, which would give coherence to its disparate material and spiritual patterns and harness new economic forms unleashed by a growing population. The discovery of America was the event which created a new world order. Perkin Warbeck, who might hardly seem a footnote to this process, touched and was touched by all the people who made the discovery of the new world possible: bankers, explorers, princes, charlatans; greedy men bent on disciplining a continent emerging from the chaos of civil wars.

All over Europe in the latter half of the fifteenth century civil wars had been fought, in Scotland, France, Portugal, Spain, and in the ashes of the Burgundian state. The Wars of the Roses were the English experience of a common phenomenon. The last thirty years have seen an enormous outpouring of published work on the Wars of the Roses. Families, administrations, counties and regions have been described minutely to provide an understanding to the nature of and reasons for the Wars. But with the exception of the attention given to the loss of England's French lands, in the 1450s, because of the furore this caused within England, most of what has been written is myopically Anglocentric. In their earliest manifestation the Wars of the Roses were a consequence of Henry VI's disastrous mishandling of foreign affairs. Yet, such was the nature of politics in the 1450s, there was little of a foreign dimension in England's troubles except Richard, Duke of York's retreat to Ireland, and Warwick the Kingmaker sweeping the sea before withdrawing to Calais with

Edward, Earl of March. But when the dam burst and civil war broke out in England, between 1459 and 1465, Scotland and France became bases for the exiled Lancastrians. During the Readeption crisis and the renewal of the wars, between 1468 and 1471, Burgundy and Brittany became involved, the former as supporter and financier of Edward IV, the latter as home in exile for Jasper Tudor and his nephew, Henry, after Edward IV's return to England. The Yorkist triumph meant France's failure to install its client candidate, Richard Neville, Earl of Warwick as King's Lieutenant in a restored Lancastrian regime.

The most complex configuration of the internationalization of the Wars occurred during the period 1483 to 1509 when no fewer than five major powers, Brittany, France, The Holy Roman Empire, England and Spain, were at loggerheads over French ambitions: first in the Burgundian Netherlands, then in Brittany and then Italy. In an effort to maintain their domestic and foreign policies each power in turn was sucked into the civil war and political instability wished on England by Richard III's seizure of power. In 1485 the French were for once successful in having their client candidate, Henry Tudor, placed on the throne after the Battle of Bosworth. But Bosworth did not simplify the drift of European politics the complexity of which, if anything, intensified so that further interference in English politics by France and its main rivals, Spain and the Holy Roman Empire, was to be expected. In 1487 Imperial intervention in England came through Margaret of York, dowager Duchess of Burgundy. Imperial mercenaries fought, unsuccessfully against Henry VII in battle at East Stoke.[3]

Such intervention by powers intent on the short term neutralization of England's military capacity had the inevitable effect of increasing contacts between man and man in what was already a cosmopolitan situation. Margaret of Anjou, unsuccessfully, used the French commander Pierre de Brézé against Edward IV in the early 1460s. In 1470 Edward lived in the home of Louis de Gruuthuse at Bruges. Once Edward was back in England he showed his gratitude to Louis by giving him an English title, Marquess of Winchester, and by showering him with gifts, some of which were his own personal belongings. Henry VII's period of exile resulted in his penchant for employing Bretons, Frenchmen and, at times, anyone he could woo from foreign service.[4]

The fighting which took place during the wars has been shown by Anthony Goodman to have involved all classes of people from almost every region of England.[5] But the combatants were by no means limited to Englishmen alone. The early battles may have been fought only by interested English parties, but from 1485 onwards the conflict engaged many outside the English ruling élite. Bosworth is a nice case in point. There a French-backed candidate supported by a mixture of English exiles, Scots and French troops (lent by Charles VIII), joined with native English and Welsh supporters against an English army, but one which contained observers from Spain and one of the most prominent Burgundian mercenary captains of the day, Jean Salazar. At East Stoke the position was reversed. At that battle Henry VII's English forces fought Irish, Scottish, Swiss mercenary and English troops led by the Earl of Lincoln and Martin Swart.[6] This was only one side of the coin. English kings were happy to employ mercenaries from the Netherlands, France and Switzerland in England, and they were equally happy to employ, as Edward IV did in 1471 and Henry VII did in 1492 and 1497, artillery personnel who had experience of European, particularly Flemish, warfare. The other side of the coin was the desire of European monarchs to staff their forces with England's élite force, its archers. Charles the Bold deployed English archers in specially trained units in battle, and staffed his bodyguard with them. In 1478 Margaret of Burgundy successfully recruited men from Coventry to serve as archers in Flanders. In the 1490s the French were said to quake at the thought of English troops entering their country against them.[7]

Men saw service widely in Europe, a Europe that was not yet one of nation states, but rather a place of lords and men personally attached to each other, not inviolably to their 'patria'. Political relations were peculiarly personal. Loyalty, a key concept in the period, was not given, forever, irreversibly. If loyalty was dishonoured the wounded sense of honour would dictate service elsewhere, where true, truer, loyalty was recognized. The tension between loyalty and honour is one cause of the otherwise bewildering shifts in the politics of the time, their apparent and real irrationality and lack of sequence. Thus could Louis XI offer the slighted kingmaker, Richard Neville an apanage in north-eastern France to betray Edward IV. Thus could Louis support such unlikely allies as Margaret of Anjou, George Duke of Clarence and Warwick the Kingmaker at Margaret's court at Angers. It was a feature of the Wars of the Roses that between 1460 and 1525 England spawned a number of satellite courts, the courts of the dispossessed and exiled in European states. The internal exile of the Lancastrians began at Coventry and York in the 1450s. Thence they fled to Scotland, briefly, before settling at Angers. The House of York saw its noble progenitor forced to a self-made court in Ireland in 1459, while in 1470 his son, Edward IV, fled to Burgundy. Pensions and gifts maintained these royal guests against the day when the debt would be repaid with an attack on their native country. So, for fourteen years, Henry Tudor lived in prison and at ease in Brittany before gathering his band of exiles at Vannes. Then, caught in the welter of European politics, he crossed into France and for a brief period was established in Anjou and at Paris.[8]

After Bosworth the most notorious haven for English exiles was the household of the dowager Duchess Margaret of Burgundy. Margaret, the remaining politically independant member of the house of York, was the patroness for many who questioned Henry Tudor's right to the throne of England. Prior to Bosworth it was reported that the Calais garrison firmly expected Clarence's son to inherit the throne. When he did not inherit, over two hundred of the garrison transferred their allegiance from England to Flanders. They fought at the siege of Therouanne for the Archduke of Austria, Maximilian, in 1486.[9] A similar transference of loyalty was exercised by Sir Richard Harleston in the Channel Islands and, when he was forced to surrender the Duchess Margaret's usurped jurisdiction to Henry, he fled to her household in Malines.[10] A year later he was joined by Francis, Lord Lovel and John, Earl of Lincoln. This period, in the approach to the Lambert Simnel plot marks a, perhaps the, high point in Margaret's life. She could be confident of financial aid from Flanders and the Holy Roman Empire, as well as aid to arm and transport some of Maximilian's beloved mercenaries to Ireland. At East Stoke this all came crashing round her ears. The core of her rebel force led by Lincoln and Lovel, including the ex-Calais garrison men was annihilated. Lincoln was killed, Lovel forced into permanent exile and political extinction – dying where and when we know not. Some loyalists remained, Harleston was one; and some stragglers from the rout at East Stoke reached her the following year.[11] For them the Warbeck adventure awaited. But in 1488 her cause was all but finished. Her Irish allies, who had lent their military support at Stoke, suffered a furious onslaught from Henry who took from them massive bonds to ensure good behaviour. Future communication with the Duchess would be punished severely, as would any breach of their primary loyalty to the English, Tudor, King.[12] For Margaret, worse was to happen at home in England. In May of that year, in what might have been the forerunner of an emergent policy, Henry VII allowed Edward Plantagenet, Earl of Warwick, to witness a document in Warwickshire. Was this to be the beginning of a political rehabilitation for Warwick; the beginning of restoring him, a political non-person, to his rightful place in the realm, just as Edward IV considered doing, but did not do, to Henry himself.[13] It did not happen, and we will see why, but it might have.

In Flanders Margaret could no longer count on Maximilian's automatic support against Henry. European politics had made the cooperation of England and Flanders against France a matter of necessity. Between November 1488 and February 1489 the Treaty of Dordrecht was negotiated and concluded. The old friendship with Flanders was revived; the unstated aim of the treaty was to safeguard Brittany and defeat French ambitions there and in Flanders.[14] For disappointed subjects of Henry VII, Malines promised less and less. In April 1489 Yorkshire rebelled against paying Henry's taxes for a war to defend Brittany. The only politically motivated rebel, Sir John Egremont, found virtually no support in the north and his flight to Malines ended in similar disaster. He returned to England a disillusioned man.[15] Malines was a political wilderness. True, Margaret kept up a desultory correspondance with James IV of Scotland: in December 1488, September 1489 and February 1490. And, true, these dates may be significant, in that the last two coincided with a new plot against Henry. But in the late eighties Henry VII enjoyed the summer of his reign: alliances with Flanders and Spain, successful war with France, and an intelligence system which stopped Margaret's plots, if indeed they were hers, dead in their tracks.[16]

Exile for those who could not come to terms with Henry Tudor could be found without crossing the Channel. Following their defeat at East Stoke, Francis Lord Lovel, Sir Thomas Broughton, and others, were received within Scotland by James IV. In 1488 he granted them letters of safe conduct for a year, but they had probably been received in the previous year by his father James III. At the end of the year James also allowed his court to be used by a party of English exiles in transit from Ireland to the Duchess, Margaret of Burgundy. Their normal place of residence was in her household, for they were headed by the redoubtable Sir Richard Harleston. During 1488 Harleston had roamed the high seas as a sea rover for the Duchess Margaret. Some of these exiles went back home after brief periods in Scotland. John Broughton, for example, in exile in 1488, was pardoned by Henry VII in 1490. For others this was not so. Sir George Neville, banished to Scotland in 1491, spent the rest of his life as a wanderer.[17]

England, halfway between Europe and Scotland, was host to displaced persons from Brittany, Burgundy and Scotland. On the death of James III a number of particularly loyal servants fled south of the border, just as Richard III's had fled north in 1487. Among the Scots who came to Henry VII for relief was John Ramsay, the so-called Lord Bothwell. Henry gave him a pension for life and, thereafter, whether in exile or in Scotland, he acted as agent for Henry. Long-lasting loyalty, over-attachment to a lord, a possible cause of exile, could indicate the sort of behaviour which would result from speedy pardon. Hence Sir John Ross of Montgrenan was welcomed back from England by James IV within a few years of his flight.[18] Brittany sent exiles to Henry's court. Some were voluntary, men who had followed him back to England in 1485, and stayed. Others, like Master Pierre le Penec in the 1490s, had been highly placed in the Breton government, but, on the conquest of Brittany, in taking action against the French to defend their duchy, were forced to leave it. Penec became a royal councillor, was given a position in the English Church and served Henry loyally at home and abroad. Even before the duchy fell Henry had manipulated the loyalties of exiles to undermine the French. In December 1491 Henry appointed Master Oliver Coetlogon Proctor General of the Duchy of Brittany (a meaningless title), called him councillor and gave him an annuity of 1,000 gold crowns. Since this was an attempt to undermine the French, Henry also promised to indemnify him if, due to war, he lost his property in Brittany.[19] Henry Tudor's penchant was for Bretons and Frenchmen. Edward IV used Burgundians. The most recently exposed career of an exiled Burgundian is that of Stephen Frion. In many ways Frion's career resembles that of Penec. He began as a civil servant in Flanders and was French secretary, successively, to Edward, Richard III and Henry. Yet he acted as a spy for the Flemish court before defecting to France.[20]

The epitome of the court which patronized exiles, and the most feared in Europe even by the Ottoman Turks, for its manipulation of faction, was France. Louis XI is well known for his manipulation of Richard Neville's ambition, and twenty years later Charles VIII, as we will see, exploited the legitimist longings of old supporters of York in much the same way. Expanding east and west, into Flanders and Brittany, the French monarchy encouraged disappointed factions to serve France. After 1477, with the Burgundian state in terminal decline, Louis XI and Charles VIII were served by men whose parents or grandparents had left France for Burgundy a generation earlier. Pierre d'Urfé, Guillaume and Guy de Rochefort, Philippe de Crèvecoeur, Philippe de Commynes, Philippe de Savoie and Jean de Chalon all abandoned Burgundy and rose to eminence in France.[21] In many cases those who defected from Burgundian service in Flanders and the Low Countries came from what is now north-east France, principally Picardy.[22] The very provinces they abandoned they then conquered for France and defended with all their expertise. Nor did they have any regrets. When the wars between Flanders and France ended, in 1493, many of the exiles opposed French acceptance of the peace at the Treaty of Senlis.[23]

Each new political crisis brought its new defector. Nowhere was this more clearly seen than in Brittany just before its fall. At the end of its life, with a crippled economy, occupied by its Swiss, Flemish, and English allies and assaulted by the French, the Breton government was riven by faction. On a number of occasions the French accepted at their court Jean de Rieux, Marshall of Brittany who, unable to obtain the preferment he wanted there, then

Anne de Beaujeu, Regent of France for Charles VIII until the French annexation of Brittany in 1491

returned to Brittany to lead its forces against the French.[24] Cases like this were not uncommon. In 1492 a disappointed Breton nobleman, Guillaume Carreau offered to transfer his loyalty to Henry VII and deliver the strategically important town of Brest to English forces. When his sense of honour was slighted by the paltry reward he was offered he opted for service with the French. They confirmed him in power in Brest and he exposed his dealings with the English and their agents in Brittany.[25] The final conquest of the Duchy was made possible by one such defector. Having oscillated in his allegiance between France and Brittany for seven years Alain, Seigneur d'Albret, a councillor of the French regent Anne de Beaujeu, delivered the *coup de grâce* to Brittany by surrendering the key to the town of Nantes to the French army encamped outside it.[26]

THREE

The Breton Wheel of Fortune

The besetting preoccupation of every European power during 1490 and 1491 was whether or not Brittany had any viability as a duchy independent of France. For a while, during 1490, it appeared that this was possible. But when the diplomacy aimed at ensuring Breton independence collapsed, France used every means at her disposal to undermine the major powers – Spain, England, Burgundy, Austria – ranged against her. The Perkin Warbeck Conspiracy was one part of these schemes by which France was able to occupy Brittany in 1491. By the end of 1491 a coalition of powers had decided to declare war against France, but it was only when Warbeck appeared in Ireland, as Richard, Duke of York, that Henry VII began to lobby European powers for a grand alliance against France. In January 1492 he wrote to Ludovico Sforza:

> Were we not of the opinion that the extent of the tyranny of the French and their wicked lust for aggrandising others is manifest and well known to you we should endeavour to demonstrate it at full length; but . . . Everyone knows by what right they harassed the Duchess and Duchy of Brittany by protracted and grievous war, and at last brought it into their power. The art and craft they employed to induce Ghent and several other towns of Flanders to revolt from the King of Romans . . . Who is unaware of the snares they are preparing so that they may bring all Flanders under their yoke? If we wished to give you examples nearer home, we might remind you with what perfidy they supplanted the princes of Savoy . . . To such an extent does this insolent licence wander in every direction and move hither and thither with impunity at will. We pass over in silence the mischief the French are contriving against us and the snares they are spreading, as we have decided to avenge our injuries not by words but by arms.[1]

Already, on 8 December 1491, Henry had informed the papacy, that France was encouraging the Scots to make war on England, and that they had bribed members of the Breton nobility to secure delivery of the duchy, and that 'They have also by many promises incited certain barons in Ireland and in our kingdom to rebel against us; and to this end they hostilely invade our borders, commiting acts of plunder and conflagration.'[2]

To understand both Henry's fury, and the origins of the Warbeck conspiracy it is necessary to understand the events leading up to the complex French moves against the allied powers. By the Treaty of Le Verger, 1488, France secured virtual control of Brittany, and in January 1489 she took possession of the towns of Guingamp, Concarneau, Le Conquet and Brest.

This action prompted a massive allied response. Swiss, Burgundian, Spanish, and English troops poured into Brittany so that by August of 1489 only Brest remained in French hands. Away in the east, on its border with Flanders, Henry VII and his new ally Archduke Maximilian threatened to roll back the twelve years work which the French had expended in pursuit of conquering Flanders, Franche Comté and Burgundy. Suddenly the French regime was faced with the harsh reality that it could not simultaneously acquire Flanders and Brittany. In order to conquer Brittany it therefore decided to make peace with Maximilian. The peace of Frankfurt of July 1489, between Charles VIII and Maximilian, temporarily detatched Maximilian from the other countries ranged against France, and it ushered in a year and a half of diplomatic and military uncertainty.[3]

French diplomacy was at its height in 1489. As well as negotiating with Maximilian France also sent ambassadors to England and Brittany. In each country the French blackened the reputation of the other in an attempt to weaken the allies and allow her inevitable conquest of Brittany. By August 1489 it was widely believed war was over, so the papacy turned its mind to brokering a peace between England and France. The Pope sent Leonard Chieragato, Bishop of Concordia, to France to conduct negotiations between Henry VII and Charles VIII. Quickly a number of sticking points emerged. On the French side it was felt a true peace would, in the circumstances, take too long to negotiate. On the English side Henry VII knew that the Breton war had cost over £120,000 and that the Breton economy was so crippled that Brittany could not repay her debts. A deal was struck therefore whereby France became *de facto* governor of Brittany and undertook to repay Henry's war costs. The amount of money Henry VII was demanding was colossal. Early on in negotiation he demanded the resumption of payments due to England under the Treaty of Pécquigny of 1475. Then he said he had no intention of appearing inferior to Edward IV. Edward had received 50,000 crowns annually from France; he was being offered a mere 200,000 over three years. However, after a gruelling five months of bargaining, Chieragato had negotiated a truce, a sum, and the possibility of a permanent peace with France. The most complex part of the negotiation was how to achieve a peace which recognized Brittany's integrity as a duchy. By 16 September the intricate negotiations, which left Chieragato feeling 'very fatigued and languid', were over and it was agreed that there would be an independent truce between France and Brittany to last until 1 May 1491.[4]

It would be wrong to imagine that these negotiations succeeded because of papal arbitration alone. When the French stalled the negotiations, in the summer of 1490, Henry sent troops to raid Normandy. In July it was rumoured that they would attack the Cherbourg region. In early August twenty English ships disembarked between five and six thousand troops in the La Hague region of Normandy and set fire to the villages there. For about two weeks they pillaged and took prisoners, and burnt the town of Quettenhou.[5] By the time Henry's ships withdrew from Normandy events had developed elsewhere. On 18 November 1490 it appeared that the Duchess of Brittany, Maximilian, the Spanish, and Philip the Fair had formed an alliance of mutual defence. Despite this, which was said to have infuriated them, the French made public that the truce was to run till May 1491. However, when on 19 December 1490 it became known that Maximilian had contracted to marry Anne Duchess of Brittany it was only a matter of time before matters came to a head. Charles VIII aborted the Anglo-French negotiations and, by February, England and France were locked into a war of words. By mid-March 1491 the French chancellor let it be known that France was 'threatened with a serious war by the three most powerful kings – of the Romans, of Castille, and of England'. The Bretons meanwhile added insult to injury by claiming, in an embassy to the French court, that they knew that Maximilian's marriage to their duchess 'would be most agreeable to his most Catholic Majesty by reason of his very close connection with his father in law, the king of the Romans.'[6] Charles VIII it should be remembered was betrothed to Maximilian's daughter.

The French reply to what they regarded as the betrayal of the treaties of Le Verger and Frankfurt was to prepare a comprehensive plan to annex Brittany. Supreme command of the projected army of invasion, between thirty and forty thousand men, was vested in Louis de la Trémoille. In the event it met with virtually no opposition. Brittany, wasted by war, rebellion and faction, could not defend itself. Spain, England and Flanders, on the other hand, could mount some sort of defence for Brittany. Of the three, Spain presented France with fewest problems. It was a long way from Brittany and was distracted by war against the Moors at Granada. Henry VII and Maximilian of Austria were another matter. If French plans for the invasion of Brittany were to succeed then they had to be sufficiently diverted so that they could not come to Brittany's aid.[7] France had dabbled, and more, in the politics of the Low Countries since the death of Charles the Bold in 1477. In the first phase of the war against Brittany, in 1484 and 1485, it had allied with Bruges and Ghent; both were towns jealous to protect their independence from Maximilian and thankful to find a French protector. Across the Low Countries Maximilian waged a frightful war to secure the Netherlands for his son. Fighting ceased temporarily in July 1485, but it flared up again two years later growing gradually less intense from 1489, when France abandoned its Flemish allies to concentrate on conquering Brittany. In November 1490 Bruges, the last French ally, capitulated. But the French needed a diversion to tie Maximilian down while they took Brittany, so they prolonged the war.[8]

That diversion was Philippe de Cleves. In the early 1480s Philippe had been Maximilian's chamberlain but by the late 1480s the two men were estranged. Ostensibly this estrangement related to the rough justice meted out by Maximilian on rebel towns. In reality Philippe regarded Maximilian's intrusion into the Low Countries as intolerable. Philippe accused Maximilian of wishing to annex the Low Countries to his hereditary domains and regarded Maximilian's son Philip the Fair, alone, as heir to Burgundian Flanders. In this Philippe found wide support, until 1489. Then, denied wholehearted French support, all Maximilian's rebels except Philippe de Cleves had made peace with him. Philippe remained loyally wedded to his chivalrous ideal of Burgundy and refused to have any dealings with Maximilian, who had stripped him of his rank and title. Under the direct protection of the French, Philippe set himself up in Sluys castle. From here he led a rebellion which killed the trade in Bruges and damaged that of Holland. He encouraged Danish pirates to use Sluys as a base from which to pillage Channel shipping. Late in 1489 he stirred up a revolt in Bruges, and in 1490 promoted political murder in Ghent. His relations with the French were close and cordial. He supplied them with intelligence from the heart of Flanders, Malines, and they began to pay him a pension of 8,000 livres per year. In May 1491 the French government decided to send troops to de Cleves and on 5 June the *Sante Barbe* sailed for Sluys with reinforcements for de Cleves. Four days later he declared that peace with Maximilian was impossible because the Flemish estates and de Cleves had sworn loyalty to the regime of Philip the Fair. Within a month Charles VIII of France was addressing de Cleves as his 'faithful counsellor and chamberlain' and, in token of his gratitude, sent him 3,000 livres to maintain his rebellion. Four French officers, Andre de Fontaines, Guillaume Bongars, Bernard Urdoulx and Jean de Bournonville were sent to help him at Sluys. More payments from France followed, as did promises, secured by France, that more Danish privateers would join de Cleves's rebels.[9] There followed a long and expensive siege into the summer of 1492 when not even the aid of English troops could shift de Cleves. Eventually Sluys was surrendered not because of any military action but because the death of Philippe de Cleves further necessitated a successful negotiation with Maximilian to save the family lands. The

French had had their diversion in Flanders and had occupied Brittany for virtually a year before Sluys surrendered. Tying Maximilian down in war also produced profitable by-blows. The towns in Holland and Friesland rose in rebellion against his war taxes. This was the pattern of events to be hoped for as the French turned on that other power likely to defend Brittany, England.[10]

French policy toward Henry was always coloured by a backward glance at 1485. Even if Robert Gaguin, France's ambassador to England in 1489 and 1490, never made the speech credited to him by Bacon it illustrates the point. Bacon has Gaguin say that his master, King Charles, 'rememberith their first acquaintance at Paris with so great contentment; nay, never speaks of him, but that presently he falls into discourse of the miseries of great kings, in that they cannot converse with their equals, but with servants'.[11] Henry was assured that the first thing the French desired in their dealings with him over Brittany was his good affection. In fact it was a kind of supine compliance, born of gratitude, which France was requiring. The cheapest weapon in any struggle was insincere diplomacy. At the beginning of 1491 Charles VIII sent a Herald, Champagne, to Scotland, apparently to renew the Franco-Scottish alliance. He was in Scotland at the beginning of March 1491 and he returned to France at the end of that month to deliver the news that the Scots would send an important embassy to France. For James IV this embassy was part of his search for a wife.[12] For the French it was about breaking a possible English marriage alliance with Scotland and persuading James to declare war on England. By May 1491 it was said in France that Charles VIII intended sending financial aid to James just as he had done to Philippe de Cleves. When the Scots ambassadors arrived at his court Charles VIII treated them incredibly casually, sure in the knowledge that he had obtained a way 'to make trouble in England by way of Scotland'. The ambassadors achieved next to nothing. They agreed a treaty which in due time, within a year, the French effectively tore up, and they failed to negoitiate a wife for James.[13] This diplomacy masked Charles VIII's real purpose which had been to send his personal messenger, Seigneur de Concressault, Alexander Monypeny to Scotland. Monypeny was one of those expatriate Scots, like his late father, William, and Charles's Chamberlain Bérault Stuart, who actively intervened in the Wars of the Roses on behalf of the French.[14]. Monypeny's business was to announce one of Charles VIII's 'great schemes' to James IV, and the timing of his visit, which coincided with French aid to Philippe de Cleves, suggests that the great scheme was action against England. James IV in Scotland was to be one leg, Maurice FitzGerald, Earl of Desmond in Ireland was to be another, and the disaffected within England would be another. The French, as in Flanders, would supply men, arms, boats and, wherever necessary, would harry English shipping. With a convenient east and west coast, Scotland was vital to the French plan for it provided France with a safe haven from which to direct and observe the diversion in Ireland.

These preparations against England were not taken lightly by Henry VII. He organized a number of Scottish dissidents to capture James IV and his brother, the Duke of Ross, and deliver them to England. This kidnapping was financed to the tune of £266. 13s 4d, and one of the conspirators, Sir Thomas Tod, even left his son and heir in pledge with Henry at Greenwich on 17 April 1491 when the agreement was made. The intention seems to have been to capture James IV in April or May as he attended Parliament. In the event this came to nothing. Instead Henry chose to pursue military action against James, coordinated with open disaffection against him by Archibald Douglas, Earl of Angus, and his son George. Two years previously, disaffected subjects of King James, seeking revenge for his part in his father's death, had sent the Earl of Angus to Henry to pledge their loyalty in any event by which Henry chose to execute God's wrath against the murderer of James III.[15]

In the spring of 1491 Henry VII sent Berwick, Carlisle and Durham £5,000 to bolster their defences. What military action transpired is not clear, but at the beginning of June it was reported in France that the Scots had been routed in battle by the English. On 29 July the Earl of Angus was confined to his castle at Tantallon, in Scotland. In September 1491 James IV besieged it. Heavy guns were brought up for a major assault by land and sea. Tantallon is on the coast, between North Berwick and Dunbar; it is possible that Tantallon and the nearby Bass Rock were about to be turned into English bridgeheads in order to raid the east coast of Scotland, or used as safe havens from which to intercept shipping to and from France. Whatever the case, the whole business was over by the middle or end of October, but it was not without a sting in its tail.[16] By 22 October full diplomatic contacts had been resumed with Scotland, and the Scots sent an embassy to negotiate a truce with England. The English Parliament was not to be placated and expressed rabidly anti-Scottish sentiments, declaring that whatever promise James IV made he was sure to break it, and that it was better to be at open war with the Scots than feign peace between England and Scotland. In point of fact a five-year truce was negotiated with James, but in the glacial political climate of winter 1491 it was never ratified.[17] Thereafter, until James IV's support for Warbeck brought matters to a head, Scotland and England existed in a limbo of feigned peace: at war one way or another.

That Anglo-Scottish relations broke down in 1491 had more to do with France. During most of 1491 Henry forebore from full-blooded war with France. Instead most of the

Timbers of the Sovreign, *a ship used by Robert Willoughby de Broke. General view of the excavation of 1912 which revealed the remains of a large carvel-built ship. The* Sovreign *was built in 1488, rebuilt in 1509 and abandoned in 1621 in a dock at Woolwich*

southern coastal counties were placed on military alert, and naval patrols were sent out to defend English fishermen.[18] Nevertheless it was important for Henry to show that he had some credible policy toward Brittany, so in mid-February he began to put together a powerful raiding party. In April Sir John Haliwell, a Devonian, was appointed Admiral of the Fleet, and on 2 May artillery trains began lumbering from the Tower of London to Dartmouth, the port of muster.[19] A week later, in his flagship the *Regent*, Haliwell and a force of two thousand men sailed for Brittany. As this party also contained, in the *Sovreign*, Robert Lord Willoughby de Broke, this was a force to be reckoned with. De Broke was England's finest maritime commander. But by the beginning of June much of Brittany had fallen and two thousand marines could not retake it. They managed, however, to run the gauntlet of the French blockade and landed English troops in Normandy in late July. In mid-August they again landed, this time in Brittany, at Cancale, 5 miles east of St Malo, and 35 miles north of the beleguered Duchess, in Rennes. They offered her safe passage to the Low Countries, but this, like a good Breton, she refused. The landing caused the French such alarm that a squadron of ships commanded by Louis Lucas was sent from Honfleur to maintain the French garrison at Brest lest the English, who had designs on the town, took it. However, instead of going toward Brest, Haliwell went up channel, eastwards. In late August his fifteen or sixteen ships were rumoured to have landed near Harfleur and raided villages there. It is far from clear whether this was true or not.[20] However, the ports in the mouth of the Seine, Harfleur, Honfleur and Rouen, contained important naval establishments and dockyards. At Harfleur the French were preparing two ships disguised as English vessels so that they might land an expeditionary force of one hundred and twenty troops in English livery in Ireland.

French attitudes to the Wars of the Roses rested unequivocally on the principle of ruthlessly advancing French interests. Of sentiment they knew nothing. Thus, on the eve of the war with Brittany, in 1484, the Estates General were treated to a description of English politics 'as a record of incessant change accomplished amid orgies of crime'. Edward IV's children had lately been 'murdered with impunity, and the crown transferred to the assassin by the goodwill of the nation'. contrast this, said the speaker with the loyalty and devotion of the people of France to their child king Charles. A year later, hardly that, and they sponsored the English claimant to the throne, Henry Tudor, and encouraged a further acute crisis in English politics. Another turn of the Breton wheel of fortune, in 1489 and 1491 the French King and his Council were reported to be offering Edward, Earl of Warwick help to place him on the throne of England because they had done wrong in placing Henry on the throne in the first place. And when, in September 1492, this had misfired, but Warbeck appeared recreated as the Duke of York, Charles VIII then told his subjects that he had sent ships to Ireland to 'our cousin the Duke of York' because he was 'true heir to the kingdom of England'.[21]

The leader of the expedition the French were preparing was an Englishman. When John Taylor went to France we can only guess. The last time he was referred to as domiciled in England was 2 January 1489.[22] We hear of him, next, in France in September 1491. He was a man of critical importance, for without him there would have been no Perkin Warbeck conspiracy. In the reigns of Edward IV and Richard III he was a yeoman of the King's Chamber, an important but not exalted position. His connections before this were to the Duke of Clarence. Taylor may have been involved in the plots which resulted in Clarence's death, and he was probably an estate officer of Clarence's. More than this, he was a Devonian, an Exeter man, and a clothier. Three years after Clarence's fall he was appointed surveyor of the customs for the south-western region with duties which ran in the ports of Poole, Exeter, Dartmouth, Plymouth, Fowey and Bridgwater. He proved a loyal servant of

Edward, corrupting juries for him in Exeter, and a true servant of Richard III by staying loyal to him when most of Edward's household in the south-west joined Buckingham's rebellion. Rewarded by Richard with rebel lands he proved too loyal for accommodation to the new regime of Henry Tudor. He lost his customs' post to James Boneython late in 1485 when Boneython was rewarded by Henry for his loyal service to him in France, Brittany and at Bosworth. Once more, what happened is not clear, but Taylor was granted a pardon in September 1489.[23] Possibly this was merely precautionary. Conceivably Taylor had been mixed up in some way with the south-western sector of the Lambert Simnel plot, for he made no secret of his belief, in 1491, that Clarence's son was rightfully king of England. It is notable that early 1489 saw much coming and going between France and England, and it is possible that Taylor and others of his association in the west were supplying the French with intelligence about Henry's shipping. Taylor was a man of immense political potential because his relatively humble position opened onto a huge political hinterland. As king's yeoman he faced toward the court. Within his region he was important to anyone with political connections. As a merchant and customs official his world opened onto almost unlimited horizons: up channel to Flanders and the great trading cities of the Hanseatic League; down channel to Normandy, Brittany, Spain, Portugal and West Africa; westward to Ireland, Scotland and Iceland, even to America. Taylor was at the great interface of politics and mercantile finance, state power and capitalism. Humble he may have been, in his status, but he was indispensible to royalty. His flight to France shows a hardheaded judgement of political reality. No dissident with the slightest understanding of European politics would have preferred Flanders to France. There was nothing Margaret of Burgundy could offer that France could not outbid a hundred fold.

All that is left of what became the Perkin Warbeck conspiracy is a letter and an account, but the conspiracy which eventually involved Warbeck had been more ambitious in conception than the minor diversion which took place in autumn 1491. What John Taylor wanted to promote was an English rising on behalf of Edward, Earl of Warwick staffed by disenchanted middle-ranking survivors of the affinities of Warwick's father, the Duke of Clarence, his grandmother, Anne Beauchamp Countess of Warwick, Richard III, and John Howard, Duke of Norfolk. Something of this is contained in the well-known letter he wrote to John Hayes in 1491. But the shadow is there six months before. The French had their agents already in Scotland, and in 1490 made contact with two English dissidents Sir Robert Chamberlain and Richard White. The intention behind the Chamberlain affair which resulted in 1491 in his near defection to France cannot be divined. But in Chamberlain we may suggest there was a socially humbler, though politically more significant, version of what the Earl of Lincoln had been in 1487: a figurehead for Yorkist loyalists. Chamberlain had followed Edward IV to exile in Burgundy and served in the garrison at Calais in the 1470s. He had been Chancellor of Ireland in the same period. So Taylor may have hoped for a French-backed version of the Stoke invasion complete with Irish rising, important past political figures and another pretender.

The whole thing began well enough. In the summer of 1490 the French had made contact with Richard White, a gentleman, of Thorpe by Bellingford in Norfolk. By 24 August White had agreed to aid the French and, so it was said in his accusation, to help murder Henry VII.[24] White was probably a go-between for Charles VIII's government and their main target, Sir Robert Chamberlain. Chamberlain was difficult to approach directly because ever since 1487 he had been under suspicion of treason. In that year he had been placed under house arrest at Chertsey unable to travel more than a mile from his home without permission from the king. Each consecutive year following he had been bound over to maintain his loyalty to Henry VII. He was *persona non grata* for good reason. His father, Sir Roger Chamberlain, had, with a young Sir John Howard, served John, Duke of Bedford in France. As a critic of Henry VI's government he had like Richard, Duke of York supported Humphrey, Duke of Gloucester. In 1447 he had been part hanged for treason. At the end of the rope his life was saved by a last minute reprieve. He nevertheless continued in opposition to Lancaster as a steward of one of Richard, Duke of York's Kentish manors. Sir Robert fought for Edward IV in the civil wars in the north in the 1460s, probably under Sir John Howard. It was he and another, later, Chancellor of Ireland and East Anglian, Sir Gilbert Debenham whom Edward landed in 1471 to scout out the Cromer district. He served both Edward and Richard III as knight for the body and was one of only two from East Anglia in Richard III's retinue to serve him outside his own sphere of influence. In the emergency of 1485 he and his son Ralph were sent to guard North Wales, and he was promoted to Sheriff of Anglesey, Receiver of North Wales, Keeper of Snowdon and Constable of Beaumaris castle.[25]

By 17 January 1491 he had entered the plot against Henry VII and within ten days he and a group of rebels including his two sons Edward and Ralph attempted to defect to France. They were seized at Hartlepool by Sir Edward Pickering. They had attempted to save themselves from arrest by entering the sanctuary of St Cuthbert at Durham. But sanctuary was ruthlessly cast aside by Henry VII who justified Pickering's violation of St Cuthbert's rights on grounds of necessity: the necessity of seizing their correspondence with France.[26] Chamberlain was executed in March 1491. His co-conspirators all survived, one way or another. His sons were pardoned in July 1491, but lost estates which were granted to Henry Wyatt and church patronage to John de Vere, Earl of Oxford, who was the mortal enemy of their father's lord, John Howard, at Bosworth. [27] White, the go-between who had contacted Chamberlain at his manor of Barking in Essex, was tried for treason and found guilty, but was reprieved on Tower Hill at the point of execution. He failed to draw the obvious conclusion from this and, in 1495, was captured and executed after invading England on behalf of Richard, Duke of York – Perkin Warbeck.[28]

It is difficult to identify others outside Chamberlain's immediate entourage drawn into this plot. Possibly Sir George Neville, the so-called Bastard, may have been involved. Certainly he had the right background for Taylor to appeal to him. In 1484 Richard III had deployed him in Wiltshire and Dorset as one of the northerners running a rebel region, and he married Lord River's widow. He was formally rewarded in July 1485 with large tracts of land which had belonged to the Tudor loyalist Sir John Cheyne and was given the office of Master and Keeper of Cranbourne Chase. The week before Henry Tudor landed at Milford Haven Neville was commissioned to take ships and men from the West Country to intercept Henry. Nonetheless he seemed to have accommodated himself with Henry VII in 1486 and 1487. He was knighted after the battle of East Stoke, and then returned to the North to live there. Yet some time after 1488, his last recorded sighting, in York, he passed out of favour. He was banished from England about the time of Chamberlain's plot, and in early April 1491 arrived at the Scottish court where James IV gave him a £50 gift.[29]

That a rising on the Earl of Warwick's behalf was a concern of the king is indicated in the military preparations of 1491. To defend England against the French attack in East Anglia and Hampshire was perfectly normal. But in the July in which he arrayed coastal defences he also arrayed Warwickshire, not a county with a coastline, against the French.[30] Was this array against a real threat, or an imagined one? Two months after Henry called for the defence of Warwickshire John Taylor wrote to John Hayes, of Tiverton, recommending that through one John Affright, a servant of Anne, Countess of Warwick the Countess should be asked to join a rising against Henry Tudor in the autumn of 1491.[31] Nothing came of this plan. But more of a threat might have come from members of the group which had schemed against Henry in 1486 and fought against him at East Stoke: northerners who had come down from the

Neville estates in Yorkshire to serve in the Midlands. Christine Carpenter has argued that despite real support from gentry in the north of the county after 1487 Henry VII exhibited very little trust in those from central and southern Warwickshire. From 1490 till 1500 the county sheriff was invariably a Leicestershire man. Outsiders held most of the royal grants, and in 1493, when Warbeck threatened to invade England, Richard Empson was appointed Recorder of Coventry.[32] Yet despite this suspicion 1491 was too late for most committed Neville men who had been transplanted from Middleham to Warwick. They were making their way under a new regime and had no interest in rocking the boat.

John Taylor was of different stuff. He worked tirelessly for his French sponsors. Secretly he came to England to visit his old friend Thomas Gale at Stokenham park, in Devon's South Hams. They talked about the Earl of Warwick. On the same visit he met his old friend John Hayes in Exeter.[33] Hayes was approached because he was a long-standing servant of the Duke of Clarence. He had worked in the west of England for twenty years as a highly placed royal official. In the 1460s he had served the Courtenay family and probably Richard Neville, Earl of Warwick. After Neville's death, in 1471, Hayes began to work for Clarence when Clarence was given Warwick's lands in the west. On Clarence's downfall, he was appointed receiver of all Clarence's western lands, and this was followed by promotion to regional receiver of the King's lands under Edward IV. He survived Richard III's reign with such good political credentials that after 1485 he was returned to work for the restored Courtenay family, as well as for the Earl of Northumberland, for Margaret Beaufort, and also Edward, Earl of Warwick as receiver for his lands during his minority. Taylor approached Hayes through their common past. They must have been about the same age, and had friends in common. When George Neville was sent by Richard III to catch Henry Tudor in 1485, he liaised with Thomas Gale of Dartmouth and John Hayes, who provisioned and financed the voyage. They can be associated with another group with a maritime background: Sir Richard Harleston, Governor of Jersey from 1468 until his defection to Margaret of Burgundy in 1486 and Sir Edward Brampton, Governor of Guernsey. They can even be associated with Sir James Tyrrell, active at Calais and in the Low Counties in Richard III's reign, and like Chamberlain an East Anglian. Taylor knew his quarry. During Buckingham's rebellion, John Hayes had supplied money to Edward, Earl of Warwick's guardian, Richard III's traitor Thomas Grey, Marquis of Dorset. Hayes had kept his post in the west by the skin of his teeth.[34]

Thomas Gale of Dartmouth, the other man whom Taylor had visited, had been appointed Clerk of the King's ships in the last year of Richard III's reign, the spring of 1485. He had helped provision Neville's expedition against Henry Tudor that year and, like John Taylor, was removed from his post immediately Henry became king. Yet he was, in 1491, not a young man. Probably in his sixties, his public career had begun in 1456. He had preceded John Taylor as customs official in Exeter and Dartmouth until 1462. Around Dartmouth he was important. He had been mayor, bailiff and MP on more than one occasion, and he had trading links with Ireland. In 1477 two factors of his, making for the port of Youghall were captured by pirates, held in gaol and abandoned, naked, on the Irish coast. This took place as a consequence of Gale's good service to the king. Because he had supplied vesssels at his own cost during the 1475 war against France, Edward IV recompensed him with the right to import goods to the value of his costs, free of customs dues. His unfortunate factors were attempting to capitalize on Gale's gift from Edward when they were captured. Gale's career was that of a careful bourgeois, but one of obvious loyalty, and such men were useful.[35] Thomas Wrangwysh of York, a loyal supporter of Richard III, was convicted of treason following the 1489 rebellion in Yorkshire during which, by deliberate negligence, he had allowed the rebels to enter the city.[36] Men like Gale, and the others mentioned in John Taylor's letter, John Attwill of Exeter and John Aleyne of Poole were, like Wrangwysh,

Arithmetic, shown in its use in commerce, on a fifteenth-century tapestry

successful bourgeois. They might, in the event of a landing, have been persuaded to immitate Wrangwysh and even perhaps prepare landing places at Dartmouth, Exmouth or Poole.

When Taylor visted Hayes at Exeter they walked a while together, in the cloisters of the cathedral, and then entered the church. Entering St Peter's church, Taylor gave Hayes a secret sign by which he would be able to recognize Taylor's messengers. True men alone would take Hayes by the thumb as he did then. Knowing who was the enemy was essential, the most innocent of visitors might be a spy sent down from court. Thus John would be 'assured of all thinges, and fere nothing, and so ensure ye all youre frendis and myne'. When Hayes's treachery was uncovered he was accused of having allowed William Warde of Topsham, Taylor's mesenger, to deliver him a letter without making any attempt to arrest him. It is more than likely that Hayes's actions had been uncovered by Hugh Oldham. Oldham was Hayes's deputy as receiver of revenues from lands which belonged to the Earl of Warwick. On Hayes's fall Oldham became Deputy Receiver, under Sir Reginald Bray, one of the king's closest advisers and like Oldham an associate of the king's mother.[37]

William Warde delivered Taylor's letter to John Hayes at Winchester on 26 November 1491. The letter from Rouen, on 15 September, had been written a month and a half before its delivery. It was a paean to French charity which Taylor hoped would encourage Hayes to defect to France. According to Taylor, Charles VIII had decided to support the Earl of Warwick, his 'Lovers and Servants', and to accept these people as his friends. As long as they were 'knowen for true men to the quarell' they could defect to France safely. Charles would support anyone who defected like this and ask nothing in return, doing this for the 'wrong he did in making Henry King of England, and for the gode he oweth unto the Sonne of youre maister (Clarence) for they be nere of kyn'. After sounding out other committed supporters of the Earl of Warwick, Hayes was asked to determine a time and place for a French landing in England. Taylor also requested estimates of the numbers of troops needed and raised the possiblity of defections from England by, 'any man of gretter name'; yet he cautioned against too many defections which would give the game away, because everything was prepared. According to the letter he was convinced that the hour of Henry VII's downfall was come,

> Sir, ye shall here by othre frendis, Sir the convenable tyme of helpe is come, and therfor nowe endevour your self, and put to your hand and spare no coste, for there shall be helpe in thre parties oute of Royalme, but here (Rouen) is the place most metely for you, and where ye shall lak nothing . . .

Yet nothing happened. Hayes did not defect to Rouen. There was no French invasion, not much Scottish action and no rising in England. It is not hard to see why nothing was achieved in England. Suspects like Hayes were watched. One of the king's key loyalists had been established as Hayes's deputy, and a number of specially employed spies were at work in the west. On 18 January 1492 an anonymous spy was paid £1, perhaps as a month's wages. Hayes was picked up sometime in December 1491, and on 1 January 1492 the king reimbursed one Morley £2 for his expenses for transporting a man accused with Hayes to court.[38]

Security, however, was not the major reason for the failure of this apparent plot. Firstly, there was a question mark about the calibre of those Taylor wished to involve in the plot. With the execution of Sir Robert Chamberlain an obvious message had been sent out at home and abroad. With men like Chamberlain and George Neville out of the running, Taylor could find plotters only among the humblest of Richard III's supporters. Taylor was dabbling in politics not trading, and he knew it. He suggested to Hayes, either seriously, or to prompt him into action, that the Countess of Warwick be encouraged to stir men against Henry VII. This was pure fantasy. Possibly Taylor knew that Rowland Robinson, one of those attainted after East Stoke, and an officer from her manor of Berksewell, was serving Margaret of Burgundy. Or perhaps he thought, in the words of Joel Rosenthal, that great widows who survived to become matriarchs were bastions of political and partisan devotion.[39] If so he had forgotten the events of a lifetime. This was the widow of Richard Neville, Kingmaker, who after her husband's death had been removed from sanctuary, and incarcerated in Middleham castle. She had watched her own, and her family's, estates be divided between Clarence and his brother the Duke of Gloucester. Edward IV's last word, in 1474, was that she was to be treated, 'now', as if 'naturally dead'. To believe that she would support a coup on behalf of those who had thus buried her alive was the height of folly. Worse still was it to believe that she bore ill will to Henry VII, for in comparison with Edward and Richard he had treated her with some degree of courtesy. Though Henry had deprived her of a huge number of manors and settled on her an estate about a quarter of the size that was her due she was no longer 'as if naturally dead'.[40] Taylor wanted her to write to

Charles VIII or to any councillor of his that she knew offering assistance. Wise woman, if she ever received such a message it was ignored.

It is difficult to know what to make of Taylor's letter and the circumstances of its discovery and survival are peculiar. It was claimed, in the act of attainder in which it is recorded, that it was snatched from the fire into which Hayes had thrown it. If this was true clearly he was a marked man. Equally, though less plausible, it may be that some or all of the letter was reconstructed or invented in the absence of hard evidence. Yet the individuals mentioned in it belong to Taylor's and Hayes' world. It is possible that the letter took so long to reach Hayes, a month and a half, that though it indicates intent, by November of 1491 events had overtaken its suggestions.

As a result of his failure to reveal the letter Hayes was stripped of his royal offices, and punished, but there is no evidence that he took Taylor entirely at his word. Taylor and his tiny band of exiles were isolated from mainstream opinion in England, lacked any independent ability to create concerted actions elsewhere, and were blinkered about the real motives the French had for supporting them. The French, on the other hand, as they sent out Taylor's expedition, had timed matters to perfection. On 15 November they signed the treaty of Laval with the Duchess of Brittany. This guaranteed her and her councillors pensions and arrears for war damage and finalized what the French had angled for all summer: a repudiation of her husband by proxy, Archduke Maximilian. On 6 December she was contracted to marry Charles VIII, and on 2 February entered Paris to be blessed at St Dennis.[41]

Compared to the money ploughed into Philippe de Cleves's operation John Taylor's cost remarkably little: 1,737 livres. Yet it was thoroughly and ingeniously organized. It was to be presented in Ireland as an English expedition. One hundred and twenty surcoats were

Three large ships full of English soldiers entering a port. Counterfeiting English ships and uniforms was common French practice in this period and into the 1520s

embroidered with the cross of St George. One hundred and fourteen shields were made and similarly painted. A considerable quantity of armour was supplied: ten brigantines, ten sallet helmets, four suits of armour and sallets, nine bows and cases of arrows, and five halberds. Forty-nine livres were spent on 'un harnois blanc', white armour: a suit fit for a prince. The English prince's soldiers were to be taken to Ireland in ships which belonged to Adam Nyvelet. For this hazardous enterprise he was paid 1,500 livres.[42] Hazardous it was, for no coastline was safe this year. In 1492 Charles VIII informed his subjects that the English controlled the seas off Brittany, Normandy, and Picardy as well as Guienne. In the winter of 1491 privateers kept up a lively war: English against French, French against English and Spanish vessels, the Bretons threatening the towns on the rivers Charente and Gironde.[43] At the beginning of October 1491 Henry VII, aware of the likelihood of French action in Ireland sent Robert Symmonds to act as naval intelligence off the Cork–Waterford coast. Symmonds, master of the *Margaret of Barnstaple*, had served under Robert Willoughby de Broke in the Breton wars since 1489.[44] De Broke, like John Taylor a West Country man, controlled all naval operations against the French; so in order to get Nyvelet's ships, the *Marye Margot* and the *Passerose*, past de Broke they were decorated as English vessels and flew English standards. Nyvelet was paid to take Taylor and his rebel band to Ireland, land them in an Irish haven and remain in the vicinity for two months for resupply and to ensure good communications with France. The rebels were to disembark at will in Ireland, and if necessary to land in England.

They left Honfleur in mid-November 1491 and arrived off Ireland towards the end of the month. They had probably made one landing in England, when John Hayes was sent Taylor's letter. Off the south-east coast of Ireland they had rich choice of 100 miles of natural harbours from Wexford to Baltimore, a landscape much like Taylor's native south Devon. Their goal was the town of Cork, the principal town of Munster. Cork and Munster had been chosen for two reasons. From a personal point of view Taylor had contacts there. Cork provided markets and raw materials for the Devon cloth trade. Irish merchants traded with Somerset, Devon, and Cornwall and some settled in England to trade between Ireland and France. Shipping from western Europe congregated in Irish waters, and the coasts of Ireland, east and west, were profitable markets for Portuguese, Spaniards, Normans and Bretons.[45] Taylor's contact in Cork was John Atwater, bourgeois, merchant and sometime mayor. When, in 1499, Henry VII tactfully reminded Louis XII who had begun the Warbeck conspiracy, Atwater took the blame as inventor of the scandal,[46] though not as its organizer, that was Taylor. The second reason for choosing Munster was the semi-permanent state of disaffection of the FitzGerald earls of Munster from the English Crown at the end of the fifteenth century. The FitzGerald Earl of Desmond, Maurice the Lame, 'Bacagh', so called because he was carried everywhere in a chariot, ruled a swath of lands in the south and west from Wexford to Kerry. Munster was a Desmond province. Cork was a Desmond town, and among its mayors it boasted illegitimate sons of the Earls of Desmond. Prior to Taylor's mission there had been diplomatic contacts between France and Munster. French governments repeatedly played the Geraldine card in the sixteenth century, and the earl remained attached to Warbeck's cause until 1496.[47] There could not have been any rebellion in Munster without his connivance, and by the end of November he and Taylor's French expedition had, in the name of Richard, Duke of York, raised Kilkenny, Tipperary and part of Meath against Henry VII. The duke, Perkin Warbeck, had not travelled to Ireland with Taylor. He had been taken there, independently by Pregent Meno, his Breton master. Meno had arrived in Cork at about the same time as Taylor, for Thomas Furgon, a Cornish yeoman of the Crown, took him to Henry VII as a prisoner with another man, an Irishman, in the first week of December. Furgon was master of the *Anne of Fowey*, and may have been part of de Broke's force off southern Ireland. On 6 December he was paid for bringing to the king the Breton who 'conveyed the childe unto our lande of Ireland that causeth the abusion of our subgiettes there'.[48] From then on, for the next eight years, Henry disparagingly referred to Warbeck as 'the garçon' and 'the feigned lad'.

News of the landing had reached England before the end of November. Henry's first reaction, on 30 November, was to send James Norwiche, Doctor of Theology, to Ireland. Norwiche's task may have been to ensure the loyalty of the politically wavering among the Irish bench of bishops. The year of 1487 had shown just what Henry could expect from them when left to their own devices. They had crowned Lambert Simnel as Edward VI. Norwiche took with him 'especial messages' about the king's great matter. Ad hoc diplomat he may have been, spy he must have been. But he did not go without a struggle. Claiming his expenses were too small he refused the 20 marks Henry had apportioned him and insisted on £20, while the king told the exchequer to do it for as little as possible.[49] Indeed the response to the rebellion in Ireland was marked by ineptitude and delay. On 1 December the king appointed Thomas Garth and Sir James Ormond, an Irish esquire for the body, to the command of 30 sailors and 200 soldiers to suppress the Munster rebellion. They would leave from Bristol, initially posted for three months. Half the force were archers, well supplied with weapons, and further provision was made for raising mounted men from among Irish loyalists. Ormond was to be given 800 yards of scarlet cloth to issue as livery, the uniform of the genuine English King, so to distinguish his forces from the rebels in their St George's cross coats. Ormond and Garth were given sweeping powers: to array troops, to make statutes and proclamations, and to arrest and imprison anyone who disobeyed them. Ormond was granted lands in Ireland, in Meath, Kilkenny and Tipperary, which had belonged to the Earl of March. This was a reward, but it was one with a political point, for it aimed at undercutting any claims by the rebels to Yorkist legitimacy through the title of Edward IV as Earl of March. Finally, and most tellingly, they were to command absolute obedience within Ireland and supersede the King's Lieutenant there, Garret FitzGerald, the Great Earl of Kildare, from whom Henry absolved all his Irish subjects of their loyalty. Things had gone badly wrong in Ireland when both FitzGeralds, Kildare and Desmond, were said to be in arms against the Saxon King Henry. Yet in England there was procrastination. Neither Garth nor Ormond were given money or material with any urgency, and on 8 December Henry wrote, confessing his 'great mervaill', that Garth had not been supplied with his weapons, and remained in England unable to leave for their lack. Ormond had fared no better. All he been paid in hand was 100 marks. He was 300 marks short in wages and was without his scarlet livery cloth.[50] When the expedition eventually reached Ireland it was full five months before it restored order to Munster.

By supporting Philippe de Cleves and John Taylor the French succeeded in mounting diversions which prevented both Archduke Maximilian of Austria and Henry VII from defending Brittany. Yet there was a price to pay. In July 1491 Henry VII took the first steps towards an invasion of France. He proceeded slowly, almost reluctantly, at first, even after he had agreed to a joint declaration of war on France, on 15 April 1492, and an invasion two months later. What changed Henry from a reluctant participant in a punitive but fruitless war to a man intent on involving against France the maximum force Europe could muster, and in the event going it alone, was the news which reached him from Ireland at the end of November. At the same time as he sent Garth and Ormond to Ireland he wrote to the papacy, to the Sforza Duke of Milan, to the Electors of the Holy Roman Empire and others. And his fury against the French leaps from the page. It is in this anger that the statement, if Henry found France standing up to her neck in water he would place his foot on her head and drown her, originated. At Christmas 1491 Henry began helping well-placed but discontented Bretons in a plan which aimed to deliver the town of Brest to the English. By the end of

Irish soldiers, early sixteenth century. Contemporary descriptions refer to these soldiers as 'naked', meaning that they lacked body armour

January England was girding its loins for war, a war which eventually saw France invaded by an army of just over 15,000 men and the use of over 600 boats for transport.[51]

The reasons for Henry's war with France have always escaped historians. The recovery of an independent Brittany was beyond him, well intentioned as he might be. The recovery of his war expenses was a more realistic goal. But Henry's war, like Edward IV's in 1475, was also a war of revenge to punish the French for their egging on the Scots to war with England, and for their rekindling of the dynastic problem in England. In June of 1492 Henry VII sent a squadron of about thirty-five English ships under Willoughby de Broke to devastate Normandy. Despite being rebuffed they landed 1,500 men on the coast, terrorizing Normandy for a month and a half before burning forty-five ships in the harbour at Barfleur.[52] Henry also intended invading France to secure the expulsion of Warbeck from Charles VIII's court where he went in March 1492. But this was a critical error, for by May of 1492 Warbeck had become all but an irrelevance in European politics. The French had more or less given up his cause. Acccording to Laurent Breton, who was interrogated in France about Warbeck, many people now believed there was no such person as Richard, Duke of York. Others thought that he might be the son of the brother of King Edward. The Earl of Warwick? In any case, said Laurent Breton, at that moment (summer 1492) nobody really cared.[53] By invading France and forcing Warbeck's flight, Henry drove him to Flanders and to Margaret of Burgundy's adoption of his cause as a point of truth and honour. That the conspiracy was so successful after 1492 has to do with this action of Henry VII's, and the fact that in Perkin Warbeck, John Taylor had found a pretender of incomparable ability and facility.

FOUR

But to be Young

What was Perkin Warbeck? Facing this question, how was it possible for Perkin Warbeck to impersonate Richard Plantagenet, we are confronted by two problems. Firstly, was Warbeck indeed not Perkin Warbeck, but the person he claimed to be, Edward IV's second son? We deny this only to meet the second problem. How could an adolescent, generally credited with being nothing more than a boatman's son, a wage labourer's son, successfully maintain for eight years the impersonation of a prince? The temptation to accept the first fantastic solution, Warbeck was Richard Plantagenet, is considerable but should be resisted. However, if it is resisted how do we explain the conundrum of the impersonation? Ever since James Gairdner, in the nineteenth century, produced information from the Tournai archives about Perkin's family it has been clear that Warbeck was not a Plantagenet[1]. But such factual knowledge compounds rather than diminishes the interest of the Warbeck problem, for the question of how Warbeck's identity, both real and assumed, was constructed and maintained; and about why it was, and still is by some, believed that he was Richard, Duke of York, is ignored.

Since the nub of the problem is the nature of Warbeck's identity it is to literature that we ought to turn for the truest answer. Yet only one work, John Ford's *The Chronicle History of Perkin Warbeck a Strange Truth*, confronts this problem.[2] The rest, and the works of history which deal with him, fall into two camps: those which dismiss Warbeck as a fraud and those which believe him to have been Duke of York. In the year 1830 two novels appeared with Warbeck as their subject: Mary Shelley's *The Fortunes of Perkin Warbeck* and Alexander Campbell's *Perkin Warbeck; or the Court of James the Fourth of Scotland*. In her preface Shelley confessed that she had been driven to the beief that 'Perkin was, in reality, the lost duke of York . . . no person who has studied the subject but arrives at the same conclusion.' Campbell had no such qualms. For him, though Warbeck was an imposter, he was a Yorkist Bastard.[3] This happy coincidence, two novels in one year on the same subject, illustrates the persistence of the two diametrically opposed traditions. The roots of Campbell's view can be traced to the official histories of Henry Tudor's reign beginning with Polydore Vergil. For Vergil, Warbeck was 'of low birth and embarrassed by poverty in his childhood, he had begun to wander in foreign lands'.[4] From Vergil runs a line of descent to his translator and popularizer, Edward Hall, in 1547, and thence to Francis Bacon in 1622. It is in Bacon that an ostensibly true narrative of Warbeck's life is created out of misunderstood evidence. Here is Warbeck's father, a converted Jew, working in London, known by Edward IV, who stood godfather to the man, John, whose name was not Warbeck at all, but Osbeck. Here is the family's return from London to Tournai and Perkin's fantasy that being godson of Edward IV he might be 'base blood of the House of York'. Here is the fantasist – seductive notion – the boy who began 'to entertain such thoughts in his head'.[5] It is a short distance from Bacon to David Hume and from there to James Gairdner. Gairdner purged Bacon of his misreadings of

Bernard André, and pointed up Vergil's mistakes, but kept the essentials of their tradition: Warbeck was an imposter, pure and factually simple.

The equal and opposite reaction to this school is epitomized in Mary Shelley's novel, dubbed by one critic a 'barely readable fiction'. Despite drawing information from the Tudor chronicles she stands in the line of the seventeenth-century reaction against the damning criticism of Richard III. Here, usually as part of an attempt to exculpate Richard from guilt over the murder of the Princes in the Tower an argument that Warbeck was Duke of York was developed. Thus George Buck, in 1646, wrote a section in his History of Richard III entitled 'Counterfeit Prince detected, young Prince marvelously preserved. Many testimonies for the assertion that Perkin Warbeck was Richard Duke of York; his honourable entertainment with forraigne Princes vox populi.'[6] In 1768 Horace Walpole's *Historic Doubts on the Life and Reign of King Richard III* examined the case, and stated in the summary, 'That there is no proof that those children were murdered . . . That . . . Henry's . . . whole behaviour in Perkin's case was mysterious, and betrayed his belief or doubt that Warbeck was the true Duke of York.' Seizing on Bacon's prima facie weaknesses he continued, 'That it was morally impossible for the Duchess of Burgundy at the distance of twenty-seven years to instuct a Flemish lad so perfectly in all that had passed in the court of England, that he would not have been detected in a few hours. That she could not inform him, nor could he know, what had passed in the Tower, unless he was the true Duke of York.'[7] Much of Walpole is sophistry of the worst kind, a kind of prissy rationalism that finds the behaviour described in the previous chapter beyond its ken. Walpole's challenge, that the documents would prove him true, was trumped by Gairdner, in 1898, using the Tournai town archive. Still the argument persisted. John Bayley's *The History and Antiquity of the Tower of London* (1825) took the claims of the Yorkists that Warbeck was York at face value.[8]

The debate on Warbeck's identity was carried on in general works of history, or in work on Richard III. There have been few books devoted to him *per se*. But the split exhibited above is found in those few works there are. The oldest, a life by Thomas Gainsford, was published in 1618. This is a remorseless copy of Hall's chronicle, plodding and derivative, and a paean to the absolute value of obedience to princes. Nothing redresses a tedium which alternates conventional narrative, set piece speeches and Latin quotations from Lucan and Euripides to indicate the mood of the speakers. Its conclusion that Warbeck was a fake is never in doubt.[9] In the same camp is Jean-Didier Chastelain's 1952 life *L'Imposture de Perkin Warbeck*. Despite being published in Brussels, disappointingly it drew on only a little more than Gairdner, and on no European archive.[10] The most modern work, in 1990, *Richard of England*, by its title alone leaves no doubt as to what its author considers Warbeck's real identity. For Diana Kleyn, Buck on the Princes is her gospel: 'these young princes were embarked in a ship at Tower wharf, and . . . were conveyed from hence into the seas, and so cast into the deeps and drowned. But some others say that they were not drowned, but were set safe on shore beyond the seas.' Thereafter, that villain of Tudor calumny, Sir James Tyrrell, is turned from the murderer of princes into the saviour of the Duke of York, spiriting him to safety in Tournai. Once there, with his stepfather and mother, the Warbecks, York is maintained first by Richard III's pension and then through the good offices of Sir Edward Brampton until the fateful day he attempts to recover his throne.[11]

All this, on both sides of the division, is shutting the door after the horse has bolted with a vengeance. As we have seen, Warbeck's arrival in international politics had little to do with the English political scene and everything to do with France's desire to annex Brittany. To present one truth about Warbeck which was believed by others consistently over the ten years of the conspiracy is an impossibility. No such thing ever existed. Over the ten years of the conspiracy he became a prism through which the desires of others were refracted. Nor can we be sure of consistency in Warbeck himself. Although, between 1491 and 1497, he played his assigned role to the hilt in the autumn of 1497 he claimed that, 'for two years', 'he had longed to escape from these troubles but Fortune had not allowed him'. Indeed the one thing about Warbeck which becomes clearer as the sources become more numerous is an almost pathological need to dissemble, act and dissimulate. That this resulted from his ordeal cannot be doubted. But it was also innate to him.

The question of this type of pathological personality is brilliantly explored in John Ford's *Perkin Warbeck* of 1634; in the words of T.S. Eliot, 'one of the very best historical plays outside the works of Shakespeare in the whole of Elizabethan and Jacobean drama.' Ford tracks the twin fates of Henry Tudor and Perkin Warbeck across the years 1495–9. Henry opens the play: 'Still to be haunted, still to be pursued/ Still to be frighted with false apparitions/ Of pageant majesty . . . / As if we were a mockery king in state . . .' and proceeds via hard work to master the state. Warbeck only appears at act two in the full dramatic expectation of his imposture. His passage from this entrance to his execution is a virtuoso performance which all but convinces us he is Richard, Duke of York. By the end of the play Henry possesses the State, but the other category set up by Ford in his prologue, Truth, is possessed by Warbeck. To Warbeck, by a dramatic sleight of hand, falls the lot of demonstrating nobility through the exercise of free will. He wills to die rather than admit he is a false duke. And in this position, faced with certain death, his motivation is commented on by those who surround him, Henry, the Earl of Oxford, Giles Lord Daubney, Christopher Urswick; in one breathtaking scene in conversation with Lambert Simnel. This chorus reflects the different judgements on Warbeck, that he was self deluded (Bacon), that he was simply another Lambert Simnel, that he was demonically possessed, or that he is a failed version of Henry Tudor. The genius of the play resides in making Warbeck 'appear as quite convinced that he is the lawful heir to the throne of England. We ourselves', says Eliot, 'are left almost believing that he was; in the right state of uncertainty, wondering whether his kingly and steadfast behaviour is due to his royal blood, or merely due to his passionate conviction that he is of royal blood.'[12] It is Ford who, despite the liberties he takes with the facts, comes closest to the historical–psychological reality of Warbeck. In the drama we are forced to confront him as his contemporaries would have been, and like them make a judgement: prince, madman, victim, hero. What was Warbeck?

Perkin Warbeck was born in the parish of St Jehan des Cauffours, on the east bank of the River Scheldt, in the city of Tournai. The Scheldt there is slow moving and not very wide, and the river bank still has on it houses from the fourteenth century that would have been old when Perkin was born. His parents, Jehan de Werbecque and Nicaise Farou had their house near the river and, like others of their class had connections outside Tournai, at Pipaix, 8 miles from the town and also at Lannoy. The Farous can be found in Tournai before the Werbecques as early as 1413, when a will mentions Regnault father of Nicaise; but not our Nicaise, whose father was Pierre. Given the names and the length of time the Farous had lived in Tournai it is highly unlikely as has been suggested that they were Portuguese Jews. The Werbecques arrived in the town when Diericq de Werbecque emigrated there from Béarne les Oudenaarde, up-river towards Ghent. Diericq was an artisan, a boat builder, who in June 1429, became a burgess of the town. He died sometime before 1474, but well before then this *arriviste* family was on its way to prosperity. His widow remarried to Pierart Flan, Dean of the Guild of Boatmen and Receiver of Tournai. Like Diericq he too had emigrated to Tournai, from Conde. We, like Warbeck at his birth, are in the reaches of the political dynasties of successful artisans and bourgeois who ran the prosperous towns of Flanders in the late fifteenth century. Diericq had three children, Noel, Jehanne and Jehan, Perkin's father. We do not know who Noel married. But Jehanne married Jehan Stalyn of the parish of

Tournai, Pont des Trous – Water Gate, thirteenth century. Built across the river Scheldt it is the only remaining gate of eighteen which originally surrounded the city of Tournai

St Piat (a local saint), south of the Scheldt, in the shadow of the cathedral. Her brother, Jehan, became a burgess in May 1474 by right of inheritance from his father, and was, subsequently, Comptroller of Tournai. How many legitimate children he and his wife Nicaise had is not clear. It is clear that Jehan sired two bastards, Nicolas, brought up at Pipaix, and Innocent, as well as two children named Thiroyan and Jehanne, who died of plague. Jehanne's two legitimate and surviving children were Perkin and his sister, another Jehanne. This sister and her husband, Jehan Cambier, were alive as late as 1517.[13]

What were these people? Not, certainly, the sort of poor artisans who inhabited the shanty towns on the outskirts of most Flemish towns, they were entrepreneurs – pilots and merchants. When Nicaise Werbecque sold the family home in 1498, after the death of Perkin's father, it was purchased by Jehan Vallois the son of a merchant. When she died in 1513 she left a will sixty centimetres wide and a metre long. She was buried in the chapel of St Julien in the parish church of St Jehan des Cauffours. Her bequests show her to have belonged to the prosperous middling sort: chantry masses were to be sung in the hospital of St Jehan de la Plancque; she left bequests to the poor, and bequests to the almshouse near the castle of Laplaigne and Mortaigne. Laplaigne, 10 miles from Tournai, is on the river Scheldt, so the Werbeques may have had land there, reached by boat. Warbeck's grandmother's second marriage was to a receiver of Tournai. His mother's to one of its comptrollers. Her father was a minor civic official – keeper of the gates of St John. John Styenbek of Antwerp, the cousin with whom Warbeck stayed with in 1484, was also a town officer.[14] Studies of this sort at Ghent show them to have been an élite 'well educated, highly mobile, associating with the princely court and sometimes using town office as a spring board to higher positions'. By 1400 the most highly paid officers in Flemish towns were the guild deans,

Tournai, Cathedral of Notre Dame said to have been founded in the third century by St Piat, the most important Tournaisian saint. Warbeck's uncle lived in the parish of St Piat

men such as Pierart Flan, Warbeck's grandfather by adoption, Dean of the Guild of Boatmen of the Scheldt. Such men had been well educated, sometimes to university level. By 1500 the guilds they headed were no longer purely craft associations. At Tournai the Guild of Boatmen included among its number rich lime merchants and quarry owners, and entry to guilds was strictly regulated. At Tournai two charters of 1424 recognized the existence of these guilds as a force in government and granted them a direct participation in ruling the city. The deans and subdeans of guilds formed a college of seventy-two representatives, a new consistory court in a town which already had three old courts. From this new court recruitment was made to the aldermanic and other functions of town government.[15] It has often been wondered how a simple boatman's son could masquerade as King of England. The answer is that Warbeck came not from among the lowliest boatmen of Tournai but from its governing classes.

Philippe de Commynes, who held lands in Tournai, said that in the 1470s Tournai enjoyed great prosperity. Forty years later the same thing was said by the Milanese ambassador to the Holy Roman Empire. He described its wealthy families, its population 'who could not be more French',[16] its multiple defences and its suburbs. It had a market place large enough to be the site of the annual tournament (where the most prestigious commercial families took on the parts of fictitious kings of chivalry) surrounded by large, rich houses.[17] The churches of the town were fine; and the Scheldt kept it supplied with abundant food and merchandise. Assessing it for its potential as a war prize Brian Tuke, one of Wolsey's underlings, noted, 'It manufactures excellent carpets and table covers, and will prove very useful to the king, as Burgundian and Rhenish wine can conveniently be brought thence to England.'[18] It was a cosmopolitan town attracting emigrants from all parts of Flanders, Artois and Hainault as well as Germans and members of the Hanseatic League. Tournai had a flourishing industry in stone images and also boasted a school of painting. In 1468 Jacques Daret, its principal artist played a leading part in painting the decorations used to celebrate Margeret of York's marriage to Charles the Bold. But it was cloth produced in the town 'Dornix' – Tournai which provided it greatest commercial wealth.[19]

By the end of the fifteenth century the main driving force of Tournai's economy was its manufacture of canvas, says and satin. Perkin Warbeck's maternal grandfather, Pierre Farou, was in the canvas trade. So when a trade for young Pierrechon was chosen it was into cloth he went. The towns to which he was sent either by his mother, or, subsequently, by his masters: Antwerp, Bergen-op-Zoom, and Middelburg, were all places which traded in English woollen cloths. Bergen and Antwerp both had international cloth marts, Bergen's at Easter and Christmas, Antwerp's at Whit and in August and September, the so-called Bavons Mart. Antwerp was beginning to outstrip nearby Bruges as the rising star of the Netherlandish economy. It had markets of one sort or another in season all year and was the centre of trade between England and Germany through the Hansa and down the Rhine.[20] As a native of Tournai, Warbeck's mother tongue was French. Tournai considered itself French. The banners of its guilds had symbols on them protesting their loyalty to the French Crown, and the city won a prize for its composition in French at a literary contest in Ghent in 1430. But Flanders as a political entity was split between the French-speaking south and the Germanic north, where commerce was so vital. To take any part in commerce Warbeck would have to acquire Flemish and possibly German.[21] Given the polyglot nature of Antwerp and Bergen- op-Zoom he could also be expected to pick up a smattering of English from English quarters in both places, as well as a nodding acquaintance with the Italian of bankers, and the Portuguese of the long-haul Atlantic trade. Before he went to Antwerp he had been educated. Literacy was widespread by 1400 and many children, not just those of the wealthy, went to school. Pierrechon and his sister had tutors, whose names we know,

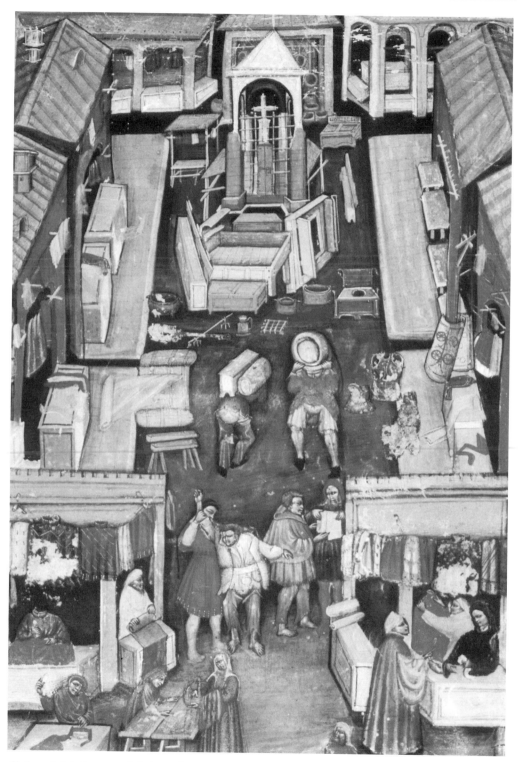

Cloth market, in the street of cloth merchants, 1470. Towns in Flanders still sell cloth like this at annual fairs such as the Braderie at Lille in early September

Pierart or Pierre Flan and Adrien Carlier. Once again the question of the simple boatman's son evaporates. This was an educated boy, and if he was in commerce he would be expected to manage Latin, however perfunctorily, as well as his other languages.[22]

Perkin Warbeck's date of birth is not known, but if he was about the same age as Richard, Duke of York he was born between 1472 and 1474. This tallies roughly with what we know of his life and what we can reconstruct from his confession. The first date we can suggest with any hope of its accuracy is December 1484, when he was sent to Antwerp to learn Flemish. He only stayed six months in Antwerp, because of the terrible wars then afflicting the Low Countries, and went back home for a year. Since he was six months in Antwerp, and a year at home, the eve of his second visit to Antwerp was, again probably, June 1486. Before he went to learn Flemish in Antwerp he had boarded with his aunt and her husband, Jehan Stalyn, for 'a certayun season'. It is impossible to be certain why he did so, but his boarding may have been to gain experience before beginning work in the cloth trade importing business.[23] If so it was a rude awakening to the realities of international politics.

The death of the French king, Louis XI, opened the long process by which Maximilian of Austria reconquered the Low Countries. In September 1483 he overthrew the French government around his son at Antwerp and made war with Ghent and Bruges. Ghent and Bruges replied by building a blockhouse to halt trade on the Scheldt, to strangle the trade of Antwerp and much of Flanders. Maximilian was so poor that he raised cash for his war by ransoming prisoners and auctioning captured cattle in the market place at Antwerp.[24] English trade of wool to Antwerp dropped dramatically in the years 1483–5, cut by piracy in the channel and the harassment of merchants attempting to enter Antwerp by both French and Burgundian troops.[25] Given the circumstances of the war, Warbeck's return to Tournai was perfectly natural. But it was a war which went Maximilian's way and by July 1485 both Bruges and Ghent had capitulated to him. For seven months there was peace. Maximilian went to Germany for election as King of the Romans; his nobility preserved peace with France; Warbeck returned to Antwerp to work for Alexander. Alexander's man in Antwerp, Berlo, placed Warbeck in lodgings with a skinner, in a house close to the English Merchant Adventurers' Hall near to the Great Market and the Old Bourse. Warbeck came back to Antwerp to learn Flemish, instead, he fell ill and took five months to recover. If he returned to Antwerp in June 1486, when peace seemed assured, then the end of his illness was October 1486, for we are moving from his confession as our only source to safer territory. His illness, from its duration, and timing, may have been plague. Plague had been rife in Flanders since 1467. In the worst years of the century, 1480–2, when freezing winters and meningitis epidemics swept France, Amiens, Lille, Rheims and Cologne were affected by plague, but not, apparently, the Flemish towns. In 1487, when the plague in France was mainly recorded in the south and west, Antwerp, Ghent, Brussels, Ypres and Sichen were afflicted. Brussels, Louvain and Sichen were afflicted in 1488 and the same places along with Lille and Maastricht were in 1489. Plague is not recorded in Tournai in 1487, but its proximity to Lille, and the letter which Warbeck said he received from his mother, suggest that it was in 1487 that the plague killed his brother and sister, Thiroyan and the first Jehanne.

Warbeck was lucky to survive, but neither his experience of commerce nor the Flemish language was advancing much. He had not attended any of the principal marts of the region. In Antwerp his illness may have coincided with Sixen mart at Whit and also Bavon mart, which ended in October. However he was sent to Bergen-op-Zoom in October 1486, perhaps to work at the Cold mart – neither healthful nor merry – which began in December each year. He stayed here for two months before Berlo, his master, placed him in service at Middelburg, another cloth town. Once more he was to 'lern the langage', and this time he lived with

Antwerp, the Scheldt Gate, 1520. Drawing by Albrecht Durer. Warbeck's family may have acted as pilots between here and Tournai

another merchant John Strewe. Strewe is the last of the trio of obscure merchants with whom Warbeck began his career.[26] Arrived in Middelburg at Christmas 1486, by May 1487 he was in service at the Portuguese Court. This move is critical to Warbeck's story, and much has been made of it, not least in attempting to find links between this part of his life, the Yorkist court of the 1470s, Margaret of Burgundy's Flanders of the 1480s and his later impersonation. The reality which emerges from behind Warbeck's confession is more prosaic and more extraordinary than the vague hints of the confession which contain it.

Antwerp in the 1480s has been described as 'an economic innocent: other people came knocking at the door, moved in and made her fortune for her'. It had none of the complex banking mechanisms of Bruges, its near neighbour, but it had the same mix of peoples. Ships of all nations anchored off the Isle of Walchern and on the Scheldt: Dutch Portuguese, Spanish, Italian, Ragusan, Catalonian, English and Breton. The Hanseatic, English and French merchants were important in Antwerp, but it was the southern merchants: Potuguese, Spanish and Italians, particularly the Genoese and Florentines, who dominated the scene. Working in Antwerp was working in one of the most important towns in Europe, on the eve of its success. This was a cosmopolitan world where mark up profits of 250 per cent were possible in the cloth trade, and Bruges was the centre of this world of wheelers and dealers as she was the centre of the world markets, the junction where north met south, where the long-haul galleys of Italy met the Hanseatics from the Baltic, and where eastern Europe met the west. This world market town was a huge service industry of money changers, bankers, and innkeepers-cum-brokers. The population of Bruges at beginning of the fifteenth century was reckoned to consist 50 per cent of foreigners. They found recreations in taverns, gambling houses, bath houses and brothels. Foreigners were allowed to own houses in Bruges but only people of their own nationality could lodge with them. Other nationals had to lodge with innkeepers, and were closely supervised. Their landlords daily provided the government of Bruges with lists of their guests.[27]

One of those who owned a house in Bruges was an Anglo-Portuguese Jewish merchant, Duarte Brandão, alias Sir Edward Brampton. Warbeck knew his wife, Lady Margaret Beaumont, and took ship with her in the *Queens Ship* for Portugal, at Easter 1487, 15 April. More ink has been spilt on the subject of Warbeck and Duarte Brandão than almost any other facet of the story. Partly this is the result of Brandão's fascinating career, and partly it is the result of wishful thinking, the attempt to find an absolute link between the Yorkist court and Warbeck, to provide Warbeck with a teacher for his imposture. It reaches its height in Cecil Roth's articles, the first of which was entitled 'Perkin Warbeck and his Jewish Master'.[28] Warbeck never claimed to have served Brandão, only to have known his wife. Certainly Brandão owned a knowledge of him, and they probably knew each other, but how closely they were associated is an open question. It is important to remember that our knowledge of the relationship comes from the confession, and one of the jobs of this confession was to provide clear pointers to the living who knew Warbeck. Brandão was a well-known figure in England, the Low Countries and Portugal. To associate Warbeck with him tied Warbeck to an inescapable and verifiable reality, commerce.

Supporters of the notion that Brandão was the *éminence grise* behind Warbeck, like to stress his fidelity to York, to both Edward IV and Richard III, and thus by extension to Margaret of Burgundy and to Warbeck. In reality Brandão was more typical of his time, his place, his class and his accident of birth than fits such an easy idea. His driving force was not an attachment to one national dynasty but a desire to self aggrandisement, to bettering his postion, to wealth, honour and prestige, and perhaps, a desire to return to Portugal, the land which by law, religion and accident of birth had disowned him. He was born the illegitimate son of a Jewess and a blacksmith, and in the late 1460s was forced to flee from Portugal to England. In England by 1468 he caught the eye of Edward IV who sponsored his baptism in the Domus Conversorum, as a Jewish convert to Christianity. How else could he get on? Between 1468 and 1475 he was loyal to Edward, and served him well at several critical junctures. He was well rewarded: in land, and marriage to his first wife Isabel Pecche.[29] In 1475 his career took an abrupt upturn, based albeit on years of hard work. Following Edward IV's invasion of France he came to the notice of Charles the Bold of Burgundy. He remained in Burgundy until after Charles's death when he was lucky enough to run across the penniless Alfonso V, King of Portugal. Charles had been Alfonso's patron, but was now dead. Brandão, who by this stage was a well-off merchant lent Alfonso the money to return to Portugal. In 1479 Alfonso demonstrated his gratitude by naturalizing Brandão, creating him king's counsellor, exempting him from customs on imports, and, most lucrative of all, giving him a monopoly of malagueta pepper, the so-called Grain of Paradise drug that was so fashionable at the time. Brandão was made, and his life developed as a triangular enterprise between England, Portugal, and Flanders.[30]

In 1480 he was back in England, involved in shady dealing concerning his wife's lands. Though it is assumed that his first wife died prior to his second marriage evidence exists to suggest that, as with other aspects of his career, marriage was for financial gain: Duarte Brandão may have been a bigamist.[31] Next year with 160 men and his own ship, a Portuguese carvel, he took part in the naval action under John Howard against Scotland. In what spirit was this undertaken? He was rewarded with a grant of the export of wool from

Bruges, the 'Old Hall'. This late thirteenth-century Guildhall is testimomy to the wealth and power generated by cloth production and subsequently maintained by a world market

London, Sandwich, and Southampton to the straits of Morocco, the essential prerequisite to his whole commercial enterprise, as we will see. At the same time he was promoted: 1481, Esquire of the body; 1482, captain, keeper and governor of Guernsey. The accession of Richard III saw no slackening of his career, political or commercial. In May 1483 he was sent by Richard against his rebel Sir Edward Woodville, and throughout the reign he was in receipt of lavish gifts of annuities and favourable commercial grants, the shipment of wool, for example, to the value of £200 in 1484 and the rewarded lands of Tudor partisans.[32] By a stroke of good fortune he was sent out of England in March 1485. For some years he had acted as informal diplomatic agent between Portugal and England and in that fateful year Richard III dispatched him to negotiate a marriage with a Portuguese princess. Duarte was still in Portugal in August 1485, and still there as late as October that year. For the next three years, like any man with sound judgement he stayed well clear of England and developed his commercial ventures.[33]

By 1486 he was living in Bruges, where he had an agency, employing an Italian, Arnaldo de Recaselli, as his factor. In 1487 he was the means by which King João II of Portugal paid the outstanding portion of the Infanta Leonora's dowry to Frederick III, father of Maximilian. The negotiations took all of 1487, one way and another, and it seems likely that Brandão travelled backwards and forwards between Portugal and Flanders that year. However, on 5 May 1487, Brandão was given leave to settle in Portugal. According to the charter of admission, Brandão, João's counsellor and a knight of his household had 'informed us of his desire and will to leave the Town of Bruges, where he now has his seat, and (bring) his wife and children to our realms, and here establish himself to live . . .'. The mechanics of all this we are unsure of but his wife at least, with Warbeck made the voyage at Easter 1487, three weeks before the date of this charter. Brandão's move from Flanders to Portugal again speaks volumes about an acute commercial nose, and his consistent instinct for survival.[34]

Flanders in 1487 was turning into a charnel house. Maximilian had returned to the Low Countries with his father in May 1486. His father came to live off the Netherlands while the Hungarians occupied Vienna; Maximilian came not to make peace but to open war against the French. The war was carried on by mercenaries hired from Germany and Switzerland, and paid for out of specially levied war taxes. While his mercenaries plundered the Low Countries Maximilian's Burgundian nobility conducted the war like a tournament, and between them they spread plague to the major commercial centres of the Low Countries. By 1487 Flanders and Holland were reduced to a chaos worse than the wars of 1482. Trade was impossible, and frequent spy scares saw to it that merchants were liable to summary arrest and ransoming by both sides.[35] Seven months after Brandão and company left Bruges, William Cely wrote to his brothers that the war between Maximilian and Ghent was so bad that 'ther maye noo man pass be londe to Barow [Bergen-op-Zoom], for they of Gaunte take them presonners, what maner men somever they be . . . wherffor ther dars noo merchauntys resorte to nor ffroo . . . Syr wee thyncyth the world goyth on whelys yn Flaunders, Godde better hytt . . .'.[36] During these years the natural trading links with Portugal were severed and the merchants of Bruges looked elsewhere for imports to survive on. The lucky ones, like Brandão, got out before the situation deteriorated completely, and ran their businesses personally from Lisbon instead of using agents and factors there.[37]

The economic links between Flanders and Portugal were well established by the time Warbeck went to Lisbon. There had been a resident Portuguese factor at Bruges since 1441 and, when Bruges went into terminal decline after 1493, he was moved to Antwerp. The Portuguese sent oil, wine, dried fruits and cork to Bruges, and once West Africa was opened up slaves, gold, ivory, cotton, skins and feathers followed. Sugar was first sold in Flanders in 1468 and malagueta in 1472. When the Azores were opened up in 1430 the Flemish helped settle them and by the 1450s Bruges merchants were favourably placed in Lisbon. In 1468 duties on Flemish cloth entering Lisbon were reduced. And in 1472 Flemish merchants in Lisbon formed a brotherhood paying a levy on exports of oil, honey, soap, wine, wax, cork, sardines and malagueta pepper to support a chapel. For Warbeck to travel with the wife of Duarte Brandão to Lisbon was entirely natural. It removed him from the immediate dangers in Flanders. It gave him wider experience in trade, and it placed him in a town with a large

Lisbon, the centre of international trade from where you could go anywhere

Flemish community.[38] What could have been more conducive to a young man. He came to Portugal as far from being a nobody, but as one who the counsellor and household knight of João II, Duarte Brandão, could willingly recommend to his fellow, Pero Vaz da Cunha. Warbeck took service with da Cunha for a year. But what a year. Portugal trembled on the verge of discovering the sea route to India and the Far East, and of establishing its economic empire. She was the most outward looking power in Europe, and Lisbon, for these few years, was the most important city in Europe. 'Bliss was it in that dawn to be alive, / But to be young was very heaven!'

Columbus had settled in Portugal in 1481; Warbeck arrived in 1487. Every spring fleets of lateen-rigged carvels were bringing to the Tagus bags of malagueta pepper, cords of elephant tusks, coffles of Negro slaves and chests of gold dust. In the autumn they set forth again with holds full of red caps, hawks' bells, Venetian beads and assorted truck that the Negroes bought for gold; and deck loads of horses for which native chiefs paid extravagent prices. Along the quays and in the narrow streets of the old town all the languages spoken from Iceland to the Cameroons could be heard; seamen from Scandinavia, England and Flanders jostled Spaniards, Genoese, Moors, Berbers and converted Negro potentates. New churches and palaces were being built, Italian bankers and Jewish money changers had offices all round the square; Lisbon was enterprising, opulent and sanguine.[39] In 1482 the Congo river was discovered, and in the year of Warbeck's arrival João II sent Pero da Covilhã and Afonso de Pavia to Alexandria in search of the legendary Prester John. Pero reached India and settled, eventually, in Abyssinia where he lived, still, in 1526. This was the world of Perkin Warbeck.[40]

Of the five people whom we know knew him in Portugal, two were fidalgos, from their renown probably Cavalerios fidalgos, the top ranking officers of the royal household; two were king's counsellors, higher ranked than fidalgos. The last was King João II himself. Duarte Brandão was settled in Lisbon by 22 May 1487. He immediately received a huge annuity, title to two lordships and a tithe of a customs duty. With this he set himself up in a splendid house facing the Serro dos Almirantes, adjacent to the Paço de Madeira. The next year he exchanged his annuity of 50,000 reals for marsh lands and the year after this, in 1488, he visited England.[41] What was he up to? Securing his business ventures. Brandão was one of those who made the Portuguese economy what it was. He sold malagueta pepper in London, through Antwerp, buying cloth in return, for barter on the Malagueta coast, in Guinea. When, in 1489, he secured a general pardon from Henry VII it was for his usual purposes of furthering his business. He had been disassociated from York long enough to be once more *persona grata* in England, and in 1489 had acted as informal intermediary between the English embassy and the Portuguese court when Henry VII made João II a knight of the Order of the Garter.[42] Exploration and Africa are the connecting factors common to all who knew Perkin.

Brandão obtained for Warbeck his entrée to the Portuguese court, and in the 1490s, when Warbeck fascinated all Europe there were many who could claim recognition. In 1494 João himself was interested enough to commission Martin Behaim, a Nuremberger in his employ, to report back to him, from Flanders, on 'the young King of England'.[43] Behaim had gone to Flanders ostensibly to collect money due to his father-in-law for sugar. His father-in-law, Jobst Hurter, a Fleming, was captain of Faial and Pico, islands in the Azores. Behaim had emigrated to Portugal from Nuremberg at the beginning of the eighties. He was made a Cavalerio in 1485 and married in 1488.[44] He was one of those extraordinary men who by dint of their talent for self-advertisement cause others to doubt

Martin Behaim's globe. The first globe of the world made by Behaim in 1492. Behaim was a native of Nuremberg the most important centre of science and technology in fifteenth-century Germany

their real ability. With connections in trade, in Portugal and in the scientific centre of Nuremberg, Behaim made a fundamental contribution to exploration. He claimed to have been instrumental in rounding the Guinea coast and discovering malagueta pepper. But whether this is true or false his real contribution to exploration was that in 1492 he made the first ever globe of the world. Behaim, like Brandão had the trust of the king, for he was a member of the royal maritime commission which scrutinized all exploration projects tendered to the king.[45]

In 1496, when the Spanish offered to send Henry a declaration from the King-at-Arms of Portugal concerning Warbeck's status they named as principal informant one Rui de Sousa. De Sousa had been on embassy to Spain in 1495 and had been identified by Ferdinand and Isabella as a man who knew both Warbeck and the real Richard Plantagenet, Duke of York.[46] De Sousa was one of the most highly placed of João II's household. In 1482 João had sent him to England to warn Edward IV off his projected exploration of the Guinea coast. Sent to England in February he successfully completed his mission and returned to Portugal in mid-September.[47] When Henry VII sent his ambassadors to Portugal in April 1489 it was de Sousa who greeted them on João II's behalf with the Grand Seneschal of Portugal and the Captain of Portugal. The ambassadorial report designates him 'baron'; he was a Fidalgo, one of a remarkable nobility of service who served their kings in discovery as well as diplomacy.[48] In August 1489 de Sousa was sent to Morocco to finalize a peace which the King of Fez had forced on João II confirming former treaties between Fez and Alfonso V. Three years later he was sent from a Portuguese fort, Pinda, (present day Santo Antonio do Zaire) to conclude a treaty with the Mani-Congo as part of the search for Prester John. He and his party penetrated two hundred miles inland, up the Congo river, chasing the black Christian king.[49]

Warbeck lived for a year in this remarkable country. And if he later gave as his reason for leaving Portugal the desire to see other places it is no wonder. The talk around him must have been of little else. His master was Pero Vaz da Cunha, fifth son of Tristao da Cunha the man who in 1506 sailed up the East coast of Africa and Madagascar, to take control of the Persian Gulf and the Indian Ocean.[50] Pero Vaz, nicknamed O Bisagudo – sharpface – gained notoriety in 1490 for his murder of a Portuguese ally: Bemoi, prince of the Jaloff tribe in the Senegal. It has been suggested that Warbeck was on Bisagudo's expedition to the Senegal, but this is unlikely. Bisagudo did not leave Portugal until late 1489 or early 1490, and Warbeck says he only served him as far as summer 1488. What Warbeck would have been privy to was the arrival of Bemoi at the court of João II. Bemoi came to Portugal as a result of the establishment of the fort of St George of the Mine on the Senegal river. In a contest over the throne of the Jaloff, in 1486, Bemoi appealed to João. João agreed to help Bemoi in return for the conversion of his entire people to Christianity. Within a year Bemoi was forced to flee from his enemies and came to Lisbon, amid great pomp and ceremony in 1487. Bemoi charmed João, and after listening to his tale João concluded that through Bemoi's agency he might find Prester John. Bemoi agreed to convert to Christianity, the Portuguese royal family stood as his godfathers and he took João II's name as his own given Christian name.[51] After his baptism he was knighted and given a coat of arms. 'During the celebration of the baptism . . . there were continual tournaments, bull-fights, farces and great evening-parties . . .' Bemoi's men were baptized too and they put on displays of horsemanship 'with one hand on the saddle bow they jumped to the ground, with the horses at full speed, and returned to the saddle . . .'. This happened in fact in November 1489, but Warbeck may have seen similar things, for these were the usual Portuguese celebrations for visiting dignitaries. Bemoi returned to Senegal in 1489/90 and Warbeck's old master da Cunha disgraced himself. As head of the expedition of twenty carvels returning Bemoi to Senegal, he feared treachery, or the plague, so he slew his charge in the mouth of the Senegal river.[52] Miraculously, or perhaps not so miraculously, this did not blight his career. In 1500 the converted Jew, Master John, King Manuel of Portugal's personal physician wrote from Brazil to the king as part of the expeditionary voyage which had just discovered Brazil. He recommended the king to 'order a mappa mundi to be brought which Pero Vaaz Bisagudo has, and on it Your Highness will be able to see the location of this land'.[53] Bisagudo had not been to Brazil, but his maps, like Behaim's stood as the tools behind the Portuguese advance over the globe. He continued as diplomat and explorer. With his father, in 1514, he was part of the embassy to Rome by which Portugal dedicated its Eastern empire to the papacy; and he died (still in search of Prester John?) at Mombasa in 1527.[54]

Sometime in 1488 Warbeck transferred his service from Vaz da Cunha to Pregent Meno. He claimed he wanted to visit other countries, and the Bretons did a lively business between Portugal and Flanders. How this transfer of service was effected we do not know. Meno's name does not appear in any of the remaining Portuguese documents. We know that in 1494 it was a Breton vessel which João II hired to take the Portuguese factor, figs and raisins to Bruges. According to Warbeck, Meno traded in silks. Certainly, in the late fifteenth century silk was becoming the fashion item of luxury and status, replacing fur; and cloth flooded into Portugal. The country had a very primitively developed cloth industry and this was a weakness which the Bretons exploited. Until the last quarter of the century there were few Bretons in Portugal. It was the growth of the sugar trade from Madeira which brought Breton ships to Portugal in greater numbers. It was Breton ships which delivered sugar to Bruges in 1468, and we know that men of Blavet and Quimperlé freighted it to Bruges in the seventies. Trading like this Warbeck could have travelled almost anywhere. Boats from St Pol de Leon took cloth from Flanders to Lisbon and thence to Madeira. From Madeira they shipped sugar back to Arnemuiden, for sale in Antwerp.[55] By 1500 Breton linen was being sold in Tenerife.[56] And in the next century there were voyages from Brittany to Seville and from there to Arnemuiden and Middelburg. Given the amounts of silk used in European courts it may be that Warbeck was taken on by Meno because during his year in Portugal he had built up contacts of his own with visiting dignitaries.[57]

In the 1480s and '90s Ireland was a bit off the beaten track, economically. Her trade was not as healthy as many other parts of Europe, but with much of the Channel and North Sea trade tied up by the Normans, Hansards and Flemish the Bretons were obliged to break into Irish trade or perish. They considered the country 'pays estraunge et sauvage'.[58] This conventional view, however, disguises the fact that in the late Middle Ages Ireland traded with every principal port in Europe, including all the Flemish ones, from Lubeck and Danzig on the Baltic to Pisa in the Mediterranean. Bilbao, Santiago, Oporto and Lisbon traded regularly with Ireland, and Ambrogio Lomellini of the Genoese banking family which dominated Nantes organized voyages direct between Lisbon and Ireland.[59] Generally Bretons traded on the east coast of Ireland to places like Drogheda, Dublin and Waterford, though occasionally they strayed to Dingle, Limerick and Galway. Some even settled permanently in Ireland. Garcinus de Mon Reall traded salt from Nantes to Ireland, his adopted country. Jenico Marks arrived in Dublin from Gascony at the age of eight, and stayed the rest of his life.[60]

The greatest Irish exports of the period were wool, wool-fells and hides, and fish. The wool exports were handled mainly by the southern ports, Waterford and Ross. In the fifteenth century Irish cloth coming to England increased, especially that entering England via the south-west, John Taylor's region. Her imports from Brittany were wine, iron, salt, resin, cork and liquorice. An active cloth trade existed between England and Ireland, financed and dominated by Bristol, Coventry and London; but Bretons too traded cloth to Ireland: the *Sebastian* of Vannes, for example, freighted canvas. And salt, the major Breton export to Ireland, was traded for horses.[61] Luxuries like silks and spices, also reached Ireland, so Pregent Meno's voyage to Cork is not improbable. The difficulty was the financial risk involved. Irish merchants were poor and did not always pay their debts in coin. When merchants at Waterford defaulted on payment in coin they made good their debts in leather hides. At Cork, in December 1499, Thomas Leboulyn took eight days to pay, and then paid part in leather and part in coin. Being given white herring as part payment for goods was not out of the question.[62] Eight years, to the month, before Leboulyn's transaction Pregent Meno sailed up the River Lee and docked at one of the many quays on the island which is now the historic centre of Cork. With this he sealed Perkin Warbeck's fate.

FIVE

The Resurrection of Richard Plantagenet

Cork was the point of intersection for those three men with a common background in commerce, cloth and the sea: John Taylor, John Atwater and Perkin Warbeck. It was a substantial urban community whose prosperous merchants, men like Atwater, built themselves good solid houses. Atwater and his ilk maintained extensive links with the West Country, Bristol, France, Spain, Portugal, and the Low Countries.[1] They were mayors and town officers, men of the same social standing as Warbeck. And like Warbeck's relatives they built up their cities, embellished them with beautiful churches and died wealthy. A sixteenth-century view of Carrickfergus shows a castle, a friary, rows of single storey stone houses, clusters of windowless mud cabins, town walls and a number of fine tower houses. Cork harbour was surrounded by just such merchants' tower houses – twenty feet square and forty feet high – and in the late fifteenth century Belvelly castle, a substantial eighty foot tower, guarded it. At roof level tower houses had wall walks. On the top floor they had residential quarters. Below this were the servants quarters, and below this an armoury. In the countryside, ground floors of the houses of the Gaelic chiefs protected their livestock, just as they did in many Irish homes until the middle of the twentieth century. Such were the homes of the élite in Ireland.[2] And in some such house, it is possible, Warbeck was transformed from boy to princeling.

On arrival in Cork, according to the only account we have – Warbeck's own confession – he was obliged to model some of his master's silks, to attract customers.[3] Seeing him, a group described anonymously as 'they of the town', said they recognized him as Edward, Earl of Warwick whom they had seen in Dublin, presumably refering to 1487 when Lambert Simnel had been crowned there. This tallies with what the French were paying John Taylor to do, raise rebellion on behalf of Warwick. However, Warbeck vociferously denied he was any such person and in the presence of citizens of the town, including the mayor, John Lewellyn, swore on the gospel and the cross that he was not Warwick. Who 'they of the town' were led by we do not know, but they had been set on to do this by John Atwater, and it is just conceivable that among his men was the ex-prior of Kilmainham, James Keating, an Irishman and head of the Irish Order of the Knights of St John, to whom Henry VII refused an automatic pardon after Stoke.[4] Warbeck's oath was not good enough to satisfy his assailants, for a second group, this time led by Atwater himself, arrived and maintained that he was Richard III's bastard son. Eight years after the event Henry VII described Atwater as an 'Iralandois qui fut le premier motif & Inventer de mectre sus labusion dudit pierequin'. Taylor may have fixed the whole scheme in advance, sending Meno to place his

The Charter Roll of the City of Waterford, c. 1372, showing the mayors of Dublin, Waterford, Cork and Limerick

unsuspecting apprentice in the political firing line at Cork, but if he did Warbeck was unaware of this, as he would have had to have been to remain convincing. We do not know how many times Warbeck had been to Ireland, or where else he visited between 1488 and 1491, but the generous grants of customs rebates, the payment of £300, and the position of constable of Carrickfergus castle with which Henry VII rewarded Pregent Meno suggest (apart from anything else) a man with previous interests in Ireland. Warbeck denied Atwater's suggestion that he was Richard III's bastard, and took oaths on the Holy Evangelist and the cross, again, that he was not a Plantagenet. Still he was pursued and told not to be afraid but to take on the royal role; to take it upon him boldly. To persuade him to adopt the persona of Richard, Duke of York, Atwater and others told him that if he did so they would make rebellion against the King of England, and that they would have aid from the most powerful in Ireland: the Earls of Desmond and Kildare. At this point Warbeck gave in, and his imposture began. But it is one thing to act a role for a three-month rebellion, quite another to act the same role for eight years. How was this possible?

Part of the answer lies in the enormous force and onslaught Warbeck was subject to. He later told his mother he was not sure whether he had been confused into taking on his role, or deceived into believing he was the Duke of York.[5] However we should not treat this as balanced recollection, for when Warbeck wrote this, in 1497, he was suffering the strain of maintaining imposture, and the sudden vertiginous release from his role. To be seized in the street and forced like Warbeck to take on a role was by no means unknown. Victims of brainwashing have talked of being worn down and stripped of their own identity in order to accept a confession compounded of lies which are, nevertheless, closely related to their own life.[6] Warbeck shares with two fellow citizens of Tournai just this the doubtful privilege. In 1225 a Tournaisian was forced to impersonate Count Baldwin of Constantinople; and in 1308 a faction of the French court seized another Tournai citizen to impersonate Jean de Brabant who had died in 1302.[7] Yet such people always, as did Warbeck, admitted who they were in the end. Warbeck's was not a case of complete psychological distortion as a result of brainwashing. His was a case of dissimulation. Such phenomena were by no means unknown in the early modern period for this was a society where ego boundaries were not as rigidly fixed as today, and where sanctioned inversions, through lords of misrule and play, produced imposters. In 1533 a Mary Baynton gave herself out to be Henry VIII's daughter, 'put forth in the world to shift for her living'. In 1587 an Ann Burnell claimed to be the daughter of Philip II of Spain, and in the same year 'Arthur' who entered Spain claiming to be the offspring of Elizabeth I and Leicester. Most bizarre of all was the youth who, in 1612, ran naked into St James's claiming to be the ghost of Prince Henry.[8] Warbeck's case, however, was unlike these in not being self-imposed. But it was so prolonged that without some degree of collusion it would have been impossible. To play his part convincingly for so long Warbeck would have had to have the psychology of an actor, and a good one at that.

Warbeck was chosen, because it was believed by Taylor and Atwater that he could carry out his appointed task. Witness the way he describes his discovery: acting out the task his master had given him to such a degree that it was not too far-fetched for him to say they thought I was a noble. He was a highly educated, literate member of the bourgeois class. He looked like a prince of the house of York, and other people thought he did so too. He had a working knowledge of court life, its rituals, nuances and niceties, and from his experiences in Flanders and Portugal a knowledge of political conditions reminiscent of the Wars of the Roses. In Portugal he had been courtier of King João II who had taken power by striking down the Duke of Braganza and ordering his execution, and by assassinating with his own hand his brother-in-law. What greater education did Warbeck need about the courts of Edward IV or Richard III than this? Nor was it at all odd for a child of humble background to travel so far or rise so high. Shipwrecked off Portugal Christopher Columbus had subsequently served in Portuguese and Spanish ships, visited Ireland, and married a member of the Portuguese aristocracy. His brother-in-law was Pedro Correa da Cunha. Warbeck was just what Atwater and Taylor were looking for. Like the fictional Hyckescorner who could boast he had been everywhere and done everything, Warbeck was already playing a part when Atwater found him.

> Syr I haue ben in many a countre
> As in fraunce Irlonde and in spayne
> Portyngale sevyll also in almayne
> Freslonde flaunders and in burgoyne
> Calabre poyle and erragoyne
> Britayne byske and also in gascoyne
> Naples grece and in myddes of scotlonde
> . . . Thre myle out of hell
> At rodes constantyne and in babylonde[9]

Such a list is the key to Warbeck's life, the point about which everything else turns. One side is Portugal and his life beginning at St Jehan des Cauffours: on the other side stands the imposture. The sentence of his confession which joins these two parts is, 'then becawse I desired to see other Cuntrees I took lycence of hym [Pero Vaz da Cunha], and then I put my sylf In servyce with a breton . . .'.[10]

Warbeck was not the stuff of which adventurers were made. But he was a risk taker of another sort: an actor. It was Wilhelm Busch who first noted that Warbeck's childhood and adolescence was marked by a rapid transfer from one master to another. 'From his very childhood he lived a life of constant change and adventure; . . . he had already served under five different masters, when still seventeen, he entered the service of Pregent Meno . . .'[11] In fact the changes were more extreme than Busch granted, seven changes in ten years. In his letter to his mother, in 1497, the incident he selected to convince her that he was her son was the rupture of his relations with her as he left her in tears at the Marvis gate of Tournai to take the road to Antwerp.[12] From this point on his life had been a series of abruptly terminated relationships. That these were short, and that they could not be anything else other than shallow we should not doubt. By the time Warbeck met John Taylor, he was already practised at presenting to the world whatever image it desired to see. His advancement in the mercantile world had depended on his ability to please his masters: he was already the great pretender by the time he reached Cork. Part of necessity for this ability lay in the necessity of survival. As a kind of social orphan he had no other tools. But part lay more deeply in his character as a need for approbation, forced on him by the ruptured relations with his parents, the adaptation of insecurity into a drive to please. That he had climbed as high as minor courtier in Portugal suggests that he was successful at pleasing his masters. A sojourn at court would only have reinforced this ability: the need to dissimulate, cover up real feelings, pretend, fawn, and flatter. Where did the actor end and the courtier begin? It was, paradoxically, his decision to break out of this world which saw in the fullest flowering of his gifts. Till his death Warbeck was the servant of Taylor and his Yorkists. In the years of his imposture Warbeck was in a role which seemed stable: Master, but Servant, the actors role, in control of his audience yet dancing to the tune of the playwright and the money of the audience. What Warbeck had given up was what most of us take for granted, the personal nature of thought and action; that what we think and what we do is not determined for us by others, that our thought processes are not constantly subverted by the life script of another or others. And that, within limits, we are free to act as we choose. Yet these losses are what made Warbeck so convincing. Having lost one sort of freedom he invented another, his role: acting. He was able and willing to do and try anything, losing himself in the new persona. Mimicking life, experimenting, pushing at the boundaries of reality, being Richard Plantagenet because he could no longer be Perkin Warbeck.

Immediately after he was presented to the world as Duke Richard, Warbeck says the earls of Desmond and Kildare promised to aid him. It is doubtful, whatever he believed, that this was so, but Taylor and his associates managed to convince Warbeck that he was to receive aid from both the Midlands and the south of Ireland and subsequently both Henry VII and Margaret of Burgundy accepted that this was what had happened. Both believed that Warbeck was in arms with the earls of Desmond and Kildare, and that they had recognized him as king. Of Desmond's involvement we are in no doubt. It was admitted by all, and two years after the Warbeck affair in Cork, Desmond and his brother Thomas de Desmond were pardoned. So, at the same time, 30 March 1493, was Kildare, and so, two months later, 29 May, were Hubert Burke and Edward Ormond.[13] Both the Burke and Ormond families were allies of Desmond; and the Burkes of Clanridick were clients of Desmond. One of the septs of the Burke clan was called MacHubert Burke. So Hubert Burke was probably one of Desmond's men.[14] Between them Atwater, Taylor, Burke and one Stephen Poytron or Poteryn of Meonstoke in Hampshire, a rebel executed in 1495, forced Warbeck to learn English; no great hardship for one already bilingual.[15]

Taylor badly needed Desmond involved in his schemes. Desmond belonged to a family alienated from the English Crown by the foolhardy execution of one of its members in 1468. The disloyalty of the Desmonds became notorious over the next hundred years, but in the period 1483–8 they were wooed by opposing factions. Richard III wrote to a Desmond reminding him of his father's years in Ireland, sending him royal livery and a Yorkist collar with a white boar pendant.[16] It did little good. Though he was probably involved with Simnel in 1487 he was murdered by a relative in December that year. During 1487 much of the south, and parts of Munster had stayed loyal to Henry VII. Most southern towns were exempted from swearing the oaths of allegiance required by Henry in 1488, in marked contrast to the region of the Irish Pale. In the aftermath of 1487 Maurice the Lame, the new Desmond earl was used as commissioner against the Yorkist rebels by Henry, and made Constable of Limerick castle. The south emerged as a region of counterbalance to Kildare, and Desmond may have believed that the recovery of his family influence was at hand. But nothing more followed, and in 1489 Kildare began the slow recovery of his power.[17] This game of political duplicity, rewarding one then reverting to the former, superior, power was typical of Henry VII. And if his actions were perceived by Desmond as a slight, the roots of Desmond's alienation and Warbeck's plot lie in a characteristic deeply ingrained in Henry VII.

What of Kildare? The year after Warbeck's arrival he was accused of complicity in the plot. In June 1491 he was in Munster, as arbitrator in a dispute. It is conceivable that this was a cover for negotiations with Desmond, or the French. French ships were in the Irish Sea in the autumn that year taking messages to and fro between Scotland and France. The opportunity for treason by Kildare was very present in 1491.[18] Yet in 1493 he wrote to Thomas Lord Ormond defending himself vehemently against charges of having aided Warbeck.[19]

I am accused to the kyng, as I understand, that I sholde have layn with the French lad that was supported with your cosyn and myne therle of Desmound, and that I sholde ayd, supporte, and comforte hym with godes and messages; where as I never lay with hym ne ayded, comforted, ne supported hym, ne yn none other manner wyse, as the lordes of this land have certified his highnes at this tyme.

This has been dismissed by some historians as a case of 'the lady doth protest too much', on the grounds that Warbeck's confession, and a letter of 1493 to Isabella of Castille, states that Kildare aided him. In fact Warbeck's confession says only that he was told that Kildare would aid him, not that he was aided in person by Kildare. As far as the letter of 1493 is concerned we have always to be aware who its author was or was not. It was not Warbeck, but rather his master, Taylor, or one of the rebels at Margaret of Burgundy's court in 1493. Her information about Kildare also came from the same source as Warbeck's, Taylor. We are forced therefore to reflect not on why Kildare was involved but why it was said he was involved.

In the seventeenth century Sir James Ware saw the letters sent by Taylor *et al* on behalf of their protégé to Desmond and Kildare 'wherin he trusted them to side with him against King Henry, and to send him auxiliary help to recover his right'.[20] Desmond responded with military aid. Kildare responded in writing but nothing more. Part of Taylor's plan may have been to suggest to Margaret of Burgundy that Richard Plantagenet was backed by all Ireland, that he was more than Lambert Simnel and that he was who they claimed he was; given the manner in which the expedition was launched, with disguised ships, the use of seals obtained under false pretences is not impossible. Indeed the whole purpose of seizing Warbeck may only ever have been to use him as a cover to involve the earls, and Margaret of Burgundy with the French-inspired plot to cause maximum embarrassment to Henry VII. It is equally possible that, by writing to Kildare, Taylor hoped to precipitate a rupture of the very sort which did occur between Kildare and Henry VII between 1491 and 1498. In 1491 the earl was still under heavy bond – £4,000 upon himself, and £4,000 on ten others – that he would maintain his allegiance to Henry and never privately or openly assent to anything contrary to Henry's well-being. Any messages from Burgundy were to be sent immediately to the king, and Kildare was to seize any messengers or any person stirring rebellion against Henry in Ireland.[21] In 1491 or 1492 he was sent precisely the sort of sensitive material he was supposed to seize. That he was regarded by Henry as a traitor is not surprising given his past. Yet in behaving as he did, driving Kildare from office, and forcing another humiliating bond on him, Henry obligingly fell into the trap laid by Taylor. The Irish sources hint at as much when they maintain that in 1492 Kildare resigned his office because of the behavior of Henry's appointee in Ireland, Sir James Ormond.[22] The political quagmire which persisted in Ireland for a further five years was thus the result of Henry's politically untutored response to Warbeck.

Warbeck saw out the Christmas of 1491 in Munster. Where he was we do not know. His confession suggests that he stayed in the Cork area, but he may have travelled west. He could have gone as far as Tralee, or even further into the Desmond dominated Dingle peninsula, or he could have stayed at Adare, a town which boasted a Desmond Castle and numerous ecclesiastical foundations. Christmas, though, came in with howling gales, as well as bringing Sir James Ormond and Thomas Garth back to Munster.[23] Warbeck was learning English. Henry's rebels were sending out letters to involve those whom they could. Their missive to Margaret of Burgundy reached the Low Countries at the end of January or beginning of February. Its arrival caused such a stir at the Burgundian court that on 8 February Philip the Fair's council sent a messenger as speedily as he could to take the news to Maximilian's lieutenant, and brother-in-law Albert of Saxony. As the council recognized, the cat was truly well among the pigeons; and when Pierre Puissant left on embassy to England in the same month he was followed there by a succession of messengers each carrying him letters on secret affairs of state.[24] Bearing in mind the reaction of Maximilian and Margaret of Burgundy to Lambert Simnel an enormously embarrassing situation had been created by the mere act of writing to Margaret. A year later, on 25 August

Perkin Warbeck's letter in 1493 to Queen Isabella of Castille informing her of his wanderings as Richard, Duke of York, prior to his discovery

1493 Margaret wrote to Isabella of Castille informing her of the contents of the letter. According to her letter Desmond and Kildare had written to her informing her that the second son of Edward, her beloved brother, Richard Plantagenet, Duke of York, who everyone reputed as dead was alive and living safely in Ireland in great honour. This was attested by their seals and by the affirmation of their oaths. This may have been what Taylor wrote to Margaret from Ireland or we may discern these as invention. Yet to have interested Margaret, Taylor would have had to have produced something very like this, for she claimed that when this news reached her from Ireland she thought it was an outburst 'of insanity and like a dream'.[25]

But Margaret was not alone in receiving letters from Richard Plantagenet. On 2 March 1492 Edward Ormond arrived at James IV's court carrying letters from 'King Edwartis son' and Maurice, Earl of Desmond. The letters to Scotland and Flanders were a considerable achievement for Taylor. While they cost him no more than two messengers their effect on the international diplomatic scene was out of all proportion to their cost. In the Low Countries his action enormously complicated relations between England and Burgundy which were in the process of being normalized after years of strain. In Scotland the letters arrived exactly when the French desired. Since the beginning of December 1491, or before, there had been a French embassy resident in Scotland. The ambassadors were still there in January and may have been there in February when James's 1491 embassy to France returned to Scotland with the news that they had achieved something of a treaty with France.[26] Hard on the heels of this came the appeal from Warbeck. What Warbeck/Taylor told James we can only guess at, but to judge from later events they mentioned their correspondance with Margaret of Burgundy. Two months after Edward Ormond appeared in Scotland one of the most trusted of Margaret's supporters, Rowland Robinson, was welcomed there. This was not coincidental, since to reach Scotland in May 1492, he would have had to have left Malines immediately Warbeck's letter reached Flanders.[27] Drawing together France and Burgundy, Taylor wove his worst. After a period of three years in which conventional European and English politics had seemed to be reasserting themselves he had succeeded in transforming events in Ireland, Burgundy, Flanders and Scotland sufficiently that a pattern of hostility toward Henry VII was created which endured until Warbeck was executed.

What Desmond and Warbeck said to James IV we do not know. They may have been offering alliance with Scotland in return for James's aid to Duke Richard. Kildare was accused in 1494 of transferring his allegiance from England to Scotland. Margaret of Burgundy said that she was asked 'to give support and help . . . by virtue of kinship and blood, they [Desmond and Kildare] promised to give assistance as well'.[28] Letters from the pretender arrived in pairs, one from him, one from a sponsor, both prepared by the same secretary. What would Richard Plantagenet have written to James? In 1493 Isabella of Castille was told that after Edward V was murdered.

I myself, then nearly nine years of age, was also delivered to a certain lord to be killed, (but) it pleased Divine Clemency, that that lord, having compassion on my innocence, preserved me alive and in safety; first, however, causing me to swear on the holy sacrament that to no one should I disclose my name, origin, or family, until a certain number of years had passed. He then sent me therefore abroad, with two persons, who should watch over and take charge of me; and thus I, an orphan, bereaved of my royal father and brother, an exile from my kingdom, and deprived of my country, inheritance and fortune, a fugitive and in the midst of extreme perils, led my miserable life, in fear, and weeping, and grief, and for the space of nearly eight years lay hid in divers promises. At length, one of those who had charge of me being dead, and the other returned to his country, and never afterwards seen, scarcely had I emerged from childhood alone and without means, I remained for a time in the kingdom of Portugal, and thence sailed to Ireland, where being recognised by the illustrious lords, the Earls of Desmond and Kildare, my cousins, as also by other noblemen of the island, I was received with great joy and honour.[29]

Again it is the form rather than the content that we should attend to. There is enough of Warbeck's life in this account of Richard's for Warbeck to play Richard convincingly. Here is early parental abandonment; here is the solicitous care of strangers, the childhood, and a sojourn in Portugal. The new life Warbeck had taken on was, significantly, close enough to his old life for there to be little internal discrepancy, even if between the two, new facts were at odds with old.

Outward fact could be overcome with good tuition. Taylor knew Edward IV, and he knew George Duke of Clarence. Also, possibly, he knew Ireland in the late 1470s. But he did not have the intimate knowledge of the English court necessary to Warbeck's education. For this there had to be another source. Conventionally this source has been seen as Sir Edward Brampton or Margaret of Burgundy. Yet the earliest history of the conspiracy, that of Bernard André in his life of Henry VII, attributes it to Stephen Frion.[30] Recently Frion's role has been the subject of intense scrutiny in an attempt to link him directly to Margaret of Burgundy and thus to suggest Margaret of Burgundy and Flanders sent Warbeck to Ireland.[31] But the unresolved problem of Frion's importance can be resolved if we assign him a short, limited, but significant, part in the story. According to Warbeck's confession after he had learnt English, Charles VIII sent an embassy to invite him to France. This is only half the story, for Taylor's transport and supply to Cork, Adam Nyvelet, had been commissioned to remain in the vicinity of Ireland for six weeks.[32] If he remained there for the whole time he would still have been at sea in early February, about the time the rebels despatched their letters to Flanders and Scotland. But Warbeck was greeted in Ireland not by a minor sea captain but by one of Charles VIII's most reliable naval commanders, Louis Lucas: the Loyte Lucas of Warbeck's confession. In the summer of 1490 Lucas was stationed in the Seine, at Honfleur, from where, on 18 August, he was sent with a number of other captains, including George Doria, who was then stationed at Rouen, to maintain the French garrison in Brest. Two years later in July 1492, in the opening phase of the war with England, Lucas was in the company of French privateers attacking Spanish merchantmen off the Breton coast.[33] In the meantime he had been despatched on the command of Charles VIII, perhaps after the correct signal to France had been given by Taylor, to take Frion to Ireland and then withdraw all of Taylor's men and Warbeck to Harfleur. Why Frion? Not, I think, for his then connection with Margaret of Burgundy. In the past he had served Richard's aunt. He had begun his service to Flanders in servicing her husband, Charles the Bold. By 1480 he was in her entourage and came to England with her, and secured, through her good offices, the post of French secretary to Edward IV. He remained in this office serving Edward IV and his brother, as well as Henry VII, until his flight to France in 1489. Who better was there to educate Warbeck in the ways of the family, their ties to the Low Countries, their peculiarities, their affections, those personal details unknown to all but the most intimate: Frion, a man observant enough to be trusted by the Burgundian regime as their spy at the Yorkist court in the 1480s. Once he had schooled Warbeck, Frion played no further part in the conspiracy. Instead when he had done his job he continued to serve France, until we lose sight of him in 1509.

Between them Taylor and Frion turned Warbeck into Richard Plantagenet.[34] Margaret of Burgundy described him thus to Isabella in 1493. Her letter is disingenuous, ingratiating, and in places palpably false. Yet not even she would have been able to write what she did if Warbeck had been less of a congruent prince than he was. 'I recognized him (for the reason that I had once seen him in England) as easily as if I had last seen him yesterday or the day before that . . . this man is the one whom they once thought dead.'[35] The initial process of schooling Warbeck took about two months, though it is doubtful that it stopped until after the autumn of 1493. But when the primary act of recreation had been accomplished Warbeck, Taylor and his rebel band were escorted from Ireland by a flotilla of French vessels under Louis Lucas. They were greeted at Harfleur by Bérault Stuart, Seigneur d'Aubigny, Charles VIII's chamberlain, who spent 500 écus making ready the occassion.[36] Alexander Monypeny, Seigneur de Concressault, French ambassador to James IV, and part of the French end of the plot, was placed in charge of Warbeck's bodyguard. Warbeck's letter to Isabella of Castille catches the mood, 'I came to the . . . King of France, who received me honourably, as a kinsman and friend.'[37] Both Richard Plantagenet and Perkin Warbeck had been reborn.

Part Two: At Large

SIX

The Dreadful Deadman

The withdrawal from Ireland of what had become the Perkin Warbeck conspiracy turned a useful diversionary tactic into an embarrassment of questionable value. In the person of Warbeck Charles VIII had acquired a plausible Plantagenet prince and a group of dedicated anti-Tudor rebels who would stop at nothing to overthrow Henry VII. Their natural language, fanaticism, sat at odds with that of international politics, short term self-interest. The only value they possesssed for the French monarchy was as a bargaining counter in France's consolidation of its hold on Brittany. Long term they had no future. Short term they could be kept on a pension, as Richard de la Pole would be, and either used for sabre rattling against England or offered to Henry VII as an appetizing morsel for which to exchange Brittany. Brittany would be bought with money – the Étaples pension to pay off Henry VII's

Charles VIII, King of France

war debts on behalf of the new Queen of France, and gratitude. In 1485 Charles had placed Henry on the English throne, now by surrendering Warbeck Charles could make Henry secure from overthrow. Through the summer of 1492 the two kings pursued an elaborate and erratic course of accommodation by diplomacy, piracy, raiding, or the threat of invasion. Richard Plantagenet was forgotten. As Laurent Breton said, either there was no such person or else, faced with an English invasion, nobody really cared.

Breton said his piece on 1 May 1492. Three days later one who cared very much, Rowland Robinson, was rewarded £4 10s 8d by James IV of Scotland. This was Robinson's second visit to Scotland on behalf of Margaret of Burgundy. His first was in 1489, and there may have been others as well, either late in 1488 or in the spring of 1490 when Margaret wrote to James. Robinson had fought at Stoke, had survived and then been attainted. Somehow, in 1488, he got into the service of the duchess and remained with her until 1497 when we lose track of him. Under Warbeck, during the years 1495 to 1497, he assumed some sort of role as treasurer. He arrived with a party from the Low Countries including a messenger from the King of the Romans, Maximilian. The whole group stayed in Edinburgh from the beginning of May till 19 July, and James housed them and paid for their upkeep.[1] The letters which John Taylor had sent from Ireland, in February 1492, had found their mark. Both Maximilian and the Duchess of Burgundy wanted confirmation from James regarding the discovery in Ireland of Richard, Duke of York. Who provided the necessary information in this situation is a moot point. James may have done so but it is more likely that he was primed by the French. Early in December 1491, while Warbeck was in Cork, a French herald took up residence in Scotland. James paid for his lodgings in January 1492 and in May, when Robinson and his party from the Low Countries arrived, he was present at court.[2] According to Margaret she had at first regarded the rebels' letters to her as 'outbursts of insanity', but when 'the Duke of York was summoned to France as a blood relation', she sent, 'some men who would recognise him as readily as his mother or nurse, seeing that from his early youth they had been in service and very close contact with King Edward and his children'.[3] Sending observers from Malines to France in spring 1492 was very easy. In April that year a powerful Flemish embassy headed by Englebert of Nassau, Jehan le Sauvage and Paul de Baenst was engaged in negotiating what became the Peace of Senlis. They took up residence in France between 1 April and 5 July, at the same time that Robinson and his company were in Scotland. All year highly placed Burgundian household officials and heralds travelled back and forth between Malines and France. In July Emot le Sergent, Limbourg Herald, took messages to the ambassadors. In September Maximilian's secretary went to the French court.[4] When Margaret's men returned from France they affirmed, 'with a most sacred oath, that this man was King Edward's second son. If he were discovered to be an imposter, they cursed themselves with great execrations, prepared to endure all torments and tortures.'[5]

Margaret's letter was intended, in 1493, to impress Isabella of Castille with the miraculous nature of Richard's survival. Parts of it are exaggerated and misleading, yet it does not contradict the other sources relating to this period. Margaret was placed in a quandry by this discovery at the court of her enemy. She could not openly support France against Burgundy's allies, the English, yet if it was, as it appeared to be, true that her nephew was alive neither could she stand passively by. She appears to have acted by inaction. Toward Duke Richard she took no action herself, but she allowed members of her household to make common cause with the English rebels at Charles VIII's court. According to Edward Hall, a unique source, because he spoke to 'some men . . . whiche were there attendynge' on Warbeck, he was joined by about a hundred English rebels headed by Sir George Neville, Rowland Robinson and John Taylor.[6] Taylor's whereabouts we have located; he was in France from

March 1492 onward. Neville's whereabouts are problematic, in that we lose sight of him after April 1491, when he was in Scotland. It is possible he went from Scotland to Margaret. Robinson we know was in Margaret's employ in Scotland in May 1492. In the identified leadership of the now one group, we have the names of what were previously two groups of malcontents, one stemming from the rump of Stoke, led by Robinson, the other, formed at Charles VIII's court in 1489. Given the time taken for Robinson to travel from Scotland to Burgundy and then to allow time for all the news gathered from France and Scotland to be coordinated, it seems unlikely that this group was established in France much before the beginning of August 1492.

Throughout 1492 the main thrust of activity in England had been dictated by the planned war against France. Henry had responded to the Warbeck diversion in Ireland by planning one of his own in Brittany, and by keeping up military pressure on France by raiding Normandy.[7] Yet by the summer of 1492 all this, and his planned invasion in conjunction with Maximilian, had come to naught. The Breton plan had been discovered, the English attacking Normandy had been given a bloody nose, and Maximilian was pursuing his own agenda, leading to the Peace of Senlis. Against all military sense Henry insisted on invading France in October. He attacked into an oncoming winter, and against a town, Boulogne, which was far better fortified than his intelligence had told him. Partly he did it to secure his war debt. More significantly, he intended to impel the expulsion of Taylor and Warbeck from France. In 1499 it was said that Henry placed the capture of Taylor above the value of the pension he agreed to accept on 6 November 1492.[8]

By the agreements made at Étaples, and after, Charles VIII secured Brittany and established such ties with England, that he secured English neutrality toward France for the foreseeable future. Taylor and Warbeck were of no further use to him there. On 13 December 1492, in the negotiations relating to the matters supplementary to Étaples, Charles VIII ratified an agreement renouncing all aid to Henry's rebels and traitors. In Bacon's words, 'upon the first grain of incense that was sacrificed upon the altar of peace at Boulogne Perkin was smoked away'.[9] According to the eyewitness in Paris there were fears in Warbeck's camp that Charles would go even further than he was obliged and hand Warbeck over to Henry. Thus, before the clause was signed at Amboise, Warbeck was employed to dupe the captain of his guard, Alexander Monypeny, the Seigneur Concressault, to allow Taylor and their whole company to flee from Paris to Flanders, by night.[10]

They arrived at Malines before 12 December 1492; but it was nearly a case of out of the frying pan into the fire. What had been a group Charles VIII had used to get what he wanted from Henry VII, now became a group which Maximilian used in the same way. Regarding England, it was said that Warbeck's residence at the Burgundian court so disturbed Henry VII that Maximilian could have obtained any agreement he sought from Henry. In France there was considerable agitation as the final stages of the Senlis treaty were approached. Just before another embassy arrived from Flanders in April 1493 rumours circulated at the French court that Maximilian was contemplating making Warbeck King of England, marrying him to his daughter Margaret of Austria, and, with a restored Yorkist monarchy making perpetual war on France. This may not have been taken seriously in France. Possibly it was a ploy by a court faction so that the French delegation would take a hard line with the Flemish negotiators.[11] None the less, the expulsion of Warbeck from France had boomeranged on the Étaples signatories. In summer 1493 both the French and English courts believed that an imminent invasion on behalf of Richard, Duke of York was likely, first against England then, later, France.[12]

Richard, Duke of York's arrival at Malines was regarded as a miracle. Whatever Margaret of Burgundy came to believe about Warbeck in later years, both she and Maximilian believed, in the winter of 1492 that Richard Plantagenet had survived the Tower of London. Both Polydore Vergil and Edward Hall, having confused the origins of the Warbeck plot assert that Margaret's reaction to Warbeck was dissimulation. Yet they have great difficulty in doing so, and while their description of the duchess greeting Richard rings true, their assertions, Hall's particularly, that she was dissembling, are strained. According to Vergil she received Richard, 'as though he had been raised from the dead and as if (so she dissembled) she had never cast eyes on him before; so great was her pleasure that her happiness seemed to have disturbed the balance of her mind. So that her rejoicing should be noted by all she publicly congratulated her nephew on his preservation and took pleasure in having him repeat the tale of how, having been saved by a ruse from death, he had wandered among many peoples, in order by this means that she might convince all that he was indeed Richard the son of her brother Edward.'[13] She herself wrote thus to Isabella,

> I recognised him . . . not by one or two signs . . . but by so many particular signs that one man who has clues of this kind would scarcely be found among 10,000 individuals. Then I knew him from private conversations and acts which had taken place between him and me, and which assuredly no one else could guess at; finally I knew him from the questions and conversation of others, to all of which he replies so correctly and expertly that it is clear and certain that this man is the one whom they once thought dead. I, in fact, when I considered that he is the sole survivor of our family through so many calamities and crises, was very much moved, and in that affection . . . embraced him as an only grandson or an only son.[14]

There can be no mistaking in these accounts the highly charged nature of the atmosphere, the emotion, passion and lack of balance, and the instability, bordering on temporary derangement, caused by Warbeck's advent. The reasons for this lie in Margaret of York's tragic life. Wim Blockmans has explored the devotion of a lonely duchess in search of insight into her personality. He has examined her pious and charitable acts in the light of her political career, and the results are startling and illuminating. Blockmans concludes that Margaret regarded her marriage to Duke Charles the Bold as a failure. In all but name it ceased to function as a marriage in 1472, four years after they were married. By then the duke was giving himself over obsessively to warfare. In the first six months of their marriage they had only seen each other 21 days, in the first year 96 days. By 1472 they lived apart, and after 1475 they never saw each other again. Margaret and the duke's daughter, Mary were close, and Margaret represented her husband during his absence from Burgundy in 1475 and 1476. After his death she was forced into temporary political retirement, but then refused to be lionized by either Louis XI or Edward IV, rejecting their attempts to create political matches for her. Instead she chose the Archduke Maximilian of Austria as a consort for Mary, and had, for the rest of her life, cordial relations with him. Maximilian protected her from all problems she had over her dowry. Blockmans draws attention to the paradox of Margaret's eight and a half years as duchess, comparatively powerless, as opposed to her twenty-two years as dowager, when she was very powerful. His examination of her books shows that the most significant of them were purchased in the period 1475–7 when she was ruling Burgundy in her husband's absence. One, particularly, he considers helps us to understand her more, *The Vision of Tondal*. This tale concerns a knight, Tondal, who is concerned only with his good looks and the world. He gives no thought to the salvation of his soul and so is sent to Hell. From there he visits Heaven where he meets former enemies who promise reform. One will enter religious life. One will give all to the poor. In the next stage of Heaven Tondal visits the Faithfully Married. Blockmans suggests that Margaret saw

The Lonely Duchess. Margaret, dowager Duchess of Burgundy. Jean Molinet in his 'Faictz et Dictz' characterized her by listing those she had lost, her husband, her brothers and her nephews

in Tondal the Type of husband who should have repented his martial life and returned to a faithful marriage. He suggests she used her copy of Tondal, in her prayers, to persuade her husband to turn to spiritual values as she herself had done.

Blockmans argues that Margaret regarded as most hurtful the realization that she would never have children of her own by marriage. He has analysed her devotional attachment to saints either in art, or in the practices of religious guilds; and he concludes that they are united by the common theme of childbearing and pregnancy. Thus, for example, Margaret gave to the Poor Clares of Ghent, a Life of St Catherine, a saint revered by pregnant women or those hoping for pregnancy. In 1473 Margaret became a member of the guild of St Anne in a Ghent church. The frontispiece of the guild register, newly commissioned in 1476, was on a theme of pregnancy. Both Margaret and Mary also belonged to St Barbara's guild, the patroness of those confronted with sudden death and often associated with Margaret of Antioch, Margaret's patron saint: patron of pregnant women and the unprotected.

Thus in her religious devotions Blockmans lays bare Margaret's longings for children. Yet she was an immensely practical and active woman, and in the period after the death of her husband her life was partly fulfilled so that, Blockmans argues, her response to her situation provided a role model for women rulers in Flanders over the next hundred years. In 1480 she took up a full political life negotiating alliance with England and one manuscript illustration shows her placed between Maximilian and Edward IV, mediating. 1485 saw the vindication of Margaret's rights through Maximilian's victory in the civil wars in Flanders. Thus when war broke out again, and Maximilian was captured at Bruges, it was she who organized his release by summoning his father Frederick III and an Imperial army. In this period she took care of Maximilian's son Philip the Fair and in 1493 welcomed his daughter Margaret home from France. Her court at Malines became again a princely nursery in 1501, when Philip the Fair's children were educated there while he was in Spain. In this special attention to the children of Mary and Philip she found some compensation for her own childlessnes.

Blockmans review of her charitable bequests reveals a unique confirmation of this, charity to orphans. For example, in 1478 Margaret paid a priest at Binche to oversee the education and feeding of a five-year-old orphan. She went to the length of paying for his clothing and for surgery to a broken leg. It is not surprising that in England rumours abounded that she had in her safekeeping the Duke of York. His survival was expected, and her charity could be interpreted thus. She placed an orphan daughter of the Count of St Pol, in a Ghent convent, founded reformatories for repentant prostitues, and educated them in her own houses at Mons. Most extraordinary of all, in view of its date, 1499, the year of Warbeck's execution, she took up a young English child on whom one Pieter van Temple was ordered to spend a large amount of money, for his work and profit. Blockmans concludes that the remarkable number of children Margaret helped surely must have been higher than the examples quoted here, and may be connected to the fact that she bore no children herself.[15]

Very clearly she was vulnerable to the appeal Warbeck's masters might make. Philip the Fair was still in his minority. His sister Margaret had returned from France, and her beloved nephew was miracuously found to be alive. If her Flemish role is transposed to an English context her response to Warbeck is understood. She had played the role of the faithful matriarch, and been vindicated, personally and politically in Flanders. That she was governess at the court of the young Philip, Margaret and Richard, and pursued the right of her nephew would have been quite natural for her, and percieved so by others as such. He was the son of the late King of England, and cousin of the imprisoned Edward, Earl of Warwick, her favourite brother's son. Once she was sure that Richard was who he said he was, she assigned him a personal guard of thirty retainers dressed in Yorkist colours of murrey and blue, honoured him highly and called him the White Rose, Prince of England.[16]

Malines. Margaret's palace lay behind the street façade marked by the stepped gable. Malines was the administrative centre of Flanders, and an important arms manufacturing town

Margaret's powerful position in Flanders and the fact that she believed Warbeck to be a Plantagenet legitimized him in the eyes of the Flemish nobility.

Warbeck played a convincing duke. According to Bernard André he could 'recall all the circumstances of Edward IV, and recited by heart all the names of his household and servants, as though he had been taught these and had known them from the time he was a little boy. In addition he gave details of locations, dates and persons . . . He even (as fine player he was) fortified these facts with a veil of such deceit that . . . men of wisdom and great nobility were induced to believe him.'[17] Warbeck's aide-de-camp in Flanders was no less than Hughes de Melun, Governor of Dendermonde (one of Margaret's three Flemish dower towns), knight of the Toison d'Or, a highly placed ducal advisor who had been rewarded for his part in the late wars with France with an annuity of £1,800.[18] There was about this much of the case of the emperor's new clothes. In Polydore Vergil's words, 'The more deceit was given the appearance of truth the more people professed that they believed the youth had escaped the hand of King Richard by divine intervention and had been led safely to his aunt.'

The effect in England of Warbeck's acceptance by Margaret and the Flemish establishment was galvanic. Burgundian politics and culture was very important in English life. The news 'came blazing and thundering', says Bacon,[19] and it set up an immediate debate among all classes of people, common and noble alike. In Bruges the town authorities issued an ordinance to maintain public order which was threatened by affrays among merchants, 'especially those of the English nation', who were ordered to, 'conduct and behave themselves peaceably and quietly . . . without wearing any badges, either secretly or openly, of white roses or red roses, which might occasion . . . any trouble, quarrel or partisanship, nor also to abuse, reproach or offend one another by word or by deed in any manner, forbidding the carrying of any arms . . .'[20] Across the channel, in Hampshire Sir Thomas Tyrrell, talking to John Kendal, the Master of the Order of the Knights of St John of Jerusalem in England, in Avon castle, recalled the good old days when Edward IV had visited his house, and made good cheer. Hopefully, said he, Edward's son should make like cheer there. And just as that house had been built with money from the Hundred Years War he hoped for another war for profits to build another house.[21]

Warbeck's reinvention as Duke of York resurrected the political debate about Henry VII's right to the throne. That it did so has everything to do with the political conditions of the moment, which according to Polydore Vergil were a factious nobility at Henry's court: foolhardiness, opportunism, loyalty to the house of York and feelings of being hard done by. Yet at the root it owes its origins to the expectation in early modern Europe that past political leaders would return from the dead and deliver their people from bondage. Warbeck's appeal lay in the fashion in which two strands of this returning hero story were combined: that of the leader who had not died but had merely fled abroad to return one day; and that of the apocalyptic hero who would bring peace after decades of civil war.

The tradition of the hero fled abroad but returning was a common inspiration in the Middle Ages. In 1330 Edmund, Earl of Kent was executed for conspiring to overthrow Edward III in favour of his murdered brother Edward II, whom he belived to be alive. Subsequently Edward III himself visited Cologne to view an individual who claimed that he, Edward II, had escaped thence via Ireland and France. Present in this type of survival story is a journey through Ireland, Flanders and a wandering through other European countries.[22] During the Wars of the Roses this story surfaced in the accusation against the Duke of Clarence that he had suborned three of his household, 'to cause a strange child to have been brought into his castle of Warwick, and there to have been put in likeness of his son and heir, and that they should have conveyed and sent his said son and heir into Ireland, or into Flanders, out of this land, whereby he might have gotten him assistance and favour against our said Sovereign Lord.'[23] The most curious example of this phenomenon, which echoes Warbeck's imposture, was the persistence of the belief in the survival of Edward VI. His return was vigorously prophesied for the year 1556, and by the late sixteenth century such expectations were rife. In 1581 a yeoman was executed after a career which had been begun disseminating the rumour of Edward's survival and ended in full scale impersonation. In 1587 a smith denied that Edward was dead and claimed that he knew the man who had carried him into Germany in a ship called the *Harry*. Two years later he was reported living in France or Spain. By 1599 this hope had become an intricate contrivance whereby Edward had been spirited away to become King of Denmark; in which capacity he had saved the commons of England, Wales and Ireland by supplying them with corn.[24]

The second tradition to which Warbeck's story appealed was that of the returning apocalyptic hero, the sleeping hero. In 1485 Sir Thomas Malory noted, 'the opinion of some men of the death of Arthur', in *Le Morte d'Arthur*: 'Yet some men yet say in many parts of England that King Arthur is not dead, but had (i.e. taken) by the will of our Lord Jesu in (i.e. into) another place. And men say he shall come again, and he shall win the Holy Cross. I will not say it shall be so, but rather I will say, here in this world he changed his life. But many men say that there is written upon his tomb the verse, "Hic iacet Arthurus Rex quondam Rex que futurus."'[25] This tradition informed the conscious and unconscious fantasies of the ruling élite. The pedigrees which they constructed for themselves linked them to the mythic histories of Arthur, Merlin and Brutus. These stories belonged to a common heritage of prophecy, stemming from Geoffrey of Monmouth, which promised a leader who 'shall rise out of his sleep like a live man whom all thought to be dead'. During the Hundred Years War, Edward III's propagandists represented their king as that leader. Later both Henry IV and Henry V worshipped at the shrine of the political prophet John of Bridlington who had prophesied a Lancastrian reign of peace after years of civil war.[26] The one who was to reign in peace was variously named, the Son of Man was one such name; and, just as apocalyptically, the Dreadful Deadman was another. In one version of the prophecy the reign of peace would begin after terrible wars, and the invasion and destruction of England by six foreign kings. Those involved were the kings of Flanders, Scotland and Ireland, indeed most European monarchs. In another version the Dreadful Deadman brought peace by ending the turmoil of six disastrous kings' reigns. These prophecies and the rumours they generated were taken seriously by both high and low during the Wars of the Roses. Edward IV and Henry VII appealed to a British past in which an angel had prophesied to Cadwalader of the return of a hero. In certain of his propaganda exercises Edward IV had himself called the Son of Man.[27]

And when John Leland toured England in the 1540s he was shown rolls of descents in which Henry VII appeared as a descendant of Ivor, son of Cadwalader, with his right to the throne prophesied by Henry VI.[28] These stories, rolls and prophecies were a shared set of mind. At one extreme lay highly wrought literary prophecies of the high Middle Ages. At the other lay anti-Tudor prophecies of the common people in the mid-sixteenth century. In between lay Henry VII with his elaborate claims upon the past and his son Arthur, the hero returned. But alongside him was that other hero, returned from the dead, Richard, Duke of York; son of the Son of Man, the Dreadful Deadman, returned to haunt him. This is the meaning of Bernard André's statement, 'Certain prophecies concerning him were falsely spread far and wide by pseudo-prophets, and these totally blinded the minds of the common and ordinary people.' Warbeck's backers skilfully equipped him to make the claim that he was the 'live man whom all thought to be dead'. Indeed he had been discovered in Ireland, one of the locations from which the deliverer would come. In 1497 one of his banners was said to show a little boy emerging from a tomb; the other, a little boy, escaped from the jaws of death, coming out of the mouth of a wolf.[29] They also joined the possibility that he might be a resurrected Richard, Duke of York to the perennial tale of the true child conveyed overseas. That this was their ploy is hardly surprising for it was none other than the John Taylor, Clarence's servant, who had been charged with spiriting a false child to Ireland, who provided Warbeck with his origin story in Cork.

The acclamation in Flanders of Richard, Duke of York as the White Rose was a political disaster for Henry VII. The political dissolution caused by Richard III's usurpation had been painfully ended by a political nation which had come to accept that the legitimate king was Henry Tudor. His kingship was based on the understanding that since Edward IV's sons were dead he inherited Edward IV's mantle, and his political establishment was staffed mainly by Edward IV's ex-household. The possibility that one of Edward's sons was alive turned the political clock back to before 1483, and created a wide constituency for the supposed Duke of York. Thus when, in response to the events in Flanders, a conspiracy against Henry VII began to emerge, its principal proponents were from those parts of the Yorkist establishment closest to the king and his family, and included men who had fought against each other between 1483 and 1485. It is possible that the most coherent group were men who were possessed of some residual loyalty to Richard, Duke of York, Edward IV's son, and it seems that Warbeck's masters targeted such men for their support. They also developed a propaganda of non-obligation to Henry VII in order to undermine his authority. In 1496 it was stated that even Henry knew he was in the wrong: he 'hath not openly deprived us of our kingdom . . . knowing in his own heart our undoubted right'. A year earlier it was said, by Margaret of Burgundy and Maximilian, that Papal ignorance of English constitutional law and the facts pertaining to Richard's survival had allowed Henry to manipulate the then Pope, Innocent VIII. Had it been known that the Duke of York was alive the Pope would never have sanctioned the excommunication of Henry's rebels. Finally it is present in Polydore Vergil's account of William Stanley's supposed treason. According to Vergil, Stanley's treachery amounted only to having said that if Warbeck was genuinely Edward IV's son then he would not oppose him.

Vergil suggests, and the indictments of the conspirators are sufficiently one-sided to confirm his view, that the plot to dethrone Henry VII began among his household officers and was not imported from Malines. The first reported treasonable conversation was said to have been at Windsor on 12 January 1493 between the King's Steward of his Household, John Ratcliffe, Lord Fitzwater and Sir Robert Clifford.[30] Clifford was a northerner, brother of Lord Clifford who fell on the Lancastrian side at Towton. Robert had made his way under Edward IV in the 1470s, rallying to him at York on his march to Barnet in 1471. Retained by the Duke of Gloucester thereafter he was one of Edward IV's esquires for the body by 1477, and, significantly, won the prize for best swordsman during the festivities at the marriage of Richard Plantagenet and Anne Mowbray in 1478. By the 1490s he was married to Elizabeth, daughter of a William Barley who joined him in conspiracy. Barley's wife was a Darcy, and he was related to two other East Anglian families the Tyrrells of Gipping and the Harlestons. The Darcys belonged to a group of East Anglian families associated with the last Mowbray, Duke of Norfolk, whose title Richard, Duke of York had assumed in 1478. In 1481 Clifford fought with members of the old Mowbray retinue commanded by John Howard against the Scots.[31]

Fitzwater, an East Anglian, and Clifford discussed this son of Edward IV and concluded that they would support him, and would offer their support to Margaret of Burgundy. Fitzwater agreed to furnish fifty men-at-arms to support Richard, Duke of York in whichever quarter of the realm he landed. Clifford would act as go-between and inform the Duchess Margaret of Fitzwater's intention. However, the problem of accepting this, and Vergil's version, of events wholesale, is that it is very obviously only one half of a strategy to include an insurrection within England to coincide with an invasion from Flanders; and we know that in 1493 Margaret of Burgundy made attempts to raise a mercenary army similar to the one used in 1487. It is also clear that English contacts with Flanders were many and varied. Messages entered England via Calais. Some members of the old Yorkist Calais establishment with interests in Calais were later punished for their part in the plot; and Clifford was well known there. Equally messages could have been sent through Calais via Lord Fitzwater's in-laws, the Whetehill family. The Whetehills were an important Calais family, who had been mayors of Guisnes. Adrian Whetehill was Comptroller of Calais charged with handling the Étaples pension money.[32] In any case we know that, in 1493, messages were brought to England by John de Lysa, a merchant, and Peter, a servant of a Flemish hospitaller who lived near Douai.[33]

On 10 February, two more men agreed to follow Warbeck, Sir Gilbert Debenham and Sir Humphrey Savage received a messenger at Westminster from Warbeck, and sent him back with verbal assurances that they were committed to his cause. Savage would remain in England while Debenham defected to Malines. Debenham, like Clifford, had associations with the old Mowbray affinity. Savage was an in-law of the King's Chamberlain. Thus finally, on 14 March, Sir Robert Clifford obtained a similar assurance from the King's Chamberlain, Sir William Stanley, that on receipt of a signal from Clifford, in Flanders,

Stanley would assist Warbeck with all his resources. The weakness of Henry VII's political position was manifest. His principal household officers, appointed to their positions by way of reward for their behaviour during 1484 and 1485 were showing themselves every bit as loyal to him in the 1490s as John Earl of Lincoln had been in 1487.[34]

The summer of 1493 was marked by a scare of invasion like that before Stoke. Henry was aware that his household, and his Stanley and Savage relatives, could not be trusted. He anticipated invasion from Flanders and trouble in Ireland. He therefore began to build bridges to the Anglo-Irish establishment, and to anyone else who had been involved in the first Warbeck insurrection in Ireland. There had been a good deal of violence in Ireland since Warbeck's departure. In June 1492 Kildare had been removed from the deputyship of Ireland under the guns of Thomas Garth's men, and though Henry's new Irish deputy lieutenant did not visit Ireland, in the winter of 1492–3 James Ormond, the new Treasurer, and Garth were involved in personal feuds with Kildare of such intensity that Kildare killed Garth's son. With Warbeck in Flanders Ireland was a disaster in the making.[35] In February 1493 ships were readied at Bristol for a substantial English force to impose a peace. Cannon and powder were got ready and on 8 March Sir Roger Cotton was commissioned to go to Ireland. His second in command was Henry Mountford son of Sir Simon Mountford of Coleshill in Warwickshire. Cotton took with him 11 men-at-arms and 188 archers. Mountford had his own retinue of 100 men. And from payments to James Ormond, for twenty lengths of cloth, it is clear that Ormond was to add his men to theirs to create a powerful military presence.[36] Within two months they had begun to repair some of the damage wrought by the French the previous autumn. At the end of March 1493 Kildare was pardoned; and on 10 April both Desmonds, Warbeck's backers Maurice and Thomas, his brother, were restored to the king's grace. At the end of May Hubert Burke and Edward Ormond, two Warbeck intimates were pardoned, and despite another atrocity from Kildare he was pardoned further.[37] Even in England such restoration was possible, given the circumstances. On 19 June John Hayes, Taylor's friend was pardoned for his non-disclosure of Taylor's 1491 plot.[38]

Henry pursued the defence of Ireland with vigour over the summer of 1493. In mid-June he sent Henry Wyatt with reinforcements to Garth and Ormond and set up his government in the shape of the new deputy, Walter FitzSimmons. This carrot and stick approach worked. Ireland did not waver over the summer, and by the autumn of the year it was possible to withdraw Cotton, FitzSimmons and Ormond to England and wind down the military presence to 100 men. In November Kildare travelled to England to purge himself of his past sins, and stayed while Henry attempted to reconcile the warring Anglo-Irish, until May 1494. By this time Henry had achieved as much as was possible. On 18 March 1494 Maurice Earl of Desmond swore fealty to Henry, and Garrett FitzGerald, Great Earl of Kildare was bound for his loyalty to enforce Desmond's bond. Ireland, it appeared, was saved against the Duke of York.[39]

Since 1488 Flanders and England had been allies. During 1492 Albert of Saxony, Maximilian's lieutenant and Henry VII were in frequent contact. In November 1492 all parties, Maximilian, Margaret of Burgundy and the ducal council were kept informed of English affairs. But in December 1492 and January 1493, when Warbeck was fêted in Flanders, contact with England dried up. However, on 26 February the courier Thomelin Hazart took letters from Albert of Saxony to England. Henry VII's reply was sufficient to prompt letters from the ducal council to Albert of Saxony; and from Albert to Margaret and the Flemish chancellor about English affairs. On 15 April, three weeks after Hazart's return, Maximilian sent a pursuivant to the English court, where he arrived on 3 May.[40] This marked the beginning of the diplomatic moves against Perkin Warbeck which culminated in the Poynings and Warham mission of July.

Henry VII, King of England

By the summer there is no doubt that Henry VII believed he faced a challenge like that of Stoke. As early as 25 April he was at Warwick castle, and after touring the west Midlands for the whole of May he took up residence in Kenilworth castle for two months. With the King was a retinue of twelve field gunners who operated falcons, light artillery for rapid deployment in emergencies. Only after the invasion scare was over, in August, did he move south, to Northampton, where he remained during September. Throughout this period Henry, personally, was prepared for battle, and his harness, battle armour, was returned to London only at the end of October.[41]

According to Polydore Vergil, the aim of the conspirators was to raise popular insurrection against Henry by disseminating rumours that the Duke of York was a true Plantagenet, saved from the Tower. In order to counteract their claims about Warbeck, Hall, who spoke to eyewitnesses of Warbeck's career, says that in the spring of 1493 Henry scoured the Low Countries to discover Warbeck's exact origins. During one of these forays, according to Hall, a group of Henry's spies reached Tournai, and were told by its citizens that Richard, Duke of York was Perkin Warbeck.[42] Thomas Gainsford, Warbeck's first biographer goes further preserving or, more probably, inventing a story that Nathaniel Osbeck, a member of Warbeck's family, was rewarded by Henry for supplying the information Poynings and Warham used to cast doubt on his veracity in front of the Flemish council.[43] Whoever it was that supplied Henry with information on Warbeck by June, he possessed enough information to mount a propaganda campaign against the so-called Duke within England. Thus for example, he could write to Gilbert Talbot comparing Warbeck's career to that of Lambert Simnel, and drew parallels between the dangers from Lovel, Lincoln, the Irish and the Germans and the present danger. The blame he laid on the 'greate malice' of Margaret of Burgundy in dressing up Perkin Warbeck to play the Duke of York.[44]

The threat of invasion was taken very seriously. Unauthorized travel was forbidden to prevent defection and espionage and subversion.[45] Around the king the mood was one of grim defence. On 20 March the six-year-old Prince Arthur was appointed chief justice of Oyer and Terminer to investigate conspiracy in Shropshire, Herefordshire, Gloucestershire, Worcestershire and the Welsh Marches, with powers to array men for military service. Too young himself, these measures were undertaken on his behalf by the king's uncle, Jasper Tudor, and the prince's most important household officers. A month later similar commissions were appointed in every county between Yorkshire and Oxfordshire, from the Marches to Cambridgeshire (and later Surrey), staffed by the king's most trusted officers and the Chief Justices of the realm. When Warbeck's supporters were attainted in Parliament in 1495 their treason was dated from 20 April 1493, a fact which suggests action was taken against them before the commission was recorded on the patent roll on 13 May. A number of the appointees, Edward Courtenay, Giles Daubney, Robert Willoughby de Broke, and one of the ecclesiastics, Richard Fox (Lord Privy Seal), to say nothing of the already appointed Jasper Tudor, had been in exile with Henry in 1483, and were his most trusted servants. A week later, 20 May 1493, these officials, household, chamber, legal officers and justices were appointed Commissioners of the Peace in the fifteen counties they were already appointed to investigate by Oyer and Terminer. A week later the king ordered the arrest of eight men, some of whom, from East Anglia may have been harbingers of rebellion there. This process, in R.L. Storey's words, marked the 'most dramatic purge since Bosworth' of local commissions. How effective the measures were is less certain. One of the major commissioners, John Kendal, was later accused of plotting on Warbeck's behalf; and one of the Warwickshire commissioners, Sir Simon Mountford, was later executed for engaging in the sort of treason he was supposed to identify. On the other hand the whole operation was being directly supervised from Kenilworth by the king, and it was backed by military forces held there. So, while such a display of power did not stop defections to Warbeck it did uncover supporters.[46] On 20 May Humphrey Savage and a Middlesex yeoman, John Burton, led a group of armed commoners in taking oaths to support Warbeck against the king. The behaviour of Londoners was every bit as unpredictable in 1493 as it had been in 1486 and 1487 when some citizens had supported Edward, Earl of Warwick's claim to the crown. Thus in order to blunt the appetite of the Londoners for treason there was at least one public hanging, of four traitors drawn through the streets and hanged for treason at Tyburn, just before Savage's oath taking.[47] But it was impossible to create complete security in England and mistakes were made. For example, on 14 May 1493 the king was obliged to give 6s 8d to John Smethe, a man wrongly accused of treason and brought to the king for examination. Nor could ports be secured totally against defectors. Thus, when they believed sufficient promises of support for an insurrection had been obtained, Sir Robert Clifford, William Barley of Albury in Hertfordshire and Thomas and John Brampton of Albury defected to Margaret of Burgundy on 14 June.[48]

From his actions it seems that Henry believed an attack would be made on the east coast. East Anglia was the region where two of the conspirators, Fitzwater and Debenham were most influential. And in spring 1493 Margaret had been sending messages to Scotland, where Henry had spies employed. Naval forces were ordered to be prepared in the mouth of the Orwell. And Ipswich was designated to maintain resupply of a patrol under the command of Stephen Bull, John Clerk and William Walshe who stood ready to put to sea. They were expected to remain at sea for at least six weeks (12 July till 23 August) in order to cut lines of communication between Scotland and Flanders. Sandwich, Ipswich and the Thames estuary were searched for supply vessels, and soundings were taken from Sir Reginald Bray and John Lord Dynham about whether it was then necessary to send more powerful ships, such as the *Sovreign* and the *Regent*, to sea.[49] Great Yarmouth, a town later in the rebels sights, was also probably placed on alert. The refortification of its defences, begun in 1488 under the King's Attorney James Hobart and Henry Heydon, was given a further boost that summer as the king remitted taxes to the tune of over £17 per annum for a further three years.[50] As we have seen the king already had field artillery on standby and at the end of July and beginning of August he wrote to trusted counsellors ordering them to have mounted retinues placed on one day's notice. Gilbert Talbot, for example, was ordered to provide 80 men at the king's expense – as many men-at-arms as possible, with archers and foot soldiers to make up numbers – and John Cheyne twenty men.[51] Others would have received similar instructions.

But despite the scare, a real one, nothing happened. The rebels seem to have been defeated by the king's countermeasures, and a lack of money. As the summer wore on they sent messages not to East Anglia but to Kent. The area they picked was the Kent–Sussex border between the Romney Marshes and the Weald. Here, Roger Harlakenden of Woodchurch and others were asked to stockpile armour. Harlakenden was found out and accused of having received a messenger, allowing him to return to Flanders, and destroying the letters from Warbeck. It was said that he had promised eighty brigantines to the rebels but at his trial, two years later, he was found not guilty.[52] It is probable that the man the rebels were really interested in was Harlakenden's neighbour Gervase Horne of Appledore, ten miles from New Romney. The Horne family were long-standing supporters of York, but Gervase Horne died at the end of July and was posthumously accused of treason. Had not powerful friends, Cardinal Morton and Sir Richard Guildford, intervened, the Horne family would have lost their lands. Horne was a veteran of Buckingham's rebellion, having risen against Richard III; and then two Hornes had had to buy back their grace. It is possible that the rebels were switching their strategy, from East Anglia to Kent. But it is more likely that they were floundering for lack of money and support.[53]

By the time Henry had all his precautions in place the danger had passed. Messages were sent to England calling off any planned insurrection. The Merchant of Ruby, such was Warbeck's code name, could not raise the capital necessary to finance his invasion. This was not 1487 when military activity in the Low Countries was so intense that Maximilian could throw Margaret of Burgundy one of his finest mercenary captains and hardly notice it. Though peace with France was a real prospect there was fighting in Flanders and Artois. Swiss mercenaries still garrisoned towns such as Courtrai and the expense of Maximilian's taxes had provoked popular insurrection. By July 1493 Maximilian was switching his attention to the far west of his domains, to Croatia and Styria, which were under threat from the Turks.[54] Margaret was so unsuccessful in her attempts to raise cash that she was reduced to appealing directly for aid to a war-weary Flemish nobility and to making extravagant promises to the mercenaries in Flanders that they would have duchies, counties and baronies in England if only they would invade on her behalf.[55] Not even the Bruges bankers, who had financed the salvation of Flanders from the French could be induced to lend her the funds necessary for so hare-brained an enterprise. There was then a chance that with correct handling, diplomacy could be used to bring Perkin Warbeck's imposture to conclusion.

Diplomatic feelers had been sent out in May 1493 for Henry to send an embassy to Flanders. Yet such was the snail's pace of early modern diplomacy that it was only on 9 June that Malines despatched a reply to Henry.[56] When the reply reached England at the end of June, Henry responded immediately by despatching the two ambassadors he had previously prepared. They were well chosen. William Warham was a fine orator and Sir Edward Poynings, Deputy Lieutenant of Calais and commander of English forces at Sluys was well known and well regarded in Flanders. They were ordered to Malines on 5 July and arrived in Bruges by 17 July.[57] They had arrived at a time of heightened political activity brought about by the meeting of the Estates General called to ratify Senlis but, as the ambassadors of a friendly power, were well received. According to Polydore Vergil, who may have talked to Warham about this embassy, they were there to assert in public that Richard, Duke of York was the assumed persona of a commoner; and that it was beyond doubt that Richard had perished along with his brother. 'And to assert or believe otherwise would be the height of folly since it was sufficiently obvious that King Richard would have in no sense safeguarded himself in killing Edward the eldest son of King Edward . . . if he had spared Richard the second son, who would have been equally able to claim rightfully the kingdom in his fathers name.' Philip was to be told who Perkin Warbeck was and reminded also that during the recent civil war Henry had helped him against the French. All this was outlined by Warham in his speech. He then went further, grossly insulting the Duchess of Burgundy by saying she 'regularily contrived to discover scoundrely nephews from among her brother's children. Not many years earlier . . . [she] had pretended that Lambert was the son of George Duke of Clarence . . . who . . . became a turnspit in the royal kitchen before he was promoted to be trainer of the royal hawks. Now she feigned that Peter Warbeck was the other nephew, a son of her brother Edward, a fellow who also was fit to wash the dirty cooking dishes in the royal kitchens.' Hall invents an earthier version of this speech. But it was so hurtful, touching the raw, that Vergil maintains she wished to harm Warham.[58]

Given the events of the previous eight months it is not surprising that Warham's assertions sparked off debate among the archduke's councillors, or that Warham and Poynings remained in Malines till 14 August.[59] The verdict reached was Solomon's judgement in reverse. Instead of coming to a single judgement, however unpalatable, the council attempted to steer a middle path in order to offend neither Henry VII or the Duchess Margaret. According to Vergil there were long debates on the council about whether Perkin was or was not King Edward's son. Ultimately it was agreed, out of respect for Henry,

Flanders would no longer actively assist Warbeck.[60] But it could not prevent the duchess doing so since she was a free agent and was completely responsible for the administration of her dowry lands, in one castle of which, Dendermonde, Warbeck resided. This was a moment of extraordinary ill luck for Henry. The summer of 1493 marked the end of Maximilian's regency for Philip in Flanders. In October 1493 Albert of Saxony, Maximilian's lieutenant was replaced as head of Philip's council by Engelbert of Nassau.[61] In giving the answer to Henry that it did, Philip's council may have been attempting to avoid insulting Maximilian and Margaret, while hoping that, given Maximilian's distractions in the west, his support for Warbeck would fade.

Poynings and Warham returned to England in late August and went straight to confer with the king at Northampton. Once matters had been discussed, and a course of action agreed on, Poynings left Northampton and went to visit his Paston relatives in London. There he delivered himself of a sanguinary judgement of Warbeck's chances of making trouble for England. 'As for the matier beyond See', William Paston told Thomas Cary, having talked to his nephew who had just then, 9 September, come from the king, 'be ye sure ye may slepe in rest for any trouble that shall be this yere or the next.'[62] It had been decided to embargo Flanders to produce by economic strangulation what diplomacy could not. Thus on 18 September it was proclaimed that no one in the realm except those trading in wools and wool-fells through the Staple of Calais was allowed to export goods to Philip the Fair's territory. Nor could anyone import goods from Flanders except under special licence, upon pain of forfeiture of all the goods. Those charged with implementing this proclamation, customers, controllers, seekers and searchers, were told that if they did not arrest those who infringed this proclamation then they were to be treated as little less than traitors, losing their offices, and forfeiting their goods.[63] It was presumably prior knowledge of these measures which led to Poyning's optimistic judgement that Warbeck would not be causing trouble in the foreseeable future. Nothing was further from the truth.

Henry VII's interdict in restraint of trade did ultimately dissuade Philip the Fair from his support of Warbeck but this took three years. In the meantime Warbeck's status had grown to such a degree that he could marry a cousin to James IV of Scotland. Henry VII's actions were like those of an imprudent gardener, whose pruning, far from curing the problem, causes ever more florid growth. In taking the hardest line possible with Charles VIII Henry had created a legitimate duke, in Flanders, where one had never been before. In not acquiescing in the equivocal judgement given by Philip's council in August 1493, Henry created in Margaret of Burgundy an improvident *alter regina*, the Juno of Tudor propaganda, who took it upon herself to internationalize the plight of her nephew far outside Flanders. In the space of two years the Warbeck conspiracy had advanced from a diversion to allow the French annexation of Brittany to one which was about to involve every European monarch, and the Roman pontiff, in the revival of Yorkist claims to the English throne. Henry VII, of all people, was not the man to underestimate the likelihood that such a far-fetched claim might succeed in overthrowing a King of England. Again, therefore, he took action against the supporters of York. Again he acted too harshly. The years 1494–5 saw not the approach of easy victory but the re-entry into England of the threat of civil war, a state caused by Henry's ever harsher attempts to defeat its by-products: an ageing dowager, a group of political zealots and the belief that peace was finally possible because Richard, Duke of York had survived the Tower of London.

SEVEN
A Wood of Suspicion

When Warham belittled and insulted the dowager Duchess of Burgundy, the die was cast. The death of the Holy Roman Emperor Frederick III, on 19 August, created the perfect opportunity for Richard, Duke of York to meet the emperor elect, Maximilian, who had been Margaret's protector since 1485. Warham and Poynings had achieved nothing. Margaret could still do as she pleased, so on 25 August, she appealed for help to Queen Isabella of Castille. The result of the Poynings–Warham mission was that it internationalized support for Warbeck, and it may have changed the nature of the conspiracy.

If Warham knew who Warbeck was and where he came from, and produced evidence to back up his assertions, it may have been hoped that this would cause a breach between the duchess and Warbeck's masters; men who would then be seen to have duped her. But if there was a crisis of this sort, now, it had no effect on the degree to which Margaret was willing to sponsor her so-called nephew. Indeed the relationship of the two, as expressed in documents a year apart could hardly have sounded more harmonious. At the end of 1494 Richard, Duke of York talked about 'my very dear beloved aunt my lady Margaret of England'. He was more effusive when he mentioned, 'the great love and affection in which she always holds us', and the way this was manifest, 'by aiding us to recover our right'.[1] The key to the relationship is in Margaret's letter to Isabella. 'But what can I do a woman and a widow, bereft of father and so many mighty brothers? For after so many disasters in our most unfortunate House, after the fall of our family from the pinnacle of Royalty, what aid, what help still lies in me?'[2] This as we have seen is exactly her mental world. The Duchess's tragic situation was mitigated by her patronage of religious orders, and especially those which helped orphans. What then of Warbeck and she: she a childless widow, he a motherless child? Bernard André, in a muddled account of Margaret's instructions to Warbeck, prior to his visit to Maximilian, has her say that Warbeck was to go to the emperor, 'always concealing with caution in your mind and in your heart what has been arranged between us concerning my brother's son'.[3] On this point, her knowledge of the imposture, Warbeck confirmed that she knew he was a fake. It may be that one other unintended outcome of Warham's insults was to convert Warbeck from genuine pretender into stalking horse for Edward, Earl of Warwick. The pressures on Margaret and the exiles to reach such a compromise were enormous. Personal motives aside – some of them were ex-Clarence men – they had, with Warbeck's talents, conjured up a conspiracy in England which it would have been next to impossible to ditch. Already prophets talked of York's likely recovery of the throne. And Robert Clifford reported to the conspirators that, in Hall's phrase, 'he knew him to be king Edwards sonne by his face & lyniaments of his body'.[4]

Margaret attempted first to drive a wedge between England and Spain. On 25 August, Margaret sponsored a letter from Warbeck to Isabella of Castille. Her letter described what she had seen of Richard, Duke of York, and her belief that he was her nephew. She flattered

Isabella of Castille, Queen of Spain

Isabella as a queen surpassing all others, appealed to their 'kinship and closeness of blood', and begged her to 'take pity on our destitution, misfortune and losses, and not allow the throne of England to be tyrannically usurped by a supremely wicked enemy . . .'.[5] Such aid would bring an Anglo-Spanish alliance much firmer than that of Edward IV. Warbeck, as Richard, also wrote, from Antwerp, on the same day. Like his aunt he said nothing that was not strictly limited by what he had actually seen and done. With the exception of his escape from murder and his orphaned wanderings the letter was substantially his own life: eight years in divers provinces, Portugal for a time, Ireland, France, the flight to Flanders and his reception by Margaret. Subsequently he had received envoys from Maximilian, James IV and King Hans of Denmark. Would Isabella not join with these monarchs and aid him? He too promised friendship closer than that of his father. Spanish scepticism endorsed the missive, 'From Richard the one who calls himself King of England', and did nothing.[6]

From Antwerp Margaret returned to her town of Dendermonde, where, twice in the second week of September Albert of Saxony sent her news from England.[7] Where was her nephew? Probably at Malines with Albert. Very shortly after this he, and Albert of Saxony's entourage began their long journey to Vienna for the funeral of Frederick III. Saxony, who was Maximilian's brother-in-law, entered Vienna on 5 November, alongside Warbeck. Ludwig Klinkhamer reported to Sigismund of Tirol that he took him for Margaret of Burgundy's brother,[8] so the apparent likeness of Warbeck and York must have been considerable. Frederick's funeral was a sumptuous and solemn meeting of princes and dignatories from all over Europe. Molinet tells us that between his lying in state and the day of the funeral 5,412 masses had been heard for him. The cathedral was decked in black, and lit reputedly by over 600 candles. In the middle of the church the emperor's tomb was covered by a sheet of white damask, itself covered by black damask. About to bury his father, Maximilian was accompanied by representatives of the Imperial household and administration: Albert of Saxony, his son Henry, and the Imperial Electors. In the next rank of mourners were found representatives of the Flemish nobility, Venetian ambassadors. Round the tomb stood two highly placed French representatives; two from Hungary; Rene of Lorraine's representative, and that of England: 'Richart, filz de Edoart, roy d'Englterre'. This huge concourse of imperial luminaries, lay and clerical, buried Frederick with all pomp on 7 December. And at the end of the service the representatives of the Empire made their final offerings of achievements and banners, and then the visiting dignatories, among whom were Philip the Fair's party and the Duke of York, did likewise. Once this was over the socializing began with a dinner – most exquisite, reported Molinet.[9]

Warbeck had been sent to Maximilian for one reason and one reason only, to obtain financial backing for his invasion of England. He was called to meet the emperor for one reason and one reason only, to satisfy Maximilian's curiosity. From the time he met Warbeck, with the exception of a brief period of two years between 1498 and 1500, Maximilian believed wholeheartedly that he was the Duke of York. All his public utterances were to this effect, and even at the end of Warbeck's career, when he was totally discredited, Maximilian gave instructions to his ambassador to England to ignore suggestions that he was anything other than a Plantagenet.[10] It is not clear on what basis this judgement was made. Margaret's recommendation of Warbeck as York and the evidence of his eyes would have counted for much. And then there was the famous story of Richard Plantagenet's escape from death with which Warbeck must have felt more and more at ease as he worked for the maximum response from his listener. From what we know of Maximilian's mentality he existed in a world of astrology, horoscopes, zodiacs and pseudo-scientific Platonism. To have accepted Richard's resurrection in this mental world was not a great aberration. For Maximilian the early 1490s were a halcyon period: after the civil wars in Flanders, before he was defeated by European politics. Perhaps like James IV of Scotland, who also embarked on his adult political career at this time, the pursuit of the Duke of York's cause was more important than its end. He was robust of health now, as healthy as he ever was, before decline began in 1497.[11] Warbeck entered the emperor's entourage at Vienna and became his intimate. For Warbeck this was the first time since his Portuguese days when he lived the untroubled life of the courtier. He acted as imperial go-between for Maximilian and Bianca Maria, delivering letters between them in the first days of their life together. Bianca Maria Sforza had waited ten weeks in the Tirol to see Maximilian since marrying him by proxy.[12] Their marriage was solemnized at Innsbruck, in the spring, a celebration at which Warbeck is likely to have been present.

Warbeck, though, had come about serious business, and in this respect he, or his masters, could not have come at a better time. The Fugger bankers were at this moment transferring Bianca Maria's dowry to the imperial coffers, and Maximilian was about to cream off the feudal dues of his confirmation of imperial and Netherlandish privileges and grants.[13] In visiting the emperor the Yorkists charmed him and convinced him of their rights. This gave them access not just to the fruits of marriage and office but opened up to them connections with the Bruges money markets and the courts commercial contacts. The Medici bank at Bruges had financed Charles the Bold on a huge scale, and after his death spent £20,000 artois keeping the Burgundian state, and Bruges banks, from ruin. When Warbeck went back to Flanders with Maximilian, his finances were underwritten at Bruges and in Amsterdam.[14] The death of Sigismund of Tirol opened up another financial avenue, and before he left on his Imperial progress Maximilian instucted the Staathalter und Regenten of his newly aquired province to find 16,000 florins for Warbeck. But this was never paid, and the

Innsbruck Castle, the Courtyard, 1494. Drawn by Albrecht Dürer on his journey to Italy in the same year that Perkin Warbeck visited Innsbruck

imperial fiat was not enough to ensure finance for a quarrel in a far-away country. Despite chivying from Maximilian, in November 1494, the Tirolese refused to part with their money.[15]

Sir Edward Poynings's judgement that for the next two years there would be no trouble from Warbeck was ridiculously optimistic. If not wilfully misleading it was based on a typically one-dimensional soldier's view of politics. By the interdict of 18 September all trade with Flanders and the Burgundian Low Countries was forbidden. Flemings were expelled from England, their goods seized, and the Merchant Adventurers' textile mart transferred from Antwerp to Calais. Cloth, for the forseeable future, would be sold to the Netherlands via Calais, but this did not have the expected effect of bringing Philip the Fair to heel. Over the following three years Flanders imported increased amounts of wool in order that native looms replace the shortfall in English cloth.[16] At home there were immediate repercussions. In under a month the lay-off of labour and loss of markets resulted in a race riot in London. On 15 October 1493 two servants of the mercer John Pykton led eighty of their fellows in an attack on the London headquarters of the Hansa, the Steelyard. They did little real damage, but they threw the city into turmoil and obliged the mayor to defend the Steelyard with guns and crossbows. Once the riot had been contained a mayoral enquiry revealed the rioters to be unemployed covenant servants, thrown out of work by the ban on trade with Flanders. Normally these men were retained by the London merchant community to broker their imports from Flanders to the city. Unemployment meant loss of customers because of a lack of goods to sell on, and whereas previously merchants had taken servants on at £20 per annum, plus food and drink now they could not find even a five mark retainer. The Hansa on the other hand imported what they could not, and while the Hansards grew fat on importing goods prohibited to English merchants the covenant servants could not meet their everyday expenses. Enquiries by both the mayor and king revealed no more sinister cause than the above: that the rioters were genuinely impoverished. They spent two years in a number of gaols, including the Tower, before the king pardoned them.[17]

The Hansa, however, were dealt with more quickly in order to remove the cause of the grievance. On 21 October, six days after the riot began, Robert Hill and Richard Buckberd appeared before the king in chancery and stood surety for twenty-seven Hanseatic merchants in the sum of £20,000. By this bond the Steelyard merchants agreed not to trade with Burgundy, except via Calais, and were obliged to forbid any of their agents or servants from doing so on their behalf. Also, since only two months earlier the merchant John de Lysa had been found carrying messages to Warbeck's band, the Hanseatics were forbidden under forfeit of their bond any association with Henry's rebels.[18] Though the Flemish government was in touch with Henry VII in February on secret business, possibly giving warning of what was to come, on 8 April 1494, as Warbeck was returning from the Tirol with Maximilian, Maximilian and Philip issued the Flemish counterpart to Henry VII's interdict banning all trade and ordering the seizure of English merchants' goods.[19] As relations between England and Flanders deteriorated even further Henry VII resorted to policing his mercantile community with bonds. In this period, up to within two days of lifting the commercial interdict in February 1496, merchants visiting Calais had their date of return to England fixed in advance and entered bonds that they would not extend their visit or visit anywhere in the Burgundian Low Countries. London was the main target of this enterprise, with twenty out of forty-two bonds, but merchants from King's Lynn, Hull, Lincoln, Shrewsbury, Stafford, Wolverhampton, York and elsewhere were among those caught in the political crossfire.[20] Maximilian, at the height of his support for Warbeck, replied to these measures accusing Henry of destroying the employment of the poor of Flanders, depopulating the country, and in January 1495 by issuing a reinforcement of his interdict of 1494.[21]

The importance of commerce in this war of nerves was one facet of the trade embargo. The other was the chronic weakness to penetration by espionage of a realm whose secondary administative centre, Calais, adjoined Flanders. Calais was a hundred miles from Malines, but only forty from the duchess's dower lands of Cassel and la Motte. Given the linkage between the civil and military functions there was much coming and going between Calais and Flanders. Spies were best disguised as travellers, clerics or merchants. Merchants leaving and entering Calais were examined on the state of affairs elsewhere, and garrison soldiers were disguised as merchants in order to reconnoitre areas outside the March of Calais. Calais had part declared for the Earl of Warwick in 1485, and its garrison had then split, part remaining loyal to Henry Tudor, part taking up service under Maximilian. When the conspiracy against Henry VII was broken in 1494 a significant element was found to be connected to Calais. William Lounde, who defected to Warbeck in 1493, may have lived here in the 1470s with his master.[22] Robert Clifford, the go-between between England and Malines was overheard in Calais enthusing to a lady that Warbeck was the Duke of York.[23] Treason spread from Malines via Calais. When, in 1495, Warbeck appeared off Deal, Edmund Wode and Edward Ashley, merchant and gentleman of Calais respectively, were with him.[24]

Throughout 1493 and 1494 a propaganda war was fought between Malines and England and it was not until the end of 1494 that Henry VII began to win it. Malines sent across agents to canvas opinion in England, Henry replied by bringing people who knew Warbeck to court and threatening to bring his childhood friends from Tournai thither. Of the time when Henry claimed that, 'there is no noble man, gentleman, or person of any condition . . . who does not well know that it is a manifest and evident imposture . . .'. Polydore Vergil later wrote, it was a time when many noblemen conspired against the king, 'and persons of the lowest birth maligned the king himself . . .'.[25] In the winter of 1493–4 Edward Cyver, of Northampton, a hatmaker, also known as English Edward, slipped into England from Flanders. Given the size of the English population at Calais he could have come from there, but in view of the charge that he had visited, 'all the towns along the sea coast', before he was captured he may have come in through Poole, Portsmouth or Southampton. All three ports were used by Warbeck's messengers. Cyver travelled the south coast 'discovering the state of mind of the people . . . and influencing and converting those well disposed . . . from that state of mind . . .' and then relaying this to Malines. Apart from making contact with sympathizers this was probably reconnaissance for a landing on the coast. But he over-reached himself in London spreading the good news. He was taken outside the Temple Bar on 8 February and indicted a week and a half later.[26] With him, in a round up of London dissidents, were four sanctuary men from St Martin le Grand in the city, a yeoman of the Crown, Robert Bulkley, an unnamed Flemish man, possibly a messenger from the rebels in Flanders. Four of this group, Thomas Bagnall, John Scot, John Heth and John Kenyngton had distributed bills, probably defamatory vernacular rhymes attacking the king and selected members of his council, all over the city. They were forcibly removed from sanctuary, and tried before an oyer and terminer commission at the Guildhall on 22 February. Bagnall managed to have himself restored to sanctuary, but the Flemish man, and the other three who had previous counts of treason to answer, were executed on 26 February at Tyburn.[27] Gilbert Debenham, Humphrey Savage and John Burton who had attempted recruiting in London for Warbeck a year before were to have been tried with this group. They were indicted along with Cyver on 20 February, but only Burton went through full legal process, to emerge alive, and pardoned on 1 April.[28] According to their attainders Debenham and Savage fled to sanctuary in Westminster Abbey. Here they both remained for over five years till Debenham was pardoned in 1499 and died in 1500; and Savage, pardoned in 1499 died at an unknown date. Both had been declared outlaws.

Though a sanctuary man like the others, Robert Bulkley was not executed. A yeoman of the Crown, he was from a family who were long-standing clients of the Stanleys. One of Cardinal Wolsey's correspondents in the 1520s described Henry VII's method at this time. He 'would handle [treason] circumspectly, and with convenient diligence for inveigling, and yet not disclose it, to the party nor otherwise, by a great space after, but keep it to himself and always grope further having ever good wait and espial to the party. I am sure his highness knew of the untrue mind and treason compassed against him by Sir William Stanley and other great men, two or three years before that he laid it to their charge, and kept it secret and always gathered upon them more and more.'[29] It is possible that Bulkley bought his life with information about Sir William Stanley. Yet the difficulty lay not in placing spies in this or that man's household, but that like a cancer it was not clear, where in the body politic the next tumour would appear.

Malines made a determined effort to mine Henry's household by exploiting its inherent weakness that it was essentially the construct of Edward IV: part of his great political connection extending well down the social hierarchy, and their efforts resulted in a gradual lowering of tolerance among the political élite to the suggestion that Warbeck was not Richard, Duke of York. This can be seen in the cases of some of those who defected to Flanders. There was a degree of residual loyalty to York which leached men away from the royal households. The Queen lost Edwards, one of her yeomen. In the same year, 1493, Henry lost his sergeant furrier, whose loyalty to Warbeck became so pronounced that he was viciously punished when captured.[30] Richard Lessy, who was chaplain to Cecily Neville is a case in point. Not actually punished for treason he was nevertheless complicit with the plotters, for he was accused of misprison.[31] Charles Ripon, Constable of Portchester Castle, near Portsmouth and later an adherent of Edmund de la Pole, may have had a relative, Robert, in Warbeck's camp in 1494.[32] Two examples here can show how the rebel claims affected the political élite. In 1493 William Lounde was steward to Sir Ralph Hastings. Lounde was from Doncaster, and of a family with Neville connections. Hastings regarded him so highly that not only did he control his household, but he had access to his master's jewels and plate. In late summer of 1493 he absconded to Malines taking with him all of Hastings money and a considerable quantity of plate. He was subsequently promoted to acting as chancellor to Warbeck's court in exile. In the meantime, because this was precisely the method used to indicate to Malines a readiness to support their duke, Hastings was immediately, wrongly, identified as a traitor and placed under bonds that he remain loyal to the king.[33] Even the apparently humble had important connections. Thomas a Wode, of Faversham in Kent, defected to Warbeck and was captured in Ireland, possibly in 1495. On the discovery of his treason his lands were forfeit and the king granted them to John Norton, gentleman, also of Faversham. Norton had the ear of Sir Edward Poynings, which may be how he acquired the grant. He, however, immediately sold the lands on to Thomas Malpas who agreed to sell them back to a Wode.[34] Given the way messages were transmitted it is clear that even the most impeccably loyal – Sir Edward Poynings – might in fact be treacherous. Neither Hastings nor Poynings were traitors, but John Ratcliffe, Lord Fitzwater was, and so was his steward Thomas Cressener, servant of William Daubney, ex-Clerk of the Jewel House to Edward IV.[35]

The ease with which men entered England spreading propaganda and carrying intelligence could not be overcome by Henry. There were just too many creeks and harbours for any early modern state to police effectively. Attempts were made to police the channel. At the close of 1493 Martin Behaim was sent by King João II of Portugal to Flanders. As we have seen, Behaim came from the circle which knew Warbeck as a Flemish servant not Duke of York. He had risen high in service to the Portuguese monarchy, but was, by birth a

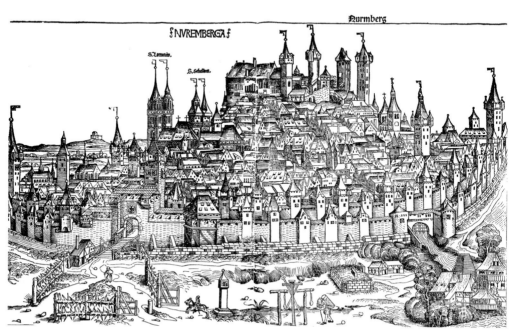

Nuremberg in 1493. In 1494 Martin Behaim wrote to his cousin Michael, in Zistelgasse, Nuremberg, recounting his capture while on the way to Flanders to visit Richard, Duke of York

Nuremberger. He was personally known to Maximilian, had lived in Flanders for a number of years, and knew the Portuguese Factor at Bruges. João II sent him to Flanders on a mission of sorts, embassy or information gathering, it is not clear which. Behaim was taken prisoner on the high sea by one of Henry VII's naval patrols and in December 1493 detained in England with his servants. In his capture he lost 160 gulden, all his travelling expenses, but was lucky to keep his life. While he was captive in England he caught a fever and at one point was so close to death that he was given the last rites – he had a lighted taper placed in his hands. But he did not die, he recovered; and when he was well enough paid a pirate to secrete him in his ship and take him to France. By the second week of March 1494 he was safe in Antwerp, going about family business, and writing to his cousin in Nuremberg giving him the news.[36]

There was no need for melodramatic entrances to England. Personal servants passing backwards and forwards carried news quite adequately. Enough gossip took place among England's political élite to justify Polydore Vergil's statement that 'there was no one who was not deeply concerned over such an affair'.[37] John Kendal, Prior of the Order of the Hospitallers in England had links with the dissident community in Bruges and Flanders because of his hospitaller connections. He was Lieutenant for the Master of the Order of St John, in Italy, Ireland, Flanders and England and was friends with a small group of Englishmen who had spent the 1480s and early '90s in diplomatic service in France and Rome. Some of these friends were brothers of the English Hospice of St Thomas in Rome.[38] A fellow hospitaller Guillaume de Noion, who acted as secretary for Warbeck kept Kendal up to the minute with news about Warbeck. Every time Kendal received a letter from Flanders he sent a news message to Thomas Langton, Bishop of Winchester, or to John Husee, or the Archdeacon of Northampton, Peter Husee (who were members of the confraternity in Rome) or to Sir Thomas Tyrrell. Sometimes Kendal visited Langton to give him the news, sometimes Langton and the others received information from Flanders and they circulated it likewise. In 1494 or 1495 Noion's servant arrived with a letter addressed to Sir Thomas Brandon, a member of a family with an impeccable record of loyalty to Henry VII, since Thomas's uncle had been killed as king's standard bearer at Bosworth. The servant was so terrified of giving the letter to Brandon that he delivered it to Kendal, and fled.[39]

The existence of these friends networking information should make us aware of a difficulty in dealing with the conspiracy of 1494–5, that we assume those few names which we know represent the bedrock of conspiracy. It is much more likely that the reverse is true, that they are only the more important who would not or could not be reconciled to the government. The treason of William Stanley is notorious, and has provoked much discussion. Practically unknown is that of his bastard son Thomas, who emerges into the light of the historical record, in 1510, after fifteen years incarcerated in the Tower of London.[40]

Among the political élite there was any amount of loose talk, but what the king demanded, always, was proof. When Richard Nanfan, a long standing Cornish loyalist heard Robert Clifford say 'Perken Warbeke was kynge Edwardes sone', he understood the full weight of such disloyalty, 'Never wordes went coldre to my hart then they dyd.' Yet the king sent him 'sharp wrytyng agay that he wold have the prouffe of this matier. I hade no wittnes then but my sylfe; but as hyt hapned afterwardes I caused hym by good crafte to confesse the same he had said to me be fore hym that was marshall here at that tyme, and els I hade lykly to be putt to a grett plonge for my trothe.'[41] This can be read as another example of Henry VII's obsessionalism, but given the nature of the Warbeck problem as a focus for unfulfilled dreams, as a cultural curiosity, or a focus for dissidents and the discontented, it was vital to Henry VII that he distinguish the gossips from the conspirators. Repeatedly, later, in 1495, 1497, 1499, 1500 and 1502 Henry kept lists of rebels, fined men, executed men and reprieved men in order to use this knowledge to whittle away support from the opposition. It was important to know who to contact, who to offer pardons to, and who to entice back to England with money. It was important too to know the rebels' plans, so that they might be spiked. Henry used spies in the established fashion, sending men off in pairs and threes so that they might return to him not singly, leaving gaps in his knowledge, but remain at Malines and by continually replenishing Warbeck's stock of supposed defectors, have a continuous flow of intelligence from Flanders. Returning spies, and returning defectors were funnelled through Calais. By a letter dated 22 October 1494 Henry ordered his administration there to repay Richard Nanfan his costs, £2, incurred when he sent to Henry three rebels who had 'forsakyn the ffeyned lad', and were appealing to Henry for a pardon.[42] It was by this means that Henry would 'always grope further having ever good await and espial to the party', the clear implication being that he placed spies in the households of those in England he suspected of having sent men to Warbeck.

Such use of spies was neither novel nor foolproof. Edward IV had attempted to mine households with spies, paid as 'unnamed', only to find that he had already been undermined, and that some of those he used as spies were double or triple agents.[43] Francis Bacon, who preserved the oral history of this period, conjures up its terror: the king's attempt to obtain proof absolute of involvement in treason from within England and Malines. Bacon reports, 'a strange tradition that the king, being lost in a wood of suspicions, and not knowing whom to trust, had intelligence with the confessors and chaplains of divers great men'. This bizarre

A petition to the Lord Chancellor of England, Cardinal John Morton, in which the story of Thomas a Wode of Faversham, Kent, one of Warbeck's followers, is related breach of trust was in fact normal.[44] Having escaped the Battle of Barnet with his life, John de Vere, Earl of Oxford wrote to his wife ordering her to imprison his chaplain if the chaplain returned home, 'for I undyrstand . . . [he] wold have destroyed me . . .'.[45] Those the king sent to Flanders, said Bacon, 'he did use to have them cursed at [St] Pauls, by name, amongst the bead roll of the king's enemies', so that their incognito was preserved. Unlike the melodramatic spy of Edward IV, one 'we wol not be named', Henry VII's spies were so anonymous in 1494–5 that the only traces they left were those of his chroniclers repudiating the gossip that individual x or y was a spy.[46]

Yet spies there were, controlled, like the returning defectors from Calais. Their work uncovered an extensive and well-developed plot involving all types of people, ecclesiastics, merchants, politicians, artisans, labourers, yeomen; and a variety of commitments. According to Molinet the plot in which William Stanley was involved numbered forty people who had promised Warbeck 40,000 florins.[47] Molinet's figures are suspect, more verisimilitude than veracity, and in any case we know the names of more than forty plotters. His forty means, 'sufficient of the élite to be dangerous'. That money was sent there is no doubt, it is a recurrent theme in all sources. Stanley was rich and sent money, said Bacon. Mountford was a supporter of York, so he sent his son and money. A number of important clerics were convinced of Warbeck's claims and sent money, themselves or through a third party, said Bernard André.[48] The same had been done for Henry Tudor in 1483 and after. Money seems to have been particularly forthcoming from emminent clerics whose treason is otherwise difficult to explain: most of them were too old to fight, and could not offer men. But what they could offer was legitimation, for they sent Warbeck their letters of credence and these in turn bought him belief in Flanders and real credit in the money markets. Promises of men were made by Stanley, Fitzwater and others, and the letters embarrassingly sent to Thomas Brandon, and others, in Kent for example, begged for military support. What Henry's spies found at Malines was a small English court in exile, much like his own, in Brittany, in 1485. This one, headed by an English duchess, was possessed of a pretender, had its own chancery through which promises had been obtained in England of support in the event of invasion, and was gathering an army of invasion from all over England. A list of those executed in 1495 gives details of over fifty men from twenty-four counties and two towns: Bristol and London.[49] The most heavily committed of the counties were Yorkshire, Northumberland and Shropshire. Warwickshire contributed Henry Mountford, armiger and Richard Malory, gentleman. All told, the list named four gentlemen, thirty-six yeomen, two chaplains, a goldsmith, a merchant, four labourers, a mariner and two grooms. This was a typical fifteenth-century retinue. And while some, following Polydore Vergil's description, may have been sanctuary men, some were there to represent their master's interests.

In the summer of 1494 Maximilian and Warbeck made a leisurely return to Flanders from the Tirol. They left Innsbruck in March, and by the end of June were as far north as Cologne. In July they reached Aachen and Maastricht.[50] The rebels who had stayed behind in Malines had engineered a considerable success. In mid-June 1494, after ten months of peace in Ireland, the Earl of Desmond broke his oath to Henry and raised Munster in rebellion.[51] In England Henry's spies had achieved as much as to make restive some of those executed and imprisoned later in the year. On 3 July William Daubney, Edward IV's old keeper of the Jewel House took out an extravagant pardon of all crimes committed since the beginning of time. Thomas Thwaites furnished himself with a pardon against accusations of embezzling the government in Calais.[52] Some part of the plot may have been uncovered, or miscarried at this stage, because on the day of Daubney's pardon William Graunte, kitchener of Westminster Abbey also took out a pardon. He was charged with feeding Gilbert Debenhan and Humphrey Savage. Two days before his pardon he found ten men who stood bond for his loyalty.[53] The repeated pattern of every summer in the 1490s began to re-form: threat of invasion, threat of insurrection, trouble in Ireland, the Scots in alliance with the regime sponsoring rebellion.

In mid-July Henry VII's spies in Flanders informed him of the dramatic turn of events there, the deliberate attempt to destabilize England. Maximilian's arrival was daily expected in Malines and the rebels there were spreading the story that there were 'certain persones', in England, 'which wol not long tarye from theym, but goo unto them in hast uppon knowledge of the comming of the (King of the) Romayns . . .'.[54] Henry immediately increased security in English seaports, ordering his customs officers, on 21 July, to keep a watch for any suspicious vessels entering ports. All creeks or small rivers, where small boats could put to sea, were also to be watched. Any suspects attempting to leave the realm were to be arrested and sent, with a report of the circumstances, to the king.[55] At about the same time reports were circulating in France that Maximilian had assembled a large force to invade England and that he was hiring transports from Breton and Norman ship masters.[56]

This information was supplied to Henry by Charles VIII. In July two of his most highly placed servants, Robert Briçonnet and Louis la Trémoille had visited Flanders on embassy. Passing on what they had observed there, was part of a larger French plan to drive a wedge between the normal anti-French configuration of England and Flanders. In the approach to Charles VIII's invasion of Italy the French had assiduously courted England. There had been a French embassy in England over Christmas 1493 and correspondence between Henry and Charles in March and June.[57] In June Henry was still in communication with Philip the Fair's government at Malines,[58] but the French were desperate to prevent the development of a possible scenario in which Warbeck, as a restored Yorkist Richard IV, married Maximilian's daughter Margaret and both countries declared war on France. In fact their fears were groudless, for at this stage Maximilian, though he was supporting Warbeck fancied not opposing France, but with France partitioning Italy. Nevertheless so heightened were French fears on the eve of their campaign to Italy, in August 1494, that they adopted a pro-English stance, with much talk of alliance, and promised, as payment for English non-intervention in Italy, that if Scotland were to threaten England they would desert their ancient ally. On 10 August Henry VII drew up instructions for a diplomatic reply to Charles VIII in which he stressed the peaceful condition of his realm, mentioning only the problem of revolt in Ireland. Maximilian's behaviour was written off as a fit of pique over Étaples and the damage the trade embargo was doing to the Flemish economy. Regarding Warbeck: no one believed a word of truth in his claims, everyone knew he was an imposter. These were brave words, given the circumstances in England, and a smokescreen of deceit.[59] Henry had imported to his court Warbeck's childhood friends and others who knew him to disabuse his court of the tittle-tattle and gossip surrounding the pretender. Nor, despite brave words about Scotland can he have been ignorant of the comings and goings between Flanders and Edinburgh which saw James IV sending his herald Snowdon in reply to a visit from Petit John, a name common among messengers at the Flemish court, and the same as that borne by a Breton executed alongside Sir William Stanley in 1495.

The situation was far from good. In August Maximilian and Warbeck reached Malines, and during August and September progressed through the Flanders duchy for Philip the Fair's recognition as ruler of the Flemish federation. On 10 September a huge retinue of Flemish and German nobility decended upon Louvain for Philip's reception as Duke of Brabant. Entering the church with his nobles as witnesses Philip swore on the Gospels to respect the privileges of St Peter's chuch just as his predecessors had done. Then Berthold von Heneburg, the Imperial Chancellor swore to maintain the privileges of Brabant. Warbeck was considered of such importance that in the official account of the visit he was listed a mere two names behind Von Heneburg, and in front of Albert of Saxony, Philippe de Cleves, now Seigneur de Ravenstein, and well in front of Hughes de Melun, Bauduin de Lannoy and various Burgundian royal bastards. A month later Warbeck's importance to the Flemish state was signalled much more clearly at Philip's entry to Antwerp. The same retinue travelled with Philip to a town crazy with festival. The town authorities, and the various trading groups, or nations – Spain, Portugal and England, had built a monstrous thunder-making castle six feet above the ground. At the moment the noise was made three naked women were exposed, as three graces, to the astonishment and joy of all concerned. Richard Plantagenet was received with a guard of twenty archers with white rose badges and lodged in the Hotel des Anglais, the Merchant Adventurers' redundant headquarters. The exterior of the building had been hung with armorial bearings and the whole bore a designation in Latin proclaiming, 'Arma Richardy principis Walie et Ducis Elborati, filii et heredes Eduardi quarty, nuper dei Gratia regis Anglie et Francie, dominy Ybernie.' From a court which had transformed spectacle making from entertainment into an art form to make political points, the message was clear and, to passers by in this most public of places, shocking. For two Englishmen it was too much. They armed themselves with staves, and carried a large pot of dung up to the buidling. They strewed the excrement all over the steps of the building and plastered it on the armorial devices. In the hue and cry which developed they got clean away, but, like Cinna the poet in Shakespeare's *Julius Caesar*, an innocent Englishman was murdered by Warbeck's supporters issuing out of the house.[60]

In England, in a parallel series of celebrations, a second Duke of York was created. To create focuses of loyalty in Ireland and England to a genuinely royal Duke of York the king's three and a half year old son, Prince Henry, received royal office and ennoblement. On 11 September he was created Lieutenant of Ireland, and two days later Sir Edward Poynings was made his deputy.[61] The king had decided to deal decisively in Ireland to prevent any possibility of a coronation and invasion in the manner of Lambert Simnel. Poynings was appointed to do what ever was necessary to resolve the Irish situation by force. At home the king himself moved against dissidents. Throughout September and October he moved restlessly between Oxfordshire and Kent. At the beginning of October he was at Westminster. Later in the month he was once again at Woodstock, where he had been in early September.[62] Here he had Garter King-of-Arms proclaim that the creation of his second son as Duke of York would take place on 1 November. Two weeks of celebrations were announced, to culminate with the most spectacular jousts to date of Henry's reign. The whole court with observers from abroad would participate, and the king's daughter, Margaret, would present prizes to the winning combatants. The model for this sort of celebration was Burgundian, so Henry was sending the court at Malines a message, in the language it had invented, that the English court was united, round the Duke of York, that its king presided over a model court which bore arms for him, not against him.[63]

On 27 October the king and queen were at Shene, and on the next day they and Prince Henry, who came, symbolically from Edward IV's palace at Eltham, entered Westminster to begin the festivities. On 30 October the three and a half year old held the towel at his father's table at a huge feast before he and a select band were, next day, made members of the Order of the Garter. Then, on 1 November, with most of the nobility of England, perfoming ceremonial roles, Henry was created Duke of York. When the patent of creation was done everyone, including observers from Milan, Scotland and Flanders processed to a dinner which was finished with the words, 'Largesse . . . de treshault puisant et excellent prince second filz du roi nostre seigneur duc de York lieutenant general Dirlond counte marishall Dangleterre, et gardien de Cinqu Portz . . .'. On 9 November the jousting began. And on

11 November combatants entered the lists in Yorkist blue and murrey on horses decorated with black velvet embroidered with white and red roses. On 13 November an emerald and gold ring, the last of several prizes of this sort – gold and diamond, gold and ruby – was awarded to the finest jouster. On 14 November the king began to arrest the ecclesiastics who had sent money to the other duke, in Flanders.[64]

The celebration at Westminster was not just a political statement for foreign and domestic consumption. It provided a magnificent smokescreen behind which the king could disguise the arrests of the conspirators. Some may have been flushed out in July, but in October serious arrests began. By the beginning of October Henry had received sufficent information to place four people under bond for their future good behaviour. That some were merchants bolsters Molinet's claim that the merchant community in England sent money to Warbeck, and suffered for it. Between mid-October and mid-December twenty-four men were bound over to appear before the King's Council, and in December three at least were bound over for their loyalty.[65] About three weeks after the initial measures, on 22 October, the arrest of Charles Ripon was ordered.[66] And the following day a veteran of Buckingham's rebellion, Long Roger, who had risen in Kent against Richard III in 1483, was brought to the king for interrogation.[67] Such moves were aimed not just at revealing conspirators under interrogation, but by a calculated display of the arrested to confirm suspicions. Lord Fitzwater, the King's Steward was concerned enough about his position to take out a pardon on 28 October, for previous misdemeanours in Calais.[68] The celebrations also allowed close observation of men the king suspected. Sir Simon Mountford attended, the Stanleys were in evidence, the Lord Steward's table was named as next in importance to the king's during the banquets. Even so, who plotted and who did not? During the religious services attending the celebrations the cross was borne by Thomas Langton, who received news from Flanders, and circulated it to his friends.[69]

The king had placed spies in households in England and at Malines, and the French monarchy also kept him up to date through the diplomatic network. More French intelligence was supplied by the governor of Picardy, Philippe de Crèvecoeur, Seigneur d'Esquerdes, an acquaintance of Giles Daubney, Lieutenant of Calais.[70] Jean Molinet suggests that Henry's spies were under instruction to obtain written proof of conspirators' involvement, and if possible to obtain copies of their letters and seals. Furthermore Molinet reports that Henry sent Garter to Flanders to assess the military threat posed by the Burgundian Duke of York. As early as 18 October some sort of communication was carried from Malines to England, possibly safe conduct for Garter. Officially his mission was to deliver a verbal message to Maximilian, Philip, and Margaret of Burgundy that however they had celebrated Richard Plantagenet's entry into Antwerp, in reality he was Perkin Warbeck of Tournai. Like Warham's message a year earlier this was not well received by Margaret who had Garter imprisoned. He was released only because he was held to be Henry's representative, stating the king's view, not his own. This, according to Molinet, had little affect on him and he proceeded to make his view of Warbeck well known throughout Malines, even in the presence of Flemish officials. What lay behind this visit is difficult to assess. Undoubtedly it was a simple spying mission, and it was probably aimed at sowing dissent in the rebel ranks; but it may also have been the signal to Henry's spies in Malines that the end of the conspiracy in England was nigh.[71]

EIGHT

True Men

While the celebrations for the creation of Henry, Duke of York continued, the king and his council met in full session. The records of their meetings exist for 7 and 11 November. But unlike the scares of 1499 there are no references to treason in these records. Despite a mention of legal fraud by John Kendal, of state security there is nothing. It was the essence of Henry VII's strategy that this be so.[1] Arrests had already been made the day after the jousts were over, on 14 November. Legal action began against at least one man, William Worsley, and some, like Sir Simon Mountford may never have gone home. Such was the gravity of the treason that the king had offered a pardon to Sir Robert Clifford, to guarantee immunity from prosecution and persuade him to provide proof of the identity of the conspirators. When Clifford had fled England in the summer of 1493 it was because he believed Warbeck was the Duke of York. However, after about a year or more with Warbeck he became sure that Warbeck was not Richard Plantagenet. The Great Chronicle says he saw 'by many lyklyhode' that Warbeck was an imposter.[2] Molinet implies that he had been admitted to the inner circle of the rebels, so his discovery may have been made there, possibly he ran across Duarte Brandão pursuing his business deals in Flanders. Clifford had fought beside him in Scotland in 1481.[3] It is possible that this unfortunate coincidence alone unmasked Warbeck, but whatever it was Clifford was certainly disabused of his support for Warbeck. Just after he. arrived back in England he let it be known that Richard Plantagenet was a bastard, begotten on the Duchess of Burgundy by her court confessor and Bishop of Cambrai, Henry de Berghes. And this scurrilous story found its way back to Warbeck's then patron, Maximilian.[4]

In 1471 Clifford had become a retainer for life of Richard, Duke of Gloucester, and he had served Edward IV loyally in the 1470s and early '80s. Clifford does not seem to have been close to Richard, and when Richard III seized power and defeated Buckingham's rebels Clifford's brother, Sir Roger was executed. Sir Robert subsequently opposed Richard and led a rising against him in Hertfordshire. He was pardoned, in April 1485, but the condition of his pardon was that in future he act as informer for Richard.[5] His career seems to have been punctuated by impetuous acts from which he recovered using the only thing he had at his disposal, information. After Bosworth Henry VII used his northern origins to good effect. He was made Chamberlain of Berwick, a JP in Yorkshire, and commissioner in his adopted county of Hertfordshire. By 1490 he was knight for the body to Henry VII. He was used on diplomatic missions and acted as a French–English interpreter in 1492.[6] His loyalty to York had been real enough, but his *amour propre* was uppermost. Polydore Vergil's discussion of Clifford identifies his motive as 'probably' self preservation. Moreover Vergil's denial that Clifford was sent over to Flanders as an agent of Henry VII is explicable in the light of his previous career. Clifford had a reputation for informing which needed denying, and which grew worse after the Warbeck incident. After 1495 the king never trusted him or held him in much esteem.[7]

Clifford's reputation was such that he would not have been accepted at the English court as even a reformed rebel, let alone the pariah he became, without some indication of his bona fides. At best he would have been viewed as a double agent. Once he had decided to defect from Warbeck he stayed in Malines until he got his hands on the proof of who had declared for Warbeck in England. Then his friends in England petitioned the king for his pardon and return.[8] This was successful, for Clifford and his gentleman servant Richard Walter of Aspenden had their pardons recorded on 22 December. Given the length of time such matters took, Clifford's return had been planned for at least a month, probably two, before he arrived in England. Nor had his friends escaped scot free: they had had to pay for his pardon.[9] The day after his pardon was recorded in England, Clifford was in the Duchess of Burgundy's entourage, with Warbeck, in Antwerp.[10] Three weeks later he confronted William Stanley in the Tower. According to Molinet, Clifford's escape was coordinated at Calais, from where Clifford was recalled to England. The minute Henry's man (from Calais?) arrived at Malines, Clifford and two others took the letters and seals of Warbeck's supporters to England as proof of treason and rode to Bethune. At Bethune they waited and then went to Calais and thence to England.[11] It was an escape made, said the Great Chronicle, 'not with owtt som danger'.[12] It is impossible to tell if Molinet's version of events is fact or fiction, but the sense of danger implied by the London chronicler is borne out by the fact that the king gave William Hoton and Harry Wodeford £26 13s 4d, a reward equivalent to the income of a prosperous gentleman, for getting Clifford out of Flanders.[13]

Just after New Year, on Twelfth Night Henry VII took up residence in the Tower. Polydore Vergil says that Henry did this so that the conspirators could be tricked into coming to this royal residence which they would have regarded innocently.[14] This *faux naïf* explanation does not accord with the king's expenditure. This shows that men were arrested by members of his household and his most loyal followers: the Digbys, the Earl of Oxford and the Earl of

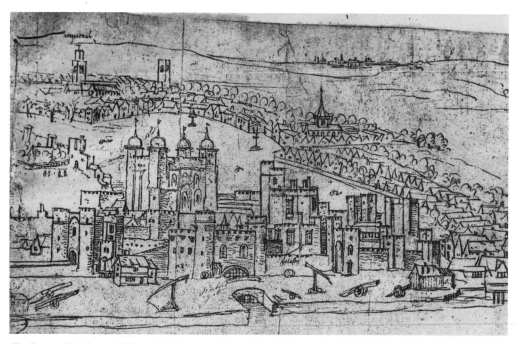

The Tower of London in 1550. In 1501 and 1502 Henry VII added to the Tower, extending it with domestic apartments. Among his improvements was a garden

Surrey.[15] When Clifford arrived he was thoroughly debriefed. Hall says he knelt down and besought grace and pardon, which is quite probable.[16] What is improbable is Vergil's assertion that the king was shocked to learn of his chamberlain's treason. He had known of it for two years at least. What is more probable is a public show of incredulity aimed at tying the hands of his council by forcing them to agree to Stanley's execution. Those who, like Vergil's Henry, confess themselves unable to believe in the chamberlain's treason, like the king's council have been gulled by the ingenuity of the age. What the king knew was Stanley's guilt, what he needed was Clifford's personal testimony and the material proof he brought with him. Possessing these, Stanley was placed under house arrest in his chamberlain's quarters in the Quadrate Tower, and examined by a small number of councillors.[17] Whether he reacted with the arrogance reported by Vergil and Hall, or whether this is the hubris necessary to their tale is impossible to tell. It may be that Stanley attempted to brazen out his treason, feeling that his office, and the debt of gratitude under which he had placed the king, when he had saved his life at Bosworth, would be enough to save him. He was wrong. Clifford was rewarded with £500 on 20 January, the day John Ratcliffe Lord Fitzwater, the Lord Steward, was brought to court.[18] Clifford's may have been an outright reward, but his return to England had been engineered by his friends there, themselves under suspicion of treason, who had had to pay for his pardon. Clifford's £500 was possibly their quid pro quo. No reward was ever simple in Henry VII's England.

By the time Stanley and Fitzwater were under arrest they and their co-conspirators faced the biggest show trial since Clarence's attainder in 1478. On 25 January 1495 two enormously powerful judicical commissions of oyer and terminer were appointed, one to London, the other to Middlesex. They were headed by the king's uncle Jasper Tudor, Duke of Bedford and eleven magnates, some too young to serve, but they were reinforced by a second rank of lords, mainly Tudor loyalists, some, like Giles Daubney and Robert Willoughby de Broke, stepping into the positions of men they were about to try. Also present were Reginald Bray, Thomas Lovell and others from the council and eight principal judges. Their sitting at the Guildhall lasted for three days.[19] On the first day, 29 January, they heard indictments against the main group of conspirators, lay and ecceliastical. The ecclesiastics were nationally known: William Worsley, Dean of St Pauls, William Richford, Provincial of the Dominican Friars in England, Thomas Powys, prior of the Dominican friary at King's Langley, William Sutton, parson of St Stephens in Walbrook in London. The lay members were national figures too: William Daubney, Clerk of the Jewels to Edward IV and Richard III, Thomas Thwaites, ex-Treasurer of Calais, Robert Ratcliff, Porter of Calais; and an important Warwickshire gentleman Sir Simon Mountford of Coleshill. Obscured by this group were two minor officials, Thomas Cressener, Lord Fitzwater's steward, Thomas Astwode, steward of Marton Abbey in Yorkshire, and Robert Holborn and Hans Troys. On 30 January, having procured the verdict of guilty, the commission sentenced them all to death. However, Richford, Powys and Worsley were pardoned, (for the sake of the Church, said Bernard André), and their sentences were commuted from death to imprisonment and fine. According to a London chronicler shame led to the premature deaths of Richford and Worsley. Less poetically, we know Worsley was very heavily fined and plunged into real financial hardship from which he never recovered, losing house and lands. Their fellows did not have to wait so long for death. On 31 January William Sutton, Thomas Thwaites, Robert Ratcliff, Simon Mountford, William Daubney, Thomas Cressener, Robert Holborn, Hans Troys, and Thomas Astwode were sentenced to death, but then Sutton and Thwaites had their sentences altered, possibly on account of their advanced ages, and were imprisoned in the Tower. Four days later this wheeling and dealing saw their charges redefined as misprison of treason and, with another cleric, Richard Lessy, they were imprisoned until they paid the king a fine. The following afternoon the party for execution, Mountford, Daubney, Ratcliff, Cressener and Astwode, left Newgate gaol for Tower Hill. The first three were beheaded without much ado, but Astwode and Cressener, both young men, were pardoned at the block, to the delight of the crowd of onlookers. That morning some of the smaller fry were dealt with. Petit John, a Breton, had been examined at the Guildhall. The next morning he was sentenced to be hanged, drawn and quartered at Tyburn. In the afternooon Holborn and Troys were taken from Newgate to Tyburn and hanged, eviscerated and hacked into four pieces. Next morning, 6 February, Petit John was hanged.[20]

Petit John's execution was a sideshow to the real event of 6 February 1495. That day Sir William Stanley was indicted before the Duke of Buckingham, the Marquess of Dorset, the Earl of Arundel, Simon Digby and the Chief Justice of the King's Bench in Westminster Hall. He was charged with conspiring against the king with Clifford, sending Clifford abroad to wait with Warbeck to invade England, and promising to rise for Warbeck at a prearranged signal. Asked how he pleaded he denied all the charges, and pleaded not guilty. Process was resumed the following day and the jurors found him guilty as charged.[21] There and then he was sentenced to a traitor's death and taken up to the Tower. His execution took place nine days later, on 16 February. At 9 o'clock in the morning Stanley was led by two servants of the Sheriff of London from the Tower gate to a scaffold on Tower hill. On this he was executed. He was buried at Sion and his funeral expenses were borne by the king. £10 0s 0d on the day of execution, £15 19s 0d for his burial, £2 0s 0d for its supervison by the Lieutenant of the Tower, and £31 0s 1d to meet the wages due to his household servants. The question which remained to mystify the citizens of London, and historians ever after, was why he had thrown away enormous power, 'ffor a knave that aftyr was hangid'.[23] Yet he was not alone, and the trials continued.

Two days before Stanley's execution, 14 February, four commissions of oyer and terminer appointed the king's chief supporters, and his judges, to make judicial scrutiny in every county south of Shropshire, Staffordshire and Nottinghamshire, except the six south-western ones, Cornwall, Devon, Somerset, Dorset, Wiltshire and Hampshire. Two years later this exception may have been viewed as a cardinal error, but on the morning of Stanley's execution the London commissioners resumed work in the Guildhall. In Berkshire William Hody, Thomas Tremayle, William Norreys, John Isbury, Thomas Say, and William Besyllis held their session at Grauntpount-juxta-Oxford where William Stanley's co-conspirator, the Lord Steward John Fitzwater was indicted for treason. Like Stanley he was accused of promising to aid Warbeck and of sending Clifford to Flanders. On 23 February a true bill was determined, and Fitzwater's fate hung in the balance.[24] He was sent not to the block, instead he was imprisoned in Guisnes castle, in the Marches of Calais.[25] This was lenient punishment, for Fitzwater knew the town, because he had served there in the 1470s. But was more intended here than lenity? Was Fitzwater sent to Calais as bait, to catch those in the march who were suspected, but not yet identified, as supporters of Warbeck. Enough support came from Calais to make this feasible, the more so since at the end of 1496 Fitzwater attempted to abscond from his imprisonment.

Cases unearthed by Henry's commissioners continued to be heard throughout the spring of 1495. In May two Suffolk yeomen were tried for acting as messengers for Warbeck. And the Kentish gentleman Roger Harlakenden's 1493 promise was discovered, and he was tried. But, in what has been called 'probably the most massive and effective security operation ever to have been mounted against sedition within the realm', what had Henry VII smashed? Was there ever a coherent plot against the king? Or were these measures taken, as David Starkey suggests, against a figment of the king's imagination, as Steven Gunn suggests, to purge competing factions at court, or as Christine Carpenter suggests, to remedy a situation of gentry feuding in the west Midlands. The names of the conspirators have always looked incoherent. Stanley, Fitzwater, Daubney and the clerical element appear to lack any centre. So was this no more than the opportunity that foolish political gossip gave to Henry VII to strike down those he chose: for other reasons? The answer: no, lies in the fact that despite superficially appearing unconnected, the names of the conspirators are grouped round the major surviving personalities of the Yorkist royal family, Cecily Neville and her daughter Margaret of Burgundy, and are drawn from those personally associated with Edward IV. Most striking is the East Anglian connection, which, with its associations with the Mowbray Dukes of Norfolk suggests a possible residual loyalty to Richard, Duke of York, Edward IV's son. There is also a point made by Margaret Condon, that the middle years of Henry VII's reign display an alarming number of defections from those loyal to him previously. Hence Fitzwater, and Robert Ratcliff, had both been bound over for their loyalty; and Sir Simon Mountford too, in £1,000 for his good bearing, on 28 January 1494.[26] This is what one would expect from an increasingly unpopular monarch: it happened to Edward IV in 1468 and 1469. And it goes some way to answering those who find Stanley's behaviour inexplicable in the terms of a commitment to Warbeck. He was not a single eccentric political figure, but one of a large number of people, 150, tried over four years 1494–9.

The way in to this political connection is via the will of Cecily Neville, dowager Duchess of York. Cecily, mother of Margaret of Burgundy, erstwhile grandmother of Perkin Warbeck, made her will at Berkhamstead castle, Hertfordshire, on 31 May 1495, six months after the plot had been smashed, a month before Warbeck landed at Deal. Among her beneficiaries are two, possibly four people with direct connections to the plot. The most well known is Richard Lessy, the dean of her chapel and steward of her household.[27] Accused of misprison of treason he was pardoned on 12 March 1494. Like many in this plot he seems to have been involved in the dynastic convulsions of 1483, when he obtained pardon in the wake of Buckingham's rebellion. His pardon in 1495 cost him £200.[28] The nine men who stood surety for its payment were from Berkhamstead, and four were officers of Cecily's household. His mistress made bequests in her will to cover Lessy's fine – debts, or money – to the value of 500 marks willing the hope that Henry VII would expedite the collection of her, now Lessy's, debts. Connected by geographical proximity to Lessy and Cecily Neville was Thomas Powys, prior of the Dominican priory of Langley. King's Langley was five or six miles from Berkhamstead castle and Powys probably knew Lessy, for Lessy bequeathed money from his will to the church there.[29] It is difficult to know if the connection to William Richford is the apparent one of being fellow Dominican, since Richford was head – Provincial – of the English Dominicans or whether, like others, John Kendal and Thomas Langton, he was one of a number of English diplomats who were alienated from Henry VII's claim to the throne. Richford was in Italy in 1484, 1486 and 1487.[30] The connection to Cecily Neville's household is more pronounced when we realize that William Barley, Thomas and John Brampton and Robert Clifford also came from Hertfordshire as did two men executed in the summer of 1495, after the Deal landing. And it is possible, since the Lounde family were part of the Neville affinity, that the Anne Lounde to whom Cecily left bequests was related to Warbeck's so-called chancellor, William Lounde.

There are direct links between Margaret of Burgundy's household and that of her father's. Richard Harleston was a servant of Margaret of Burgundy and Perkin Warbeck. Harleston, who defected to the Duchess of Burgundy in 1486 is always said to have been brought up in her father's, Richard, Duke of York's, household and was in Warbeck's fleet off Deal in 1495.[31] At his death, in Flanders, it is said that Margaret paid for his funeral expenses and tomb. But there is a more direct link between Cecily Neville's household and her daughter Margaret's. One of the men who stood surety for the payment of Richard Lessy's fine was

Richard Boyvile, to whom Cecily left bequests, and who was used in 1468 to take a present of eight horses to her son-in-law, Charles the Bold. Subsequently Edward IV rewarded him for his good service to Margaret of Burgundy, and he and his wife waited on her when she came to England in 1480.[32] Alongside them were the future conspirators Thomas Thwaites and Thomas Brampton.

English connections with Burgundy, and Margaret's household were maintained through Calais. Flanders supplied the European art market and Edward IV's servants travelled to Flanders for arms, art and jewels. In the early 1460s Thwaites held an important position as clerk of the Staple and supervisor of Rysbank. As a reward for his good services in 1468 he became Bailiff of Guisnes. He followed Edward IV into exile and was his clerk of war. By 1472 he was Deputy Treasurer of Calais for life, and he picked up property and more offices there in the late 1470s. By 1482 he was chancellor of the Duchy of Lancaster and one of a select group in Calais trusted by Richard III. Thwaites was on active diplomatic service in Burgundy in 1475 and had represented the English government in the diet at Bruges in 1469.[33] Similarily William Daubney was found in Flanders in 1479 with Piers Courteys, Edward IV's Keeper of the Great Wardrobe receiving money from the then Archduke Maximilian.[34] Calais men knew Flanders and Margaret's household, and were rewarded with positions in it. John Ratcliffe, Lord Fitzwater, was married to Margaret Whetehill of Calais. The Whetehills were the most important family in Calais occupying its principal lieutenancies and turning the office of controller into a hereditary position for two generations. Richard Whetehill, whose daughter Fitzwater married, was an 'escuyer panetier' in Margaret of Burgundy's household by 1474, and lieutenant of Guisnes till 1476. In this year he was replaced by Sir Ralph Hastings, William Lounde's master.[35] During the 1470s Fitzwater lived in Guisnes, and the Paston Letters preserve a demand from William Lord Hastings in which Hastings is desirous of acquiring a new clerk of his kitchen. The man he named spoke English, Flemish and French and had served both Whetehill and Fitzwater. Inasmuch as the Whetehills can be aligned in English politics in 1471 they followed Warwick the Kingmaker. Adrian Whetehill, Fitzwater's brother-in-law was pardoned in 1471, after Warwick's defeat. But then the family was assimilated into the Yorkist establishment, ultimately serving the Tudors.

Those of the rebels not closely connected to either of the surviving York matriarchs can nevertheless be associated with the Yorkist royal family. Though the Croyland chronicler noted the inability of the three royal brothers – Edward, Richard and George – to avoid argument, Warbeck's supporters did not come exclusively from one brother's retinue. John Taylor had been a Clarence man, Thomas Gale of Dartmouth a late supporter of Richard III. William Barley, Robert Clifford's father-in-law, a fellow defector in 1493, may have been a retainer of the Duke of Clarence. However, both in 1494 and in the 1498–9 plot we can locate a core group of Edward IV's intimates who, with Thomas Thwaites shared their king's exile and returned with him to England in 1471. Robert Chamberlain and Gilbert Debenham gained an immortal reputation among their fellows for scouting out Norfolk in 1471, and warning Edward of the danger to him from the Earl of Oxford. Robert Clifford and William Stanley, were men considered loyal enough by their actions in 1471 to warrant naming by the author of the Arrival Chronicle, the Yorkist account of the retaking of England by Edward IV.[36] With the exception of Clifford, this group endured as whole into Richard III's reign. For in the latter days of Richard's regime William Stanley and Robert Chamberlain were appointed to keep the castles of Caernarfon and Beaumaris against Henry Tudor. Of four appointees to castles in North Wales, the others being to keep Conway and Harlech, three of them, Stanley, Chamberlain and Sir Roger Kynaston, later rebelled against Henry VII.[37]

A scene at court. From a book of poems by Charles of Orleans. Thomas Thwaites may have intended to give this volume to Edward IV. In October 1487 Thwaites had an anthology of French chronicles written out as a gift for Henry VII. Neither of these books was finished, and they now form part of what was the royal library; so they may have been seized when Thwaites was arrested

The proximity of Warbeck's followers to the royal family is indicated by the fact that a number of them were associates of Elizabeth Woodville or other Woodvilles. William Sutton, rector of St Stephen's Walbrook in London, was allied to the Woodville, Rivers and Neville families. He was an executor of Elizabeth Woodville's will in 1492, a feoffee of Dame Joan Ingoldesthorpe, widow of the Neville Marquis of Montague, and a feoffee of George Neville, the bastard, supporter of Warbeck, husband to Lord Rivers' widow and great nephew, albeit illegitimate, of Cecily Neville.[38] River's widow Mary Fitzlewis, was a member of a family which linked the old Mowbray affinity – Brandons, Wingfields, Darcys – which the real Richard of York had inherited from his wife to the royal family.[39] Robert Clifford himself was married into a family, the Barleys, which as we have seen had connections with the same families, the wider Mowbray connection and with one of the nurses of the royal nursery. Robert Ratcliff, the so-called Porter of Calais, had the same connection to the East Midlands and East Anglia. His early offices were held in Lincolnshire, Norfolk, Suffolk, Essex, and Hertford. In 1471 immediately prior to the murder of Henry VI, Ratcliff guarded him in the Tower. In Edward IV's household he rose to become, by 1480, Porter of Calais, responsible for its security. The faction fighting over position in Calais at the end of Edward's reign reveals him allied with the Woodville faction, supporting Rivers and Dorset against Lord Hastings. Ratcliff followed Sir Edward Woodville into exile in 1483, but redefected to Richard III who rewarded him on his return. The year 1485 saw him removed from office by Henry VII.[40] Such intimacy with the court is shown by the fact that several of Warbeck's supporters had a common background spanning court, diplomacy, Europe and service to Edward V. The common link is found through William Caxton.

Caxton was patronized by Margaret of Burgundy and mentioned her in a number of his printed books, the History of Troy being the best known. As an English merchant he was well known in Flanders as Governor of the English Nation at Bruges and was at Margaret's wedding. On embassy to Flanders in 1464 we find as his co-commissioner, Richard Whetehill, a relative of Lord Fitzwater. Caxton's books were favoured by the royal family. At Earl River's behest Caxton printed works for the education of the prince. *Jason*, translated by Caxton was dedicated to the Prince of Wales by permission of Elizabeth Woodville. It has been suggested that when the Yorkist royal family fell from favour Caxton looked to merchant friends to keep his presses employed and it is notable that he dedicated his translation of Charles the Great to Warbeck's supporter William Daubney, 'a good and synguler frende of myn'. In the latter days of Richard III's reign Daubney raised loans for the king by pawning jewels to his friends in the city, where for a number of years he had been a port official. Daubney links Thomas Cressener, one of the sons of a relative of Cecily Neville, Alexander, to Fitzwater. Thomas was, probably, a lawyer and an associate of William Daubney, and is named as having been Lord Fitzwater's steward. Caxton's press also provides a link between court and diplomacy. As a jobbing printer he printed papal indulgences in England. Two ecclesiastics for whom he is known to have worked – John Sant, Abbot of Abingdon, and John Kendal, Knight Hospitaller – were involved in conspiracies against Henry VII.[41] Sant was the abbot in the so-called Abbot of Abingdon's plot in 1489, a botched attempt to free the Earl of Warwick. As a diplomat in 1474 he had been befriended by Margaret of Burgundy. Kendal, as we have seen, was involved in treasonable conversations about Warbeck with Thomas Langton, bishop of Salisbury. In the 1470s Langton too had been an active diplomat. On two occasions, 1476 and 1478, he was used to negotiate possible marriages for Edward, Prince of Wales, in Spain, and Elizabeth of York in France. He was regularly used to negotiate with France and Flanders, and in 1484 and 1485 represented Richard III in Rome.[42] However, a quite extraordinary connection exists through one of the surviving Caxton indulgences. Purchased from John Kendal to aid the hospitallers in their fight against the Turks, one of the two surviving indulgences for Kendal is made out in favour of Sir Simon Mountford and his wife.[43] The names of the plotters are thus in no sense random, but closely associated with the world of the royal court and its children.

Close association with the court at regional level is the key to understanding support for Warbeck. It was Colin Richmond in 1983 who asked how the royal household and the politics of the years after 1485 appear if viewed from the south-west Suffolk vantage point of those three Yorkist stalwarts Robert Chamberlain of Gedding, Sir Gilbert Debenham of Little Wenham and Sir James Tyrrell of Gipping. And what relation did they have to their south Norfolk neighbour and steward of the royal household Lord Fitzwater? The answer appears to be found in the particular nature of loyalties in the region. Rosemary Horrox has shown that in East Anglia the core connection of politics was provided by the queen's possession of the Duchy of Lancaster estate. After 1475 the queen's interest was regarded as the main instrument of royal authority, and this political connection was boosted in 1478 when Anne Mowbray, the heir of the last Mowbray Duke of Norfolk married Richard, Duke of York. This allowed the Mowbray retinues to be amalgamated with the royal interest in East Anglia and the result was a very strong and long-lasting affinity bound by ties of kinship which linked its leading members to the queen's family. Thus can we find common ground between Calais and East Anglia, for when John Howard was deputy lieutenant at Calais in the 1470s, East Anglians, among whom were Fitzwater and Robert Chamberlain, staffed the march.[44]

In 1483 the usurpation of Richard III split the bond between those East Anglians loyal to the Crown and those who threw in their lot with opponents of Richard III. In fact neither Richard nor his chief ally John Howard, Duke of Norfolk could dominate the two main affinities of the region: the de Vere retinue and the old Mowbray connection. Both these affinities organized a number of serious plots against him. During 1484 and 1485 the Brandon family, old Mowbray men, mobilized a number of former Mowbray retinues on behalf of John de Vere, Earl of Oxford and Henry Tudor. A number of important local families belonged to the Mowbray tradition. The Debenhams, Brandons, and Chamberlains were all counsellors of the last Mowbray duke, and though they found themselves on either side of the political divide during Richard III's reign, once Oxford returned from Bosworth to rule East Anglia the political situation stabilized.[45] The arrival of Warbeck on the scene threw all this into the melting pot again since he, as Richard, Duke of York, could claim otherwise dormant loyalties within the region. This factor explains why men antipathetic to each other in the years 1483–5, and loyal to Henry VII thereafter, suddenly, apparently, renounced their loyalty to Henry on Warbeck's arrival on the political scene. It also explains why the conspirators at Malines wanted to draw Thomas Brandon into their conspiracy (and why Sir Thomas Tyrrell, East Anglian and ex-Master of the Horse under York, was so interested in news of Warbeck). Despite the well-known heroism of William Brandon as Henry VII's first standard bearer at Bosworth the Brandons were Mowbray adherents. William's father, another William was a ducal counsellor. Both Brandon brothers led the East Anglian sector of Buckingham's rebellion. In Thomas Brandon, Warbeck's masters were targetting the right type of man, nominally, through the Mowbray retinue, a retainer of their Pseudo Duke.[46]

John Lord Fitzwater may have played a role in East Anglia similar to the Brandons, during 1484–5. In January 1485, one of Richard's men in East Anglia, Robert Chamberlain, was in some sort of dispute with Fitzwater and both were bound over by Richard III not to attack each other.[47] Fitzwater was not part of the Mowbray affinity. His career advanced via Calais, the Earl of Warwick and Lord Hastings. But his agreement to maintain peace toward Chamberlain seems to place him alongside the Brandons. After Bosworth, Fitzwater emerged enormously enhanced in prestige, though still a man of very modest means. He was appointed Steward of the Household, Steward of Duchy of Lancaster lands in Norfolk, Suffolk and Cambridge, and Warden and Chief Justice of forests south of the Trent.[48] He may have been casting his eyes on the Howard family's position in East Anglia, for in October 1485 he began to bully and terrorize ex-Howard servants and the Howard dowager duchess. Oxford at the time acted as patron, a good lord, to the duchess. In 1487 Oxford was given virtually viceregal power to raise soldiers in East Anglia to fight at Stoke. Fitzwater appears to have contested his authority and caused two men, Henry Heydon, Steward of the Household to Cecily, Duchess of York and William Boleyn, an ex-retainer of Richard III who had been his deputy admiral for Norfolk and Suffolk and a Knight of the Bath at his coronation, to hesitate in giving allegiance to the new king.[49] Stoke was a sufficient shock to Henry VII to render behaviour such as this politically suicidal. Though Oxford controlled East Anglia others were brought in. Fitzwater lost his stewardship of the duchy in 1489 to Thomas Lovell and James Hobart, highly placed servants of the king; and in the same year the political resurrection of Thomas Howard began. This was a sound move, for Howard went on to serve Henry loyally, and the Howard lands in East Anglia were gradually restored to him. By 1495 he had made as good a recovery as could have been expected.[50] Fitzwater's hopes of succeeding Howard, if such they were, were dashed. By February 1490 Fitzwater was in trouble with the king's council,[51] and in January 1492 he agreed to aid Warbeck.

Gilbert Debenham had been a Mowbray man, and his father, another Gilbert, had been Steward of the Mowbray Duke of Norfolk. In 1484 news of the projected East Anglian landing, led by the Earl of Oxford reached Richard III. A number of Edward IV's ex-officers in East Anglia, like Debenham, ex-Mowbray men, linked up with Edward IV's men in France to plan a landing at Harwich. At first, possibly because his father had been a feoffee of the Countess of Oxford, the mother of Henry VII's faithful earl, Debenham was not trusted by Richard III. But after the plan came to nothing, Debenham was used to defend Harwich and to seize land and property belonging to Sir William Brandon.[52] By March 1486 Debenham was back in favour with the new king. Despite removal from the commission of the peace and the loss of a stewardship at Donyngton in Yorkshire, his father's service to the Countess of Oxford may have told in his favour.[53] Having been part of the Mowbray and then Howard affinity in East Anglia he continued in its service: to its new master, Oxford. What Debenham did before Stoke we do not know, but when Henry VII called on Oxford to go north in July 1487, Debenham was with him.[54] He was beginning to make his way in the new regime. Within a year he was nominated to serve against the French, and in 1489 he was sent under Giles Daubney to fight in Flanders, at Dixmude.[55] Loyal service brought its rewards, two grants in February 1491. By the first Debenham became, during the king's pleasure, the Constable of Carrickfergus castle and Lord of Carlingford. By the second as, knight for the king's body, he was granted the governorship of all mines in Ireland for seven years.[56] Just as his seamanship had proved useful to Richard III in 1483 so it recommended itself to Henry VII. Unlike Fitzwater, against the grain of 1483, Debenham successfully re-entered political life.

William Stanley's reputation has always been that of the traitor of Bosworth, whose treachery was his undoing. His was the name blackened by Polydore Vergil as the man who claimed huge rewards after saving Henry VII's life at Bosworth, was made chamberlain but who, said Hall, coveted the Earldom of Chester and was so encouraged by his capture of Richard III's booty, and his popularity, that 'he set naught by ye kyng his sovereign master'. He was the isolated Icarus of treachery whose pride finally took him too near the sun. Modern analysts have painted a different picture. To Christine Carpenter his folly is inexplicable in such an experienced politician. Her explanation of Stanley's execution is that Henry needed to execute Stanley as an example: to prevent anarchy in Warwickshire and elsewhere between members of Henry's household. For Christine Carpenter there is no case of Stanley or Simon Mountford being serious rebels and for her the very existence of a Warbeck conspiracy, let alone involvement in conspiracy by Stanley, is questionable.[57] Michael K. Jones on the other hand, is prepared to accept both some conspiracy and Stanley's involvement in it. Stanley, jealous of the Earldom of Chester, coveted power and property because he was a younger brother entirely dependent for his continued good fortune and the growth of a hard-won estate on royal goodwill. To Jones, Stanley's desire for tenurial security is the driving force behind his treason in both 1485 and 1495.[58]

These readings – provincial power and pursuit of property – are the staple diet of fifteenth-century studies. Yet, while they may be the necessary adjuncts to understanding Stanley they are not sufficient in themselves. Nowhere in either reading does Stanley's behaviour register, and in a set of events such as the ones we are dealing with, behaviour is everything. William Stanley's reputation has always suffered because insufficient distinction is made between his attitudes and behaviour and that of his brother Thomas, Earl of Derby. Thomas acquired and richly deserved a reputation as a trimmer and time-server. It was a reputation still vivid at the end of the seventeenth century. But where in the civil wars, 1459–85 Thomas was careful to align himself with no one party in the fray, and accommodate himself to the victor immediately afterwards, William maintained loyal service to York. The initial conflict in their region, Cheshire, at Bloreheath in 1459 set the pattern, one repeated twenty-five years later, at Bosworth. Thomas refused to be drawn into action, but William committed himself to Richard, Duke of York and took with him both his and his brother's retainers. His reward, after a war in which both brothers benefitted from Neville patronage, was to be made Steward of Lytham and Lord of Skipton. In 1469 he became constable of Rhuddlan, Caernarfon and Beaumaris castles, and in February 1470 Steward of Denbeigh for life. During the Readeption, 1470–1, his brother Thomas accommodated himself with his Neville relatives. William, on the contrary was identified as a partisan of York. On 7 November while still serving as Chamberlain of Chester and Sheriff of Cheshire, fifteen gentlemen leading a mob of 400 armed men attacked William in his house at Nantwich with war cries of, 'King Henry, Prince Edward, a Warwick, a Warwick.' Shortly after, he was removed from his offices as chamberlain and sheriff.

Edward IV's restoration found the same pattern played out. Thomas stood on the side lines. William was one of the first to rally to Edward's side. He may have entered London with Edward, and members of the Stanley affinity, including the Savages, fought for Edward at Tewkesbury. William was knighted after the battle. Thereafter he expanded his power and estates in North Wales eventually becoming, by 1483, Chief Justice of North Wales.[59] His intimacy with York continued. He was made Steward of the Household of Edward, Prince of Wales, the future Edward V and brother of Perkin Warbeck's surrogate. The degree of intimacy of William and the royal family is indicated by their mutual exchange of household servants.[60] And when, in 1495, Holt castle was seized, the garnishing of Stanley's collar of livery, suns and roses, perhaps his collar of office, was found among his possessions.[61] Viewed from this perspective, William fits the pattern of those who supported Warbeck: committed early to York and intimate with the royal family, especially Edward IV's children. 1485 marked a turning point for the Stanley brothers. Thomas's behaviour at Bosworth was as it had always been, but his relationship to Henry Tudor opened the floodgates to patronage and power. William, in character, revenged himself at Bosworth on Richard III, the murderer of his master, King Edward V. Thereafter his career was secondary to his elder brother's. He might well have expected after Bosworth to be treated for his loyalty by Henry VII as he had been by Edward IV. To a degree he was as Chamberlain of the Household, but he was not ennobled. The contrast between William Stanley and Thomas Howard is

Part of an inventory of Sir William Stanley's castle at Holt. Coin in bags was recorded amounting to almost
£10,000. The inventory of the Treasure House, shown here, lists the garnishings of a Yorkist collar of livery

instructive. Howard was loyal, to one king after another, but in such a fashion that the loyalty, which was to an institutiun, the Crown, flattered the man. Stanley was a different order of man. Possibly it was easier for Howard. His lord, Richard, was known, unequivocally, to be dead. He himself was lucky to have been spared execution by Henry. Loyalty and gratitude might reinforce each other. For Stanley things were different. He had saved Henry Tudor's life. The debt of gratitude lay awkwardly with the king, and honour demanded loyalty be rewarded. But to what degree? Commentators make it clear that William Stanley emerged voracious for reward after Bosworth and desirous to some degree of playing the role of kingmaker. To a man of Edward IV's temperament such a one might have been made an ally. But to Henry Tudor, never. He preferred the coolness and caution, even perversity of Thomas Stanley to the heat and commitment of William. Very quickly relations deteriorated.

The nature of William Stanley's treason has always been debated. The chroniclers present two versions of his crime, and his indictment a third. According to Polydore Vergil, Stanley said that if Warbeck was Richard Plantagenet he would not oppose him.[62] This in effect was a denial of his fealty to the king, if true, and at his trial he was accused of sending Clifford to Flanders and of agreeing to rise in favour of the Yorkist pretender upon a signal given. In the circumstances of the 1490s to suggest that none of these amounted to treason is naïve. We only have to look at Richard III's reaction to Collingbourne sending a messenger to Henry Tudor. He was executed. It has been argued recently that Stanley's was an isolated act of folly since he acted without any support from his family or affinity. This we may doubt. A bastard son, Thomas, was taken in 1494 and held in the Tower of London till after Henry VII's death. The yeoman of the Crown, Rowland Bulkley, taken in 1493 for spreading defamatory bills has been identified as belonging in the Bulkley family, long-standing retainers to Sir William Stanley.[63] John Warren of Poynton who was pardoned on 5 February 1495 committed some misdemeanour before 25 November 1494.[64] On the tenth of that month he had been bound over with two others in the sum of 500 marks for his true allegiance. The Warrens were a Stockport family who, two generations previously had married into the Stanleys. He too, though he escaped lightly was involved with Stanley, the dating alone would convict him of that.[65] Sir Humphrey Savage, another of Warbeck's supporters, was the product of a Stanley marriage.[66] His father, Sir John, was married to Sir William Stanley's sister Catherine. Stanley was by no means alone in his treason, nor was he caught as Vergil suggests by idle gossip. Jean Molinet and other chroniclers repeat the story that Stanley sent money to Warbeck.[67] In Warbeck's retinue was a Lancashire gentleman, William Ashton of Ashton-under-Lyne, from a family of Stanley clients and a near relative, if not the son, of Sir Ralph Ashton.[68] Sir Ralph had been a Neville feed man, and a loyalist of Edward IV during the Readeption, like William Stanley. Sir Ralph passed into service with Richard III and Richard used Ashton and two of his sons as supporters in Kent. William sat as a JP in Lancashire in 1483.[69] Was William Ashton, executed after invading with Warbeck at Deal, at Malines on his own account, following family loyalty? Or was he the man Stanley sent to act as messenger for him ?

Collingbourne's behaviour is a useful analogy to pursue, in that both William Stanley and Sir Simon Mountford were said to have sent messages to Warbeck. Mountford was a very well-connected Warwickshire man: Constable of Kenilworth, a Hastings retainer and he had been a counsellor of Richard, Earl of Warwick. Christine Carpenter sees Mountford as an experienced, skilful, politician who thought he could survive any upheaval by backing both sides while doing nothing. This had been his ploy during Richard's reign and, says Dr Carpenter, he kept his hands sufficiently clean in 1485 to be among the first to be rewarded by the new king. But Mountford was accepted so far and no further. He was deprived of his office as Constable of Kenilworth, originally his for life, and was then relegated to the outer circles of royal favour. From here he watched a new and suspicious King Henry remake Warwickshire in his own image. Out went Mountford and in came the king's relatives by marriage: the Stanleys, and his uncle Jasper Tudor, Duke of Bedford. Bedford's agent in Warwickshire was his chamberlain Edmund Mountford, a long-serving Lancastrian much out of favour under York, but restored to power under the Tudors, and uncle of Sir Simon. In the north of the county Simon Mountford saw Henry Willoughby take control. Power may have ebbed away from Sir Simon but the burden of everyday government did not. He worked very hard for little reward and became increasingly alienated.[70]

Yet exactly how detatched from politics was Mountford? In 1486 we find him associated with men who had been opponents of Henry Tudor and some who would become so. In that year seven men, eight if we include the subject of the bond, John Lord Zouche, stood bail for Zouche's future loyalty to the king. Zouche had fought against Henry at Bosworth. Included in this agreement were Simon Mountford and Gilbert Debenham, Lord Zouche's stepfather. There also were William Berkley of Uley, another who had fought for Richard III at Bosworth; and another future supporter of Warbeck, John Brampton. Among these names Mountford's political neutrality appears less certain.[71] According to the Warwickshire antiquary, William Dugdale Mountford sent £30 to Warbeck via his son, Henry, who then became a convinced rebel. Henry had been sent to Ireland with his retinue to root out John Taylor and his French supporters in 1491. Christine Carpenter has connected him to Stanleys' relatives, the Savages; and, as we have seen, Henry's father was bound over for good behaviour in January 1494.[72] Henry was not the only Warwick gentleman at Malines in the 1490s, another was Richard Malory of Monks Kirby, strictly speaking from the manor of Newbold Revel, in Monks Kirby. In 1480 Newbold Revel was held from Richard, Duke of York through the right of his Mowbray wife, Anne. Thereafter, due to the assumed death of Edward IV's son, the manor changed hands. But is there an indication in Richard Malory's presence among the invaders at Deal in 1495 of feudal loyalty to an overlord?[73] The Malory family of Litchborough, in Northamptonshire, fought against Henry VII at Stoke, and possibly also at Bosworth.[74] Two years later, an officer of Edward, Earl of Warwick voiced treason during the rebellion of 1497. It is worth recalling that the region all these men came from was the one John Taylor wished to involve with the Countess of Warwick against Henry VII in 1491, and one which Rowland Robinson knew well.

This apparently random group of gentlemen and ecclesiastics punished by Henry VII is in fact a coherent group. That coherence is clearly provided by links to the queen, court and children of Edward IV and in some cases to Edward, Earl of Warwick as well. Even the most colourless figure among them, Fitzwater, owned a father who had lost his life, fighting for Edward IV before Towton.[75] Simon Mountford's public advancement under York began in 1459. By 1462 he was knighted. He was a commissioner of the peace in Warwickshire from 1464 to 1470 and was appointed Lieutenant of Carrisbrook castle in 1469. During the Readeption of Henry VI he was removed from office as a Warwickshire justice of the peace. Restored in 1471 he became sheriff that year, a Hastings' retainer by 1470, and the most powerful man in Warwickshire.[76] Yet however coherent a group it was, it was not able to mount, or participate in, a coup against Henry VII. It is this inability which has led some to question its coherence, and portray these men as disappointed careerists. That alienation played a part in predisposing men against Henry VII there can be no doubt, though for his part Henry VII's inability to understand the need to treat all honourably and not restrict and divide trust, led to a very dangerous situation. The inability of the plotters to topple Henry, and Warbeck's subsequent failure to find support in 1495 and 1496 is probably the result of an accident, that Atwater and Taylor named Warbeck after Richard, Duke of York and not another royal child.

On the one hand, attachment to York was invited and, because Margaret of Burgundy accepted Warbeck as York, given because of pre-existing personal loyalties which overrode those created by the civil wars of 1483–5. The weakness of the Warbeck/York claim lay in the fact that Richard, Duke of York, Edward IV's son, never had a regional following, nor a power base of land from which men might rise on his behalf. The nearest we approach to this is the old Mowbray affinity, in East Anglia. Yet this was split by the civil wars. Additionally when Anne Mowbray and Richard, Duke of York were given lands for a livelihood, they were given lands in Sussex, not East Anglia.[77] Edward IV showed no inclination to create a following for his son, and his son, as Duke of Norfolk, did not live long enough to create enduring loyalty. Thus when Warbeck arrived in England he could not exploit a large pre-existing power base. He had no mass support until 1497. In 1495 and 1496, Henry had his most loyal lieutenants in positions to reinforce his authority as king: the Earl of Oxford in East Anglia; Cardinal Morton and Sir Edward Poynings, as deputy to Henry, Duke of York and as Lieutenant of the Cinque Ports, superintending Kent; and Thomas Howard, Earl of Surrey as King's Lieutenant in the north. The breakdown of political discipline which happened in England in 1497 was the result of foreign intervention of a sort like that seen in 1470 and 1471. Those powers which backed Warbeck so circumscribed the king's course of action that only war seemed to offer a solution, either through battle or as a diplomatic weapon to force Warbeck's surrender. In fact what happened was a regression to civil war so that some of the people who had fought against Richard III now opposed Henry VII. In 1497 a number of the rebels had fought with Henry's men during Buckingham's rebellion and at least one had joined him in exile in Brittany. This phenomenon had already been prefigured in support for Warbeck in East Anglia and Hertfordshire, places which had opposed Richard III in 1483 and now produced disloyalty to the Crown again.

Stanley, Debenham, Savage and Fitzwater were struck down because as members of Henry VII's household they had agreed to aid Warbeck. Subborning Fitzwater and Stanley gave them access to the king's person and destroyed the wider security which the military function of the household provided. It is clear that in 1495 Malines was considering the landing in East Anglia which they had planned for 1493, and Fitzwater and possibly Debenham could have been called upon, if not to join a landing, to abstain from attacking rebels. Considered thus, from a strategic point of view, Stanley provided Malines access to the North Wales coast, to the castles of Flint and Holt and the town of Chester. Men might have been landed anywhere here from Ireland or Scotland and Stanley was notable for his command of many powerful men in this region 'Soo that he myght arere a myghty people In a short seson.'[78]

Equally worrying was the fact that through their contacts Malines had access to royal palaces and to the king's chamber. Fitzwater as Steward, and Stanley as Chamberlain of the Household, controlled the hiring and firing of all royal servants providing for everyday needs and staffed the guards to the king's chamber. This opened up the horrifying prospect not of mere intelligence gathering but of assassination. For example in October 1494 two Suffolk yeomen, William White and John Pylkington, agreed between themselves to act as messengers for Warbeck. On 20 February 1495 they were caught at Greenwich, in the vicinity of a royal palace, distributing letters from Richard Plantagenet.[79]

Attempts were made to control those who were identified as threats to the king. In January 1496 a Warwickshire esquire of the body, Gerard Danet, was bound over in £500, with two others, not to come within one thousand paces of the king without special licence. This was revoked, feelingly, after the battle of Blackheath, when Danet's loyalty had been proved by service on campaign.[80] Possibly this was punishment for some infraction of household duty, but at about the same time that White and Pylkington took up service with Warbeck, one

Bernard de Vignolles, servant, slipped quietly back into England. Bernard was returning from an errand for his master, John Kendal, Prior of St John of Jerusalem in England. Some time, perhaps two or three years before Warbeck was captured in Cork, English men in Rome had discussed assassinating the royal family. They had begun through an astrologer, a Spaniard, Rodrigo, to obtain poisons, but he had proved inadequate and they had then hired a second Spaniard, John Disant. Nothing had come of the plot. Perhaps it was not serious. More possibly, as was later revealed, they did not possess the cash to finance Disant properly. Warbeck's advent changed everything. Kendal was Lieutenant for the Hospitallers in Flanders, Italy and Ireland. He had connections with Malines, and a fellow hospitaller, the Irishman, James Keating was in Warbeck's retinue. Rodrigo, perhaps on the make with Henry's diplomats, circulated rumours of the first plot, so de Vignolles was sent to Rome to kill him and re-enlist Disant to help assassinate Henry. Disant, it was felt, was too well known to come to England himself, but he might provide some method the plotters could use. To their surprise Disant said he would come incognito, disguised as a friar on pilgrimage to St James's shrine at Compostella, and with two ivory false teeth to disguise his characteristic gap-toothed look. Lack of money to sustain the journey stopped Disant's plan.

Unable to go himself, Disant gave Bernard a little wooden box to deliver to John Kendal. It contained ointment which, said Disant, when spread along a passage or door which the king passed would cause those people closest to the king to kill him. Bernard returned to his quarters, went into his chamber, opened the box 'and when he saw that it was a vile and stinking mixture, he closed it again and threw it into the jakes'. The next day he left Rome for England. When he had got as far as Orleans he began to worry that Disant had already informed Kendal about the potion, and so he would be be in trouble. He therefore went to an apothecary and bought a box like the one Disant had given him, and also some mercury. He returned to his lodgings and from the chimney of his chamber took some soot, from the floor some earth and mixed them with water. This he added to the mercury to make an ointment about the same colour as Disant's concoction. By this time Bernard had decided he had no intention of being implicated in treason. When he arrived in England he took the box to Kendal, told him what the astrologer had said, and added that it was dangerous to the touch and that if the Prior kept the box in his house for twenty-four hours it would imperil his life. Understandably Kendal ordered de Vignolles to take the box to some out of the way place and throw it and its contents away. Part of the prior's insistence that Bernard ditch the potion was that Bernard had arrived back in England just when Mountford, Stanley and all the other ecclesiastics were being seized. Kendal was terrified he might be arrested. About a month after his servant's return to England he gave him a horse and money so that under pretence of visiting family in Normandy, de Vignolles would leave England, and not incriminate Kendal. Bernard did not leave England instead, he had, by the time Kendal visited him, contracted an illness from which he did not recover for a year and a half. Fortuitously, under cover of the sick room, Kendal and Bernard de Vignolles remained undetected.[81]

Kendal was a very highly placed diplomat. He had been papal chamberlain in 1491, had been captain of the guard to the heir to the Ottoman Empire, Djem, during Djem's captivity in Rome, and had represented Henry on diplomatic missions: he spoke Italian and French, we know.[82] He had access to the king in a way barred to most of his subjects, but meddled with Warbeck. Following Stanley's fall Henry determined to safeguard his person. Sweeping away the informality of his Yorkist predecessors, Henry reverted to more rigid Lancastrian practice to control access to the royal person. Where before all public court departments controlled by the chamberlain had one staff, now Henry hived off what had been the Privy

Chamber, which became known as the Secret Chamber, and gave it its own staff headed by a gentleman directly accountable to him. In this way he could protect himself and, after 1502 when his firstborn, Arthur, died, control all access to his second son Henry, Duke of York. He also appointed new household officers, and this time there was no accommodation with dubious loyalty. Almost to a man Warbeck's support had come from men who had stayed at home in the years 1483–5. Giles Daubney was promoted to chamberlain, and Robert Willoughby de Broke became steward. Both these men had fled England to join Henry in Brittany after Buckingham's rebellion.[83] Francis Bacon described the atmosphere after Stanley's fall as one of terror because, he says, Stanley had maintained no more than was generally believed, that York had better title to the throne than Lancaster. For this reason none thought themselves secure, 'and men durst scarce commune or talk with another, but there was general diffidence everywhere, which made the King rather more absolute than more safe'.[84]

NINE

The Red Rose and the White

Richard Plantagenet had been resurrected in 1491 because of the intense diplomatic and military activities among the European powers. Though he and his cause were taken up by Charles VIII and Maximilian I at different times and for very different reasons, their actions resulted in a similar threat to Henry: in the words of John Taylor, a threat from 'three partes out of royaulme'. In 1494–5 just as in 1491–2 the destruction of a projected English conspiracy did not end Warbeck's career. Warbeck existed as a parasite on international diplomacy, the most important product of which was the Holy League, created for the defence of Italy on 31 March 1495. England was not a signatory to this league though Spain dearly wanted her to be. Part of the reason for Henry VII's neutrality lay in the threat to England's internal stability which Warbeck posed, and part in the agreement worked out at Warbeck's advent, the Treaty of Étaples. Such neutrality was tolerated by the Spanish, who believed they could inveigle Henry to join the league, but it was not tolerated by Maximilian I. After Charles VIII's first year in Italy he had become too rabidly anti-French and too convinced of his own Herculean self-image to tolerate Henry's equivocal behaviour. Convinced that Warbeck was the Duke of York, Maximilian believed that while Henry VII promised that England might side against the French, Richard IV would guarantee absolute English commitment to the Holy League, or to some sort of league. International relations created some stange bedfellows, for in 1495 Maximilian believed he could persuade Spain, Flanders, Scotland, and Plantagenet England to ally against France.

By the end of 1494 Yorkist and Imperial agents had secured promises of support for Richard Plantagenet in Munster and Scotland as well as England, and in Flanders funds were obtained to equip an expedition more formidable than the one sent to England in 1487. Some of the money came from sources associated with the Flemish court. Bankers in Bruges, such as the Medici partner Tommaso Pontarini were councellors of Margaret of Burgundy's late husband and it is possible that Daniel Beauvivre, a Brugeios merchant who corresponded with John Kendal was involved in obtaining funds for the rebels.[1] The most fully documented loan is the 8,000 French écus which Richard acknowledged in a series of agreements made with his aunt, in December 1494. In fact he obtained more than this from her, but we do not know how much because the documents refer vaguely to 'other sums' and 'other obligations' and to the duchess's liberality in her private capacity, 'nom privé', to him and his servants, Taylor and Rowland Robinson, who were more probably his masters if the Scottish experience is anything to go by. The security against which these loans were obtained was, in essence, the recovery of his kingdom.

By letters patent of 10 December Richard acknowledged a series of promises to his aunt, including one to repay her for her financing of the 1487 expedition which had been made 'pour la recouverance et reduction a notre lineage et en expulser Henry qui a present illicitement l'occupe . . .'. By a protocol of the same date he agreed to pay her 81,666 écus d'or, the sum outstanding still on her dowry of 1468. Edward IV had gone some way to meeting these expenses in 1481, with grants of privileges in exporting wool and the revenues from the manor of Hunsdon. Now Richard agreed to meet all outstanding debts, honour all previous agreements, obtain for her any property or goods seized during Richard III's reign, and grant her both Hunsdon manor and Scarborough castle. These agreements were finalized on 24 December and were witnessed by a group representative of Warbeck's backers in Flanders. A mere week and a half before he fled to England, Robert Clifford stood witness with William Barley and Robert Ripon for their master's good intent. Alongside them were Baulduin du Grospre, a principal member of Margaret of Burgundy's council, possibly a lawyer since he was one of the executors of her will, and Jacques d'Yvregny, esquire – possibly of her household. Richard Plantagenet made this agreement, he said, for the help of God in recovering England, love of his aunt, and to acknowledge the help given to him by Philip the Fair and Maximilian I. It is also more than likely that armed with this formal loan agreement the rebels could obtain further loans elsewhere.[2]

We know that they borrowed directly from Paulus or Pouwels Zachtlevent or Saftleven a Pomeranian cloth merchant, resident in Amsterdam, who numbered among his patrons the Danish royal family. His house still exists today as 48 Warmoesstraat, Amsterdam, now part of a police station. In the fifteenth century the Warmoesstraat was the eastern dike of the River Amstel. Alongside it lay the Damrak, Amsterdam's first harbour. All the houses now on Warmoesstraat were then advantageously placed for access to the small craft which brought Amsterdam's trade from sea to land. Those who lived here were wholesale merchants or rich artisans, and they were Amsterdam's wealthiest citizens.[3] Pouwels concluded agreements to lend Richard Plantagenet money, 'under the signe and seal of the duc of Yorke'.[4] Some of the debt outstanding on this loan, which remained unpaid as late as 1510, was recouped when James IV of Scotland granted Pouwels the right to export cloths to Scotland free of customs duty.[5] But what his motivation for making such loans was remains mysterious, because real princes, let alone imposters, were notoriously bad at repaying debts. Nonethelsss he continued for twenty years to lend money to Tudor rebels.

When the rebels obtained their loan from Saftleven is unknown, but about the same time that they obtained credible financial backing from Margaret they also received advancement from Maximilian. Maximilian's financial contributions were bound to be limited by the constitutional arrangements of his domains, but in order to secure more than token backing Maximilian needed something with which to convince his sceptical administration. It may have been with this in mind that on 24 January 1495 Richard Plantagenet issued an even more extraordinary set of letters patent than those of a month before. These were fronted, appropriately enough, by a discourse on fate which asserted that the work of Providence removes all errors made by mortal man. The error to which Richard was referring was the occupation of his realm by another and his profound belief that with Maximilian's aid 'We will recover our heritage.' It was allowed nonetheless that he might die before he was reinstated in his realm, and so after hard deliberation, and because of the immense benefits he had received from Maximilian he ceded to Maximilian and his heirs all his rights to the realms of England, France and to the Duchy of York, the Lordship of Ireland and the Principality of Wales. He also renounced any right to papal arbitration by which the terms of this agreement might be overturned. Such is the nature of this topsy-turvey world of Perkin Warbeck that this is a document that cuts both ways. It may have provided Maximilian with

POTENTISSIMVS · MAXIMVS · ET · INVICTISSIMVS · CÆSAR · MAXIMILIANVS
QVI · CVNCTOS · SVI · TEMPORIS · REGES · ET · PRINCIPES · IVSTICIA · PRVDENCIA
MAGNANIMITATE · LIBERALITATE · PRÆCIPVE · VERO · BELLICA · LAVDE · ET
ANIMI · FORTIDVDINE · SVPERAVIT · NATVS · EST · ANNO · SALVTIS · HVMANÆ
· M · CCCC · LIX · DIE · MARCII · IX · VIXIT · ANNOS · LIX · MENSES · IX · DIES · XXV
DECESSIT · VERO · ANNO · M · D · XIX · MENSIS · IANVARII · DIE · XII · QVEM · DEVS ·
OPT · MAX · IN · NVMERVM · VIVENCIVM · REFERRE · VELIT ·

Maximilian I, Holy Roman Emperor

something to convince his subjects, but it also allowed for the quiet disposal, if needs be or the invasion of England was successful, of Warbeck/Richard Plantagenet and his substitution by another, perhaps nominated by Maximilian – Edward, Earl of Warwick – on the advice of the dowager Duchess of Burgundy. For the moment though the agreement remains testimony to the seriousness of Imperial intent. The letters patent were witnessed by the Imperial Chancellor Berthold von Heneburg, Margaret of Burgundy, Thomas de Plaines, a councillor of both Margaret and Philip the Fair, and Ladron de Guevara a ducal councillor who sent one of his sons in the invasion of England in July 1495.[6] It was with this document signed and sealed that Maximilian went to the Imperial Diet at Worms in March 1495. Here at length he lectured the Electors on the necessity for war with France, and canvassed their support for Warbeck, stressing that by descent the Duke of York had a better claim to the thrones of England and France than Henry VII.[7] Maximilian remained, as we have seen, York's residuary legatee.

Unsuccessful as he was in persuading the Electors to finance his enthusiasms, when he was in Flanders Maximilian was financed by the Receiver General of the Duchy of Burgundy. Much of this money was spent on routine matters, but the emperor also received money used in politically sensitive ways. During 1495 Maximilian received in excess of 11,000 livres nominated 'for secret affairs'. Some of the cash went to pay for the war against the Duke of Ghelders, but some may have gone to Warbeck. For example, in February 1495, 6,000 livres was allocated to Maximilian for the purchase of a vessel. Each time a part sum of this 6,000 livres was paid, the quittance for the money was authenticated, by Maximilian, in code.[8] We know also that on three separate occasions, 1 April, 7 April and latterly on 23 April 1495, he badgered Albert of Saxony and Casius Hagkeney, a Cologne bourgeois, his argentinier, into financing Warbeck.[9] In retrospect it is clear also that rewards ordered in March and April to Rodigue de Lalaing, the bastard son of a family of important ducal counsellors, for fighting in the Ghelders campaign, were as much payments in anticipation of service to Richard Plantagenet as for Rodigue's present service in the ongoing war.[10]

Once they were sure that the necessary financial preparations had been made, messages were sent to England that 1495 was to be the year of invasion. Warbeck's hospitaller secretary, Guillaume de Noion passed the news to John Kendal via Daniel Beauvivre that the Merchant of Ruby, code name for Richard Plantagenet, had got ready nearly all his money to the amount of 9,000 or 10,000 francs, and that he would shortly send it to him *par banque*, and that the Merchant of Ruby would take it with him. This should not be read as a financial statement. But can it be decoded as the Merchant now has 900 or 1,000 troops and will shortly invade by boat? Certainly it is a message saying, 'The plan is complete.'[11] Unfortunately we do not know the date of Beauvivre's letter, but it was probably sent between April and June 1495, because on 22 March Henry VII's government felt sufficiently worried by the threat of an attack from Scotland and elsewhere to commission the Vice Warden of the West and Middle Marches, Thomas Howard, Earl of Surrey to muster and array infantry, mounted men and all able-bodied men between the Trent and the Tweed. Likewise Richard Fox, Lord Privy Seal and Bishop of Durham was commissioned to raise men in his bishopric, in county Northumberland, Tynedale, Redesdale and the marches.[12] Together they were to resist the Scots and other enemies. At the same time news arrived in England that the army which had been sent to Ireland in 1494 was inadequate and needed reinforcement.[13] For the first time since the Warbeck affair had begun John Taylor's scenario of 1491, a tripartite invasion of England, looked distinctly possible.

After Warbeck's appearance in Ireland it had taken eighteen months to restore order there. Maurice, Earl of Desmond, his principal backer, had sworn allegiance to Henry VII on 18 March 1494, but in mid-May Desmond forswore his oath and led a rebellion against

Henry. The threat of another pre-Stoke situation, or worse, developing in Ireland was very real. Immediately Henry heard of Desmond's disloyalty he deprived Desmond of his key post as Constable of Limerick castle cutting him off from easy acccess to his allies in the north and west of Ireland. Sir James Ormond was appointed constable and given grants of land in Meath, Kilkenny and Tipperary. In September the king's son Henry, new Duke of York was created Lieutenant of Ireland. The old Anglo-Irish administration was replaced by an English one and Sir Edward Poynings was made Deputy Lieutenant at the head of an army of 653 men. This was a signal of the solution intended: drastic military action to reduce Ireland to loyalty before it was handed lock, stock and barrel to Warbeck.[14] Those who would not swear voluntary alliance to Henry Tudor, and surrender lands and sons as bond, had their lands fired. Between 13 October and 30 November 1494 Sir James Ormond carried out such a devastating scorched earth raid 'against Perkin's abettors who with other rebels and abettors had fled thither' to Ulster. One O'Hanlon of Orior in Armagh blocked the deputy's route to the north. But such was the fury of James Ormond's attack on O'Hanlon that he submitted. In Tyrone – central Ulster – O'Neill, a Kildare relative, submitted voluntarily. Both Desmond and his Ulster ally O'Donnell refused to have anything to do with Henry Tudor. O'Donnell refused to swear an oath, and Desmond refused the offer of a conciliatory pardon made in December 1494.[15]

Fighting stopped over the winter of 1494–5 as an Irish parliament met, and military reform was pressed further. All constables of Castles in the Pale – Dublin, Trim, Athlone,

Gallowglass figures on the tomb of Felim O'Connor, Roscommon, Ireland. Gallowglasses were Hebridean soldiers given land in return for military service

Wicklow, Greencastle, Carlingford and Carrickfergus – would henceforth be Englishmen born in England and all offices would be held as long as the king pleased and no other way.[16] The ramifications of what was believed to be a plot which undermined allegiance to Henry VII can be read in the attainder of the Earl of Kildare on charges of treason which later proved false. While Stanley, Fitzwater and company were rounded up in England, in Ireland Kildare was accused of sending messages to the king's Irish enemies, of sending men to help O'Hanlon fight against Poynings, of attempting to assassinate Poynings in Armagh while he was warring on O'Hanlon, and of reneging on his allegiance to the English Crown by agreeing to accept a Scottish army sent to Ireland in order to help Desmond and himself expel Poynings from Ireland.[17] Kildare remained at large in Ireland over the winter 1494–5 until at the end of February he was captured and transported to England. Immediately his brother, James FitzGerald raised rebellion and took Carlow castle which he still held at the end of June when Warbeck sailed from Flanders. The situation in Ireland was at a critical juncture.

The arrest of Kildare, with his enormous, prestige and connections all over Ireland alienated many from Henry VII. According to the Desmond chronicler, Perigrine O'Clery, 'there was not right nor justice, law nor rule in Errin, but everyone's right according to his strength'. The Earl of Desmond had linked up with the Gaelic chieftains of Ulster, O'Reilly of Cavan and O'Donnell of Tirconnel, informal allies of the Desmonds since the mid-1460s. Under the rule of Hugh O'Donnell and his son, both formidable soldier politicians the O'Donnells expanded their activities well beyond Ulster: south as far as Limerick where they encountered the FitzGerald of Desmond influence, and north, out of Ulster into Scotland, where both father and son concluded formal anti-English alliances.[18] Desmond's and O'Donnell's interests encompassed a great swath of territory encirling the English Lordship of Ireland, the Pale and by the summer of 1494 they were in communication with Flanders. O'Donnell of Tirconnel committed himself to Warbeck and then he allied with James IV of Scotland. At the beginning of July 1495 O'Donnell went to Scotland to see James IV. O'Neill of Clandeboy, one of the three major Ulster families – the other being O'Neill of Tyrone – also espoused Warbeck's cause. O'Donnell and O'Neill of Clandeboy also made allies of the MacMahon and O'Reilly clans. In the west of Ireland – Connaught – Seaan Burke of Clanriddick, a Desmond ally known to O'Donnell, and from the clan which had aided Warbeck in 1491, was known to be a strong supporter of Warbeck. Even in the Irish midlands and south-east, some of the clans generally favourable to the English, O'Byrne, MacMurrough, O'Connor, O'Dempsey and O'More, hesitated about who to support in this crisis.[19]

In Munster a full-scale rising was planned. According to Perigrine O'Clery, Kildare's arrest prompted Maurice FitzGerald, Earl of Desmond, to call together the Geraldines and their allies. The chronicler gave Desmond's reason for so doing as shock at the treachery of Henry VII in arresting Kildare. He told his followers that 'to them belonged of right the supremacy and possession of the country in which they were, for it was Maurice FitzGerald from whom the Geraldine's sprang that forcibly wrested the country from the Irish and Danish heroes'.[20] The message was clear enough. But it is equally clear that the earl saw a unique opportunity to advance the Desmond cause as the principal Irish power either through an alliance with Prince Richard, Duke of York, or, if he could not get what he wanted from York then he would strike a deal with the Saxon King, Henry. We do not know who made the first move, Margaret of Burgundy or Desmond, but in the spring of 1495 the Flemish court offered help for a Desmond rising. It was probably John Taylor who sent letters from Perkin Warbeck to John Atwater of Cork and the Munster William, Lord Barry. Their attainder, three years later says they received letters from Warbeck and in the aftermath of the rebellion

Barry and Atwater were denied pardons.[21] It is possible that Barry was the nobleman recruited to organize among his Munster peers. The list of those pardoned a year after the rising is an indication of its scope. Not only did the earl call upon his son, Thomas, but he also involved the sons of a previous Desmond earl, Earl Thomas, in the shape of his sons Thomas, John and Gerald. Then either he or Barry, called on the service of lords allied by marriage or fealty to Desmond: Edmund FitzMaurice, Maurice, Lord Roche, James Lord Courcy, John Lord Barret, and for aid from Sir Maurice le White, the Kerry knight, Maurice and Sir Edmund, knight of Witley. The account of the military activity following these alliances shows that west Munster Gaelic chiefs were also involved.[22] There was possibly even some complicity between Flanders and the port of Youghall, as a port where Warbeck's troops could disembark in Ireland. The rebels made landfall there in July and the mayor, burgesses, and community had to take out pardons with Desmond and the rest. In the spring there was little military activity in Munster, but the threat of war was unmistakable.

Thus when John Pympe, one of Henry's officers, arrived in England on 20 March it can have been with little else than attrocious news and a plea for more men. Within a month of his arrival he found himself apppointed Treasurer for War with William Hatcliffe and Henry Wyatt as his auditors. They were all sent post haste to Ireland. Wyatt and Pympe arrived on 3 May, Hatcliffe on 7 June.[23] By then Desmond was about to begin his attack on Waterford and Warbeck was waiting for a good wind for England. At the same time an embassy from James IV of Scotland arrived in Worms and rumours began to circulate in Europe of James IV's overt support for Warbeck.[24]

The Scots flirtation with Maximilian and Margaret of Burgundy can be traced back to 1488. When serious Scottish involvement with Warbeck and Maximilian began is in doubt, because of the loss of critical records, but it was probably some time in 1493, or 1494 when Snowdon Herald accompanied Petit John, a Flemish messenger and John Pringill, to Flanders.[25] In the winter and spring of 1495 William Elphinstone, Bishop of Aberdeen and James IV's Lord Privy Seal went to Rome to initiate a new phase of Scots diplomacy in Europe. Putting the disastrous French manoeuvres of 1491–2 behind them the Scots hoped to curry favour with Rome and the Empire. At Easter 1495 Elphinstone was in Flanders and in May on his way to Worms to see Maximilian. Elphinstone and his party arrived there on 3 June. On 9 June it was reported that Warbeck's soldiers alone numbered 1,500 and that Maximilian intended to reinforce them with 800 of his own men. The Scots said they hoped for the certain victory of the Duke of York. The next day, having thus praised Maximilian's protégé it emerged that the reason for the embassy was to conclude a treaty of friendship and a marriage alliance.[26] What James IV wanted was a wife and a league against England which would enable him to recover Berwick which the Scots had lost in 1482. Norman Macdougall believes that Warbeck was given token support at this stage, to flatter Maximilian and to threaten the English with. James IV intended to resume Berwick from England, and any prevarication by England, would be met by a threat to admit the Duke of York to Scotland.[27]

The reason for James IV's patronage of Warbeck has never been clear. The old view of James, that he was controlled by an anti-English southern Scots faction, has been shown by Norman Macdougall to be inadequate and simplistic. By 1495 James was nearing his age of majority and it was now necessary for him to assert himself. He had failed in his relations with France, and had endured the demeaning offer of an English noblewoman as wife from Henry VII.[28] Needs be, he must marry and develop a coherent foreign policy. Yet within the triangle Ireland–Scotland–England, anti-Englishness has something to recommend it. In 1488, when news of James IV's pro-English father's death reached Ireland, it greatly weakened the ability of Henry VII's servant Sir Richard Edgcumbe in the middle of his negotiation to reassert English authority in Ireland.[29] And if James was seeking to flatter

Maximilian in 1495 he did not stop at half measures. Rumours of an impending Scottish attack on England had resulted in the readying of northern soldiers at the end of March. In mid-May news reached Venice that James had sent Warbeck a number of ships and troops, and when Warbeck's men landed in Kent they were described as the king's Scottish and Flemish enemies.[30]

By May, however, Warbeck's chief backer was apparently distancing himself from his protégé. At the beginning of the month two Venetian ambassadors on their way to negotiate with Maximilian met one of his diplomats, Philibert Naturelli, in Padua. In answer to their questions Naturelli assured the ambassadors that Maximilian was not backing Warbeck. It was all the doing of his son, Philip the Fair. This was subterfuge, designed, presumably, to throw Venice and England off the scent, and place Maximilian in a stronger position for the creation of his league, for within two months he was cock-a-hoop at the prospect of bringing a Plantagenet England into his league against France[31]. Flemish diplomacy was in fact hard at work in Italy on Warbeck's behalf. On 8 May, just before Scottish ships reached Flanders, Margaret of Burgundy drew up an appeal to Pope Alexander VI. Those who wrote the appeal were part of her immediate circle. They included Pierre de Lannoy, her Head of Household and a number of eminent Louvain theologians, Nicholas Hellis, master of theology and Adrian of Florence of the collegiate church of St Peter's Louvain. Margaret had founded hospitals in Louvain, begun work on a charterhouse there and had links with the university. At one time Margaret considered being buried in the charterhouse: a decorated niche was prepared for her tomb, but never used. Her confessor, Jean Bryart had links with the charterhouse.[32] Assembled under her patronage a gathering of theologians from Tournai, Cambrai and Liege worked out a suitable form of words and then sent the petition to Rome. Margaret's appeal was an attempt to have the threat of papal sanctions against Henry Tudor's rebels removed.

A large part of the appeal related to the question of by what right kings ruled, and the nature of that right. The other main strand which emerged in the argument was about the rights of the people. A people, it is said, should be ruled by a king with true rights to rule and no other. For true harmony the right of the ruling monarch to his throne should be impeccable. At present Henry Tudor was holding the throne, contrary to English custom by right of battle and by Act of Parliament. Innocent VIII, Alexander VI's predecessor, had made a papal dispensation in order to allow the marriage of Henry Tudor to Elizabeth of York. He had also been persuaded by Tudor to excommunicate and anathematize any who did not accept this. Kings of England it is argued were recognized not by vote or election, nor by battle 'but by propagation of blood'. Thus as Richard, Duke of York remained alive, the legitimate son of Edward IV, he had good right to the throne. Even if it was maintained that, as the younger son, he could not succeed to the throne while a son, or brother's son, or even a daughter of Edward IV, survived – oblique references to Edward, Earl of Warwick and Elizabeth of York – and even if the blood of York failed altogether there are still members of the house of Lancaster with better claims to the throne than Henry VII. Henry VII's title is deemed the product of damned intercourse. Again the reference is oblique, but is to John of Gaunt's descendant, King João II of Portugal. Had Innocent VIII been aware of these constitutional points, and Richard, Duke of York's survival, he would not have confirmed Henry as King.

Nay rather they would have commanded the said lord most illustrious Richard son of King Edward, to be restored to his own kingdom and to be introduced into its possession, nor would they have forbade the bounden duty of lords and others being shown to their Lord, Parent or relative as is shown in the example of the high priest Jehoiada who restored

King Joas he who had been snatched from the hands of a bloody grandmother and secretly nourished at the house of his fathers sister in the kingdom of his father and anticipated the cruel purpose of a rebellious woman by justifiable killing.

This is the central message of the petition, and why two arguments were developed, one about legitimacy, and one about the people. The legitimate claiment should not be prevented from recovering his rightful throne nor should anyone be prevented assisting in this matter for fear of papal sanction. The sanction was, as argued, imposed in error, and Margaret's theologians argued that actions taken to restore a legitimate heir to his throne be deemed acts of piety. [33]

This petition was intended to encourage insurrection in England by overturning Innocent VIII's ruling that any rebel against Henry VII would be excommunicated. Now, according to Margaret such rebels were performing good works and pious deeds. We do not know exactly when the petition reached Rome. It may have got there in June or July or later in the summer. Whatever the case Margaret's appeal was delivered to the Curia by Philibert Naturelli, the ambassador who had maintained that Maximilian was no longer interested in the Duke of York. Naturelli's denial was a complete smokescreen. Just as the learned doctors of Louvain were concluding their arguments for Margaret, the Duke of York's expedition was being readied, superintended, and staffed by Maximilian's Flemish supporters.

The fact that Maximilian had two military operations proceeding in the Low Countries, one against the Duke of Ghelders and the other against England makes it impossible to determine what in his expenditure was laid out against Ghelders and what for Warbeck. Both were being financed during April, May and June, and both were referred to as highly secret affairs. From April to June Seigneur de Bevres supervised secret naval preparations at Veere, and ships were hired in Haarlem and possibly at Damme, on the Zwin near Bruges, by Jacques de Gondebault, counsellor, *maître de requêtes*, and secretary for war.[34] The only place we know to have contributed one of Warbeck's fifteen vessels – a hoy – was Dordrecht.[35] Where the ships whose names we know, *The Kekeout* and *Le Mare*, came from we do not know. Conceivably, as they did for the Simnel expedition, some ships could have come from as far away as Danzig.[36]

Overall command of the rebel army was vested in Rodigue de Lalaing. De Lalaing was the illegitimate son of Anthoine de Lalaing, late Chamberlain of Charles the Bold, and the Lalaings had served Margaret in the 1470s. They were one of the most highly placed Flemish families, and Rodigue's illegitimacy was no bar to the normal Lalaing *cursus honorem*.[37] He had fought for Maximilian at Utrecht and the siege of Sluys, where he was captain of sixty horses. At this point he was an esquire of the ducal household. In 1495 he was rewarded for service against the Duke of Ghelders at Namur. He was paid £60 for his work there, and for certain other matters and secret affairs – a veiled reference to his captaincy of the Warbeck expedition. His service to Warbeck was no impediment either to his later career, rather the reverse. He was granted feudal rights for serving Perkin, subsequently legitimized and became Captain of the Archduke Philip's Archers, and subsequently *maître d'hôtel* to the future Holy Roman Emperor Charles V.[38] The Flemish contingent which he commanded included his brother and a contingent of noble Burgundians, for Molinet tells us that with Warbeck was 'Rodigue de Lalaing et autre compaignons de la garde fort experimentez de la guerre.'[39] As well as his brother we can identify Pedro and Don Fulano de Geuvara. Zurita, the Spanish historiographer described Pedro as a knight or gentleman in the service of Maximilian and Philip, and brother to Ladron de Geuvara an archducal councillor. Another Geuvara nobleman, was nicknamed Diego el Coxo (the lame) when captured in Kent. De Lalaing commanded not only Archduke

Detail of a panorama of the river Scheldt from Rupelmonde to the Isle of Walcheren, 1468. Antwerp is shown centrally. Vlissingen is on the north side of the Scheldt estuary between Antwerp and the port of Walcheren on the Isle

Philip's archers but also a number of Flemish gunners as well as a large number of mercenaries.[40]

Who commanded the English force is a moot point. William Lounde, John Taylor and Rowland Robinson never dealt purely with military matters, they were the core of Warbeck's administration. It is much more likely that the overall English commander was an experienced soldier, perhaps Sir Richard Harleston, or, less likely, Sir George Neville. Both these men had backgrounds which would have prepared them for a marine assault. Harleston had been Governor of Jersey from 1468 to 1486 after having led an expedition for Edward IV, in 1468, to eject a French garrison from the island. Latterly he had been a sea rover for Margaret of Burgundy. Neville had undertaken naval patrols for Richard III in the months before Bosworth.[41] Who their subordinates were is equally uncertain, but the first people to land in England were a boatload of English soldiers commanded by Sir Simon Mountford's son Henry, and he had seen military service in Ireland. According to an eyewitness account Mountford's rebel brothers-in-arms, were Richard White, Sir Robert Chamberlain's man in 1491, John Belt of Guildford, a yeoman, John Corbet, a yeoman identified as son of a London grocer, and Quyntyne a Spaniard.[42] The account given of this soldiery by Polydore Vergil is Vergil's standard description of rebels. According to him they were all rascals, thieves, sanctuary men, and agricultural labourers: the usual Polydorian 'dregs of society'. In fact the bulk of those taken prisoner with Mountford, thirty-six, were yeomen.[43] Out of over fifty Englishmen captured only four were classed as labourer. The rest were the usual mix expected in any retinue of the period: chaplains, grooms, a merchant, even a goldsmith. A number of long-time rebels to Henry VII served in this expedition. James Keating the ex-Master of the Hospitallers in Ireland had been a rebel since before Stoke. Recruits to Warbeck's force made in 1493 and 1494 – John Brampton, Thomas Brampton and William Barley – were there. These three had been drawn to Warbeck through Robert Clifford and John, Lord Fitzwater. Identified for the first time are John Heron a London merchant, Edward Ashley of Calais, and Richard Williamson, a merchant from York, and possibly a city chamberlain.[44] More ominously there were a number of ex-officers of the king's and queen's households who had joined Warbeck. Richard Woodhouse, for example, was a gentleman usher of the chamber who along with his brother Roger, from the Chester area, may represent defections from the Prince of Wales's household. In 1484 Richard had obtained a pardon from Richard III presumably for involvement in Buckingham's rebellion.[45]

Parts of this expedition may have been readied at Damme, but it probably sailed from Vlissingen (Flushing). At the beginning of March 1495 Henry VII sent to sea five royal ships led by Stephen Bull, in the *Hermitage*.[46] It is possible that they were intended to damage the preparations being made, for on 4 April Albert of Saxony, in Holland, was informed from Malines of 'la descent des anglois en zeelan' – the English landing in Zeeland. The next day another message was sent to Albert on the same subject and within ten days a message was sent from Albert to Henry. If the inference that the English were raiding Zeeland is correct, diplomacy of some sort followed.[47] Molinet sites an account of Henry's last attempt to persuade Malines give up its aid to Warbeck in the period immediately before Warbeck's expedition sailed. According to Molinet an English ambassador, Lord Somerset – Sir Charles Somerset – who was used on a number of missions at this time, visited 'madame la grande', her nephew Richard, Philip the Fair and Maximilian. He made obeisances to all except Richard. Margaret chided him, 'It seems you do not know my nephew Richard since you did not bow to him.' The ambassador replied that Richard her nephew had already departed this world and if it pleased her to send one of her men to England he would take him to the chapel where the real Richard was buried. This nicely calculated bluff drew its response. Prince Richard was astounded and declared that when he was crowned in his kingdom, shortly, he would not forget these words. Yet, says Molinet, despite this simulated hauteur Warbeck was very scared by what had been said.[48]

Warbeck's expedition left Vlissingen at the end of June, with the intention of linking up with rebels in England. John Kendal's fellow hospitaller, ex-master of the order in Ireland, James Keating, sailed with Warbeck while Kendal prepared for the landing. The hospitallers had a commandery at Melchbourne in Bedfordshire where Kendal stockpiled livery for use by his retinue in the event of a rising. He had ordered that a set of red and green jackets with panels to display the red rose be made. According to his servant, who informed on him, they were constructed in such a way that it was easy to substitute a white rose for the red.[49] De Lalaing was aiming for a landing in East Anglia. After his failure reach to East Anglia it was said by one of his captains that they had all hoped to take Great Yarmouth, and some might yet do so. Two of Warbeck's messengers, arrested in 1495, were respectively from the village of Gisleham and the town of Easton Bavents near Lowestoft.[50] De Lalaing may have had north Norfolk in mind as an area for landing. In October 1495 Edward Sybly of Wiggenhall, near King's Lynn confessed some plan of treason to the Earl of Oxford and consequently lost his goods and his liberty. So King's Lynn may have been in their sights as well.[51] At a practical level this destination should not surprise us. What happened at Deal was so botched that it cannot have been intended. In addition two conspirators taken but still alive, Debenham and Fitzwater, were from East Anglia, and Robert Chamberlain's accomplice in 1491, Richard White of Thorpe-juxta-Bellingford, near Norwich, sailed with Henry Mountford.

In attempting to land in Norfolk, Warbeck's masters were deliberately echoing Edward IV's 1471 expedition, to reap the benefit of the propaganda of that victory. Then, Edward sailed from Vlissingen to Norfolk in order to link up with the Mowbray Duke of Norfolk. He made landfall at Cromer and sent Debenham and Chamberlain to reconnoitre the immediate area for support. He did not find support because any gentry loyal to him had been arrested or were under heavy bond for loyalty. The duke had been removed from the region, and so with this news Edward went further north.[52] There was a quite deliberate attempt in 1496, the year after their failed landing, to represent Warbeck as one who would revive 'the blessed and debonair government of our noble father King Edward'. [53] Not only this, as we have seen they tried to exploit the legacy of the Mowbray connection when they appealed for support.

The failure of the Warbeck expedition to make a landing in Norfolk was nearly Edward IV's fate too. When he had tried to set sail for England he had been prevented by bad winds for nine days. Eventually the wind had changed and he made a good crossing to Cromer.[54] But, at the mercy of the elements, this was not always possible. In 1483 Henry Tudor had missed most of Buckingham's rebellion because of bad weather. Nor was the weather kind to de Lalaing's expedition. Bernard André says that during the crossing Warbeck's own vessel became detached from the main force and only rejoined it on the morning they arrived at Deal. One vessel, at least, did not get to England. A correspondent of Sir John Paston told him that on 3 July, the day of the landing, a ship from Yarmouth had seen a Dordrecht hoy hove to off St Valery in Normandy. Its crew were Dutch, but its cargo consisted of eight horses with saddles and bridles, and eight or nine English rebels. Immediately the hoy dropped anchor the rebels took the ship's boat to the shore and disappeared in the direction of Flanders. The vessel and its contents were seized and it's Dutch crew were imprisoned.[55]

Responsibility for the defence of southern England in spring 1495 was divided between the king and Cardinal Morton. For the first six months of the year Henry stayed in the south-east, then, at the end of June, he moved to Woodstock, a favourite residence in emergencies. It was a good, centrally sited muster point. But the king did not stay at Woodstock long, he turned north, and went as far as Tewkesbury on 3 July, the day Warbeck's rebels landed, before establishing himself in Worcester for five days and then going north to Ludlow, on 12 July. Thus he was within easy reach of Bristol if immediate action was necessary in Ireland. The south was not, as is often suggested, left in a *laissez-faire* state. Morton took up residence in London and organized troops and artillery to be sent to defend the coast. The city fathers of Canterbury sent two men to Mortlake to see him about 300 soldiers to be brought into Kent to resist Warbeck. How many more men were raised in Kent and assembled near Canterbury is unknown. However, from letters in the Paston collection we know that elements of the Earl of Oxford's retinue were present at Canterbury also.[56] These men reported the threats to take Great Yarmouth to the town authorities, which frightened them so much that they summoned aid from the surrounding Norfolk country. They demanded that Sir John Paston and his retinue come to the town and that Norwich also send troops. Both these contingents were Oxford's responsibility, so they may have written to Ralph Shelton, Oxford's steward to raise other sections of this Oxford's retinue. In the event nothing happened. So, when on 12 July they knew that they were not going to be attacked by Warbeck, they again wrote to Sir John boasting about the number of guns they had readied against the invaders and then, in the true spirit of home defence, invited him to inspect them. 'Ser, if it woll please your maistership that ye myght have leyser, I desyre and pray you to come sporte you, and to see how weell we have appareld and furnyshid our town . . .' They would take his advice on how to improve their batteries.[57]

On the Kent coast, towns had also been prepared in advance of Warbeck's arrival. At Dover the mayor, Edward Hextall, who had been imprisoned himself for treason in 1486, supervised its defence. Guns were repaired, beer was bought for the soldiers about to repel Warbeck, and warning bonfires were built. There may at this time have been warning beacons throughout England. The king paid 10 shillings for one at Woodstock, but this may just have been the usual midsummer's bonfire, we cannot tell. Seven hundredweight of wood was consumed at Dover when the rebel fleet arrived in the Downs, the sea just off Deal. In Dover, on the morning of 3 July, the fleet's arrival was marked by hornblowing and a general stand to.[58] At Sandwich, five miles north and inland of Deal, town guns were positioned and augmented with the others brought from London.[59] Perhaps the bonfire at Dover relayed the news, or footmen or mounted messengers were sent to Canterbury, but from Canterbury, as arranged, three hundred men-at-arms were sent along the road via Wingham and Ash to Sandwich. By the time they reached Sandwich, de Lalaing had disembarked one boat of English rebels led by Henry Mountford on the foreshore north of Deal.[60]

The earliest account of what happened at Deal, pre-dating both André and Vergil is Jean Molinet's. He says that de Lalaing put down his infantrymen to spy out the land and pillage for stores. The beach at Deal is easily accessible: long, steeply shelved and pebbly. According to Molinet, 300 men – of whom over fifty are known to have been English – landed, established their forward positions in three villages and set up their banners there. If this is correct he may have meant Deal, Walmer and Kingsdown. All three accounts agree that they were deliberately deceived by the troops held near the shore. Molinet says that after their banners were displayed they were approached by a mounted man-at-arms on a very fine horse. He asked them who they were, and they replied that they were the Duke of York's men. Molinet reports the man-at-arms to have said 'We do not ask another lord in the world, we want to live and die with him and his whole company; all the honour help and favour we can give to him we shall give with all our hearts, bodies and power.' At this the soldiers who heard the reply thought they had already won the day and sent messages to Warbeck's vessel that they had secured good support and that Prince Richard should land. The Flemish and English commanders with de Lalaing, suspected a trick, and refused to land. The soldier, however, persisted with his ruse and offered the landing party a token of his goodwill: two barrels of beer. No sooner had the man made his offer of beer and disappeared to fetch it than well-armed forces gathered at Sandwich attacked the rebel beach head. According to Molinet, after the event 150 corpses on the beach were covered with arrows and horrifying wounds. This suggests the usual English tactic of softening up the opposition with arrows before a fierce attack. The rebels did their best to resist but, according to Molinet, troops poured onto the beach in numbers. Some rebels were killed on the beach, others were drowned as they tried to get back to the vessels of the expeditionary force. This short but harsh attack was all that the fighting amounted to, and with half its force slaughtered, on the land or in the water, the advance party under Henry Mountford surrendered.[61]

A little offshore the invasion fleet watched, aghast. When Warbeck was brought before Henry VII, two years later, he said that it was for the previous two years that he had longed to escape. Did his disillusion set in in 1495, with the sight of the carnage on Deal beach: horses and men running amuck. Men standing stock still in shock; others screaming at their wounds, bleeding onto the pebbles of the beach, while out to sea corpses, stuck with arrows, floated in ever more diluting blood? Thomas Grigge, a Kentishman, was so badly wounded that he was almost killed, but a year later was rewarded by Henry VII with five marks for his trouble, and pain.[62] One of the seriously wounded rebels, John Corbet, was taken alive but took a month to die of his wounds.[63] Or was this the greatest moment in the actor's life? Watching men kill each other over his non-existent claim to the throne, while he, as spectator Prince looked on. Whatever he felt we do not know, but his commanders decided to cut their losses, hoist up their sails, leave their fellows on the beach and regroup elsewhere. Contrary to expectations they did not go north, perhaps the wind was against them. Instead, they skirted the coast of Kent, rounded Dungeness and regrouped in Rye Bay or the West Road, off Camber. All of this, their inability to get to Norfolk, their landfall in Kent, and their hasty westward departure suggests winds consistently in the wrong direction for them. Had they failed in Norfolk perhaps they could have tried further north or gone to Scotland. Now they were obliged to go west. They went, John Paston was told in the assurance 'that one man should help them with many men'. Was this as it became, the Earl of Desmond, or was it, as it was in 1497, an assertion to keep up their morale? The invasion had been a fiasco, Warbeck and the whole expedition were out on a limb. Some of this confusion is mirrored in Vergil who asserts, wrongly, that they returned to Flanders. They went to Ireland but in a disordered and desperate fashion.[64]

The king was at Worcester when the abortive invasion took place. On the day after it he sent letters throughout the realm. To check any rebel intention to link up with disgruntled elements of William Stanley's men, and for ease of communication with Ireland, Henry left Worcester on 9 July and went, via Ludlow and Shrewsbury, to Holt castle, lately William Stanley's. From then, 17 July, until he reached his mother's palace at Colly Weston, on 4 September, he remained in the north Midlands. Principally he toured Stanley country. On 30 July he was at Lathom, the Earl of Derby's residence and in the first three weeks of August progressed in south Lancashire, Cheshire and Derbyshire. A month after he had arrived at Holt he took up residence, on 17 August in Nottingham castle.[65]

For about ten days after the fighting at Deal, watches were kept on the south coast of England, but these were redundant, Warbeck had set sail for Ireland. Even before he had left Flanders, peace in Ireland had all but collapsed. On 15 June Edward Poynings sent out spies to reconnoitre southern Leinster and the Midlands; and it is said that spies were also sent to Scotland, possibly because rumours were circulating of the forthcoming alliance between Hugh O'Donnell and James IV. A week later Desmond declared war and attacked Waterford. Defending the Pale from likely attack from Ulster and Munster stretched Poynings to the limit. At the end of June he sent a minimal force of Dubliners, raised by their mayor and bailiffs, and Thomas Garth to defend Waterford. And in the middle of July he sent undercover messages to O'Brien of Leinster begging him to defend the southern approaches of the Pale while he, the Lord Deputy took an army against Desmond.[66] At the same time he begged Henry VII for more troops. Henry was at the monastery of Vale Royal in Cheshire when news of the Munster uprising reached him. He appointed Sir Roger Cotton to the command of 1,500 reinforcements for the English army in Ireland. But such a force would be slow to assemble in so short a time. On 27 July, two vessels, one Spanish and one from

Picardy, were hired to transport 11 captains, 249 infantrymen, 100 cavalry, 50 crossbowmen and 100 horses. As they left from Chester it is likely that they were intended to reinforce the defences of the Pale. Elsewhere a second force was readied. Four hundred and seventy men were ordered out of Fowey and Plymouth to stay at sea for six weeks. Their point of origin, the far west of England, suggests their task was to find Warbeck's fleet and to engage it. This they singularly failed to do, and Warbeck's fleet is next heard of raiding Youghall halfway between Cork and Waterford. It is unlikely that this raid was anything more than opportunistic plundering, and its circumstances may explain why Warbeck was never intercepted by the ships sent after him from Cornwall and Devon. Immediately before the attack on Youghall, bad storms at sea had forced ships to take refuge in the Youghall haven. Warbeck and his fellowship entered the port and plundered the ships there. John Ilcombe of Plymouth, owner of *Le Cristofre* of Plymouth, lost 60 tons of iron he was importing to England. Another West Country vessel, *Le Sonday*, owned by an Anglo-Irish partnership from Minehead, also seems to have been attacked, and William Bourget of Harfleur lost wool-fells which he was taking to Southampton and Exeter. Ilcombe and the Minehead men were subsequently permitted by Henry to seize any ship sailing out of Youghall as recompence for their losses. Bourget was granted leave to import wool-fells free of toll. Warbeck's expedition took the goods they had plundered and sold them to the local Youghall and Cork merchants.[67] Thus provided with money, and restocked and renewed, they sailed north-west to Waterford.

The siege at Waterford began in the last week of June, with a blockade on the western, landward side of the town, and possibly some raiding into the territories of known English allies, the Butlers. Waterford was defended on two sides by rivers, the Suir on the north and the Johns on the south and east. To complete their defences the citizens dug ditches and flooded them, creating moats, or ponds as they were picturesquely called. And they placed their cannon on the top of Reginald's Tower, a mighty stone fortress built in 1003 by the Vikings. There are two accounts of the siege, a Desmond one, by O'Clery, and one recorded at Waterford. O'Clery lists those who went with Desmond to Waterford, a list very close to the pardon a year later. With Desmond were the sons of the previous earl, Thomas; Thomas, John Garret, Gerald, and Lord Barry, the White Knight of Kerry and Desmond's Gaelic allies Donough Oge MacCarthy, members of the Sheehy clan and, anonymously, others. O'Clery also lists with Desmond, James, son of the Earl of Kildare, but this must be a reference not to a son of Kildare, but to his brother. Nor is it certain that O'Clery is correct about James's involvement. If Kildare's brother was there, the situation in July 1495 was grave. But it may be that O'Clery credits his presence there in order to demonstrate Desmond's importance as Ireland's leader.[68] His account of later events includes Desmond commissioning James to take up his brother's lordship, and war against the English. But whether James FitzGerald was there or not the Geraldines and their allies arrived in numbers – 24,000 says Waterford's exaggerated account – and besieged the town. The Desmond account says that after a fruitless siege of six days Desmond took his forces to raid Butler country; the Butlers of Polestown, Cahir and Dunboyne were all Henry VII's allies. Desmond went inland and north, to county Kilkenny. He attacked Gowran, Thomastown, Knocktoper and Callan. Then he went to Five Mile Hill, west to Riccoill and from here he and his supporters raided Englishmen and Gaelic Irish allies of England. The Waterford account has none of this, stressing instead the brave defence of the town and describing daily skirmishes between the town defenders and Desmond's forces until, on 23 July, the Duke of York joined the siege, sailing his eleven vessels up the Suir, into the heart of the city.[69] By now the siege had lasted a month, and it is quite possible that Desmond's raid took place while he awaited the arrival of his Yorkist allies. This might explain the otherwise inexplicable length of the siege, and why even with a large force Desmond had not taken Waterford. Waterford was merely blockaded while he raided elsewhere before taking this jewel of a city.

According to the Waterford account two of Warbeck's ships drew in to Lombard's Wear, on the Suir, and put down soldiers there. The citizens replied by sending a retinue of their own men to attack what were presumably Rodigue de Lalaing's men. The Flemish were defeated. Some were killed outright, and some were taken prisoner. The prisoners were brought into the city, taken to the market place and beheaded. Thereafter their heads were put on public display. Atop Reginald's Tower the town gunners got their ships in their sights, fired, and sank them. Desmond and the Duke of York, encamped on the south-western edge of the city, in St Patrick's Field heard the fighting and they sent a second force to go to the aid of their fellows at Lombard's Wear, only to find their passage barred by the flooded ditches. On 3 August after eleven days of bloody activity, and after a month-long siege which had yielded nothing, the Lord Deputy, Sir Edward Poynings arrived at the head of a large relief column spearheaded by two companies of harquebusiers, 90 gunners led by Adam van Edyngton and William Warrewik.[70] Poynings had with him all the men he could raise. O'Clery and the Waterford account are in agreement here: gentry retinues from Leinster, Meath and Oriell, Sir James Ormond and his men, the Butlers – nominal Lords of Waterford, Gaelic Irish from Leinster, the MacMurroughs and possibly some of James Ormond's allies, the O'Briens.

Desmond and Warbeck were forced to withdraw their forces south-west and then depart. Not only was there a strategic withdrawal by Desmond and Warbeck, Warbeck's commander de Lalaing lost a further three ships, including *The Kekeout* and *Le Mare*, sunk by Poynings' gunners. Subsequently patched up, they were sold off for prize money and used as trading vessels. Poynings established himself in Waterford and lived off cash loans from its citizens. His victory was one of superior technology and firepower over numbers, but it was a hollow one. It may be that O'Clery's account of Desmond's raid belongs to this period, and it may be that his story about the Earl of Kildare's brother is erroneous and apocryphal, but there is no mistaking the hair's breadth nature of Poyning's victory. Despite the constitutional and administrative reining in of Ireland by the famous 1494–5 parliament, and 'Poynings Law', there would not be peace long as Henry VII attempted to rule Ireland through an Englishman, and an English garrison. The price of defeating Warbeck was the restoration of autonomy to the Anglo-Irish. In that sense then Desmond had gambled and won, though it was Kildare who became once more king's man in Ireland. While in Waterford, Poynings took the political initiative and reconciled Youghall and Cork to the king. He also put out feelers to Desmond to move him, finally, away from his adherence to Warbeck.[71] By December 1495 the possibility of some sort of reconciliation was strongly in the air and Poynings was withdrawn to England. But for the moment Desmond and the rump of Warbeck's forces, six ships only of the fifteen which had left Flanders, retreated together.

The siege of Waterford had been conducted as part of a strategy whose overall plan we do not know. It involved Flanders, and continued to do, and also Scotland, for on 7 July, just after the Deal failure, Hugh O'Donnell of Tirconnel left Ulster to parley with James IV of Scotland in Glasgow. O'Donnell was a remarkable soldier-politician. His son referred to himself as Prince of Ulster. There is no record of what James IV and O'Donnell concluded after their discussions, but some sort of offensive–defensive alliance was made, and was still in effect in 1513.[72] It is just possible, also, that plans were laid for a subsequent attack on the English castle at Carrickfergus, on Carlingford Lough. Whatever was actually agreed O'Donnell returned to Ireland on 7 August, four days after Poynings had broken the siege at Waterford. It is almost inevitable that O'Donnell and James talked about Warbeck and that O'Donnell was an intermediary between Desmond and Warbeck with James IV. Whether

O'Donnell secured an entry to Scotland for Warbeck at this point is impossible to say, but both O'Donnell and O'Neill of Clandeboy, vigorous supporters of Warbeck, returned from Scotland that August. At the same time Warbeck was being entrusted to a second Desmond ally, Seaan Burke of Galway, 'the grettest secour that perkyn hade while he was in the londe safe only therle of desmonde'.[73]

Poynings did his best to track down Warbeck, but without any success. In August he sent John Staunton, on a spying expedition to Munster and elsewhere to try to locate Desmond and Warbeck but all he seems to have found were stories. So sometime in September Owenne Eton was sent from Waterford to Henry VII with letters about these.[74] Where Warbeck was between 3 August when the siege of Waterford was broken, and 20 November, when he entered Stirling Castle, no one knows. Seaan Burke, son of Ricard O'Cuairsge, was regarded as the most powerful man in Connaught over the country round Galway. If Warbeck withdrew from Waterford by land it is possible he went west to Tralee and took a ship from Tralee to Galway. Desmond was buried at Tralee. Where his remaining vessels went is a puzzle, but, at least one got news back to the Flemish court. From Galway Warbeck's men may have been guided to Hugh O'Donnell of Tirconnel by Burke's men. Possibly they stayed in Donegal castle before beginning on the last phase of their journey. But where did they leave Ireland from? The O'Donnells controlled the Foyle valley, in north-west Ulster. They may have embarked for Scotland in Lough Foyle.

News of Warbeck's fate reached Maximilian and Margaret of Burgundy by September 1495. Maximilian was engaged in the diplomacy of persuading England to enter the league against France. And in mid-August he stalled his negotiations in Italy to await the outcome of Warbeck's mission. By 16 August it was still not known who would be admitted to the league, Henry VII or Richard IV, as King of England. Three weeks later, at Worms Maximilian was informed that Warbeck had failed, and was on the run in Ireland pursued by Henry's men. When this news was relayed to him by a Neapolitan diplomat, 'His majesty listened without making reply.' On 19 September it was reported that Maximilian had been induced by the Pope, Ferdinand and Isabella of Spain, and other signatories to the league to admit Henry VII as named King of England as a member. But Maximilian would not give Warbeck up, and included in the negotiations a clause about the Duke of York which was so unpalatable to Henry VII that it delayed further English entry to the league.[75]

In the meantime Maximilian stepped up his eccentric support of Duke Richard. On 22 September he despatched Philibert Naturelli from Worms to Rome. In Rome Naturelli presented the Pope with Maximilian's reiteration of the demands of Margaret of Burgundy's May petition. Maximilian argued that as the Duke of York was Edward IV's second son he had excellent right, *optimo jus*, to the throne of England. Henry VII had obtained letters of excommunication against anyone disputing Tudor right to the throne. But these were frivolous because others – Richard – were thereby excluded from their right when the truth about his survival had been unknown. Thus as Margaret had argued, what was granted in error should be revoked so that supporters of York would no longer be under papal censure. Naturelli was received by the Pope on 18 October, and argued his petition orally as well presenting a document.[76] But Maximilian was still backing Warbeck with more than words. Three days before Philibert delivered his petition, Casius Hagkeney, Maximilian's argentinier wrote to him from Antwerp informing him that Margaret of Burgundy had just arrived in the town to raise artillery and supplies to send to Warbeck. Casius was ordered to co-operate with Margaret and raise the money necessary to arm the Prince.[76] But time was beginning to run out for Warbeck and his Flemish backers. On 23 October, five days after Maximilian's petition was received in Rome, the Flemish began to seek a way out of the crippling trade embargo designed to end their support for the so-called Duke of York.[77]

But just as one door began to close on Warbeck so another opened. The goal which the Duchess of Burgundy had pursued for years, active Scots involvement against England was suddenly realized. James IV's quest for a credible European image involved him turning his back on France, allying with Maximilian, courting the Plantagenet pretender and attempting to enter the Holy League, against France, on his own merit. To this end, in August 1495 he despatched Bishop Blackader to Spain to negotiate with Ferdinand and Isabella. Blackader arrived at Tarazona on 12 September. He delivered his master's offer: that he would break his alliance with Charles VIII, and his threat: that if he did not get what he wanted he would wreck the league by admitting Warbeck to Scotland and effectively stop any English involvement on continental Europe. The Spanish played for time. They made noises about putting Blackader forward for a cardinal's hat and bringing James within the league, and they suggested a Spanish embassy should return, with Blackader, to Scotland. This was a critical mistake. Blackader left Spain on 23 September and returned to Scotland, very quickly, on 14 October. The appointed ambassadors, Don Martin de Torre and Garcia de Herera travelled separately from Blackader, visiting England on the way. Their mail arrived in Scotland before they did and it was opened by James IV who then realized that the Spanish had no interest in Scotland and were deluding him in order to keep the peace between him and Henry VII in order to allow Henry to invade Brittany and strike at France.[78]

On 16 October a full meeting of the Scots council, forty or more, met in Edinburgh. Its business is unknown, but Norman Macdougall suggests only two lines of discussion: how to react to humiliation by the Spanish, and whether, now, to admit the Duke of York to Scotland. Macdougall adapts as a description of this council Polydore Vergil's description of the first council held in Scotland after Warbeck's arrival. What went on here we do not know. But the result was that Warbeck was admitted to Scotland, and the dating suggests that there may have been less of a debate in council than Macdougall allows.[79] To summon Warbeck from Ireland to Scotland without knowing his whereabouts would have taken longer than the two weeks which elapsed before he is first mentioned in Scottish documents. James wrote to Ferdinand and Isabella on 8 November urging them to consider an alliance with Scotland. By this date James had decided on his method to convince them that he should be treated seriously. Two days earlier he had begun to ready his reception for Warbeck, moving cupboards and arrases into Stirling castle.[80] Making preparations like these, two weeks before Warbeck arrived suggests that immediately after the council of 16 October messages were sent to Donegal or Galway. Whatever happened on 20 November Warbeck, Prince Richard of England, rode into Stirling with his closest advisers and his Flemish retinue.[81]

In England there had already been one security scare. In the September in which Warbeck disappeared in Ireland, the king and his council had ordered an inquisition on all Irish men, women and children within the realm. Particularly the City of London was scrutinized for possible traitors, and names, ages and occupations were enrolled at the exchequer.[82] Two days in advance of Warbeck's arrival at Stirling, on 18 November, Thomas Howard, Earl of Surrey, the king's lieutenant in the north arrayed all three ridings of Yorkshire against possible Scottish invasion.[83] Two weeks after Surrey had arrayed the north a discontented female servant in Nottingham accused an employer, who had kept her in service five days longer than he should have, of saying, in July 1495 when Warbeck had just withdrawn from Kent, that if the north rose in rebellion against the king his harness (body armour) was ready and he would support them.[84] This was dismissed as the malicious gossip it was. But it illustrates that the threat which Warbeck now represented was graver than at any time before.

The gravity of the threat can be measured in the months after Warbeck's landing at Deal.

Accounts of who was responsible for defeating Warbeck varied. According to the London Chronicles it was the commons of Kent, particularly Sandwich, a view backed up by the king's own words. He thanked Sandwich, in a letter which was read out to the assembled townsmen on 12 July. This letter 'greatly thanked [them] for theyr true servyces lately don Ayenst the kinges Rebellis'.[85] And so convinced was one London chronicler that he believed Sandwich alone had, with about 500 men beaten about 600 rebels. As we know, Sandwich was not alone, soldiers from Canterbury had been involved at Deal, and the king fulsomely thanked the mayor of Canterbury for defeating Warbeck's men and capturing those who fled after the fighting.[86] Henry VII had every reason for satisfaction, and in a letter of protest he sent to Philip the Fair's council made a point of telling them that Warbeck had been 'repelled by commons'.[87] The commons of Kent had been totally sceptical of Warbeck's claims. Whereas those captured on the beach affirmed that their leader was the second son of Edward IV the people of Kent said that 'The King [Warbeck] came, and he may go again to his father and mother who still live in France, and are well known.' They asserted as Gospel truth that Warbeck was no more genuine than Lambert Simnel. They mocked those they had captured, naming one of the captive captains Diego el Coxo, the Lame, whom Zurita may identify as a de Guevara.[88] However many they put down on the beach (and sources vary in their estimates of this) the numbers killed are generally put at about 150. One third of the 163 prisoners taken were English. Dr de Puebla, the Spanish ambassador to England estimated that eight captains were captured, and gave the names of Diego and Don Fulano de Guevara. The other rebel commanders identified were Henry Mountford, Richard White, John Belt, John Corbet, a French or Breton mercenary Captain Genyn and a Spanish mercenary, Quyntyne. When Belt met Sir John Paston's neighbour Robert Albon, of Great Yarmouth, at Canterbury he said he knew well that he was 'but a dead man' Belt's fellow captain John Corbet knew this too, and was determined to cheat the hangman. He refused to allow anyone to plaster his wounds with dressings and died in the Tower of London on 24 July.[89]

Cardinal Morton ordered the transport of all prisoners from Sandwich to London, by sea and land. Those walking were supervised by the sheriff of Kent, Sir John Pecche. They were put in halters supplied by the nearby towns, tied to thick cart ropes; as horses traced to draw a cart commented a chronicler. They arrived south of London Bridge on 12 July. Here they were transferred from Pecche's authority to that of the sheriff of London, and a tally made of numbers. Newgate received a quarter of their number, forty-two English rebels. The Tower of London received the remainder – some of the English rebels and a number of Flemish mercenaries who included a group of harquebusiers.[90] Molinet says that the men taken at Sandwich expected to be ransomed as war prizes. Instead they were treated as pirates. Legal process began at Deptford on 16 July with the indictment of Henry Mountford, John Belt, Richard Malory, and William Ashton amongst a group of 51 English rebels.[91] The verdict was a foregone conclusion so the trial was stopped when they confessed themselves worthy to die and threw themselves on the king's grace. In these circumstances no such thing was offered and every indicted man subsequently died. The foreign element had to wait eight days before they were led to Westminster and arraigned in the White Hall. They were all judged to be pirates and condemned to be hanged at a place assigned by the king and council then they were returned to Newgate gaol.[92]

These drumhead trials were interrupted by news from Ireland that Warbeck had landed there. In order to obtain more intelligence on his English supporters a group of nine rebels were transported to Nottingham castle for interrogation by the king.[93] They arrived in Nottingham on 22 July and may have been there for about a month while their and others' fates were sealed. On 17 August Henry examined a list of those Sir Thomas Lovell had

Rebels being hanged. The City of Canterbury accounts show payments to men for digging holes to erect the gallows, newly made, to hang Warbeck's adherents

already executed, as well as those whose execution he had postponed, with the reasons for postponement. It is possible that some picked up at this time informed to such a degree that they were reprieved. In October 1495 Robert Say, Nicholas Palmer and Anne Courtney were pardoned of all treasons.[94] But whatever Mountford, Belt, White, Captain Genyn and the others told Henry it bought them only a month's more life.

On 30 July all those condemned to death were sorted into groups for execution and sent to the coasts of Kent, Essex, Sussex, Norfolk and Suffolk to be hanged. The mayor of Canterbury was obliged to pay for six horses, halters and lines for a group whose execution he supervised. These men (six?) were taken to Sharpness Point in Kent. Here, brand new gallows were erected and the rebels hanged. All round the south-east of England on the beaches where they were executed their corpses remained 'Long afftyr'. But there was an escape. A group of condemned men on their way to the Essex coast stopped overnight at Chelmsford and the prisoners were lodged in a stable. One Englishman in the group escaped through the stable window and eventually found sanctuary in Westminster Abbey.[95] All this was well over when, on 4 September, Mountford, Belt, White and Genyn returned to London. They had progressed with Henry to Fotheringhay from where they were sent south. Three days after they reached London the Spaniard Quyntyne, Genyn and Belt were marched from where they had been imprisoned, Newgate, to Tower Hill and beheaded. Their heads were then displayed on London Bridge for a long time. Mountford and White are not accounted for by the events in London. A Coventry annal records the execution there of Henry Mountford and another conspirator.[96] Still, though, the process of public warning was not over. On 12 September six Dutch rebels were transported through the city to Tyburn and hanged. The same day four more Dutchmen were led to Wapping on the Wose, at the east end of St Katherine's wharf. This was the usual place for hanging pirates and sea rovers. The normal punishment for such men was to be hanged at low watermark. Thus it was that this last reported group of the Deal rebels, four Flemish captains, were taken and hanged in the water 'Soo that at every ffull See the watyr fflowid ovyr theym and theyr Gebett', for the passage of three tides.[97]

TEN

A War of Nerves

Perkin Warbeck's arrival in Scotland marks the zenith of his imposture. At the court of England's ancient enemy, Warbeck fulfilled his potential as an actor. He dissolved into his role so impeccably that he was able to mimic a dynastic marriage. Warbeck's ability to be Richard Plantagenet and like a maestro break convention, and jump beyond where he had been before to marry Lady Katherine Gordon may explain his success. But by now did he or his masters know where actor ended and the man began? They were breaking new ground. On the day of his arrival at Stirling, 20 November 1495, James IV despatched letters summoning his lords and barons of Strathearn, Athol, the Mearns and Angus to meet the king and Prince Richard in Perth. The sheriffs of more remote parts of the kingdom were ordered to hold 'wappinschowings' musters of arms. At about the same time James authorized an annual pension of £1,344, and rewarded Pouwels Saftleven of Amsterdam, exporter of woollen cloths to Edinburgh, and financier of Yorkist rebels by remitting his customs dues 'ad requestam Ricardi ducis Eboraci'.[1] Two weeks after he arrived in Scotland Warbeck and James were together on St Nicholas's day, 6th December, making offerings and shortly after Warbeck and his household went north with James to lodge at Methven and Perth during a meeting of the Scottish council.[2]

There is no contemporary account of this meeting, but Polydore Vergil created one, perhaps, not very far from the truth. Warbeck publicly pleaded for support for his cause from James. If this happened Warbeck was playing in character with well-rehearsed lines, used over and over again: in Flanders, in Austria, in Ireland. Even the fears and elations of the journey from Malines to Stirling would have helped him sound more convincing. I was 'saved from death by the intervention of divine providence. My father Edward when dying appointed as guardian of his sons his brother . . .' This was a story known everywhere in Europe. When 'suddenly the cruel tyrant, seized with ambition to be king, ordered my brother and me to be killed together. However, the man to whom had been given the unspeakable task of murdering the wretched innocents that we were, loathed the abominable deed as much as he greatly feared to disobey. Being thus in two minds, he thought to fulfil the tyrant's commands while at the same time avoiding all the guilt by murdering my brother and preserving me, whom he allowed to escape from the country accompanied by but one servant. Thus Richard possessed the kingdom as the profit of his crime. I, indeed, for a time oblivious of my history, thereafter wandered for long in different countries.' At last he arrived at the court of his aunt, the widow of Charles, Duke of Burgundy, 'who received me with the greatest joy, as one raised from the dead'. This was the tale whch had startled and amazed Europe four years before. Now in view of the Intercursus Magnus all his loyal aunt had left was her dower lands, 'so that I still need the help of someone else in recovering my kingdom'. It was a story which never failed, sentimental and incredible: a fairy story, a horror story, a detective story all rolled into one.

James IV, King of Scotland

Vergil says that after Warbeck was finished James's council met. Some nobles said that this was a ruse of Margaret of Burgundy, and Warbeck should not be trusted. Others felt the facts were not proven, but that Scotland might reap advantage from the situation by supporting him, whoever he was. They might win territory or at least make an advantageous treaty with England. The former position smacks too much of Vergil to be completely true, the latter of sanitized hindsight. But, according to Vergil it was after this debate, 'the King, either genuinely misled or pretending to be convinced, began to call Peter "Richard Duke of York"; and so that all might be persuaded of his good faith he gave him a relative as a wife, Katherine, daughter of George Earl of Huntly . . .'[3] Again we need not believe Vergil's apparent objectivity. Warbeck could be completely convincing in this role. He convinced Margaret of Burgundy, in 1493. He convinced Maximilian later the same year, and he himself said that he duped James IV.[4] The reasons Vergil gives for the marriage alliance are very similiar to those given by Bernard André. André took pains to state that the marriage only took place because Warbeck's masters were doubtful of James's commitment to them and wanted some tangible proof that they were more than a pawn in an Anglo-Scottish game.[5] 'This having been done' says Vergil, telescoping events, 'they deliberated on war', probably on the understanding that help would be forthcoming from Ireland, Maximilian I, Philip the Fair and Margaret of Burgundy. It is conceivable, in the never-never politics of James and his Flemish supporters, that Taylor and Warbeck's masters believed once more that their quest for a summer action on three fronts was about to be realized. But until the peculiarily harsh winter of 1495–6 was over that would have to wait. Warbeck remained James's feted guest.

In the first three months of his residence Warbeck and James were rarely apart; having decided on a course of action at Perth, on 23 December, James and Warbeck finally summoned the Spanish ambassadors de Torre and de Herera to them for an audience. They were met in the gardens of Stirling castle and treated to a torrent of abuse about Henry VII and Spain. James had seen their instructions. He knew their position. It was expected that the Scots could be manipulated by the Spanish ambassadors who were little more than tools of the English king. Once James's tirade was over he did not dismiss the ambassadors. Instead they were obliged to remain with Warbeck and James as they decamped from Stirling castle to Linlithgow Palace.[6] At Linlithgow Warbeck undertook some public duties, witnessing a Scottish charter which describes him as the most excellent Richard Plantagenet son of the one-time most illustrious Prince Edward.[7]

In January 1496 James and Prince Richard left Linlithgow for Edinburgh. There, on or about 13 January 1496 Prince Richard's marriage to Katherine Gordon was celebrated. This marriage was a calculated insult to Henry VII's Scottish policy. Given that it took place a month and a half after Warbeck arrived in Scotland it may have been negotiated prior to this even, perhaps, in Ireland. Such political alliances allowed no place for feeling. Yet in the Spanish archives there is a curious letter which lays a claim to have been written by Warbeck to Katherine Gordon.[8] We need not believe that it represents anything of reality to find it of interest. It is not inconceivable that Warbeck penned it himself. All our sources agree he was personable and intelligent. On the other hand the style is so conventional that it might have come from a book on the etiquette of wooing rather than from an individual. Then, again, this is what Lady Katherine would have expected. Young people began their letter writing copying from letter patterns. The writer, the Prince of Wales, tells his beloved, 'the brightest ornament in Scotland' that she is admired for her lineage and rank and because of her beauty which is divine. Thus some 'believe that you are not born in our days, but descended from

Tomb of Katherine Gordon with her fourth husband Christopher Ashton, Fyfield, Berkshire, c. 1537. Due to a nineteenth-century fire all that remains is a matrix where once was a monumental brass

Heaven'. The physical attributes of the reader are praised, not an exacting task if the letter was to Lady Katherine since all reports agree she was a considerable beauty, 'your eyes . . . your neck . . . your fine forehead . . . Whether waking or sleeping, I cannot find rest or happiness except in your affection. All my hopes rest in you and you alone . . . Most noble lady, my soul, look mercifully down upon me your slave, who has been devoted to you from the first hour he saw you.' Is this Warbeck the actor, the prince of imposters, writing a letter himself? Or was it dictated to him? If purely a political matter it shows how successful Taylor and Atwater were when they picked him up in Cork in 1491. But again we come against the duality inherent in the Warbeck story. If not dictated, perhaps it was freely composed, to order. It is Bacon who says that to all her other virtues Katherine Gordon added love of her husband, Perkin. So was he really wooing, as the letter says. Or, since we are hypothesizing here, perhaps he was seeking simple seduction in an attempt to cast off Richard of England in the oblivion of the sexual act; a relief from the endless chameleon shifts of persona. Most certainly this letter is nothing like the one Warbeck wrote two years later when, as a broken man, he begged his mother for money, succour, and aid.

In January 1496 Warbeck's wedding clothes, a white 'spousing goune', black hose and velvet coat, were paid for by James IV. The wedding was followed by celebrations and a tournament, during which James provided gowns for his six servants and two trumpeters. The tournament was the conventional celebration, Scotland against Burgundy, it's new ally, gazumped from England. James himself jousted, was wounded on the hand and then bandaged up with silk. He was supported by Sir Robert Ker, Patrick Hume, Patrick Haliburton and William Sinclair. Prince Richard's side was led by Rodigue de Lalaing and his brother. According to Jean Molinet, Rodigue 'did not fight any joust or feat of arms where he did not win great honour'.[9] This anodyne remark hides a proper description of the jousts, so we do not know if Prince Richard took part in them, or indeed if he could joust. We do know that James presented him with a suit of armour covered with purple damask in honour of the celebration, and as a boy Warbeck would have seen jousts in Tournai. Once the celebrations were over, Warbeck, his new bride and entourage travelled with James to his hunting palace at Falkland, in Fife. While this may have been in the nature of a nuptial progress, it also had a political purpose, for until they were expelled from Scotland in December 1497 the Yorkists used Falkland as a base.[10] It was well inland, and protected from attack, but was within easy reach of the North Sea and Edinburgh. In mid-March James IV returned to Stirling and remained there over Easter (3 April). By now James's intention to invade England was well broadcast. At the middle or end of April messages were sent throughout Scotland to summon military tenants to a meeting at Lauder, a place dangerously near the English border. The object of this exercise was to restate the Scotish intention to take Berwick. To his guest this was the price of James's help. To stop war Henry VII would have to outbid Warbeck's masters. But despite any amount of talk this year to stop, war preparations for what became the raid of Ellem were long and unstoppable. They began after the king's council at Lauder when James ordered £80 to be paid to John Sandilands of Hillhouse as a 'fee for the kingis artilzery'.[11]

Is this credible though, that Scotland was going to war on behalf of Perkin Warbeck? Norman Macdougall is convinced that it is highly unlikely that James IV believed in Warbeck as a Plantagenet. Others were cynical, and Macdougall argues that, for example, too much has been made of the Gordon wedding. He points out that Katherine Gordon was not a close relative of James but linked indirectly to the royal family by a series of remarriages. Katherine Gordon was distantly related to the king because her father, George, Earl of Huntly, had once been married to the king's great-aunt Annabella. She was in fact no more than the earl's third daughter by a subsequent marriage. Warbeck, he argues, was the servant of James's diplomacy. He was tolerated in Scotland only as long as he enabled James to exert pressure on Spain and England to get what he wanted: a marriage alliance and the resumption of Berwick, and in order to enable a prince emerging from the tutelage of a council of minority to play the part of a successful king.[12] Yet in 1495 James and Warbeck had much in common. They were the same age, James was born in 17 March 1473 and Warbeck within twelve months of this. Both stood on the threshold of maturity. Both, ostensibly, had lost fathers while relatively young. Both were about to come into their kingdoms: James by assuming rule at the age of majority, Warbeck by restoration rights in England. Warbeck offered James IV a huge amount: the possibility of atoning for his guilt about his father's death by helping one in a similar position; the possibility of uniting his realm in a first military venture against the old enemy – England; the reconquest of lost territory – Berwick; and the possibility of reorienting Anglo-Scottish affairs to his own advantage, either by the successful outcome of his support for Warbeck, or by being bought off by Henry Tudor. Like Maximilian, James may have had ridiculously grandiose ambitions, believing that if the Duke of York was successful he would fulfil them 'ad libitum sum'.

The problem for Henry VII was twofold, how to deal with Warbeck in Scotland, and how to isolate him from his European support. It was never easier than in 1496 for the Yorkists to communicate with supporters in England, and to organize for rebellion. Henry stepped up his intelligence gathering. Berwick acted as his eyes and ears. In October and December the spy-cum-merchant Edward Coke supplied him with information. In November and December Sir William Tyler, Lieutenant of Berwick sent one of his servants into Scotland, and in February gave a priest £1, undoubtedly as a reward for spying. A Picard, a favourite English instrument of espionage since they could pass as French, went into Scotland in March, and one named spy, Thomas Scotte, was sent to Scotland at the beginning of January from Ireland and another, unnamed Scot, was rewarded in March.[13] The news these men brought resulted in the refurbishment of England's northern and border defences in March 1496.

Warbeck's isolation from Europe and his forced capitulation was never convincingly dealt with. When, on 9 July 1495, he had written to Philip the Fair's council in Flanders, Henry struck a note of compromise. Though he protested to the Flemish council about its aid to Warbeck, he stressed mutuality of interest. His letter gave them a brief account of Warbeck's failure and asked for help in informing Maximilian. Henry professed himself amazed that he had received a secret message from Maximilian which greatly touched his honour. He returned the letter (which has not survived) and at the same time gave one of the archduke's archers, possibly a prisoner of war, £4, perhaps to act as a courier.[14] This offer of an olive branch when it might have been an English raid resulted in the resumption of trade between England and Flanders. Commercial pressure inside Flanders to end the interdict was becoming irresistible. So too was Maximilian's desire to produce a workable Holy League which would declare war on France. It was also assumed, in December 1495, that Philip the Fair's impending marriage to the Dona Joanna, daughter to Ferdinand and Isabella would give the Spanish much more influence in Flanders and offset Margaret of Burgundy's power. To begin normalizing relations in October 1495 between England and Flanders, Philip sent a top-ranking embassy consisting of the Sovereign of Flanders, the Seigneur de Bevres, Artois King of Arms, and his counsellor Jehan de Courteville, to England in October 1495. By the beginning of November, the main points at issue were relayed to Brussels and a larger more powerful embassy was got ready. This consisted of the original negotiating team and Paul de Baenst, president of the Flemish council, Florence Hanweel one of Maximilian's secretaries, Robert de Melun, Monsieur d'Interville, a counsellor Thomas Fortarini, and others. Their laborious work meant numerous journeys back and forth to Brussels, and between 23 December and 13 March Corneille Piat was co-opted to work between England and

Flanders. Finally on 11 February a bundle of letters was despatched to England: the final negotiating instructions.[15]

These negotiations were only one of a number Henry VII was conducting to neutralize Warbeck. In mid-November 1495 he sent Sir John Egremont to Nordlingen near Augsburg, to confer with Maximilian. Egremont was sent to Maximilian on the Emperor's request to clarify whether even with some degree of support for Warbeck from Maximilian Henry VII could be persuaded to ally with the emperor in the Holy League, and declare war on France. It was believed by Spain that Maximilian had been glad to rid himself of Warbeck in July 1495, and that he would shortly give him up in order to bring Henry into the Holy League so as to facilitate a joint attack on France from Spain, Burgundy and England. Egremont arrived in Nordlingen on 31 December 1495 as, 'a man of not much repute', judged so because he had only ten horses with him. On 4 January 1496 Egremont met Maximilian and began by enquiring about the viability of the league in the face of recent French diplomatic activity. He was fobbed off by Maximilian and responding to felicitations sent to him by Henry, Maximilian told Egremont that he, Maximilian, had no alliance with Henry his master. On the contrary, said Maximilian, he considered it his duty to support the Duke of York, because York had appealed to him for succour. Should Henry enter the league he would expect an immediate declaration of war on France and in such case he, Maximilian, would then negotiate a ten-year truce between Tudor and York. The league ambassadors gathered at Nordlingen listened in great embarrassment to this. They wanted England in the league and there was much debate as to how to persuade Maximilian to modify his position. Their greatest fear was that England and France would ally together, and that the league would collapse. Maximilian's savage diplomacy was tantamount to telling Egremont that England was excluded from the league. Henry would be insulted by mention of Warbeck, and would see this as a way out of attacking France. These sentiments were reinforced by the Venetian ambassador who said Maximilian should drop Warbeck 'as this was not the moment for disturbing the kingdom of England'. After prolonged discussion Maximilian and his council agreed to drop the references to Warbeck but insisted that Henry attacked France. They believed that there was no hope of this coming to fruition, but without dropping the promise to arbitrate between York and Tudor, which Maximilian had wanted written into the league a harder bargain might have been driven by England, and Maximilian would have been forced into total renunciation of his support for Warbeck.[16]

John Egremont was sent back to England bearing not Maximilian's first response, support of Warbeck, but with an expression of how gratified the emperor was by Henry's salutations. Of old they were common enemies of France and their two countries – Burgundy and England – were ancient allies. All the European powers wished Henry to join the league, and in answer to the precise terms under which Henry might join the league Maximilian sent him two sets of instructions: one with Egremont, the other through Philip the Fair's ambassadors then in England. On 6 January, the day he heard all this, Egremont left Nordlingen with a gold cup and 100 florins to take this news to Henry. When Egremont reached England late in March 1496 Henry was well pleased with the outcome of his mission.[17] Coupled with what his commissioners in London had achieved with Philip the Fair's ambassadors, Warbeck seemed to have been deprived of all European support. But this was a delusion. Before Egremont was back in England Maximilian had changed his mind. On 19 February he told Venice's ambassador to his court, Zacharia Contarini, that the Duke of York had written to him stating that he was prospering and that because of the recent disturbances in England there was a possibility of recovering his throne. Maximilian said that since the duke had undertaken this enterprise at his behest, it would be most unfortunate if he withdrew his support because Henry VII was desired in the league and the Duke of York did not obtain the

Philip the Fair, Duke of Burgundy

English Crown. Indeed with York on the throne England would be more inclined to join the league not less. Contarini reminded Maximilian that the possibility of an English alliance with France was very real, and that the league had much to gain from friendship with Henry VII. None the less, Maximilian replied, he would wait for news from Philip the Fair's ambassadors in England before finally making his mind up about support for the Duke of York.[18]

Members of the Flemish delegation in London, de Bevres and Paul de Baenst, had been commissioned by Maximilian to negotiate with Henry about both the Holy League and the Duke of York. On 25 January Maximilian had instructed Corneille de Berghes, his ambassador to Philip the Fair, to press Margaret of Burgundy to force the Duke of York to conclude a truce with the King of England. He in his turn would try to persuade the members of the league to pay the duke an annual pension, and would guarantee his neutrality. But as de Bevres and de Baenst reported at the end of the negotiations in England, they had not dared to mention Warbeck's name to Henry. As for war with France – invasion of Brittany – this was quite out of the question while Warbeck was in Scotland.[19]

The treaty which England and Flanders signed on 28 February 1496 was important in ending a damaging trade war and restoring relations between two former allies. But though much has been claimed for the uniqueness of the Intercursus Magnus it was typical of Henry VII's diplomacy. In every important treaty negotiated, with Spain and France, in 1488 and 1492, and in the future, with Scotland and Maximilian in 1497 and 1504, Henry included clauses against the Yorkist rebels. This treaty was no different from the rest. Flanders and England became allies, and as such swore not to permit rebels of either to stay in the dominions of the other, but to expel them within fifteen days. Despite the fact that the treaty took the unprecedented step of naming the Duchess of Burgundy, describing her military support by land and sea for Warbeck, and threatening punitive measures against her for non-compliance with its terms it could achieve very little quickly. The trade provisions themselves opened up ten years of quibbling and recrimination. Margaret's position in Flanders was so unassailable, and her friendship with Maximilian so sound, that despite the Intercursus Magnus, Warbeck still had friends in Flanders.[20]

Within days of having achieved this agreement Henry set out to undermine these friends. It was his intention to enter the league against France, and to use Spanish help to force Maximilian to back away from his support of Warbeck. His leverage on Spain was a public flirtation with France. Just after Warbeck's landing Henry had received Picard Herald in embassy from Charles VIII of France.[21] Picard or possibly one of the other messengers Henry received from France over the winter, relayed to Henry, Charles VIII's offer that if should James IV act in any way prejudicially to Henry he, Charles, would declare himself the enemy of Scotland.[22] Flirting thus Henry hoped he would deprive Warbeck of support from Scotland and Flanders. In January the league ambassadors were said to be fearful of what this French embassy sent to England would achieve but it left at the end of February after fruitless discussions about the possibility of hiring English troops. On 5 March Richmond Herald was instructed for a mission to France. He was to discuss a projected meeting between Charles VIII and Henry, a marriage between Margaret Tudor and the Dauphin, and also, possibly, one between Prince Arthur and a Bourbon princess. Financial matters, the Étaples Pension and loans were also on the agenda. But these matters were a cover for the real reason for Richmond's visit; to tell Charles VIII that Henry had hard intelligence that James IV intended to attack England and recover Berwick, and call on Charles to fulfil his offer of the previous year to act against Scotland. Richmond was also to make a private embassy to one of Louis XI's old commanders, Guillaume Briçonnet, now Cardinal Bishop of St Malo. Briçonnet was to be informed that there was no doubt that the

Scots would attack England in 1496 and told that the Duke of Orleans had said to Sir Charles Somerset, Henry's ambassador, that should the Scots threaten England, Charles VIII would allow Henry VII access to the Duke of Albany. John Stewart, the duke, was the the nine-year-old, orphan son of Alexander, Duke of Albany. Alexander was James III's brother, the man used in his 1483 war by Edward IV as a Scottish pretender. Now Henry VII informed the French, 'No other prince could so well help the Duke of Albany to secure his rights against James IV of Scotland as Henry himself and he would treat him well, as befitted his rank, so that the king of France would be happy.' Should this be done Henry would be 'generally obliged' to Charles. What Warbeck was doing for James IV, Henry VII would do for Albany. Nothing came of this suggestion, nor is it clear whether Henry was making a real offer to France, or a sending a private signal to the French not to interfere with pretenders in England's affairs.[23]

By March 1495 Henry VII's diplomacy was strained. So, in response to Maximilian's invitation to explore whether a declaration of war on France would end Maximilian's support of Warbeck, Henry sent Christopher Urswick, his almoner and a talented diplomat, to Augsburg. But the choice of Urswick was a mistake even before he got there because Maximilian held a grudge against Urswick. Before he arrived in Augsburg Maximilian's council had decided Henry VII would probably remain outside the league. His Latin secretary, Ludovico Bruno, a supporter of the Yorkists told Zacharia Contarini that Henry had only sent an embassy out of fear that York was supported by Maximilian, or that Warbeck would find support from the French. Contarini astutely countered that to give up Warbeck would mean that Henry would join the league if only to spite France. By now there was a great deal of pressure on Maximilian and Henry to compromise about Warbeck, so much so that Maximilian had ceded power to the Spanish ambassador in England to negotiate for him. He would compromise, but he would not be seen to abandon York. Urswick arrived in Augsburg on 16 April 1496, amid much flattering ceremony. Wisely he refused any discussion until after he had conferred with the emperor. The emperor's arrival on 6 May signalled the start of intensive discussion at the beginning of which Urswick made clear to Contarini that though Henry VII considered the French to be England's greatest and oldest enemy nevertheless he was compelled to guard against Warbeck in Scotland. Though Scotland was poor she had formidable forces and was linked to France by an 'indisoluble understanding'. A week later Maximilian had Urswick interviewed by three of his councillors, and talked to Urswick, twice. After this it was given out as Maximilian's conclusion that Urswick 'was merely come to spy, and investigate the projects of the King about the League and the Duke of York'. Henry VII had no intention of breaking with France, and wished merely to enter the league without having to wage war on France.

Having delivered himself of this judgement Maximilian asked the assembled ambassadors what he should do. Should he show Urswick he disapproved, or should he dissemble and dismiss him with flattery. In the discussions which followed the ambassadors once again reminded Maximilian that the purpose of these negotiations was to bring England into the league against France. Privately Urswick confessed to Contarini that Henry did not see how he could wage war on France. He was virtually at war with Scotland, had bad relations with Denmark and was plagued by the Duke of York and rebels in Ireland. After a week of inconclusive discussion between all parties Urswick finally confronted Maximilian with the unpalatable truth of Henry's difficulties. He rubbed salt in the wound by saying that he saw no reason why Henry should go to war with France as he was the last to join this league, of which only Spain was at war with France. For himself, he said, doubtless having been instructed so to put it, he thought the discussions meaningless because there were no practicalities under discussion: troop numbers, length of war, etc., etc. This effectively terminated the negotiations. Maximilian told the league ambassadors that he had decided on further discussions in England and to offer to negotiate some form of agreement between James IV, Henry VII and the Duke of York, if Henry bound himself to attack France. The gathered ambassadors declined to offer advice, and Maximilian concluded by saying that he knew Urswick of old. He had been responsible for a previous diplomatic incident which had led to Henry abandoning a promise to attack France. Thus stalemate. Urswick could go home. Maximilian would not send an ambassador to Henry until the affair between him and York was over, nor would he attack France. Only when Henry joined the league would he patch up his difficulties with Henry. This allowed Maximilian to escape the embarrassing admission that he could not pay for a war against France, preserved his support for Warbeck intact, and placed the onus for peace in Britain squarely on the Spanish. When Urswick returned to England he reported so to Henry, that 'He has not seen the least preparation for war against France, but has seen a great many of the party of him of York; and of the Duchess Margaret, especially an Italian who is latin secretary to the King of Romans and who has great influence over him. Don Ladron (de Guevara) whom he met there has made the same observation. The King of Romans still seems very ill disposed towards Henry and is keeping up connections with the King of Scots and him who is now staying there.'[24]

But peace in Britain was beyond the ability of Spain to conclude, though the very bulk of the Spanish diplomatic papers sometimes suggests otherwise. Reading them we are confronted with a system of diplomacy which, due to chance and the vagaries of the elements, worked unsystematically. Ferdinand and Isabella had ringed their French enemy with ambassadors, Juan de Fonseca and Jayme de Albion with Maximilian, Rodrigo Gonsalves de Puebla in England, and Francisco de Rojas in Flanders. These men (and de Herera and de Torre) in Scotland were expected to broker peace between all parties, and terminate the Warbeck adventures.[25] Until the middle of the year they held the erroneous belief that Maximilian had given Warbeck up, and that if they could obtain Warbeck they could persuade Henry to declare war on France. The French ambassadors to England had implied to Henry that Ferdinand of Aragon was partially behind Warbeck, and they spread rumour and distortion about Spain and her allies. In England de Puebla was told to do all he could to counteract the French influence. At the beginning of 1496 de Puebla was commissioned to revive negotiations between England and Spain for the marriage between Catherine of Aragon and Prince Arthur. And at the same time it was hoped that they would secure an alliance between Scotland and England in which the papacy might arbitrate. At one stage, in the spring, when de Puebla indicated that he thought the Warbeck problem could be solved if the Duke of York was enticed to Spain, he was told that 'we shall not entice him', but that if he could somehow manage it so much the better. In Flanders de Rojas had been deputed powers by Maximilian to negotiate with England, and Ferdinand and Isabella expected him and de Puebla to keep Flemish and English affairs running smoothly. De Puebla was to keep Rojas fully informed of English politics and Rojas was ordered to do everything he could to prevent Margaret of Burgundy aiding Warbeck and harming Henry.[26]

It was in their endeavours to create peace between England and Scotland that the Spanish were at their most inventive. At Easter 1496 Garcia de Herera and James's ambassador Bishop Blackader left Scotland for Spain to negotiate a marriage between James and a Spanish princess. In return for a Spanish princess James would conclude a treaty of perpetual peace with England, and guarantee that Henry VII would have no further trouble from the Duke of York. The Spanish had no daughter to marry to James. One, Isabella was refusing to marry. One, Maria was to marry to Portugal, and one, Catherine was to marry Arthur Tudor. None the less Spain wanted peace, so for much of the spring Bishop Blackader was left kicking his heels at Soria and later pursuing a protracted negotiation about a non-existent

Ferdinand of Aragon (kneeling left) and Isabella of Castille (kneeling right)

daughter, the sole purpose of which was to keep the peace between Scotland and England, while de Puebla bribed Henry VII to war with France by a marriage alliance with Spain. By the end of April Ferdinand and Isabella advised de Puebla that they considered Catherine's marriage and their alliance to Henry all but concluded and therefore English affairs were as important to them as their own. The alliance was to be concluded as swiftly as de Puebla could manage and a new ambassador would be sent to Scotland in order to conclude a peace between the two countries. In Scotland James raised the stakes. Despite having given an undertaking not to move against England until his Bishop Blackader's return he called a muster throughout Scotland to meet at Lauder. By late spring the initiative began to slip from the Spanish. A new ambassador to Scotland, Pedro de Ayala was to be sent to James in order to deceive him further and maintain the peace, and at the same time Garcia de Herera in Scotland was instructed to work for James's inclusion in the league and to produce a peace between the two countries. But when Blackader and de Ayala returned to Scotland the deceit was known. There was no daughter of Spain to marry James, nor would there be any peace.[27]

Elsewhere the Spanish were in trouble. At the beginning of June it emerged that de Rojas had failed to stop the machinations of Margaret of Burgundy, and had been bribed or corrupted by her.[28] The French had become more actively involved in England and Scotland and were promising to Henry that they could deliver Warbeck to him, either from France or over the border, from Scotland. To this end they were readying an embassy to Scotland and making a fine offer to marry a Bourbon princess to Arthur.[29] By June and July Ferdinand and Isabella were reduced to making vague promises that they would induce the Pope to use his authority against the Duke of York, and that when their daughter Joanna married Philip the Fair they would have enough influence in Flanders to cut off all support to Warbeck from that quarter.[30]

By 10 July Isabella of Castille wrote a hysterical tirade against France. She reproached de Puebla, 'because we know that you have more capacity than [our other ambassadors]', for his failure to obtain a promise of an English attack on France. Next month she suggested that only thing which stopped Henry declaring war on France were his financial worries. These could be overcome with the grant of a papal crusade in England. Taxes would be gathered in England and then divided half and half between Rome and England. The Pope might even be content with a third of the cash. But de Puebla could not work miracles. Much as Isabella suggested that her ambassador was exaggerating the Scottish threat, de Puebla knew the reality. After Urswick's return from Augsburg there was no possibility of an English declaration of war against France. With months' delays between the despatches and receipt of reports, fifteenth-century diplomacy was too ill developed to stop the war. As Isabella fulminated, all de Puebla could do was recommend that she either conclude the Anglo-Spanish alliance without a clause regarding war with France or that no alliance at all should be concluded. Regarding the league Henry was about to join it with no obligation to war, or to pay for a war with France. This he did in Rome on the 18 July 1496.[31]

Reading the vast bulk of diplomatic papers generated by the Perkin Warbeck affair one is tempted to agree that Perkin Warbeck never served Henry VII better than as an excuse to keep himself free from foreign entanglement. Such a view can be held so long as we deal only in the intentions of diplomats. But if we leave the diplomatic papers behind in preference for war finance or the personal finances of the king a different picture emerges: of a conflict being played out on a number of different levels, of which diplomacy is the most evident. By the spring of 1496 there had already been one emergency in England, November 1495, and in reaction to James IV's threats at Lauder, Henry VII ordered the muster and array of Sussex, Kent, Surrey, Worcester, Lindsey and Kesteven, Hampshire, Derby, Stafford, and the Cinque Ports for the defence of Berwick. Though the muster was not recorded until 23 April there had been much activity in the previous month.[32] On 20 March the mayors of Newcastle, York and Berwick were sent letters from the king, probably about raising soldiers to defend the north. The main English ports were put on standby, from Hull all the way, via King's Lynn, Yarmouth, Dover, Sandwich, Southampton and Dartmouth to Plymouth. Letters were sent also to the principal towns in Kent and Hampshire as well as to the Lord Treasurer, John Lord Dynham, possibly about finance, and to the Earls of Suffolk, Shrewsbury, Arundell and Devon, and the Marquis of Dorset, probably to commission them to defend their localities.[33] Slowly but surely the military machinery in England was being ratcheted up for defence against Scotland.

Still the diplomacy ground on. At least six months before Warbeck was established in Scotland the possibility of James IV marrying Margaret Tudor had been raised. On 20 March Henry wrote to Richard Fox, Bishop of Durham and on 5 May, commissioning him and his most trusted lieutenants in the north, William Siver, Bishop of Carlisle and the Earl of Surrey, to open negotiations for the espousal of James and Margaret.[34] This was a promising move, at face value. It was also a prize of such importance that it might have detached James from Warbeck. Yet in 1496 James would not take what, after war, the following year he was pleased to accept. Part of the problem lay in the fashion that James had been treated by Anglo-Spanish diplomacy. Having negotiated for a non-existent Spanish daughter because Spain wished to keep Warbeck from invading England he was doubtless in no mood to believe the seriousness of Henry's offers. While James was twenty-two when negotiations were first mentioned, Margaret Tudor was six years old. Indeed as late as 1498 rumours circulated that Henry sought a marriage for her in Denmark.[35] Yet Henry put considerable effort into persuading James he was serious. He renewed the commission twice in 1496, on 23 June and as late as 2 September. And he received James IV's Lyon Herald on progress at Beaulieu in high summer, 15 July. Lyon was in the company of Henry's Scottish agent John Lord Bothwell, who was presently serving Bishop Fox.[36] What this visit was about we do not know. Given Bothwell's presence it may have been back-door diplomacy to find a formula to ditch Warbeck and revoke his guarantees of safe conduct by James IV. Possibly James's price for this was too high. In any case, by the summer matters were too far gone for such a deal.

Though James had called a 'meeting' at Lauder in April and laid out money for his artillery at the same time it was only in July that the decision was taken to prepare in earnest for a war. Bearing in mind that medieval warfare was seasonal if James intended only a 'diplomatic' show of force to rescue Berwick, let alone a campaign within the year, he had to commit himself by July. There had been no full-blooded war with England since 1482, and none in his reign, therefore a complete overhaul of ordnance was ordered on 1 July. On the same day (1 July), close carts to carry shot and ammunition began to be made at Edinburgh, and five days later James ordered ordnance spears to be made at Perth. Since James himself intended leading a large host into England, 4 July saw the first of many payments for the construction of pavilions and his siege tents, supervised by his palace staff. On 5 July the creation of a Scottish artillery train began in earnest, and throughout July huge quantities of iron were cast as shot and guns in Edinburgh Castle. In the 'Kings Wark', at Leith, new guns were made and gunchambers cast while others were retrieved from Sir Andrew Wood's ship *The Flower*. The preparations advanced rapidly. On 19 July James's gunner, Hans, was put in wage at £2, the first of many such payments, while by 30 July the canvasses on which gunpowder was dried were ready for use.[37]

War preparations were well advanced on both sides of the border. John Ramsay, Lord Bothwell was being employed in Scotland and Berwick in an extraordinary capacity as a collector of intelligence: to negotiate with the Yorkist party, to negotiate with James and the Scottish nobility, in fact to do anything to prevent the outbreak of the war. His employment was typical of the intelligence war already joined by James IV and Henry VII. In mid-April Henry rewarded the constable of Shoreditch £1 for bringing an 'Espie' to him, presumably one of James IV's men, possibly Warbeck's, if he was English. At the beginning of May he spent £19 1s 9d on armour for his Scottish spy Henry Steele, and a few days later, rewarded an unnamed 'scott' 10s. A month later, on 10 June in a singular reminder of the dangers confronting him with rebels in both Ireland and Scotland he rewarded a Manxman £1. It is possible that this man was not a spy, simply a Manxman in Thomas Stanley, Earl of Derby's employ, since the Stanleys were Kings of Man.[38]

However, it is notable that in the first week of May a group of Warbeck's men led, probably, by John Taylor and the so-called Dene of York crossed from Ayr, on the west coast of Scotland, to Ireland. The identity of the Dene is not known, but he is always found mentioned in conjunction with Taylor or Rowland Robinson, the two people who ran Warbeck. The destination and purpose of these men, whom James IV laid out £40 for, is not known either. Possibly they were not going far, only to Hugh O'Donnell of Tirconnel in Donegal, since he controlled the best native troops in Ireland: gallowglasses[39]. Possibly they were striking further south, through Seaan Burke's territory to Desmond-controlled Munster. The Earl of Desmond had been reconciled to Henry VII in the previous March (1496). Taylor, with his Atwater contact still in Cork might have been attempting to subvert this important step to barring Ireland to Warbeck by urging Desmond to renounce his new loyalty to Henry, perhaps in conjunction with the projected Scottish expedition. Whatever the purpose of their visit Taylor and the Dene returned to Scotland a month later through Ayr and Irvine. Their expenses were met, 100 crowns were paid to Rowland Robinson[40], and it is just conceivable that these movements were reported to the king from the Isle of Man. At the same time as this visit to Ireland took place, 2 May, Warbeck's Flemish commander Rodigue de Lalaing was presented with a ship bought for him from John Delphin and Guillaum Bucter by James IV. Thereafter we know that his brother remained in Scotland, and was bought hose, gown and doublet, by the king while Rodigue returned to Flanders to purchase armaments and hire mercenaries for the forthcoming war.[41] The familiar elements, Ireland, Burgundy and Scotland are all present here. And Rowland Robinson seems to have been charged with fomenting rebellion in England. Unlike Taylor and de Lalaing he remained in Edinburgh throughout May and June, but in the first week of July he left the capital 'to ryde to the bordour'.[42]

The state of the English border with Scotland, viewed through the eyes of as zealous a Tudor loyalist as Henry Wyatt, was dire. On 4 June 1496 he sent one of his servants to Henry. From the veiled terms in which he referred to the man's good services, and from the absence of detail about rebel movements, he was probably a spy, come to make oral report. Wyatt hoped the man would report the lamentable state of affairs on the border which left England open to attack because of the irresponsible behaviour of the king's local officers. The lieutenant at Berwick was criticized for sluggishness. The Constable of Carlisle Castle, Richard Salkeld was written off as loyal but past his prime. Sir John Musgrave, Keeper of Bewcastle was dismissed as a political innocent whose raids into Teviotdale were alienating Scots who would otherwise have lived at peace with England. He was also ignoring his duty to keep Bewcastle, the first line of defence on the English West March, between the border and Carlisle. Musgrave was then with the king, so Wyatt advised that he should be told that his actions did more harm to the king than good. To Wyatt's mind the only worthy peson in the whole region was Anne, Lady Clifford, stepgranddaughter of the king's mother, Lady Margaret Beaufort. It was she, with one or two other trusted men, Sir Richard Bellingham and William Layton, a gentleman, who was keeping Westmorland for the king. She had ridden round Westmorland and raised all her aged husband, Henry, Lord Dacre's, tenants so that no one could remember the last time so many men had been raised. More importantly she was loved by the commons, rich and poor.[43]

Wyatt was right to be worried about the state of the West March. Men from Carlisle were being employed to take messages to the Scottish coast from Ranulph Dacre, brother of Thomas Lord Dacre, Warden of the West March. And the Skeltons, an important Cumberland–Border family had sent one of their number to James IV's court. Robinson had fought at Stoke, alongside Clement and Edward Skelton, both of whom had been retainers of Richard III. Clement seems to have been re-accommodated to political life by 1494, when the king granted him lands, but two Skeltons and Edward, probably not the man who had fought at Stoke, and a John were in Warbeck's entourage. To control this dangerous situation Henry VII had placed a bond for £800 on two Skelton's and a Curwen, making them responsible for the loyalty of John Skelton, late of Cardurnock, twelve miles west of Carlisle. Another man from near Carlisle was also with Warbeck, John Stapleton of Scaleby, five miles to the north-east of the city. He too was 'late of' Scaleby, and four people – among them Christopher Moresby, Edward Musgrave and John Crackenthorpe – were made responsible for Stapleton's behaviour. Both Curwen and Moresby must have been old men, for they had fought for Edward IV in 1471. Crackenthorpe was a close associate of Richard III, a JP and a man who had undertaken royal negotiations with the Scots. The Musgraves, one of whom had been made partly responsible for Stapleton's behaviour were part of this same group of royal servants. John Musgrave and his brother Richard had been esquires of the body for Richard III, and John had served Richard in the south of England during 1484. Both John Musgrave and the bastard Sir George Neville, who in 1496 was serving Warbeck in Scotland, had served Richard III in Wiltshire.[44]

Cumberland and Westmorland were well represented in Warbeck's retinue if we can judge from the fiasco in 1495, for two men from Kendal, Westmorland were executed after landing at Deal. As a man with Neville connections, Robinson knew the north, and families on the West March, like the Musgraves, Skeltons, Moresbys and Curwens had long-standing connections with the Neville lordship at Penrith.[45] On the East March similar connections can be found in the Carre family back to the 1460s. Like one of the Musgraves, Nicholas, several of the Carres had fought at Stoke and been pardoned. In May 1496 an Edmund Carre, citizen and draper of London was pardoned.[46] Not only does his name suggest a northern connection, but three years later he was indicted for conspiracy to rescue Warbeck and the Earl of Warwick from the Tower of London. As a region the north and east saw more executed after Deal beach than anywhere else, seven from Yorkshire and four from Northumberland died.[47] Robinson was doing his best to rekindle loyalties which had last been fully active ten years before. But with what success he could not be sure. In late summer 1496 one defector was noted from among the Earl of Oxford's servants,[48] and there were plotters at the highest level of political life who remained undetected as late as May 1496.

The unmasking of the last highly placed conspirator occurred because of the desire of the French monarchy to ensure Henry VII's neutrality in Europe. Some time towards the end of winter 1496 Bernard de Vignolles, servant of John Kendal, recovered from his year and a half long illness. According to the deposition taken from him in Rouen, on 14 March 1496 de Vignolles swore that Kendal had tried to get him to leave England before he had fallen ill. When he recovered, so said Bernard, his first thoughts were to flee the country and then confess his master's machinations to the king, but he could not do that because he feared the conspirators. In order to leave England he devised a scheme whereby he might legitimately leave the country: a visit to his brother in France. He left England about the middle of February to meet his brother in Rouen.[49] But while at Rouen he met two 'friends' of Kendal's, 'merchants who sold stones to Rome'. In the thinly veiled language of the Merchant of Ruby, and other coded messages, Kendal confessed himself delighted at their meeting. De Vignolles should take them to Guillaume de Noion, Warbeck's Brugeois secretary, then in Artois and they would be put to good use. The language of the letter is deliberately obscure. However, Noion was instructed to treat them well and to see to it that Bernard returned post haste. To give him some protection Kendal provided de Vignolles with a letter of introduction to the Grand Master of the Order of St John of Jerusalem in France, stating that Bernard had arrived in France to visit his parents. None of this correspondence ever reached its destination. The entire set of letters, five in all, written between 17 and 28 April, were seized along with Kendal, one assumes at about that time.[50] De Vignolles's

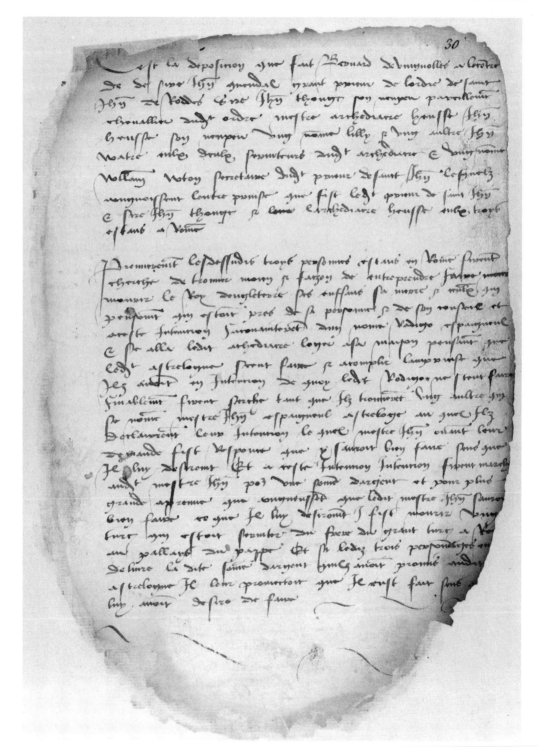

The beginning of Bernard de Vignolles's confession in which John Kendal's activities were reported. Here the pre-Warbeck plot to poison the royal family is described

extraordinary confession with its stories about plots to murder Henry VII, astrologers, conversations on the subject of Warbeck is substantiated by the letters seized with Kendal.

There was one more letter also, to Steffano Maranycho, Kendal's Sardinian servant.[51] He had been involved several years earlier buying poison for use against the royal family from a Spanish astrologer. Maranycho had reached France, bringing with him 'certain good things'. These 'good things' – poisons perhaps – were to be given to one of Kendal's servants and he would make sure that they were sold to Antwerp. Antwerp may have been Antwerp, but it could also be code for Margaret of Burgundy. Kendal had a good knowledge of Europe and the Low Countries; he was a man of European standing and an important diplomat. His official business from October 1495 till February 1496 had been to negotiate the Intercursus Magnus for Henry VII, a splendid cover for his other activities. He was related by marriage to a Yorkshire family, the Tongs, and traced his ancestors back to the Curwen family of Kendal, Westmorland.[52] How he kept his head if de Vignolles information was correct is difficult to know; probably he paid for it, like the rest. He survived, nonetheless, and on 18 June was pardoned. So too on 1 July was the Archdeacon of Northampton, Peter Husee, named by de Vignolles as one of Kendal's accomplices.[53] His secretary, William Wotton, and Husee's two servants, John Water and William Lilly, escaped scot free.[54] However, all this activity, and that on the border, indicates an ongoing drive to identify traitors and force from them if not accommodation then conformity and loyalty. There were others, also, among whom was the Prior of the Augustian Order in London.[55]

Thus when, on 13 June 1496, Dr de Puebla reported to Spain that the king had told him flatly that any war with France was impossible because 'the whole thing' for Henry was that Spain should get Warbeck in their power, we can appreciate why. The diplomatic despatches from de Puebla suggest Henry as being a man not in full control of himself, dissimulating to an ambassador, but a man experiencing quite violent swings of mood. One moment 'the whole thing' was his tune, the next, 'he does not esteem Scotch affairs more than your Highnesses do those of Portugal'. Yet in the same meeting with de Puebla, on 11 July, the king had 'opened his whole heart' to him – downcast at the inpending French embassy to Scotland, frustrated and disappointed at the hesitancy with which Ferdinand and Isabella proceeded to conclude the marriage and alliance.[56] At the time that de Puebla was hearing these confessions it was reported by the Venetian submandatories in England, merchants holding diplomatic credentials, that, 'King Henry was in dread of being expelled from the Kingdom by his nephew, the Duke of York.' James Gairdner thought this a wild exaggeration. But all the diplomatic papers are remarkably consistent. Aldo Brandini, a Florentine reported,

> the king is rather feared than loved, and this was due to his avarice . . . the king is very powerful in money, but if fortune allowed some lord of the royal blood to rise and he had to take the field he would fare badly owing to his avarices; his people would abandon him. They would treat him as they did King Richard, whom they abandoned taking the other side because he put to death his nephews to whom the kingdom belonged[57]

This is a very important despatch, for it is the first clear indication that Henry VII faced a crisis of mid-reign, a crisis of his own making since the report makes clear reference to his fiscal policies. Warbeck's masters were not slow to capitalize on this. In September 1496 when they issued their condemnation of Henry it was an invitation to rebellion because of his harsh taxes. Such rebellion was political, there was no other way of purging government. In the words of Charles Ross, 'What distinguishes this phase of political strife from its predecessors is that opposition groups or factions made it their main objective not to supplant the King's ministers, but to overthrow the King himself and replace him with an alternative of their own choice; and they sought to impose themselves by force.' These years, the Wars of the Roses, 'form the first truly revolutionary period in English history'.[58] By 1496 one prince of the royal blood was imprisoned in the Tower. A second, imposter, was supported by Scotland. The king turned to the old royal family to neutralize the emergence of a leader for rebellion from within its ranks. On 26 August nine prominent westerners were bound over for the allegiance of Thomas Grey, Marquis of Dorset, son of Elizabeth Woodville's first marriage. He was from the same group which had supplied most of the 1494 plotters, and Henry had never trusted him. He had acted suspiciously in the years 1483–5, and had been imprisoned prior to Stoke. Until after 1497 the king showed no inclination to forget, and frequently hobbled Grey's capacity for independent political action.[59] On his own behalf he could have done little, but he was guardian in minority to Edward, Earl of Warwick, and Warwick, though he had come of age in February 1496, remained imprisoned.[60] He and his erstwhile cousin, Richard, Duke of York, were critical to Henry's fate.

The engine of Henry VII's policy in the years 1496–7 was to neutralize the threat of foreign support for Warbeck. But despite all the work of the Poynings Parliament and his military success, the situation in Ireland in the autumn and winter of 1495–6 was out of control, and ripe for further exploitation by the Scots and Warbeck. Peregrine O'Clery says that Henry and his council decided 'to enter into an allegiance and friendship with the Earl of Desmond and to form a matrimonial alliance with the Earl of Kildare and to give him the representation of the Saxon King in Errin and many lordships in England.'[61] As early as December 1494 Henry had tried and failed to make peace with the Earl of Desmond. In the wake of the Munster rising of 1495 this was all the more urgent. In the autumn of 1495 there were a significant number of comings and goings between Henry and Ireland. On 9 October Henry received letters from Ireland. In the first week of November he sent two priests – spies? – to Ireland, and finally in the first week of December he had communications with the burgesses of Waterford. Two weeks later Master Richard Hatton who had tried unsuccessfully to negotiate with Desmond in 1494 was given £20 for his expenses and sent with Dublin pursuivant to Munster. It is more than likely that by the time Hatton left, all the negotiating positions had been defined, for two days after Hatton's costs were entered in the king's accounts one of the Earl of Desmond's canons was rewarded.

Until March little more was heard, and then on 3 March 1496 a messenger arrived, presumably bearing good news.[62] Indeed the news was good. On 12 March 1496 in Cork Richard Hatton concluded the first of three agreements with Desmond. Desmond was recognized as the primary power in the south with freedom from Parliament or the King's Deputy. All the status allowed Desmond by Edward IV was allowed to stand. In return Desmond surrendered his son to Cork for three years, and on 15 March swore an oath of allegiance to Henry Tudor. This was a normal oath of fealty, after which was placed a series of injunctions on not aiding rebels, traitors, or enemies of the king, whatever estate, nation or condition they hailed from, nor to tolerate their presence in any lordship, town or city – a clear reference to recent events. The witnesses to this powerful document included two of Desmond's fellow rebels of the previous year and John Lewellyn, Mayor of Cork that year, as he had been when Warbeck's imposture had begun.[63] This was a paving document for peace in the midlands and north of Ireland. It also proved a powerful indicator of Henry VII's political skill. When shown copies of it in August, James IV refused to believe it true.[64] At the time Desmond swore allegiance to Henry there was still fighting in the midlands and the north. James FitzGerald, Kildare's brother, remained in arms against the English of Leinster till July 1496. And in the north O'Donnell of Tirconnel raided a recent ally of his, O'Reilly, because he had gone over to Henry Tudor. O'Donnell ran O'Reilly into Cavan and sacked, looted and pillaged English settlements in Louth. In the summer of 1496 there was even talk of a Scottish invasion of Ireland to link up with James FitzGerald.[65] Perhaps this was what John Taylor and the Dene of York were up to. To make a peace which kept the Scots and Warbeck out of Ireland, dramatic action was needed. Henry VII's jibe at the expense of the powerless in Ireland as he restored the Earl of Kildare to power was never more apt: '". . . said the Bishop . . . all Ireland cannot rule yonder gentelman." "No?" said the King, "then he is meet to rule all of Ireland, seeing all Ireland cannot rule him"; and so made the Earl Deputy of Ireland during his life . . .'[66]

Through the early summer of 1496 Henry progessed in the south of England. On 6 August he and his party reached Salisbury. Here the king finalized an agreement between Kildare's family, the FitzGeralds and the Butler Earls of Ormond which had riven southern central Ireland. Kildare was reappointed Lord Deputy of Ireland and Walter FitzSimmonds reappointed Chancellor of Ireland. By a tripartite indenture Kildare, the Archbishop of Dublin, Thomas Butler, Earl of Ormond and Sir James Ormond agreed with the king in council that they would settle their differences and present a united front against Warbeck. This was too optimistic a view of what could be achieved, for Kildare's restoration meant the loss of power of Sir James Ormond. Ormond, whose star had risen steadily for six consecutive years, could not stomach this, and so defected from Henry to Warbeck. But the king had the greater power in his debt, Kildare. The earl's oath to Henry is proof of the situation which had induced his restoration. He swore to administer wide-ranging powers of arbitrary arrest and transport of any rebel at the king's behest. If Desmond 'or any maner of

Ormond Castle, the seat of Piers Ruadh Butler, Carrick-on-Suir, County Tipperary, Ireland.. The Butlers were Anglo-Irish allies of Henry VII in Munster

man' in Ireland rebelled he was to set aside affinity and proceed in arms against them be they Gaelic or Anglo-Irish; and should 'any Estraungiers Scottes ffrenshemen or others' invade he was to defend Ireland with the best of his power.[67] With these agreements concluded the king travelled to his Lord Steward, Robert Willoughby de Broke's Wiltshire house with Kildare, de Broke, and his chamberlain, Giles Daubney, and thence to Bristol. At Bristol the group bound for Ireland, Walter FitzSimmonds, Kildare and his new wife, the king's second cousin, Elizabeth St John began to embark for the voyage to Dublin, while Henry struck north on 19 August.[68] Kildare sailed for Ireland on 28 August taking with him a comprehensive pardon for Maurice FitzGerald, Earl of Desmond, and his followers in the Munster rebellion. Seventeen individuals were named including the Archbishop of Cashel, the Bishops of Lismore and Waterford, Cork and Cloyne, and members of the Munster FitzGerald clan. But there were limits to Henry VII's tolerance. Lord Barry and John Atwater were specifically excepted from this pardon.[69] Eventually, in January 1499 Barry was extended the king's grace and pardoned.[70] Atwater was not, and was hanged on the same gallows as his creature Warbeck.

Kildare was sent back to Ireland at the eleventh hour. In Scotland the drums of war were beaten up. By mid-August James IV's siege tents were ready and moved from Holyrood Abbey to Edinburgh Castle for completion. Work on the ordnance and artillery went on more urgently than ever. In Edinburgh and Leith the smiths worked flat out, and in the first week of August a trio of gunnery experts began to 'furnish' the artillery in the castle, which they continued right up till the invasion of England began. At Melrose, on the borders, the work set in hand in July had been completed by 16 August so the wheels and axles for the ordnance transports – wagons and gun carriages – were carted to Edinburgh. By the end of the month most of the heavy work had been done, and contracts for light ordnance – shovels, picks and mattocks –were allocated. John Lame, a Leith smith turned twenty-one waw of iron into gunsights, locks and twenty-six gunchambers. With this delivery to Edinburgh Castle on 1 September 1496 James IV's intention to war was manifestly clear.[71]

At this point Henry VII still had Bishop Fox and John Lord Bothwell involved in the intensive diplomacy aimed at averting the war. Fox pursued a possible Stewart–Tudor marriage, and the possibility of peace negotiations. As late as 22 August, Fox was commissioned to treat for a truce and abstention from war. By this time Lord Bothwell had reached St Andrews where he found James IV, hell bent on war, 'in no wyse inclinit to ye gude of peax nor amyte'. He showed James IV the Earl of Desmond's Bond of Fealty and James was so shaken that he would 'scarcely beleve it'. Yet the situation at St Andrews was far from encouraging to Henry. Warbeck's affinity was being augmented from the English border. The Skeltons were at St Andrews, and Ranulph Dacre was sending messages via Carlisle. Treason was hinted at on the East March. Some Northumberland men had arranged secret meetings with Warbeck's Scottish agents, and defectors were arriving daily from England as were numbers of letters. Intelligence was being supplied by English defectors, and one Hatfeld, a household man of the Earl of Oxford was named. Yet such a dirty war went not all one way. Bothwell was under instruction from Henry Wyatt at Carlisle to grease the palms of an English party at James IV's court to wreck the Scots war effort, and if possible kidnap Warbeck. Bothwell enlisted the help of James Stewart, Earl of Buchan and his younger brother, Andrew Stewart, Bishop of Moray.[72] Both these Stewarts had lost heavily in the coup which had brought James IV to the throne in 1488, and Buchan was a compulsive conspirator from the 1470s onwards. They were working together with another loser from 1488, the heir presumptive James, Duke of Ross. It seems likely that, in the absence of a Duke of Albany, Buchan, Moray and Bothwell saw Ross as a focus for any discontent against James IV. Ramsay presented Ross with a crossbow from Henry VII; this type of bow was Henry's favourite sporting weapon, so Ross was enormously flattered. In spite of James's demands, said Ross, he would not fight in the Scottish army, and Moray said the same. Ross seems to have been as good as his word, he was not in the host that crossed the border into England. Yet neither did he achieve anything against James, for it seems that he was kept under close supervision in Edinburgh while James invaded England.[73] The other major plan, to kidnap Warbeck came to nothing either. Buchan was supposed to capture Warbeck. But he could not bring this off because Warbeck was guarded by a watch appointed by the king himself. Warbeck was held in tight security to prevent the sort of thing Bothwell was trying to do. Even his English and continental supporters were kept well away from him for safety's sake. Possibly James IV's return to Edinburgh at the end of August meant such increased security.

Shortly after his conversations with Ross, Bothwell surveyed the preparations at Edinburgh castle. Here he counted two French Curtalds, ten falcons, thirty carted guns with chambers and sixteen close carts to transport ordnance – 'but litill' he commented and pitiful in comparison with Henry VII's massive overkill of the following year. When next he wrote to Henry Bothwell reported a worsening situation, James IV was 'safer out of reson and sa litill inclinit to gudness but all to traublen and cruelte without his wilbe fulfillit in all poincts'. Bothwell told Henry that James's war was unpopular and that the the season for war was late. Against the advice of his nobility James was wholly set on war 'in ye quarrell of yis fenit boy'. The season may have been late, but Bothwell was wrong about the war's unpopularity. It was popular with the people, despite James's difficulty in financing it adequately, and it was popular with his nobility, who supported it almost to a man. Those who did not, like Buchan and Ross were a discredited few, not a credible opposition. Bothwell was living in the past, like Warbeck's supporters.[74]

Norman Macdougall suggests that in James IV's war on England he and Warbeck had very different and distinct aims: James wished to serve notice on Henry and Spain that he should be taken seriously; Warbeck's masters wished to raise insurrection in England.[75] To this end James hoped for a war in the East March, and Warbeck's men, following their communication with Dacre and the Skeltons, were looking for a rising and war in the West March. Thus, because according to Macdougall, he knew Warbeck was an imposter, James's war aims were limited to the reconquest of Berwick. Success for Warbeck would have meant taking Carlisle and raising the West March against Henry and like the Jacobites in 1745 marching on London. Such a formulation is problematic. There is evidence of Henry's fear about a possible betrayal of Carlisle, but no attack, nor, so far as we can tell any attempt from the Scottish side of the border was made on the city. Furthermore, defectors to Warbeck came not just from the West March, but from Northumberland as well. It is quite possible for James IV to have believed Warbeck genuinely to be Richard Plantagenet, but nevertheless, his war aim was determined not by strategic considerations but by political ones. There are indications that at this late stage he would allow himself to be outbid by either party. We know from later diplomacy that Henry was desperate for James to revoke his safe conduct protection for Warbeck, but from James's point of view Henry was not prepared to match words with deeds. We do not know the full extent of James's demands on Henry. A marriage with Margaret Tudor and an amity with England was one point negotiated with Fox but because of the Yorkist's promise to deliver him Berwick, James may have demanded the surrender of Berwick from Henry as well. He may even have presumed further and asked Henry for a recompense for his expenses and for not invading England. But there was apparently no assurance over what was to become of Warbeck. James might have delivered him to Henry, but if like Maximilian he believed in his legitimacy he may only have offered to exclude him from Scotland, or have tried to arrange a truce with Henry and a pension for the 'Duke'. Fox, and certainly Henry would not have agreed to so expensive a peace without Warbeck's surrender, if to such an expensive peace at all. Thus on 2 September James demanded his due from the Yorkists: 100,000 marks payable within five years and 'ye deliverie of ye castell and towne of Berrek' and the restoration of fishing rights. After a day's deliberations Warbeck and his principal councillors Sir George Neville, William Lounde and John Heron, acceded to the delivery of Berwick but reduced James's financial reward to 50,000 marks repaid within two years. By this stage, said Bothwell, the 'zoung aventurusnes' of the king ruled him. The possibility of recovering Berwick, a thing his father had failed to do, drew him on, and so the agreement with Warbeck's council, of 3 September, was turned into a legal document. The return from Malines of Warbeck's Flemish commander Rodigue de Lalaing, on 5 September confirmed, that Bothwell and Fox were wasting their energies.

The Yorkist camp which Bothwell reported on was nonetheless in an uncertain condition. Warbeck had kept intact his force of 1,400 men, mercenaries of mixed nationality and these were being augmented by defectors from England. Robinson's work on the borders had also produced some gains. On the other hand as the situation resolved into war Bothwell reported that Sir George Neville was vacillating in his loyalty between Warbeck and Henry Tudor. He suggested to Bothwell that the advice which he had given James in council to postpone the campaign was for love of Henry. To this Bothwell retorted that Henry cared not for his pleasure or displeasure. Indeed Neville's behaviour is peculiar in the extreme. He seems to have been targeted by Bothwell for subverting, and to have partially defected from Warbeck along with a group of followers. Yet as soon as he had done this he reverted to following James IV. Was this genuine vacillation, or was Neville a counter mole to Bothwell. For a man out to recover his position in England he drove a hard bargain, and remained in exile into Henry VIII's reign. More critical for Warbeck's war effort was the attitude of Rodigue de Lalaing. De Lalaing brought with him, reported Bothwell, 'sundry pleasant things for ye wers both for man and hors', but only two little ships containing sixty 'Almans' – probably mercenaries from the recent wars in the Netherlands and Alsace. His relations with Warbeck were acid. Bothwell stood near and observed a man bound by honour and duty alone[75].

he said in Franch 'Sire I am cummyn her according to my promys, to do zuor Hightnes servis, and for non oder mans saik am I cum her, far and I had not had zour letters of warand I had ben arrestit in Flandrs, and put to touble for Perkins sake;' and than cam Perkin to him, and he salut him and askit how his Ant did: and he said 'well', and he inquirit gyf he had ony letters fra hir to him, and he said he durst bring non, bot he had to ye King

The Intercursus Magnus, and the Spanish marriage of Joanna to Philip the Fair were bringing changes to the political complexion of Flanders, which Henry had urgently hoped for in June. In October 1496 there are references to the imprisonment at Malines of mercenary soldiers.[76] So perhaps de Lalaing could not get all that he was after. Yet there was a limit to what Spain could achieve. By the time Don Pedro de Ayala, the new Spanish ambassador to Scotland (a man more cunning than learned) arrived in Scotland, James, at war with England, and his own ambassador, Blackader, feared capture, en route, as a Scottish agent.[77] Throughout the summer of 1496 Henry VII was as underhand in his desire for a full alliance with Spain as Spain was with Scotland. He was terrified of the effects such an alliance would have on his and James IV's relations with France. Yet when news of Henry's justifiable fears reached Isabella of Castille, she sanctimoniously advised de Puebla to press Henry towards war with France. It would be 'the finishing strokes to a thing of immense and universal good'.[78] Henry did not need this sort of advice. Into the political vacuum created by ineffectual Spanish diplomacy between England and Scotland stepped the French. Motivated, so it was maintained, by the desire to arbitrate between England and Scotland, Charles VIII sent two embassies to Britain, one to England and one to Scotland, each with very different missions. To England Charles VIII sent a three-man embassy charged with paying outstanding instalments of the Étaples pension, attempting thus to buy Henry's peaceful acquiescence in French policy. There was more on offer. The French, Henry was told, had sent an ambassador to Scotland for no other purpose than to obtain Warbeck for Henry. By this time Henry had good evidence of Warbeck's parenthood, and was attempting to secure his parents to visit England. But Charles VIII disliked this plan, and suggested instead that he would personally guarantee the delivery of Warbeck to Henry. Beyond this were grander promises of an alliance by marriage between Prince Arthur and the daughter of the Duke of Bourbon. All this was no more than typical French spoiling diplomacy: wily and duplicitous.[79]

The French sent another three-man embassy to Scotland: two heralds and Alexander Monypeny, the Seigneur de Concressault, the man who had set up the Warbeck business in Scotland in 1491, and captain of his guard in 1492. Concressault was received at St Andrews, where Bothwell managed to read his letter of credence. His instruction was unambiguous enough. Charles VIII was willing to arbitrate between James and Henry and said that he was aware of the offence given to England by Scotland from messages he had received from Henry through Richmond Herald and Guisnes Pursuivant. Having announced this, Concressault was brought to the Scottish council where James IV informed him of England's attacks on Scotland, its piracy and cattle raiding. Monypeny, as a Scot, understood: the auld enemy. So, said Bothwell, he became 'right soft in ye solistation of yis peax', and informed Bothwell it was no wonder there was war likely between England and Scotland.

As usual the true purpose of Concressault's visit was disguised by a falsity. He was not there so much to arbitrate as to acquire Warbeck. Bothwell taxed him on this and he admitted that he had suggested to James that he send Warbeck to France. Then he wormed out of Concressault the fact that Charles VIII was very concerned to stop James IV from fighting Henry VII. To this end Concressault's arbitration amounted to an offer to James IV of 100,000 crowns if he release Warbeck to France. There followed then an extraordinary discussion. According to Monypeny, he and Louis Malet, Seigneur de Granville had been engaged on a commission of enquiry into Warbeck's real identity, 'to onderstond of Perkins byrthe'. As a result of this confidence Bothwell showed Concressault a document relating to Warbeck's identity. It may have been French in origin, or indeed in French because Bothwell said that it was written by Henry VII's French secretary, Meautis. We know that Charles VIII knew who Warbeck's parents were and that he was tying to prevent their passage to England. Even in the light of this Bothwell might have concluded that the French knew Warbeck to be an imposter. But when Concressault saw Meautis's writing he denied that it was true and asserted on the contrary that Warbeck was Richard, Duke of York. As Bothwell dryly put it, 'I thinck his cummyn hudyr has don bot litill gude for he and ye boye [Warbeck] are everie day in counsaill'. They did after all know each other so perhaps Concressault had fallen under the Warbeck's charms much as James IV and Maximilian. But what of Charles VIII? Prima facie Concressault's mission was to return the rightful Duke of York to France. This would preserve the peace between England and Scotland and between England and France. Henry would then be at odds with his partners in the league. And Warbeck's fate? He, like Richard de la Pole, would have become a French poodle, to be prepared in Normandy with a fleet and soldiers to threaten England every time relations between the two countries deteriorated; or set free again, like de la Pole, to go into Scotland to attack England by the

Ship, late fifteenth-century French, bearing the arms of Louis Malet, Seigneur de Granville, Admiral of France. With Alexander Monypeny he investigated Warbeck's parentage for Charles VIII of France

Scottish back door. Whatever game the French were playing it was not that of selfless arbitration. But John Lord Bothwell could do little at this late stage to influence events. He withdrew from St Andrews and Edinburgh to Berwick from where he sent Henry news on 8 September: James intended crossing the English border on 17 September following a general muster at Ellem Kirk on the Scottish East March on 15 September.[80]

When James crossed the border, in fact on 21 September, he did so under the colours of Scotland and Yorkist England. On 9 September and 10 September his treasurer bought quantities of blue, red and white taffeta 'to the Duke of Yorkis banor' and linen for a standard. Books of silver and gold thread were bought at the same time to embroider them. The king's largesse to Yorkists before the raid was notable. Rodigue de Lalaing received 100 crowns on 10 September, and on 14 September a present of two horses. Rowland Robinson was given £10. To some of the more highly placed mercenaries in Warbeck's affinity, his French, Dutch and German brothers-in-arms – Lawrence the Armourer, John Deufald, 'Captain Clavis (Claus)' – James was fittingly generous. Lawrence was given £2 2s 0d, Deufald and Claus 14s each. To Richard of England he gave £36 for his purse and paid for the horses to drive his cart – a luxury carriage to go to the wars in style. With this bounty the Yorkists were sure of their war. On 9 September James's tents were assembled and stretched on Restalrig meadows. By 12 September the construction of close carts was complete, and the next day 143 carters and 196 horses were assembled and paid for two weeks' service. The discrepancy between the projected date of the muster at Ellem and its date in reality was probably due to the delay in completing the ordnance, but by 11 September all the ammunition was ready; the gunnery at Leith was marshalled and tallow to grease the axle-trees and waterproof the ropes was made available to the artificers. The same day a messenger was despatched to Haddington, 10 miles east of Edinburgh to hire carts there, and on the following day, with John Sandilands of Hillhouse and twenty gentlemen in attendance, James's artillery train joined his tents at Restalrig. The heavier guns, the bombards, were probably by now on their way to Haddington. Final preparations, packing gunpowder for example, was still in hand at Holyrood Abbey and Edinburgh Castle on 13 September, when James put into wage four of his gunners – Hans, Robert Herward, Adam Brounle and Henric – and artificers and pioneers 'to draw the gunnys in petthis and myris'. On 14 September the ordnance carts, artillery pioneers, miners, quarriers and Warbeck's band of adventurers lumbered east to Haddington, with more gunners paid for, Guyaume, two anonymous fellows and John Lame and his men, who had cast these new weapons and were now to use them for the first time. Nor were James and his duke forgetful of their obeisances. At Holyrood Abbey and Restalrig Priory, the God of Battles and the Lady Mary were invoked to lend their aid to the rightful King of England and the rightful possessor of Berwick.[81]

ELEVEN

Failure

Richard by the grace of God king of England, and of France, Lord of Ireland, Prince of Wales to all those, that these our present letters shall be sent or read, and to every of them greeting. And wheras We in our tender age, escaped by God's might out of the Tower of London, and were secretly conveyed over the sea unto other divers countries, there remaining certain years as unknown. In which season it happened one Henry son to Edmond Tydder – Earl of Richmond created, son to Owen Tydder of low birth in the country of Wales – to come from France and enter into this our realm, and by subtle and false means to obtain the crown of the same unto us of right appertaining: Which Henry is our extreme, and mortal enemy, as soon as he had knowledge of our being alive, imagined, compassed and wrought, all the subtle ways and means he could devise, to our final destruction, insomuch as he hath not only surmised us to be a feigned person, giving us nicknames, so abusing your minds; but also to deter and put us from our entry into this our realm, hath offered large sums of money to corrupt the princes of every land and country that we have been retained with, and made importune labour to certain of our servants about our person – some of them to murder or poison us, and other to forsake and leave our rightwise quarrel, and to depart from our service, as by Sir Robert Clyfford and other was verified and openly proved; and to bring his cursed and malicious intent aforesaid to his purpose, he hath subtly and by crafty means levied outrageous and importable sums of money upon the whole body of our realm to the great hurt and impoverishing of the same. All which subtle and corrupt labours by him made to our great jeopardy and peril we have by God's might graciously escaped and overpassed as well by land as by sea, and now with the right high and mighty prince, and our dearest cousin the King of Scots; which without any gift or other thing by him desired or demanded to the prejudice or hurt of us our crown or realm hath full lovingly and kindly retained us, by whose aid and supportation we in proper person be now by God's grace entered into this our realm of England, where we shall shew ourself openly unto you all . . .

Richard Plantagenet proclaimed his miraculous arrival in England in a skein of criticism two hundred years old; criticism of Henry VII's actions, criticism of his ministers and the assertion that the realm needed to be saved from evil counsel. Warwick and Clarence had used the same tactics when they had condemned Edward IV in 1468. Warbeck's proclamation accused Henry of attacking the true nobility, of murdering William Stanley, Simon Mountford, Robert Ratcliff, William Daubney, Humphrey Stafford and many others. He had wrongfully imprisoned the Earl of Warwick and deprived him of his estates in order to enfeeble his power so he could not aid his cousin Richard IV. The royal blood had been polluted, Warwick's sister and other royal ladies had been married to kinsmen and friends of Henry, of 'simple and low degree'. The low born were now favoured as councillors and a number were named as 'the principal finders, occasioners and counsellors of the misrule and mischief now reigning in England'.

There followed a list of complaints more specific to Henry VII than part of the normal language of condemnation. He abused and broke sanctuary laws. He was a traitor who murdered and robbed people. He was an extortioner with a cruel policy of taxation. All these things the Duke of York promised to set right, particularly the evil taxation. The duke promised to revert to traditional methods and to supress 'benevolences', 'unlawful impositions' and 'grievous exactions' imposed by Henry VII. To this end he asked for the support of the whole kingdom, and said that any who until then had been his enemy would be pardoned, should they aid him. He would 'redress and subdue the . . . mischief and misrule and . . . punish the occasioners and haunters thereof after their deserts in example of others.' Such general reform would be advanced by the impartial administration of 'the good Laws and Customs heretofore made by our noble progenitors Kings of England . . . according to the effect and true meaning they were first made ordained'.

Richard IV also informed his subjects that he wished to prevent bloodshed. Yet such a precaution was unnecessary; even now Henry Tudor was making preparations to flee the realm. To this end he had sent many of his supporters abroad and they had taken with them 'the treasure of this our realm'. Richard IV offered a reward of £1000 for his capture, and promised that the captor would have an estate of 100 marks, £66 13s 4d per year for his trouble. This capture would ensure the personal security of each English subject and the 'surety' of 'the commonwealth of our land your native ground'.[1] This may have been a clarion call in an honourable tradition, but it fell on deaf ears. Six months later many who agreed rose in rebellion against the shocking taxes of 1497, but they were westerners. The north, with its tough anti-Scottish border traditions, was completely the wrong place to begin a rebellion. And Warbeck's masters were obliged to justify Scottish intervention and assuage anxiety about a Scottish raid in favour of England. They said that James was helping them unconditionally and concealed their agreed deal: the return of Berwick and the 50,000 marks war debt. Instead, they maintained, when James saw Perkin's 'natural leige people according to right and their duties of their allegiances, resort lovingly unto (him) with such power as by their puissance shall move . . . he is fully set and determined to return home again quietly with his people into his own land, without doing or suffer to be done any hurt or prejudice unto our realm or the inhabitants of the same'. But real loyalty was to the king, whoever he was, and there was no political capital to be made out of old regional associations with Richard III. Whatever had been agreed with the Skeltons and Dacres no treason materialized. We have seen that the king had anticipated Robinson's work on the border and bound the friends of John Stapleton and John Skelton to maintain their loyalty. Also, if support for Warbeck, as Duke of York, came from Woodville and court sources the fact that ex-supporters of Richard III failed to support Warbeck is not surprising. Rowland Robinson's fellow Thomas Otter, from a family of long sevice to York and Neville, much invoved in earlier troubles had, by 1496, settled down to the life of a northern gentleman, loyal to the king. As Macaulay wrote, of the men who supported the Duke of Monmouth in 1685, Warbeck's masters were

under the influence of that peculiar illusion which seems to belong to their situation. A politician driven into banishment by a hostile faction generally sees the society which he has quitted through a false medium. Every object is distorted and discolored by his regrets, his longings, and his resentments. Every little discontent appears to him to portend a revolution, every riot is a rebellion. He cannot be convinced that his country does not pine for him as much as he pines for his country. He imagines that all his old associates who still dwell at their homes and enjoy their estates, are tormented by the same feelings which make life a burden to himself. The longer his expatriation, the greater does this hallucination become. The lapse of time which cools the ardour of the friends whom he has left behind inflames his. Every month his impatience to revisit his native land increases: every month his native land remembers and misses him less.[2]

Thus he becomes, 'ripe for enterprises which would at once be pronounced hopeless by any man whose passions had not deprived him of the power of calculating chances'.

Despite the air of unreality which has always surrounded Warbeck's incursion into England, Polydore Vergil said that Henry VII feared a rising. There were English traitors liaising with Scotland, and treason was feared. Vergil implies that Henry dealt with the possiblity of a rising for Warbeck by leaving the north to defend itself against its traditional enemy rather than risk arraying it before the invasion to find that his forces defected to Warbeck.[3] Such judgement cannot be faulted. The consequence of Henry's attempt to form an army against Warbeck in the following summer was rebellion, and some retinues which should have fought against Warbeck fought against their king instead. The north looked to itself, but not without Henry's command. On 12 September the Earl of Surrey instructed the Mayor of York to proclaim an array in the city for men to resist James IV, and sixty soldiers were raised. On the march, though the political and diplomatic initiative rested with Bishop Fox, Richard Neville, Lord Latimer was put in charge of the army. When Bothwell informed the king that James intended mustering at Ellem, Henry committed Bishop Fox, Surrey, the lords Clifford and Greystoke and ten of his most powerful Yorkshire officers and gentlemen – Sir Henry Wentworth, Sir William Gascoigne, Sir John Neville, Richard Cholmeley, Sir Marmaduke Constable, William Conyers, Sir John Everingham, Sir John Sayvill, Sir Thomas Darcy and Sir John Hastings – to a full defence of the north. A royal messenger, Basset, was despatched with letters to them on about 16 September and two or three days later the king established ten new posts northwards of London from Highbury and paid a messenger riding between himself, London and his posts to keep himself well informed.[4]

On 14 September the Stewart–Plantagenet host crossed the Lammermuirs guided by a man from Haddington. Their vanguard, including the artillery, reached Langton, near Duns by 17 September, but James, and therefore presumably Warbeck and de Lalaing, did not arrive at Ellem, five or six miles north of Langton, until 19 September. Why they were running behind schedule we do not know. Perhaps it was because James was over cautious, perhaps it was a delay to allow Englishmen to join the host at Ellem. Most likely it was the fact that medieval warfare was an art, not a science. Muster dates were almost always provisional and rarely kept to. By 20 September military preparations were concluded and the whole party began to cross the border, at Coldstream, a feat which took two days. 'The cobill men of Tweid' ferried the artillery over the Tweed on 21 September. But on the same day, with his supposed forces within England, Warbeck withdrew. James gave his protonotary, Andrew Forman £69 8s 0d at Coldstream for Warbeck, and then Prince Richard returned to Edinburgh.[5] Polydore Vergil wrote an account of this, based he said, on what 'men of the greatest integrity' had told him. When they entered England, Warbeck's spies reported to their commander that there was no uprising in favour of Richard IV. Warbeck, said Vergil's informant, was terrified lest he be then held in contempt by the Scots, and abandoned. To maintain their support he feigned pity for his native country, and begged James not to harry his people any further nor to burn any more places. According to this account James was incredulous, and Vergil suggests this marked a turning point in their relationship, as James began to realize Warbeck was not Richard IV. Be that as it may James is said to have replied that by all appearances Warbeck was meddling in other peoples business and not his own: for he called England his country and the English his countrymen, but no one had come to his aid.[6] With this stinging dismissal and money in his purse Warbeck withdrew but for James the raid had just begun. He was intent on demonstrating that he and his artillery were a force to be reckoned with in Europe. In his train he had observers from Hugh O'Donnell of Tirconnel, French ambassadors, and agents of the Flemish court. After abandoning Warbeck, James pushed into England raiding the Tweed and Till valleys. He went as far south as Howtel tower which he pulled down, and then returned to Branxton tower which suffered the same treatment, to arrive at Heton castle in the Till valley on the 24 September. Here he set his miners to work all night to drive a mine under the wall. The next day Hans, in command of James's artillery, bombarded Heton, and on the second night the Scottish miners prepared for another round of mining. Duddo, Twizel and Tilmouth peel towers were demolished at the same time. With these scalps to his credit, James was forced to make a tactical withdrawal. About midnight on the 25 September James heard of the approach of the English army, 4,000 men led out of Newcastle by Lord Latimer, and raised the siege. What had taken two days to enter England was taken back to Scotland within eight hours.[7]

Whatever the effect on his personal relations with James IV in the longer term, there is no indication after the Raid of Ellem that James's financial support for Warbeck slackened. Warbeck's household was maintained by a tax laid on the royal burghs north of the Forth, and its arrears were still being collected in July 1499. The rolls of the Scottish exchequer printed in the nineteenth century reveal only small sums contributed to the Ellem raid, but the roll printed in 1958 shows a payment of £1,079 11s 4d. During 1496 and 1497 James supported Warbeck and his entourage with large sums from the Scottish Crown's income.[8] The impact of James's Raid was felt as far away as Italy where Maximilian I's father-in-law, the Sforza Duke of Milan, believed war with France was likely, but that Maximilian's support of Warbeck meant that England would be unable to fight against France for fear of attack from Scotland.[9] Some discussion of this sort may have occurred while the French embassy was still in Scotland, because it did not return to France speedily after Ellem. Instead, though Concressault and his attendant herald left for France on 19 October 1496, Champagne Herald stayed in Scotland until the second week of December,[10] by which time a major war with England was a foregone conclusion.

Champagne Herald had been in Scotland when Warbeck had first appeared in Cork. The other principal actor, early on in the Warbeck story was Robinson, who visited Scotland within months of Warbeck's arrival in France. At the beginning of October 1496 James IV purchased the ship *The Cukow*, in which Warbeck later landed in Cornwall and then seems to have returned it to its French owners, possibly under hire. This may be quite innocent but, with a state of war existing between England and Scotland *The Cukow* was being readied to slip through any English ships patrolling the seas between Flanders and Scotland. Only an apparently innocent merchantmen could get past naval patrols, as Warbeck found six months later. *The Cukow* may have been one of two or three ships which Rowland Robinson provisioned on 15 October for a voyage to fulfil the obligations of 'ane indenture maid betwix the kingis Gude grace and the Duke of York'. Robinson left from Leith in mid-October. Just before this on 7 October, Rodigue de Lalaing received his last gift, 100 marks, from James IV. Flanders was their probable destination, but the reason for the journey is not known. De Lalaing is never heard of again in Scottish documents, so perhaps he was going home. Robinson may also have been bound for Malines, perhaps, to report to his mistress, and to buy arms for the following summer's warfare. Later in October, while James was in residence at Falkland Palace, with Warbeck, he paid 29s to the English 'to pas thair way to sail' from Lindores, a port deep in the estuary of the Tay. As a North Sea port, Flanders seems a likely destination for these English.[11]

But not all the vessels leaving Scotland were bound for France or Flanders. One of them was bound for Spain, or carried a messenger, Anthony de la Forsse with letters for Spain.

Perkin Warbeck's letter to Bernard de la Forsse at Fuentarabia, dated Edinburgh 18 October 1496 and signed Rychard off England

According to Warbeck's letter Anthony had 'full lovyngly geven his longe attendaunce vpon us in sundry Cuntreys' which suggests service with Warbeck from 1491 or 1492.[12] Young de la Forsse took letters from 'Rychard off England' to his father Bernard, at Fuentarabia in Spain, dated Edinburgh 18 October 1496. By this date Anthony's father must have been a very old man. He is first recorded serving Edward IV with his fellow Gascon Louis de Bretayle in 1462. De Bretayle had served the Crown, in Gascony, in 1453, so Bernard's service to England may have begun about the same time.[13] Whatever is the case he served Edward IV, Richard III and Henry VII and represented their interests in Spain. Like most of his type he was a spy, a diplomat and a merchant. Each career supported and advanced the other. On one occasion Bernard was recommended to ship Gascon wine in a ship crewed half by Spaniards and half by Gascons. This way the ship's crew would be taken as Spanish but could collect intelligence in France.[14] He negotiated all the principal alliances between England and Spain under Edward and both mercantile and marriage alliances under Edward and Richard III. His career continued under Henry VII, for our last English reference to him is to a reward of 100 marks, and a licence for him to ship Spanish goods – for espionage purposes perhaps, in 1490.[15] From the diplomacy he undertook for Richard III in 1483 it is clear that he was on intimate terms with the Spanish monarchs and it was this intimacy which Warbeck asked Bernard to exploit. Richard of England wished to discover what 'gode hert and mynde that or most dere Cosyn the kynge of Spayne bereth towardes us'; by the instrument of the letter Bernard de la Forsse would become a 'lovyng faithfull and kynde Counseillour' of Richard IV as he had been for his father Edward IV. The implication is that Bernard woo Ferdinand of Aragon from his friendship with Henry VII. It is possible that there was, as there had been to Burgundy, Scotland, and earlier to Spain, a letter from Warbeck also to the King and Queen of Spain, and it is clear that Ferdinand and Isabella saw de la Forsse's letter. Their secretary Almazan endorsed it contemptuously 'From the one who calls himself Duke of York'. Warbeck was wasting his time with Spain as surely as James IV had earlier in the year.

At the same time as Warbeck's masters aimed to revive their fortunes in Europe there occurred one of those events which may be coincidental, or the direct result of this activity, but, because of the general situation, looked sinister. In November 1496 John Lord Fitzwater[16] attempted to escape from prison in Guisnes castle. Lord Fitzwater, one of the survivors of the 1495 plot been spared execution following his trial and had been imprisoned. This may have been gentle treatment or it may have been to set a trap. Perhaps some of Margaret's supporters tried to release him. One of the Whetehills we may recall, had been a member of her household. On the other hand, given the conditions of imprisonment for political prisoners, Fitzwater may have subborned his gaoler. Prisoners were expected to pay for their own upkeep, and their personal servants could come and go from the gaol. Such conditions were ripe for exploitation as Henry VII knew only too well. William Graunte, Kitchener of Westminster monastery, was obliged to provide daily 'mete & drynk' for Gilbert Debenham and Humphrey Savage. Graunte was retained at £1 per week to do this, but in January 1495 Henry stopped the payment and Graunte was not paid for a whole month. During February Graunte paid for the rebels' food himself, and only in April did the king order him to be paid and that his payment in future be kept up to date.[17] The potential to subborn Graunte was considerable. Soon after they were corralled in Westminster, Graunte was obliged to find ten sureties for his continued loyalty to the king[18]. Two years later one of the Cornish rebels imprisoned at Exeter bribed his way out of the bishop's gaol there, and later plots involving Warbeck showed how unreliable servants in the Palace of Westminster and the Tower of London were.

Whatever lay behind Fitzwater's actions Henry VII despatched Sir Thomas Lovell to Calais. Part of Lovell's business was to collect coin. The other part of his work may have been as it had been in 1495, to supervise the king's orders about the execution of the death penalty. Lovell was cold blooded about such business. In 1502 he threatened to throw Sir James Tyrrell's son over the side of a boat anchored off Calais if he himself did not surrender, despite having promised his father a safe conduct for his son. He was in Calais in December 1496 and was paid £5 5s 8d for his costs in the Fitzwater affair.[19] Having escaped death in 1495 Fitzwater was beheaded on 24 November 1496.

The last piece of the jigsaw, France, Scotland, Flanders – Ireland – was put in position on 15 October when the messenger Hugh O'Donnell of Tirconnel had sent to observe James IV's raid returned to his master.[20] Whatever he told Hugh O'Donnell about the raid, he had another purpose also, to renew Scottish and Plantagenet associations with Munster. Though it no longer exists Warbeck and James IV sent a letter to Maurice FitzGerald, Earl of Desmond asking him to make common cause with them against the English by joining them in Scotland. The letter was seen in the seventeenth century by James Ware, who mentions it in his history of Ireland, and it was also catalogued at this time.[21] Whatever it said, its words fell on deaf ears. For the first time since his imposture began the Irish gambit was blocked to Warbeck.

Kildare had returned to Ireland on 17 September 1496 after a 'toubleous & long passayge': a crossing of three weeks. Within a few days of his arrival he swore loyalty to Henry VII at St Peter's church in Drogheda, and then summoned the principal families abutting the Pale, north, west and south, and the Ulster chieftains, to meet him at Dundalk at Michaelmas. This summons produced mixed results. At first the only northern families to submit to Kildare were O'Reilly, Magennis, O'Hanlon and MacMahon but this was success none the less, for their lands lay along the north-west border of the English Pale, so Kildare had established a defence against incursions from Ulster. They surrendered their sons as pledges of good behaviour,and signed indentures of loyalty with Kildare. Ulster was more trouble. The O'Neils of Tyrone, enemies of O'Donnell were split by a family feud, and Kildare had hoped to secure the allegiance of both sides of the family. In the event Kildare took the oath and hostages of Donal O'Neil. More promising was news that support for Warbeck from his most most convinced supporters in Ulster, O'Neil of Clandeboy and O'Donnell of Tirconnel, seemed to be cracking. O'Neil and O'Donnell wrote to Kildare promising to submit to him anywhere he cared to name in Ireland. On 2 October at Dundalk, on the River Creggan, the border between the Pale and Ulster, Kildare swore all the northerners, except O'Neil and O'Donnell, and five Irish lordships of the south and west – O'Connor, MacMurrough, O'Byrne, O'More and O'Dempsy – to loyalty to England. MacMurrough and O'Connor had not been convinced without a show of force. But two expeditions had deprived them of the king's castle at Carlow and forced them to swear loyalty. This news was sent to England by Sir Ralph Verney, a highly placed royal official, and relative of the king travelling with Kildare. He told his correspondent, Reginald Bray, that by 31 October, Kildare had established peace across the whole of southern and western Ireland and had the north under control. He was pursuing a correspondence with the Earl of Desmond who had promised to submit to him. Already there had been one missed opportunity, but Desmond agreed to meet him at Waterford in the first week of November, after the All Hallows celebrations were over. Kildare's reappointment had worked miracles. His unparalleled power and connections – already established in Ireland and increased by his marriage into the English royal family – meant that no one wishing to maintain or advance their own position could gainsay him. Thus on 26 October Seaan Burke of Galway, who had guided Warbeck to O'Donnell the year before, abandoned York and swore his oath of fealty to Henry. He and others implicated with Warbeck now offered to travel to England to meet the Saxon King. Verney confessed himself amazed by what Kildare had achieved in only a month.[22]

Kildare's achievement was enormous, he had secured the Pale, and Henry was sure that Kildare would dominate the situation. After a month with him Verney, as we have seen, pronounced his rule good. A signal of the king's pleasure followed when in December 1496 Giles Daubney was sent to Ireland to assign lands to Lady Kildare as part of her marriage settlement. Daubney, Ralph Verney and William Hatcliffe became her trustees, and Kildare formally ratified this.[23] Thus the man who had crowned Lambert Simnel put his treachery behind him. He had shown himself more than willing to make amends for his past, and in October 1496 he offered to lead an expedition against James IV from Ulster. In early October John Mor Macdonald of Isla, a renegade Scot had arrived in Ireland. He was the last remaining independent Macdonald of the Isles with pretensions to restoring the once proud independent Kingdom of the Western Isles. By force and money, James IV had reduced the legitimate Macdonald of the Isles to the status of a court ornament. John Mor had been offered terms of accommodation in 1493, but proved an intractable rebel. He was arrested in 1494, and eventually executed in 1499 with all three of his sons.[24] But in this October he was living in O'Neil of Clandeboy's lordship, with 1,000 troops, camped near Carrickfergus castle. Originally he had arrived in Ireland to recover one of his sons, imprisoned by an Irish chief. Having recovered him he was still domiciled in Ireland. This was a region of Ireland to which a large number of Scots had emigrated. Kildare quietly sounded him out on the possibility of attacking James IV so that when the war with Scotland began John Mor and Garret Og, Macdonald and FitzGerald, would fight side by side against the King of Scotland.[25] We do not know the outcome of this offer, but in December 1496 Kildare sent a pursuivant and two trumpeters to the king. This may have marked the beginning of the defence of Ireland during 1497, or it may have been merely laying the ground for Lady Kildare's grants of land. However, in January 1497 one of the gentlemen grooms of the chamber, John Parker, received £120 to retain soldiers in Ireland to fight against the Scots, and in early February naval patrols commanded by Sir Roger Cotton, reconnoitred the Irish Sea and coasts of Ireland against possible Scottish attack.[26]

By the time Parker was on his way to Ireland, England had declared war on Scotland. In June 1497 Dr de Puebla had reported to Spain that at court, 'They are very angry in England with the King of the Romans for having sent the so-called son of Edward to England.'[27] At the time James IV withdrew from Northumberland Henry's court was baying for a war of retaliation; and it was proclaimed at Michaelmas 1497.[28] Shortly after this some of the king's servants and other Londoners attacked Scots living in London or seized the goods of Scots. For about six months anti-Warbeck songs had been circulating in London. None, unfortunately, have survived, but John Skelton's line 'Lord, how Perkyn is proud of his Pohen!' may give us a taste of these scurrilous songs.[29]

Henry VII held his first council of war at Sheen, early in October 1496.[30] At this council Henry and his commanders discussed a range of options prepared for them by Sir Robert Litton, the treasurer for war. Litton had been instructed to 'make serche of the presidents of the Werres [into] Scotland aswele for the defense of owre owne marches there: as of great armees that have been made into the same land in the tymes of owre noble progenitor king Edward the third and frothens unto the days of our fadre king Edward the iiijth . . . And that ye bring all the same presidents unto us to owre manor of Shene'.

The options which the council considered we can only guess at. But the king and his captains decided 'to make by See and by lond ij Armees Roiall for a substantiall Warre to be contynued vppon the Scottes vnto such tyme as We invade the Reame of Scotland in our owne person'. Robert Willoughby de Broke, the lord steward, was appointed 'for the anoyance of the Scottes by water and land . . . wher and [as] often as he shall thynk good'. Giles Daubney, Lord Chamberlain, was to command the van, to attack Scotland from Berwick.

After the scale of response and strategy had been decided, Henry called a Great Council which met at Westminster between 24 October and 6 November. Here, representatives from all the towns and counties in England, many of whom would be back for Parliament within a month and a half, gathered to hear the king make his demands and justify his position. In resonse to his demand the council authorized a grant of £120,000, the equivalent of twenty times the annual income of James IV from normal sources.[31] It also was agreed that the king could have a loan from his greater subjects to prime the pump for financing his military. Taxes on the scale proposed could only be granted by Parliament. So on 16 January 1497 hastily re-assembled members of the council met at Parliament to listen to Henry VII's justification for war. Chancellor Morton addressed Parliament in a speech designed to unify it in righteous indignation against James IV. On the command of Henry VII himself he launched into his speech. With over three years of the truce between England and Scotland still to run James, without cause, provocation or warning, had breached it. It was against this evil man that they had all been summoned to make suitable and timely provision, since the fatherland should be no less dear to them than their lives. Morton's classical exemplum for their predicament was the recovery of the Romans, after their defeat by Carthage; hardly an apt description of the Raid of Ellem, though perhaps indicative of Henry VII's state of mind by now. Defeated then by Hannibal, the Romans had been 'strengthened by the counsel of excellent men and, as if waking from a bad dream with renewed vigour sent Scipio to Carthage with an army'. Morton fleshed out his example with later Christian proofs, but his argument was stated with admirable clarity, 'the Fatherland before all else should be protected and maintained in freedom'.[32] Asked to consider events in the light of this xenophobic interpretation, to say nothing of anger at court and riots in London, the English parliament voted Henry his taxes. With them he believed it would be possible to mount a massive strike against Scotland, the threat of which alone might cause James IV to withdraw his support from Warbeck, or else allow an easy English victory over the Scots, and the bloodless excision of Warbeck from Scotland.

From the middle of October English military activity on the borders increased dramatically. And on 2 November, in what may have been a propaganda move, the Earl of Surrey, Ralph, Lord Greystoke, John Cartington and Edward Ratcliff were commissioned to keep the East and Middle March for the King's Lieutenant, his son, Henry, Duke of York.[33] Henry intended turning the military screws on James IV well in advance of his planned invasion. Bishop Richard Fox, at Alnwick controlled local discussion with Scotland at this time. Regional military control was vested in Thomas Howard, the Earl of Surrey, and there was a constant flow of intelligence from the north to Henry. One of Sir Richard Salkeld's servants, presumably from Carlisle, received 10s in the first week of December and in the second week an 'Espiell' was rewarded £2. By now Berwick was beginning to bulge with military supplies. The masters of the *Mary Rose* of Calais, the *Anne*, the *Ann Tugee* of London, the *Anne of Dover* and the *Magdalen* were sent during November to take supplies, sailors, and soldiers north for the war against Scotland. One hundred and twenty soldiers were sent out in naval squadrons to remain at sea until the end of January 1497: this the first of several English operations aimed at securing mastery of the coasts. By the beginning of January 1497 Henry VII had put considerable resources at the disposal of Thomas Howard, Earl of Surrey. The garrisons of Berwick and Norham had been augmented in late October and November 1496 by 1,500 men; and on the turn of the year a staggering £30,000 was despatched for the food and wages of Durham, Newcastle and Berwick garrisons. By now Henry VII was coming perilously, to stake the maximum dynastic gain – the elimination of Warbeck and his supporters in Scotland – against the maximum economic disruption compatible with the identification of dynasty and realm.[34]

After the dispersal of the Yorkist messengers in October 1496 James IV enjoyed himself hunting at Falkland Palace and elsewhere in Fife, Perth and Angus. Some of the time he boated on the River Isla, and paid children to set up wild ducks for his hawks. He pursued his interest in medicine, and gave a man who had recently had a stone removed 3s 6d. But the war could not be forgotten: 5 November brought him his 'Maister Spyour'. King James broke off his recreations and by mid-November had returned to Linlithgow Palace from where he summoned his officers of state. Then on 19 November he took this august body – Privy Seal Elphinstone, Chancellor Angus, Argyll, Master of the Household and his chamberlain, Justiciar and others – to the Hume castle of the Hirsel, 12 miles from the border. It is clear that at the Hirsel, James was made fully aware of the danger he faced. He spent ten days in the castle at a council of war, and in these circumstances defence was the first priority. In the middle of December James inspected the castle of Dunglas, in the Merse, the area through which Howard would advance up Teviotdale. Dunbar, a coastal castle, had been slighted after 1488. Its restoration was ordered, but only began in March the next year. Normally James celebrated Yule and New Year at Stirling, Linlithgow or Edinburgh, but this year he went to Melrose Abbey, ten miles from the border, for Yule. Warbeck may have been at the Blackfriars in Edinburgh, or at Falkland Palace.[35] Where exactly we do not know, but he was removed from James. Yet, if James had distanced himself from Prince Richard of England he could not escape the consequences of his support for him. In mid-January 1497 Thomas Howard, Earl of Surrey, planned, weather permitting, a substantial raid on the Scottish borders. Perhaps if James IV had news of it this explains why he and his court retreated from Melrose to Edinburgh so suddenly after Christmas. By the first week of January, Surrey was poised to cross the border advancing up the Till and Tweed valleys. According to his biography his raid into Teviotdale was something the like of which had not been done 'ther in an hundreth yere before'. Surrey scorched the earth to the 'gretest losse and empouerysshment' of the surrounding country.[36] In reality no such thing took place. Thomas, Lord Dacre remembered that

> when my lord of Norfolk & my lord of Winchester then lying in Alynwyke my lord Conyers Sir William Bulmer and other captains then lying vpon thest and middill marches with garysons to the nombre of An thousand soldiours and moo over & besydes the garisons of Berwyk and Norham It was asmich as they might take vpon haunde to make a Roode in tevidale . . .

Surrey, Conyers and Bulmer barely penetrated Teviotdale. Burning of houses there was, but the earl got no further than fifteen or sixteen miles over the border.[37] In 1497 the Scots Exchequer rebated £162 13s 4d on the Earldom of March for a few areas wasted by the English.[38] Perhaps the short days and bitter cold defeated Surrey, perhaps there was 'asmoche harme to the doers as the losse of goodes and brenying of howses' were 'to the sufferers'. At the end of January Surrey retreated harried by the Scots.

When Surrey, Bulmer and Conyers marched their freezing troops out of Scotland, James ordered his artillery to be overhauled and augmented. Gunner Hans had his back wages paid and in the first week of February a small detachment of gunners and foundry workers were sent to Coldingham to defend the eastern approach to Scotland. Shortly after this, James led a retaliatory strike into England, 'the raid of Hume', aided by the men of his chamberlain, Alexander, Lord Hume. It probably did not amount to much, perhaps a face-saving gesture, and soon afterwards James went on his annual pilgrimage to St Duthac's shrine at Tain. As a sure sign nonetheless that war would continue James left his armour and some coffers at the Hirsel.[39]

The pursuit of war was for James, witness his incredible energy touring his kingdom, a young man's enthusiasm, a demonstration of his arrival as king – the fulfilment of his role. For Henry Tudor it was a destructive obsession which conjured up civil war. By February the English East March and Berwick were well defended, but he feared a surprise attack in the west. On 13 February he ordered Thomas, Lord Dacre, Lieutenant of the West March to array troops against James, 'since our enemy of Scotland, with a great array of our rebels and traitors has hostilely invaded our kingdom of England . . . and intends further mischief'.[40] Two days later he informed the mayor and his brethren at Carlisle that he was giving control of their city to the Bishop of Carlisle, William Siver. Siver was a Durham man and Abbot of St Mary's, York. By special provision of the Pope he had been appointed Bishop of Carlisle shortly before Warbeck reached Scotland in September 1495.[41] Siver was given control of Carlisle because Henry feared its loss to a sudden Scottish attack. In his letter he called Carlisle one of the keys to the kingdom. But behind this fear of attack was another, that Carlisle would simply be surrendered to Warbeck. Thus the king informed the mayor that for the duration of hostilities no one was allowed to retain men to a personal retinue. The giving of livery, badges or clothing was forbidden and it was forbidden for anyone to take their retinue out of the city, for any reason. Everyone was confined to the city for its defence, and Bishop Siver was to take oaths of fidelity to Henry from the city council. Any person contravening these orders was to be made an example of so that any trouble-makers would 'therat take feer'. The administration of these draconian measures were well fitted to Siver, a man usually employed as tax gatherer for Henry in the North. The citizens of Carlisle were not the only people whose loyalty concerned Henry in February 1497.[42] Some of those executed in 1499 were bound over to keep their loyalty to the king. On 1 February Sir James Tyrrell and John Thomas stood bail for the loyalty of one William Order.[43] A week later Sir Robert Evers was bound for his loyalty. The Evers family were Percy servants, and one, William, had helped Richard III during the *coup d'état*.[44] On 8 February two Derby gentlemen, Humphrey and Otwell Lowe, were bound to keep bound for their allegiance. They and two others – Thomas Legh and John Ireland – had to find 500 marks each as security. They were probably linked to the Stanley plot, since both their mainpernors, Thomas Legh and John Ireland, had already stood bail for Stanley's client, John Warren of Poynton. Only in 1503 were the Lowes pardoned. Finally, Sir Edward Burgh, son of one of Richard III's household, was placed under three bonds in winter 1496 and spring 1497, and specifically forbidden to leave England.[45]

Time for an accommodation between James and Henry was running out. If Warbeck could be ejected from Scotland by diplomatic means so much the better. Henry sent Garter King-of-Arms to France and on 17 February received a French herald at Westminster. This may have been assuring Charles VIII that despite the massive military build-up Henry would not be going to war with him. Or it may be that Henry was trying to get Charles to honour his old promise to arbitrate between England and Scotland.[46] February and March also saw a good deal of activity at Calais, between Flemish and English commissioners settling the Intercursus Magnus, and exchanging seals of towns ratifying the treaty.[47] But if Warbeck was discussed, we do not know. There was one other attempt made to put a brake on the impending war: by the Spanish. Ayala, who had reached Scotland by January, was ingratiating himself with James when, in April, another Spanish embassy arrived at Stirling with the aim of getting James to call his war off, and enable Henry VII to honour his obligations to the Holy League. But these ambassadors, and the normally accurate Dr de Puebla, had abandoned reality. In March de Puebla had written to Ferdinand and Isabella to say that James had abandoned Warbeck and peace could be obtained.[48] But it is by no means clear what James's attitude to Warbeck was. James did not abandon Warbeck, and another

Tomb effigy of Robert Lord Willoughby de Broke, d. 1502, Callington church, Cornwall. De Broke had a house at Bere Ferrers in Devon, near Callington, and another at Broke in Wiltshire

attempted negotiation by the English failed to induce this. These negotiations took place at Jenyn Haugh, on the Scots side of the border in May. Probably Fox led the English delegation; for Scotland, Alexander – Lord Hume – James's chamberlain, and the Earl of Angus, his chancellor were present. All we know about what happened here is that Henry demanded the revocation of the safe conduct given to Warbeck and his rebel band by James IV. There may also have been a demand that Angus, Hume and the Bishop of Moray proceed immediately to England on embassy.[49] James refused to yield to nothing less than war. How acrimonious or amicable the negotiations were, must be left to the imagination. Given the situation, the English delegation may not have done much more than threaten Scotland with their king's plans, the outcome of which was a foregone conclusion: a humiliating Scots defeat.

Robert Willoughby de Broke, that seasoned commander of amphibious forces was to lead the way. His flagship was the *Regent*, and two other royal ships appointed with him, the *Mary Fortune*, and the *Swepestake*, were built for the 1497 campaign. Indeed such was the pressure of events that when de Broke left Portsmouth the *Mary Fortune*, was not fully completed. The rest of his fleet was composed of armed merchantmen drawn from the south and south-west of England. De Broke had twenty armed merchantmen at his disposal as well as transports to the number of twenty-six. Some of these vessels would have been dismissed on reaching their destination, but twenty of them were retained for use in the later stages of the war. To serve as marines, Henry appointed 5,000 men, 2,000 of which, as soldiers, were raised in Somerset and Gloucester. De Broke also had with him 100 Cornish miners, furnished with Tudor livery, paid at 6*d* per day and provided by Henry with the tools of their trade, to undermine Scottish castles.[50]

Large numbers of retinues were being raised in England to fight in Scotland, but Henry went no further than this: he drew in mercenaries who had recently fought in Alsace for Duke René of Lorraine against Robert de la Marck. When this warfare ended, in the winter of 1496–7, the mercenaries found work in England. At the beginning of April 1497 Henry VII received one of Duke René's servants at court. Henry's agents had been at work in Calais and Antwerp. Six weeks later, on 13 May, Arnald Krantz of Grifolheim, and four others, took Henry's money, Arnald at four marks per month and his fellows at 16s 8d each. Thereby Henry recruited the commander of René of Lorraine's mercenary forces. Kranz was hired by the good offices of a German, or Danish, paymaster who also recruited two other Germans. Henry also intended using Swiss mercenaries as Maximilian I said, to wake up his enemy. During the winter Norroy King-of-Arms, Roger Machado, was sent expressly to convey 'Souchenours', i.e. Swiss, to England. The word 'Soucher' is also found in the spring, when Henry's Breton councillor Pierre le Penec was given 100 marks to convey 50 men-at-arms to England, 'from overseas'. The search for gunners from the continent also began in December 1496, when Philip Lockier, lieutenant of the ordnance, went to Flanders to buy harquebuses and halbards. Henry already had a retinue of about ten resident gunners in England of whom four were European. In the spring of 1497 Lockier recruited seven Dutchmen as 'lez principall gunners' for the king: van harlom, van Roterdam, vander Heyde, probably recruited in Antwerp. However by June, Henry had 200 gunners in England of whom 40, at least, were Europeans: van Andewarpe, van guylder, lez Breton, and van Spayne suggest their origins. They spent their time in England preparing guns, packing gunpowder and aligning the sights on each artillery piece. And then in April and May the entire ordnance corps, men and materials, was tested at Mile End on a specially built proving ground of gun emplacements and butts.

Weaponry to fight this war lay scattered in a number of arms depots: Kenilworth, Porchester, Newcastle, Berwick, Portsmouth, and Calais, and in the Tower of London damp had rotted carts and rats had gnawed horse harnesses. A complete overhaul of the ordnance was ordered, the scale of which was enormous; William Furness, clerk of the ordnance, hired 1,000 men and 600 horses to serve as an ordnance corps. The first payment for weaponry had been made to Henry Fyner of Southwark, goldsmith, on 22 December 1496, to provide iron for the ordnance foundries in the Weald of Kent. There followed quickly, on Christmas Eve, orders for 1,000 bills, bows, sheaves of arrows and more. Matters began in earnest on 4 January. We have seen that ships from London and the southern ports took men and arms to Berwick in the winter of 1496–7. Late in the year a rigid timetable was devised to supply Berwick with enough weapons to make an invasion of Scotland feasible. The first convoy of ships, largely of European vessels, left Tower Wharf on 30 April. Almost exclusively these ships carried light ordnance for the infantry. Bows had been manufactured throughout the Midlands and London between January and April. In mid-April all bows were called in, and so were arrows, called in on 10 April, and bills, over 3,000 of which were delivered from the Forest of Dean on 14 April. Shipments north (using vessels from the south coast and Calais) began on 2 March, and ended on 22 April. For those preparing siege artillery the deadline was later, mid-May. This was to be a war of guns. Henry shipped 16 named siege pieces north at the end of May, and had 28 new falcons cast for the field. Yet, in the last analysis, everything depended not upon the quality of the equipment which Henry put into the field, but on the quality of his army.

Although Henry VII intended using Swiss and Germans as shock troops, the bulk of the proposed vanguard to invade Scotland would have been English. Between January and April Henry raised 43 retinue leaders who were assigned to Giles, Lord Daubney's command. The overwhelming fact about Daubney's van is that two-thirds of its members were the king's household knights. Only ten of the 43 held no office whatsoever, but their loyalty looked secure. Some were related to householders. Others had proved loyal shire gentry. Apart from Daubney, the two peers nominated had served Henry VII loyally for years. John Grey of Wilton seems undistinguished but James Lord Audley had been knighted at Stoke, served well in France and was a near neighbour of the Lord Chamberlain's. Personal loyalty to the king was the key to this vanguard, all vanguards indeed, but to this one especially, given the nature of its mission, to root out Warbeck. Overall command was Daubney's; but Thomas Lovell, Treasurer of the Household was also assigned to him as a kind of Tudor commissar perhaps. Many men intensely loyal to Henry were placed in the van: Rice ap Thomas, Chamberlain of South Wales; Sampson Norton, Chamberlain of North Wales; and Richard Pole, Prince Arthur's Chamberlain, as well as Sir Walter Hungerford and Sir Humphrey Stanley. Between them they were to muster 7,000 men at Newcastle-upon-Tyne, and they would have taken on more northerners and garrison soldiers as a matter of course, to increase their number to around 10,000.

In Scotland the spring months had seen much the same sort of activity. In February James IV demanded a complete mobilization for forty days from 6 April. To the south-west letters went to Kirkcudbright, Galloway, Kyle and Annandale; to the west to Argyll, Lorne, Lennox, Renfrew, Cunningham and Lanark; and to the north to Perth, Forfar, Kincardine, Aberdeen, Banff, Forres, Elgin and Inverness. In the Lowlands he readied Linlithgow and Haddington and on the border, Berwickshire. On St Valentine's Day further notice was sent to Stirling, Menteith, Fife and Angus and to Dumbarton in the west. Behind the demand for men, James ordered wood, taken from Ettrick Forest, from Selkirk, Clydesdale, Aberdeenshire, and Darnaway near Inverness. By the end of March, James took delivery of new bombard wheels for the gun carriage of his Burgundian bombard Mons Meg. Gunnery of all sorts was being made in Scotland and one man had a special task, 'to take mesour of muldis of divers gunnys to send Frans to make pellokis of irne'. Shot for Scottish guns was to be imported from French arms manufacturers. In April a new master of the artillery was appointed, and James travelled from the borders to Stirling, to Fife and back to Stirling. When in the south he oversaw artillery preparations at Melrose and the refortification of Dunbar castle. Returning from Dunbar he spent his time with Ayala. Then he was in Fife, at Falkland, from where he visited St Andrews, and then went to Kincardine to oversee work in progress on material for the enormous 'Mons' bombard. We catch only fleeting glimpses of his Yorkist guests. During April Warbeck was probably with him at Falkland and travelled to the council at Stirling. The 'Inglis hors marshal' received James's gifts twice at Falkland as did five Yorkist curriers. At St Andrews Sir Johne Barree, a priest who complained he had been taken prisoner in England was rewarded £180; whether he was English or Scottish we do not know.[51]

At Easter James received information from one of his spies, of considerable English activity on the border. Possibly as a result of this he sent out letters to postpone the April muster. Though, with Henry's attack planned for midsummer, 6 April was too early to raise his feudal levy, and not all James's preparations were complete. Nonetheless 'Wapynshawyngs' were ordered in the Mounth and Ross and throughout the Scottish borders: Nithsdale, Annandale, Westland, the Merse, Teviotdale and Lothian at the end of April. And then the northern lords, the Earl of Huntly, the Earl Marischal and the Lords of Southland, Stirling, Angus and Strathearn, were summoned to muster at Stirling on 8 May. Even outmanned and outgunned as he was by Henry, James IV showed no inclination to capitulate. Activity within Scotland increased, and renewed efforts were made to involve Ireland. The borders were James's first consideration. On 14 May letters were despatched to all border lords for a muster in early June. From Stirling, where he was in mid-May, James moved to Linlithgow Palace and then on to Edinbugh on 21 May. Two days later he was at Dunbar dispensing his usual bounty and overseeing the work in progress. On Corpus Christi (25 May) he returned to Edinburgh to concentrate on his ordnance. Hans and Henry Foulis, his gunners, were still at Coldingham. In mid-May the king's second gunner, Robert Herward was sent to Hume to coordinate preparations in the forest of Ettrick and Melrose region, and in the first week of June he was overseeing the casting of shot there. From Edinburgh James took his leave to command his war from Peebles. On 1 June letters were issued throughout southern Scotland for the muster at Melrose. On 2 June Prince Richard of England, Rowland Robinson, the Dene of York, and many other long-term rebels of Henry VII's were with James at Peebles. On 6 June James sent out letters to the sheriffs of Peebles, Selkirk, Roxburgh, and Berwick and to the Lords of Lothian and the Merse warning them of the first raid. The next day Robinson and the Dene took a further instalment of the Duke of York's pension.[52]

Because of the wildly optimistic letters of the Spanish ambassadors, Ayala and de Puebla, it has been accepted that after the raid of Ellem and the spring of 1497, James IV took no more interest in Warbeck. The records of government and commerce, however, tell a different story, for James sheltered Warbeck's supporters such as William Barley and Rowland Robinson, well after Warbeck had left Scotland, into 1498.[53] In the spring of 1497 despite all their disappointments Warbeck's masters kept up the old tune: Scotland, Flanders, Ireland. In February or March 1497 Davy Rattrye, a servant of the Duke of Ross, was sent to Binche with letters from Warbeck to Margaret of Burgundy. Rattrye reached her Hainault manor in April. Since his expenses were reimbursed by the Conservator of Scottish Privileges in Middelburg he probably travelled to the Low Countries in a merchantman.[54] To get out of Scotland in anything other than disguise, for him, would have been next to impossible given the naval activity on the east coast that year. What these letters contained we do not know. They may have indicated James's predicament to the dowager duchess, and suggested that in the circumstances he would find it difficult to maintain Warbeck for much longer in Scotland. As we will see, there was still at this stage a degree of closet diplomacy, and the Spanish ambassador in Scotland, Ayala, was having some success in weakening James's resolve and frightening Warbeck about the possibility of Anglo-Scottish peace. Feelers may already have been out for an Irish escape route. For at St Andrews, on 5 May, James IV made a gift of alms to six Irish friars. Remembering that such men with merchants made the best couriers it is possible that this group had come from James IV's allies in Ulster. On 5 June one of O'Donnell of Tirconnel's men, sent to Scotland from Ulster returned to his chief bearing letters from James.[55] These fragmentary references suggest that far from his troubles being over Henry VII would have no peace until he rooted Warbeck and his band forcibly out of Scotland.

At about the time O'Donnell's servant was with James IV, Henry VII had begun to draw up a list of potential appointments to the royal ward to invade Scotland behind Daubney's van. The king's personal tents, his exchequer tents, and tents for his Yeomen of the Guard were all with de Broke. Over £11,000 was laid out provisioning de Broke's force, to remain at sea for six weeks. De Broke set sail from Portsmouth on 16 May. He made for the Downs, off Sandwich, where for a week he stayed. He took his ease, shipped arms for a second time, and waited. And waited. What he waited for was the order to proceed north. It came, eventually, on 1 or 2 June, and when it came all concerned knew that this war against Scotland would not be the one which had been planned. There was trouble in far away Cornwall. None the less Lord de Broke rendezvoused with his transports, on 5 June, and arrived at Berwick-on-Tweed on 21 June. A week later he was on his way to Scotland. The retinues due to muster at Newcastle on 25 May were about to start the long trek north. Henry and his van commander, Daubney, were at Sheen, probably finalizing their ordnances for war. The king had been most particular about them prior to Stoke and on campaign in France in 1492. Thirty years later an inexperienced Thomas Wolsey begged a then-retired Bishop Fox to tell him how to draw up such rules and regulations. Fox told him 'I neyther have nor neurer [did] see any wryting thereof'.

For while Daubney was ordained to invade Scotland from Northumberland, 'the said entreprise was broken by thinsurrexion that began in Cornwell and Devonshire by reason of the Black Smith'. No king could have been in a more exposed position than Henry VII. One third of his forces rested on their estates secure in the knowledge that they would not be needed before July. One third of his forces had just been committed against Scotland with de Broke. The final third, Daubney's van, were making their individual journeys to Newcastle. They were beyond recall of their commander and king. The only retinues assigned to Daubney and in place to challenge the rebels, refused to obey orders and defected to them. The war that Henry VII planned collapsed under its own weight. By June 1497 it had cost, at a conservative estimate £60,000, though I doubt if £90,000 would be an over- estimate. War there was, but not that efficient sort which Henry Tudor so desired. Instead the king's voyage into Scotland was the curtain raiser to six months of civil war.[56]

TWELVE

Success

If 'Bosworth was the battle which should have been fought in October 1483', then Blackheath should have been fought in July 1495. Had Clifford not returned to betray his accomplices, and had Warbeck's Flemish captains landed in East Anglia and not Kent then the events of May and June 1497, which are dynastic in meaning, but ambiguously and tenuously so, would have been crystal clear. In neither 1495 nor 1497 was Kent prepared to rise against Henry VII, and its loyalty was the key to his survival. But if, in those years, neither Kent, nor the north of England was prepared to accept Warbeck as a Plantagenet the west of England was. The nature of the events of mid-1497 have always puzzled commentators. The rebellion which occurred in that year was so dangerous, and like the flash of lightning it was, so violent and quickly over, that it appears unconnected to the wider political manoeuvrings regarding Warbeck. Most commentators consign the rebellion to a limbo marked 'Tax Rebellion, Not Political'. This is seen in the most distant chronicle accounts of events and in the most recent analysis. After describing the executions of the leaders of the 1497 rebellion, the *Great Chronicle* remarks that the cause of the rebellion 'was ffor levying of such money as ye have hard grauntid by the last parliament' and that the rebels intended purging Henry VII's government of the ministers – John Morton, Richard Fox, Oliver King, Sir Reginald Bray and Sir Thomas Lovell – who had advised him to levy the war taxes.[1] The most recent analysis, M.L. Bush's is remarkably like the *Great Chronicle*'s. That author remarks darkly that though this rebellion was said by most to be a Tax Rebellion, the rebels may have had a hidden agenda, like the 1381 rebels, or Jack Cade. Bush argues that the rebellion of June 1497 was 'directed and sustained . . . by the governments tax policies', and Warbeck's September landing in Cornwall offers no convincing proof that the June rebellion had any bearing on politics or dynasticism. He goes further to suggest that Warbeck himself may have capitalized on the earlier tax rebellion by issuing a proclamation in July 1497 (sic) condemning Henry VII's 'daily pilling of the people by dimes, tallages, benevolences and other unlawful impositions . . .'.[2] The difficulty with this argument is, as we have seen, that this proclamation was issued not, as has been suggested, in July 1497, but eight months earlier, in September 1496. It was an invitation to rebel, to purge England of a king unfit to govern because he levied taxes so harshly.

That the rebellion of June 1497 broke out in reaction to Henry VII's taxes there is no doubt. They were heavy, prolonged and novel. M.L. Bush has described the tax as 'extremely onerous. It was the quivalent of four fifteenths and tenths, all to be collected in one year . . . £120,000. And this came on top of a forced loan of £40,000 paid in February . . . and not repayable until after . . . November.' He suggests that the revolt was against the unprecedented weight of taxation, as much as its novelty, for it combined traditional tax raising methods with new ones. In fact Bush considerably underestimates[3] the weight of taxes levied. The loan demanded in December 1496 raised £51,375 1*s* 4*d* not £40,000. Very few noblemen paid a loan, they were expected to fight. But about 4,500 members of the political nation of gentry status and below made loans.[4] Moreover the clergy were assessed for taxes three times over: once for the loan in anticipation of taxes, once for their parliamentary tax, and once for a special clerical tax levied on both York and Canterbury provinces. No wonder clergy were to the fore as rebels. The border and northern areas, and Wales and the Marches, normally exempt from taxation, this year lost their exemptions. Considerably more was being demanded than £120,000; and much more in one year than at any time since Agincourt.[5] Yet tax rebellions cannot be considered non-political. Taxpayers were generally the richer members of their communities, occupying postions of key power in their locality, intermediaries between the king and his people. The tax rebellion is not the opposite of a political rebellion, it is its embodiment. The nature of events in the summer of 1497 is aptly described by Polydore Vergil when he calls them 'a civil war'.[6]

Rebellion broke out in western Cornwall on about 14 May 1497. As far as we can tell it started over the matter of excessive tax rating by a local tax collector, John Oby, Provost of Glasney College at Penryn. Oby was accused of corruption, pocketing the difference between his assessment and the king's demand. However, what may have begun as a fracas in the parish of St Keverne exploded into a rebellion of ferocious intent. It was led out of west Cornwall by Michael Joseph – the Smith – An Gof, in Cornish, and it quickly picked up support among the local gentry and clergy. Among them it found its second leader, Thomas Flamank, the eldest son of a well-respected gentleman, Richard, who was involved in assessing the king's taxes. With no opposition the rebels carried all before them, and at the end of May, arrived outside Exeter.[7] From this point on we have good accounts of their behaviour, from all sources. This rebellion can be contrasted with that of the rebellion of 1489 in which a large group of commoners murdered the Earl of Northumberland, and after this the rebellion evaporated. In contrast Michael Joseph and Thomas Flamank showed a grim determination to take their rebellion out of Cornwall into the rest of the realm: the political arena.

When they arrived at Exeter the Cornish demanded to be admitted. The frightened citizens kept them waiting, and eventually agreed to allow their commmanders into the town. Once inside the rebel captains threatened to behead the mayor, but did nothing else.[8] They had fatter fish to fry in Somerset, a county notorious in the early modern period for rising in rebellion against constituted authority. Having made contact with the men of Somerset, across the wastes of indifference of Devon, the Cornish mined a rich seam of anti-authoritarianism. Their arrival at Taunton was marked by a general rising which extended north to Devizes, in Wiltshire, south to Dorchester and east to Winchester.[9] And it was in Somerset that they aquired their noble leader, James Tuchet, Lord Audley.

Lord Audley has always been a puzzle to historians of Henry VII's reign. They do not know why he joined in the rebellion, and he was the only nobleman to do so. Suggestions have been made that he was poor, or had lost lands, or was discontented after the French campaign of 1492. We know nothing of his attitude to the 1492 campaign, but we know that he was not poor. His estates, after his death were valued as giving him an income of £1,500 per annum.[10] Recently attention has been turned on the fact that his father, John, the Treasurer of England under Richard III, was deprived of this post by Henry VII. Was Audley seeking revenge for his father? None of these explanations, poverty, discontent or closet-Yorkism is very convincing when set against Lord Audley's nondescript public career: the perfect model of a minor peer. There is, however, a pattern to which he and his father fit. John Lord Audley, James's father, like William Stanley, Gilbert Debenham, and Robert Chamberlain first served Edward IV loyally for many years and then after 1483 made an accommodation with Richard III. Unlike his near Somerset neighbour, Giles Daubney, or his close Hampshire colleague, John Cheyne, John Lord Audley did not take arms against Richard, and in 1484 he was made Treasurer of England. John's career, like William Stanley's, began early with a defection to the Yorkist Lords at Calais in 1461. He was given modest local offices in Dorset and worked tirelessly for Edward IV in the west and south. He had some gift in languages, for he served as ambassador to France, twice.[11] His personal loyalty to Edward IV may be measured in two ways. Firstly he was one of the king's advisers singled out for denunciation in 1468 by Warwick and Clarence.[12] More telling, in a family whose firstborn son was always called John or James in succession John Audley named his heir Edward, but the little boy died, aged five, and so his second son, James, succeeded John in 1490.[13] For the Audleys, father and son, the critical moment of 1483 did not pass without trauma. John's brother, Thomas, was implicated in Buckingham's rebellion. He was not attainted, but all three, Thomas, John and son James sought pardon in 1484. Immediately thereafter Audley was dropped from the commission of the peace and stripped of his Crown appointments in Somerset and Dorset. Perhaps this was the result of real treason, perhaps merely it was guilt by association with Thomas.[14] Neither John nor James were fully trusted ever again; by Richard because they may have been sympathizers with Henry Tudor, by Henry Tudor because they had not fully declared for him. When the rebels of 1483 returned to their own in the west of England, loyalists who had been supporters of Henry Tudor were much preferred to the natural families of the county.[15] Men like Audley took second place to political arrivistes like Cheyne and Daubney. Audley's motive for leading the rebellion in 1497 was said to be a grudge against John Cheyne, who had picked up his father's old offices, and was encroaching on the Audley sphere of influence.[16] For James Audley the moral of this tale may have been that he who hesitates is lost – to both sides. Nor is Audley unique to Somerset in the summer of 1497. There were others, Sir Hugh Lutterel of Dunster and Sir Nicholas Latimer of Duntish in Dorset, who had rebelled against Richard in 1483, but had accommodated themselves with him after this, only to find themselves out of favour after 1485. In 1497 Audley's supporters also included Roger Twynyho, a member of George, Duke of Clarence's retinue, the brother of Ankarette, lady-in-waiting to Clarence's wife Isabel Neville. Among the lesser lights involved was John Verney of Fairfeld, one of Richard III's Somerset officers.[17]

This group of men formed the nucleus of a political rebellion which might have drawn on similar discontents elsewhere. It was, in any case, linked to a powerful popular discontent with Henry VII. The natural focus of such political discontent lay with the alter dynasty, York in the person of Perkin Warbeck, and Edward Plantagenet, Earl of Warwick. Thus when the rebels entered Wells in the first week of June 1497 the Spanish historiographer Zurita says, 'they sent for the so-called Duke of York who was at that time with the King of Scotland . . . They offered him help in his bid to take over the Kingdom of England as his by right.'[18] Zurita had access to the Spanish royal archive and parts of his narrative can be identified as drawn from the surviving diplomatic correspondence. James Gairdner suggested in 1898 that 'messages from the disaffected population of Cornwall did not find him in Ireland, as Polydore Vergil says they did, but must have reached him in Scotland before he set sail'.[19] Gairdner realized the crucial point concerns the dates surrounding Warbeck's departure. Warbeck left Ayr, on the west coast of Scotland before 6 July. The act of attainder against the men who supported him in Cornwall states that they had sent him 'dyvers Messages and Writinges'. Possibly this described messages sent to him while he was Ireland in August 1497 but it is likely that this was also a reference to the messages sent to Scotland from Wells.[20] A letter of September 1497 said that it was Sir James Ormond, now a rebel, and then in control of Kilkenny and Tipperary, who invited Warbeck to Ireland.[21] In view of the distance between Somerset and Scotland it is plausible that Ormond himself was reacting to news from England, for Ormond was killed on 17 July, ten days after Warbeck left Scotland. For Warbeck to have heard about the uprising in England, news of it would have had to have been transmitted before 15 June.

The first week of June marked the height of rebel fervour in the Wells, Bath and Bristol area. The rebels drew in large numbers of men, estimated variously at between 15,000 and 40,000, and sent messages to Bristol that it was to surrender.[22] The mayor of the town returned them a dusty answer and 'made redy to withstond the said rebelles, and garnished the town walles with men harnessid and with gonnes, and brought shippes and botes about the marsh garnished with men, artillery and gonnes'. This demand may be indicative of the rebel frame of mind. They had ignored Exeter and were about to launch a cross-country attack on London. Bristol had close trading links with Ireland and perhaps like the 1495 rebels they too wanted to establish a 'town of strength' by which Warbeck could enter England. But the mayor's answer, and the pressing necessity to capitalize on surprise and move with speed on London, led to the abandonment of this idea. Instead of attacking Bristol, Michael Joseph An Gof, and James Lord Audley decided to march out of Wells toward London. Joseph took the road from Wells to Winchester and to Guildford via Farnham.[23] Audley followed the same route as Joseph, possibly as leader of a host composed of Somerset rebels independent of the Cornish; for while Joseph was said to be at Guildford, on 13 June, Audley was then, reportedly, at Salisbury[24]. In payments laid out by the king there are hints that Audley's *bête noir*, John Cheyne, fought some kind of military action, conceivably against Audley, in his own 'country', near to Salisbury. But, if this is true and is not a mere documentary discrepancy, he was lamentably unsuccessful. The true defence of the realm was begun by the king in the Oxfordshire reaches of the Thames.

Henry had withdrawn from London in order to muster troops at Woodstock. From here he advanced southwards staying on the north side of the Thames.[25] When he reached Wallingford he sent overnight messages to Ewelme where he knew Edmund de la Pole, Earl of Suffolk, had gathered his retinue. He wanted de la Pole to take his men to defend Staines bridge; but unbeknown to the king, George Neville, Lord Burgavenny was also at Ewelme. The king's messenger found de la Pole in bed, in fact in bed with Burgavenny. On the arrival of the messenger Burgavenny disappeared under the covers of the bed, and the messenger delivered his master's orders in ignorance that there were two, and not one, noblemen present. When he had withdrawn, Burgavenny pointedly asked de la Pole, 'yf a man will do aught What Will ye doo now it is tyme'. This question encapsulates the dilemma of the nobility of the realm. Would they support the king or renew the Wars of the Roses? De la Pole, so he said, did not hesitate, but jumped out of bed and went to obey Henry's order. To immobilize the treacherous Burgavenny he removed his shoes so that he could not ride.[26] Fifty miles to the south a similar decision was being faced by the King's Chamberlain, Giles, Lord Daubney. Daubney had been deputed by the king to guard the southern approaches to London, and in the end, so he did. He did not, however, stop the rebels from reaching Blackheath and with the exception of one brief skirmish at Guildford did not engage them in action at all. Several years after the rebellion, political gossip reported that if he had played his part fully the rebels would have been destroyed before they reached London.[27] Daubney found an acute dilemma. Many of the rebels were his neighbours, from Somerset, and their leaders were his friends and relatives. What should he do? Like de la Pole he did his duty. Unlike de la Pole he carried it out to the letter and not in spirit. The king, years later, was said to have been furious at his behaviour.

Because of the speed with which the rebellion developed, southern England was in military chaos in the first week of June.[28] However, in the second week of June the king assembled his forces and on 17 June defeated the rebels at Blackheath, the Mount Tabor of

Sketch of a hanged man. This macabre graffito was found on the cover of a book made at the command of Henry VII. It lists still active bonds enforcing loyalty, including over fifty placed on rebels after 1497

English rebellions. With the single exception of Audley, Henry's nobility rallied to him at Blackheath. Eighteen noble retinues and three others – one of a cadet de la Pole, one of a dowager Duchess of Norfolk and one of Prince Arthur – provided their king with a quarter of the troops for his army here. The rest of them came from the gentry, yeomen and city families of central southern England. Rebel positions in Deptford village below Blackheath were charged down by Henry's veteran commander of Bosworth and Stoke, John de Vere, Earl of Oxford, and Giles Daubney was wounded in battle.[29] What was the fighting about? If it was merely a bloody end to a tax protest then the battle and the punishment of the west of England, which went on till 1506, are even harsher than they seem to be. But the fighting was not just about taxes, or even to drive the king's wicked councillors out of office. The rebels' political objectives were stated in the king's proclamation of pardon issued after the battle. Their intentions were the destruction of the king's person, the subversion of the realm and 'the retracting, stop and let of his most noble voyage and royal army prepared toward Scotland'.[30] Though this is heavily propagandistic and aimed at uniting the realm behind the king by playing on its fears of anarchy, it is a description of what had happened, and what might have happened if the rebels had reached London, rescued Edward, Earl of Warwick from the Tower and proclaimed a Yorkist readeption. Even though de Fuensalida, Spanish ambassador to the Flemish and Imperial courts, runs all the events of the year together he catches the horror of June as 'a time when the whole Kingdom was against the King, and when Perequin had entered the country calling himself King, and the King of Scotland was coming in by another way, and the whole country was in rebellion, and the men of Cornwall were giving battle at a short distance from London; when, had the King lost the battle he would have been finished off and beheaded . . .'.[31]

Blackheath was the defining moment for Henry Tudor and his dynasty, for it ensured the continuance of both. But it was a paradox. At a moment when they could have destroyed him by mere abstinence in battle, like Richard III at Bosworth, his nobles and gentry rallied to him. Daubney, de la Pole and Burgavenny all played their part in defending London and ironically it was the future rebel Edmund de la Pole alone of these three who was rewarded. For the other two Blackheath marked the beginning of a fall from grace. For the king, Blackheath showed him that no one in his realm should be trusted. All that was necessary for the final years of Henry's reign to take their shape were the plots of 1498–9 and 1501–2. Having counteracted both plots Henry VII might have ruled England in peace. But he could not, 'he became preoccupied at once by a fresh care. For he began to treat his people with more harshness and severity than had been his custom, in order (as he himself asserted) to ensure they remained more thoroughly and entirely in obedience to him.' Blackheath began this slide toward repression, and it began it because despite support in depth for the king, large numbers of well-wishers had given the rebels food and weapons.

After the battle, with Henry victorious, a Sir Robert was with some of the victorious troops who returned to the Midlands. In one Harry Cooper's house he heard a Master Butlar discussing recent events. Butlar said that he believed 'we ned nott pray for the kyng bename butt pro Rege nostro tunc'. Then, having just fought for Henry VII, he said, 'for why tys hard to know who is Ryghetwys kyng.' Sir Robert, possibly Sir Robert Southwell, did not inform on Master Butlar till January 1500, and then to the king's mother, Margaret Beaufort. According to Sir Robert, Butlar was free with his opinions. Before the battle of Blackheath and frequently afterward, he had maintained (to the Prior of Stoneleigh, Warwickshire, and to Sir Robert himself), 'that he hopyd to se hys master wer the crowne or [before] he dye'. Margaret Beaufort could be relied to act on any information touching the honour of the dynasty so she summoned Sir Robert and the prior to Collyweston. On 20 January 1500 they were examined and both men confessed they had heard Butlar's treason.[32] Yet Butlar was not the only Midlands man to have doubts about supporting the king in June 1497. Given the king's route and with royal activity everywhere, it was difficult not to support him. However, after the emergency was over Everard Feilding, esquire, of Lutterworth in Leicestershire was bound over for his loyalty, and had to find security from a number of gentry families from Leicester and Warwickshire.[33] An examination of the military accounts for 1497 shows that he had not supported Henry VII in any army, projected or assembled – of which there had been four – that year. The king had written to him on 3 July, about what we do not know: non-attendance at Blackheath perhaps?[34] In 1485 Everard Feilding had been one of four members of the ex-Hastings affinity who followed Richard III's servant, William Catesby, to Bosworth.[35]

East Anglia had also supported rebellion in some form. Some individuals were bound over to keep the peace and when the sheriffs were chosen for 1498 the king took the unprecedented step of disregarding local opinion and appointing them himself.[36] Those who fought at Blackheath, like Butlar, gave Henry their support in a muddled and confused manner, some committed publicly to him, but privately against him. Charles Ripon, for example, arrested in 1494, fought on the king's side, as did Gerard Danet. Danet was forgiven his previous trespasss and brought back within the political fold. Ripon stayed outside it. Four years after Blackheath he was plotting against Henry and was then executed for treason to do with Edmund de la Pole.[37] Men like Danet and Ripon may have believed they were helping to suppress a purely popular uprising, so they were not inclined to declare for Richard IV. Some rebels also had their doubts. A few days before Blackheath a group of westerners parleyed with Lord Daubney, volunteering to hand their leaders to the king in order to save their lives.[38] By then it was too late. The majority who had reached London were committed against Henry VII: dynastic challenges such as this were not to be defeated by discussion. A battle was inevitable.

Immediately the field at Blackheath was won there followed knighthoods and celebrations. The lucky defeated were ransomed and the less lucky leaders interrogated prior to execution. Thomas Flamank and Michael Joseph were hanged, drawn and quartered on 27 June and James Lord Audley beheaded the following day. But their fellow rebels were not dissuaded from supporting Warbeck. After the battle Henry's troops chased many rebels back across the north downs, and Henry himself ordered his commissioners to Cornwall to begin punishing the rebels. But the situation in Cornwall was beyond control, and very few royal messengers ventured over the River Tamar into the county. On the continent it was rumoured that, in spite of their defeat, the Cornish were undeterred and with James IV's aid were arming for battle once again. Those of Henry's Cornish supporters known as such were at considerable risk. One of them Roger Whalley, a client of the king's gentry supporters had been one of the first to warn Henry of the insurrection. He was a native of Padstow. Several weeks after Blackheath, when leaving his parish church, he was confronted by a gang of Lord Audley's servants and other rebels, including John Tresinney of Penryn who had been one of Michael Joseph An Gof's lieutenants. Taking advantage of the lawless situation they settled a number of scores: those of their neighbours whom Whalley had oppressed for years, and their own, for he had been instrumental in the deaths of their friends and master. They beat him up and left him bleeding, and then they went to his house which they ransacked, and went off with £50 worth of goods. They disappeared from central Cornwall – Padstow – and meant to take sanctuary at St Buryan, near Land's End, to wait for Warbeck's arrival. The June rebellion began when James Oby demanded taxes at St Keverne. The unpopularity of these taxes accounts for the widespread support it attracted. It none the less had another aspect to it. Both during and after it was recognized as a rising motivated by the only action men discontented with government could take: the replacement of one king by another. That Henry VII was considered a usurper in Cornwall made the justification of their action easier, they could appeal for aid to the one who should by right be king. By 7 September, when Tressiney and Audley's servants greeted Warbeck, they had transferred their allegiance from Henry VII to Richard IV.[39]

THIRTEEN

Cat and Mouse

James IV expected to join battle with Giles Daubney some time after midsummer. For most of June, James conducted a phoney war. He led a raid from Melrose into England on 12 June and immediately afterwards called the south and the borders to Lauder on 26 June for another muster and raid: more show than substance. There may have been a small English raid into Scotland, around 8 June, but by the end of June no real war had happened.[1] For England it was no longer possible. All available manpower was needed to defeat Michael Joseph An Gof. James IV's actions are curious. The indications from his personal expenses – on armour, saddles and horse trimmings – are that he expected to campaign earlier, rather than later, in the summer and that he changed his mind about when to fight. In a set of instructions which may never have been acted on Henry VII thanked James for abstaining from attacking England during the rebellion.[2]

At this distance James's behaviour appears almost impenetrable. He did not attack England yet went to ingenious lengths to aid Warbecks's rebels. His plans to send Warbeck to England probably originated before Lauder, but, it seems, that at Lauder, it was agreed to invade England in late July. Once James had agreed a date to invade England he returned to Edinburgh. He was back in his capital by 4 July and Warbeck put to sea on 6 July.[3] It has been argued that in sending Warbeck to Cornwall, James was ridding himself of a nuisance and embarrassment who by now he no longer took seriously.[4] From the account of the diplomacy of 1497 which Zurita gives, and from what we know, it is clear that the English and the Scots were negotiating secretly up to and into the period of the war. Ayala, though he appears in the surviving diplomacy as credulous to the point of folly about James, emerges from Zurita's account much closer to Ferdinand and Isabella's description of him as an unlearned but cunning diplomat. Part of the time he acted as a go-between between James and Fox, part of the time he tried to fulfil the Spanish desire to rid Scotland of Warbeck. At some point in the summer Ayala suggested to both sides that Warbeck could be handed over to the Spanish. But when Henry VII realized what was being proposed, Zurita says that he vetoed it.[5]

Something reminiscent of this tale is present in Polydore Vergil's statement that James and Henry quarrelled about whether or not James would hand Warbeck over to Henry.[6] Henry only agreed that Warbeck would be handed over to the Spanish when, in Zurita's words, 'he realized it was inevitable', probably a reference to the military paralysis the rebellion in England had caused. Then, said Zurita, Henry VII suggested that James send Warbeck out of the kingdom with honour, but without a safe conduct, in order that he could be captured. Accordingly Ayala suggested to James that he should not arouse Warbeck's suspicions by withdrawing support from him too abruptly, but that he should keep paying his pension. Next Ayala turned to Warbeck and told him, as if he was confiding a great secret, that peace was about to be concluded between England and Scotland, and that he was likely to suffer as a consequence. Warbeck and his masters had seen circumstances like this before, in 1492, when they thought Charles VIII was likely to deliver them to England. According to Zurita it had by this time been decided that Warbeck would to go to Ireland, and Ayala encouraged him in this decision, saying that from Ireland he could apply for a safe conduct from Spain. That there was further military action between Scotland and England this year, Zurita says was due to a combination of Henry's reluctance to agree to peace terms secretly negotiated by Fox, the Spanish and James, and pressure on James from some of his nobility to continue the war against England in the light of Warbeck's successful landfall in Cornwall.

Some of this story is in error, and it underestimates the military pressures on Scotland. It is possible that even now James IV wished to continue to support Warbeck. Yet he could not, faced with the actions undertaken against him by Henry VII. The best he could do was to accept the Spanish line. Then at least he was free to prosecute whatever war he wanted to, support Warbeck, and negotiate himself out of the war without loss of face or honour when and if he needed to. Zurita's account at least rings true for Warbeck's departure from Scotland. It accords with the fact that up to the moment he left Scotland James kept up payment of his pension, and it accords with the complex arrangements James made in ushering his guest out of Scotland.[7] At Ayr James provided Warbeck with the protection of Robert and Andrew Barton, John Barton, and George Young, in two or perhaps three ships.[8] In addition to these Scottish vessels James impressed two Breton masters Guy Foulcart and Jean Peidzoun. James paid Peidzoun by exempting him from all the customs due on his goods imported into Scotland in the two years following. Peidzoun returned to Scotland in mid-August when James was besieging Norham, having taken his party to Ireland. Foulcart had the more onerous job. He had to ensure Warbeck, or rather some group of his, got to Cornwall. Thus James provided him with letters which in the event of capture would enable him to plead compulsion. Foulcart made landfall with the Yorkists in Cornwall but was captured, 'and got away with the loss of his goods – indeed if he had been without possessions he would scarcely himself have escaped'.[9]

The ships were ready by 4 July. The Duke of York was well provisioned. He was given two tuns of wine. In contrast Andrew Barton had two pipes of cider and beer. Over £15 was spent on bread. Quantities of oatmeal, seventeen carcasses of salt beef, twenty-three carcasses of mutton, one hogshead of herring, twelve large cod and six stone of cheese, were stored on his ship as well as vessels for water, drinking cans, a cooking cauldron and fuel for cooking with, peat. In the days before their departure the duke and Katherine Gordon led a retinue of thirty mounted men, infantry and carts from Edinburgh to Ayr. James provided Katherine Gordon with a rowan tawny sea gown and a black cloak. As ever these arrangements were supervised by the faithful Rowland Robinson. Their departure from Scotland was supervised by Andrew Forman, the Scottish protonotary serving James, and Don Pedro de Ayala for the Spanish.[10] According to Zurita, Ayala had even agreed with Warbeck on the day he had to leave Ireland and on the port from which Spanish ships would pick him up. Contrary to some accounts this did not cleanse Scotland of all Yorkist taint. Taylor probably went with Warbeck, but Robinson may have remained in Scotland, for his name appears in the accounts later in the year, and finally disappears in December. William Barley was also one who may not have gone with Warbeck. He is found in Scotland in September 1497,[11] and there is evidence that even while the Treaty of Ayton was being negotiated by Henry's diplomats, James IV was still sustaining rebels at Falkland Palace. None the less, James was in a tight corner, and had bought himself space.

How bad James's military situation was can be seen in the activity of the English navy off the coast of Scotland in June and July 1497. Robert Willoughby de Broke sailed north at the beginning of June. On 21 June he arrived at Berwick and, in all likelihood, had news from

Muzzle end of an English breech-loading iron gun, c. 1500, of the sort used in naval warfare

Henry of the victory at Blackheath. Such news meant that he was now operating alone and not, as had been planned, in conjunction with Daubney. There may have been consultations with Fox and Surrey but the critical part he was playing in events would not have been lost on him. On 29 June he sailed north.[12] He ignored Dunbar and, as far as we know, also ignored Edinburgh and the Firth of Forth. Aberdeen was his object and he arrived off the Burgh on 10 July. He was not unexpected, but he never landed. He was still there on the 14 July and looked likely to stay for some while, possibly waiting for good weather in which to disembark.[13] About the time de Broke arrived off Aberdeen, James crossed the Forth from Edinburgh to Kinghorn and Aberdour in Fife. Aberdeen's distress would have been known to him; a fine reward for his restraint in not attacking England in June. He stayed in Fife two or three days and was back in Edinburgh on 10 July. The following day a proclamation was made throughout all southern and central Scotland for a muster on 20th July. [14]

How closely Zurita's story of the way Ayala got Warbeck out of Scotland can be reconciled with other evidence is not clear, for, at the point at which he claims Ayala had secured Warbeck's flight from Scotland Henry VII, according to instructions sent to Bishop Fox, believed it unlikely that James would hand over the pretender to him. Fox received two sets of instructions, one set to pursue in open negotiation and a second set to adhere to as if spontaneously. The first set is a mixture of acumen and recrimination. In the second set Henry's desperation for peace is heard. Fox was to repudiate his previous position at Jenyn Haugh and demand the delivery of Perkin Warbeck. If Perkin were to be delivered and a Scottish embassy sent to England a truce might be concluded. On the other hand, bearing in mind James's neutrality during the insurrection, their status and 'nyghnes of blode', if the Scots sent an embassy or were James to come to Newcastle then Henry could conclude a peace in person. This was the meat of the first set of instructions. Fox was expected to remind James who had begun the war and to put it to him that an oath swearing peace would not be enough. The King of Scotland would be bound 'uppon payne of censuris of the Holy Cherche and an obligation of Nisi'. Henry would swear upon the Gospel. It was also expected that the Scots would send an embassy to England to revoke Warbeck's safe conduct. Henry also looked for compensation for the damage caused within his kingdom in

September 1496. In return Henry offered to countermand de Broke's orders and 'restreign our armye by londe'. This much the Scots were to know. They were not to know Henry's plight within England.

In the second, secret, set of instructions Henry repeated his first offers, though they were put in terser language, but added the following

> Our final and resolved mynde is that ye obteyn al these articles that wer treated at Jenyn Haugh and yf ye can not obteyn all theym then to obteyne as many of theym as shalbe to you possible. And if so that our seid cousyn wol not be to any of theym agreable yet sith that the tyme of this yere is so far passed and our subjects sore weried and also thissu of bataill is ful uncertayn we shalbe contented for dyvers reasons movyng us and our consaill rather than to breke in to werre to accepte such offres as wer made unto you at Jenyn Haugh . . .

Fox was a man of enormous ability and presumably Henry felt that a successful formula could be worked out through the bishop. However, it is unclear if these instructions were ever sent to Fox, or if they were, that he had time to act on them.[15] Shortly afterwards Henry received intelligence on Scottish movements from Berwick. Within four days of his instructions to Fox he had given up the idea of peace in favour of a campaign. On 9 July he wrote to Sir Thomas Wortley informing him that Thomas Howard, Earl of Surrey in place of Lord Daubney would shortly lead a van of 10,000 men against the Scots.[16] On the continent it was rumoured that the king himself would go against James but the writer admitted, 'Nothing certain is known, but some great crash will take place before the month is out. God help the right I say no more.'[17] With Warbeck about to land in the west it seemed that Henry would be caught between war and renewed rebellion.

Having set his muster for 20 July James IV held, as best he could, to a seige of Norham castle. He intended a formidable move. On the 19 July his tents began moving to the border. The gangs assembling in Edinburgh that day were as large as anything seen before Flodden: over two hundred artificers, sixty-one quarrymen and masons, twelve wrights, four smiths and thirteen gunners. Transport for the thirty-one guns was provided by ninety-three horses and the ammunition filled thirty-seven carts. At Coldingham and Hume Henry Foulis and Sir Robert Ker retrieved James' defensive artillery and began moving it towards Norham. James himself supervised workmen in Edinburgh castle before going south. Then, with a full purse and a new damask coat for the 'great raid', he made his customary prayers at Restalrig. In September 1496 James had undertaken a limited action against England. The 'great raid' was altogether different. The king coined part of his gold chain producing £571. Personal loans were made by some of his greater subjects. Towns not contributing men sent money: Perth £150, Dundee £225. Leaving aside taxes these contributions produced over £1,500. The great Mons bombard which he had spared England in 1496 began its preparations on the day that James left for Melrose. Tow ropes were purchased, and the next day, to the accompaniment of fiddle and drum, it was wheeled down to Holyrood to join the other guns. From here Mons was supposed to join James at Norham, but she was so heavy that her gun cradle shattered. For ten days she was delayed in Edinburgh while a new cradle was constructed. On 31 July, accompanied by one hundred artificers, the bombard left Edinburgh covered by a decorated tarpaulin, the whole party supervised by Lord Hillhouse. This accident, coming when it did, was crucial and contributed to the failure of the campaign. Without Mons's enormous firepower Norham was quite safe, and while James besieged Norham without Mons, de Broke and Surrey could concert the English reply. Nonetheless this campaign is indicative of James's mood. He had spent, and continued to spend, large

Mons Meg, the iron bombard used at the siege of Norham in 1497. It was made for Duke Philip the Good of Burgundy in 1449 and given to James II of Scotland in 1457

sums on his guns. At the beginning of August, Edinburgh castle was busy with the casting of iron pellets. In the first week of August cart loads of gun stones and lead pellets were taken to Norham. In this week the artillery retinue alone cost the king £200. James was established on the border by 1 August. A letter of Henry's says that he laid siege 'as well withyn his awn land of Scotland as withyn this owir land'.[18]

The siege of Norham was in every way as peculiar an event as the raid of Ellem. On both James lavished great energy. Large forces were deployed by both England and Scotland, but the campaigns which followed were static. For ten days James had a free hand at Norham, and his guns bombarded the castle. Behind its massive fortifications Fox and his captains, Thomas Garth, John Hamerton, Henry Gregory and George Matthewson sat and sniped at their assailants. At this siege people representing every element of the previous year and a half were gathered. Andrew Forman, Warbeck's guardian in Scotland was there, so was Ayala drinking and gambling with the king, so close to the action that four of his servants were killed, three more wounded. There was even a *rapprochement* between James and Sir John Ramsay, Lord Bothwell.[19] But after ten days' fruitless siege James personally withdrew to Edinburgh. Why he did so is unclear. It is possible that James did not press his advantage much, and, too, that Norham was too well defended and too impregnable to take. But there was also the problem of money. The siege had lasted two weeks, but James had only paid his forces for one. Parts of his host had been in the field since the beginning of June and he could not keep them there indefinitely. Additionally the weather was bad and there was plague in Edinburgh. By 10 August James was back in Edinburgh where he had word from Flanders, perhaps from Margaret of Burgundy, but about what we are ignorant.[20]

By 10 August his scouts were warning James of the imminent arrival of Surrey. No sooner was he in Edinburgh than he at once sent messengers to the sheriffs of Linlithgow, Stirling, Sanquhar, Ayr, Irvine, Strathearn, Yester, Hailes, Drummond, Selkirk and Peebles, and to the Earl Marischal and Lord Lyle calling for fresh troops to withstand Surrey. Great general that he was, Surrey did not go to Norham. Instead he marched from Berwick towards Edinburgh and laid siege to the Hume castle of Ayton. A second set of instructions were therefore despatched on 13 August calling the levy to oppose Surrey at the raid of Ayton. By 16 August, James had left his capital and was already at Haddington about to cross the Lammermuirs to Duns, where he spent three nights, 17 to 19 August in a house at Cattleshiel. James's failure to take Norham was the effective end of his war with England. And if we regard this failure as strategic then on the 14th the return to Scotland of Jean Peidzoun, the captain who had sailed with Warbeck, presaged the end of Scottish support for Warbeck. On 15 August James still possessed enough illusions to fight, but Surrey commanded a very powerful force and de Broke was at that moment deploying his navy in the Firth of Forth.[21]

The week after Lammas Tide saw the start of Surrey's counter-attack. He had at his disposal the ordnance which had arrived at Newcastle during June and July: two bombards, two curtalds, ten demi-curtalds, two great serpentines, two small serpentines, sixteen falcons, three hundred and thirty-six harquebuses as well as ordnance from the north. Allowing for technical staff, harquebusiers, and the border levies from Northumberland and Durham, the earl had under him an army approaching fifteen thousand men. As he moved towards Berwick, so de Broke withdrew from Aberdeen and redeployed in the Forth by the 15 August.[22] With James on the border his capital was undefended. Had de Broke so chosen he might, with an army of five thousand, have taken Edinburgh and certainly burned Leith. However, the mere presence of an English fleet in the Forth was a disruption to Scotland. The first bridge across the Forth was thirty-five miles west of Edinburgh at Stirling. Normally it was easy enough to cross from Fife to the Lothians using a boat from one of the many villages on the coast. De Broke's presence, threatening Fife and the Lothians and thereby Dunfermline, St Andrews, Kinghorn and Edinburgh, drove a wedge into Scotland lengthening its lines of communication and paralysing its trade.

Given the evident coordination of the English military by Fox, Surrey and de Broke, the short campaign and sorry showing which James made is not to be wondered at. On 16 August Surrey left Berwick on the north road towards Dunbar. It was pouring with rain so this may account for the earl's lack of progress and the fact that he took only half the ordnance with him. To move a large ordnance train quickly in driving rain on border roads was a tall order.[23] None the less, on his first day in Scotland Surrey demolished four peel towers without any opposition: Cawmyllis, Hoten Hall, Edyngton and Fulden. The following day he pressed on to Ayton, eight miles within Scotland. Here Norroy King-of-Arms and his four trumpeters were sent to demand the surrender of the castle. Bearing in mind that James was hastening across the Lammermuirs the Scots inside felt more than sure of rescue and so refused Surrey his demand. This was at midday. Surrey therefore arranged his artillery, and at 2 o'clock began to bombard the castle. From the amount of shot used, a sharp fire was kept up. Surrey was not to be trifled with and for three hours he kept this going until the Scots surrendered.

By now James and his army were within a few miles of Ayton, but Surrey proceeded in good order. On 18 August he set eleven of his miners to work on Ayton's foundations and the castle was thereafter a shell. James and his army watched apologetically from a mile's distance. With de Broke in the Forth and Surrey facing him, James' situation was desperate. The weather was sapping the morale of both armies. James thought therefore that he might repossess Berwick by calling Surrey's bluff. Lyon Herald was sent to the earl to require him to do battle with his king. The earl took this to be a serious proposition and gave commands for the army to draw up in battle order. The losses recorded later included two thousand archers' stakes, probably incurred defending Halidon Hill against James. Lyon, seeing these preparations begin, then made a second offer: one which James had prepared him to make should Surrey take him at his word. He conveyed his master's message that James would fight Surrey in hand-to-hand combat. If Surrey lost then Berwick and the Fishgarths would fall to Scotland; if James lost then Surrey would have a king's ransom. Bearing in mind the discrepancy in age between James and Surrey, thirty years, James hoped for a cheap victory. Surrey was not to be drawn.[24] He thanked his grace

> that he wolde put hym to so moche honour that he beyng a kyng anoynted he wold fight hande to hande with so poore a man as he, how be yt he said though he wanne hym bataile he was neuer the nerer Berwike ne of Fysshgarthys, for, he had no such comyssyon so to do: his Comyssyon was to do the kyng of Scottis his Master all the harme he coulde and so he had don and wold do

Not without a hint of irony, then, Surrey prepared for an engagement. But this was an engagement which James could not afford. He had, it was later said, seen the ears of the wolf and had no wish to tempt providence. Thus on 19 August he withdrew to Haddington to consider the lessons of the summer while a sickly and rain-sodden English army retreated to Berwick. The north had done its duty in deplorable weather; it was prepared to do no more. The army melted away at the moment it reached Berwick. Despite the royal command to stay in formation the retinues refused to serve any further. Neither cheap provisions, full wages nor military advantage would persuade them to fight in the bleak Cheviot landscape where 'meny of theym were ded & meny moo syke'.[25] Their leaders took Surrey's gifts of knighthoods and were gone. Henry was left to fulminate and hint at treason, and Surrey was called to Woodstock to explain this unprecedented behaviour and to name the traitors. As Surrey and James disengaged, the situation in the north began to resolve. But Warbeck was threatening to land in Cornwall and raise rebellion once again. The release of de Broke's forces from their duty in Scotland was an urgent priority. When on 20 August James IV and Sir William Tyler met at Dunbar, peace was essential. Both countries had fought themselves to a standstill. Surrey's van had disintegrated and a full invasion of Scotland though planned had never materialized. After six raids in twelve months Scotland was as war weary as England. At Berwick a truce was agreed, and the following day saw the announcement in Scotland that the English had withdrawn from the borders.[26] By 23 August Robert Willoughby de Broke's marines were back at Berwick and in a few days this force, vital for Henry's survival in the south of England, set sail for Portsmouth.[27]

If Ayala persuaded Warbeck to make for Ireland, this may partly explain the high regard in which Ayala appeared to be held after the peace negotiations with Scotland in the autumn of 1497. We know, however, that Sir James Ormond invited Warbeck to Ireland and that this invitation may have had its promptings from Henry's Cornish rebels. But Warbeck's fate was decided ultimately by accident: to be exact, by two accidents. According to Zurita, arrangements having been made for Warbeck to travel to Spain, there was a storm during which he and his closest associates ran aground on the Irish coast. Zurita named Pedro de Guevara as being with Warbeck in his ship. Once landed in Ireland Guevara disguised Warbeck as one of his servants and they roamed the Irish mountains. During this period, says

Tomb of Piers Ruadh Butler, 8th Earl of Ormond, and his wife Margaret FitzGerald, St Canice's cathedral, Kilkenny, Ireland. In killing Sir James Ormond, Butler ended Irish support for Warbeck

Zurita, Henry's nobles hunted him down.[28] Gairdner suggested that the storm element of this story related it to 1495, but it is possible that it belongs in 1497, when there are plenty of accounts of bad weather in August. Peidzoun, it will be remembered, returned to Scotland in the middle of August. The Scottish captains Robert and John Barton and George Young were also separated from Warbeck. They were driven far south to the Ile de Batz in Brittany. There the enraged inhabitants of St Pol de Leon, taking them for pirates, seized them and held them in prison for three weeks. Then they were returned to the sea in a ship's boat.[29] Only Guy Foulcart seems to have remained with Warbeck.

Zurita's storm might account for the separation of the fleet and the considerable delay between Warbeck leaving Scotland and arriving in Munster. Three weeks after his departure from Scotland, he reached Ardmore castle and demanded that Waterford should surrender. Waterford was in no more of a mood to surrender in 1497 that it had been two years before. Its burgesses notified Desmond and sent word to Kildare. At this the Yorkists fled to Cork, pursued by four Waterford ships. They arrived in Cork haven on 26 July and were received by John Atwater. On this occasion there was no insurrection in Munster. Waterford wrote to Henry telling him that Warbeck intended making for Cornwall. Henry received their letter on 5 August at Woodstock. He replied immediately, thanking them for their loyalty, and urging them to take Warbeck on the high sea. Whoever took him would have 1,000 marks for their reward.[30]

Spain and the weather may be held responsible for the length and timing of Warbeck's last journey, but its lack of success was the result of a chance killing. John Taylor had always managed to play the Munster card through John Atwater. But Kildare's new hegemony in Ireland, and Desmond's decision to accept Henry Tudor as overlord meant that there was no real possibility of Irish support any more. There was nonetheless one forlorn if paradoxical hope: Sir James Ormond, Warbeck's long-time enemy, the man who had hunted him in 1492 after his first appearance in Cork. For years Ormond had been the beneficiary of English power and wealth. But with the reappointment of Kildare as King's Lieutenant, Ormond lost his autonomy. He took up an aggressive independent attitude allying with the O'Briens of Connaught and retaining control of Limerick castle. With this power he laid claim to the Earldom of Ormond, and began to put pressure on the Butler family to aid him in his struggle. Early in 1497 Henry VII summoned Sir James to England, but he refused to come. A second letter was also ignored and, as a consequence, in May 1497 he was declared outside the king's grace, if not actually a traitor.[31]

At this point the rebellion in the west of England erupted and messages seem to have been passed to Ormond in Ireland. According to Piers Ruadh Butler, Sir James 'vpon his comfort and speciall desire moued caused Perkyn Warbek', that is, was asked to invite Warbeck to Ireland. Furthermore Butler claimed he had proof of this from 'such as were priue vnto the Counsaill of the said Perkyn'. Butler and Ormond were at daggers drawn, Ormond having said about Butler that he would kill him where he found him, and usurping Butler power in Kilkenny and Tipperary. Thus Warbeck's story came full circle, ending where it had begun. Though Butler said he met Ormond by chance, in a field near Kilkenny, this plausible excuse may hide details of a duel. Whatever happened Butler and Ormond fought for some time until, in Butler's laconic words, 'god wrought his will vpon him And now sith he is thus dede'.[32] The upshot of this duel, or ambush, was to deprive Warbeck of his last Irish supporter except his creator, John Atwater. Even protected by John Atwater, Warbeck looked likely to be captured by Kildare or Desmond before he arrived in Cornwall. However, Atwater spirited him out of Cork to Kinsale Head, ten miles south of the city. Here his party met a Spanish ship, from San Sebastian, and probably rejoined Foulcart and another vessel, possibly *The Cukow*. Hurriedly regrouped these three ships were pursued cat and mouse by

Warfare at sea. From the Beauchamp Pageant, dated c. *1485–90*

the four ships which Waterford had sent after them.[33] They must have got clear in the end, but later they were intercepted by a naval patrol and an extraordinary scene enacted. The Spanish ship was boarded and its captain and crew assembled to be addressed by the captain of the English vessel. He informed them of the close and now closer friendship between Spain and England cemented with the recent full betrothal of Princess Catherine to Prince Arthur in July that year. The patrol was searching for the pretender, Perkin Warbeck. If they had him on board it behoved them now, as Spaniards, England's new allies, to surrender him. As a further inducement a letter bearing Henry's promise of 1,000 marks reward for Perkin's capture was shown to the ship's master. To these blandishments the master swore that he had never heard of any such person. All the time Warbeck lay huddled up inside an empty wine pipe in the prow of the ship. Unable to move the Spaniard, the patrol let him pass on his way, plying a pretended trade to San Sebastian.[34] It is notable that Zurita says that Warbeck's last escape from Ireland took place from a small harbour in which he found three ships, one of whose captains came from San Sebastian. According to Zurita it was he who took Warbeck from Ireland to Land's End.[35]

Part Three: In England

FOURTEEN

In the Time of Perkin

On 7 September Richard Plantagenet stepped unwillingly ashore at Whitesand Bay, one mile from Land's End. In all the realm of England, there was no more westerly point. Nor, that year, was there a more rebellious region. Penwith hundred, the westernmost hundred of Cornwall, in which Warbeck had landed, and Kerrier, which contained Michael Joseph An Gof's parish of St Keverne, accounted for well over a third of all the major rebels later identified by the government. Penwith provided eighteen rebels and Kerrier twenty. The two hundreds were quite distinct places. Kerrier is a windswept plateau of rocky bays and green and purple cliffs. Yet by a freak of geological fate this was the only place in west Cornwall which sustained itself by agriculture. It was a populous area which bred horses up on Goonhilly and grew corn for the market. It owed its wealth to the misfortune of its poorer, bleaker, industrial, neighbour Penwith, to which it sold foodstuffs.

Whitesand Bay, Cornwall. Landfall for Warbeck, 7 September 1497

Most Cornishmen fished, farmed, and mined tin. The worse the soil, the more they fished and mined. Penwith existed principally by mining and fishing. Its landscape has an unyielding archaic quality. At St Ives, granite was used for gateposts and beams. It was so hard it allowed little decoration. The Atlantic gales lashed the coast covering its stone longhouses with sand. When John Leland visited Penwith in the 1540s he described fishing villages dominated by the tin industry, scarred hillsides stripped of soil by opportunistic tin workers, and rivers silted up by industrial effluent. In the 1490s the tin industry was booming and it was run by the sort of men who led the rebellions in 1497, well-off yeomen and gentlemen. The only large town in Penwith was Penzance, the most westernmost market in the county. Four miles east, along the shore of Mount's Bay, was Marazion, another fair-sized market; and along the bay lay a string of small fishing villages. Only St Michael's Mount in the bay could lay claim to being a place of strategic importance. The Earl of Oxford had held it against Edward IV for four months across winter 1473–4.[1]

John Taylor and his Yorkist allies in Cornwall raised their war banners against Henry VII at Penzance, about ten miles from Whitesand Bay.[2] Penzance was probably their muster point, for the ships which had taken them to Cornwall beached at a number of ports; Penzance and St Ives as well as Whitesand. Coming from Whitesand Bay to Penzance, Warbeck made provision for the safety of his wife. About halfway between the two places was the sanctuary of St Buryan, eight houses in all. Here it would appear he left Katherine Gordon. The evidence is contradictory on this point. A royal letter of 16 September states unequivocally that she was in sanctuary at St Buryan.[3] Conventionally, perhaps following tradition, or Richard Carewe[4] in his Survey of Cornwall, it has been maintained that Katherine Gordon was placed in St Michael's Mount, and surrendered there to Giles Daubney. Whatever the truth Lady Katherine remained out of harm's way until her surrender five weeks after the landing at Whitesand Bay.

Those who greeted the rebels on their arrival in Cornwall were ex-servants of Lord Audley, captains who had fought at Blackheath, and John Nankevell, Walter Tripconny and Humphrey Calwodeley, the men who had invited Warbeck to Cornwall.[5] They could not now offer Warbeck what they could have done two and a half months earlier: five counties in arms against Henry Tudor and aristocratic leadership to boot. Certainly in west Cornwall it was not difficult to raise an army. The tin industry throve on a culture of self-help violence in which numbers of small retinues were maintained to defend tin works, and occasionally riots of alarmingly large proportions erupted.[6] Equally it was only twelve weeks since the men of this region had fought at Blackheath and there is no evidence that their spirits had been crushed by Henry's measures against them, rather the reverse, that the king found it impossible to govern Cornwall during this period. On the other hand the king's victory at Blackheath had resulted in the collapse of any noble or gentry opposition within the realm. In the face of an overwhelming noble presence at Blackheath the gentry and populace in the mid-west had drawn the obvious conclusion, that by mid-September Henry Tudor had survived the most serious crisis of his reign. There was nothng for it, therefore, but to support the king and accommodate themselves with the status quo.

Given the political realities in England, the military emasculation of the Scots, and the impending peace between the two countries, the Warbeck master rebels – Taylor, Lounde and whoever else had disembarked in Whitesand Bay – were completely isolated. Immediately after the landing a full pardon for Warbeck was proclaimed by Chancellor John Morton.[7] But this was a waste of time. Whatever Warbeck would have made of such an offer, and he might have seized on it, he was still the prisoner of his masters. At Penzance the banners of Richard, Duke of York were raised, signifying wisdom escaping from death. One portrayed a little boy emerging from the tomb, one showed a child escaping the clutches of a wolf. The third bore a Red Lion of Flanders from which, in political prophecy, salvation would issue.[8] These were the emblems of the sleeping hero, the Dreadful Dead Man, Richard Plantagenet redivivus, emblems of a party of outcasts.

In contrast to the rebellion of the summer, Richard Plantagenet's homecoming was a pedantic failure. Two years' bootless campaigning had resulted in drastic reductions to the group which had left Flanders. A force which had once numbered one and a half thousand now numbered three hundred or less. But though the rebels between them raised a large army they had no commander of Joseph's quality, and Rodigue de Lalaing had long since departed their ranks. A week after Warbeck's landing about three thousand men had been mustered at Bodmin and this was reckoned by the rebel commanders to be a large enough force to march on Exeter.[9] They would have been well advised to have waited another day or two while more men joined them. But since their campaign had been a matter of speculation for weeks they had none of the strategic advantage derived of surprise. That being the case they could only hope to make up what they had lost through lack of surprise by weight of numbers.

Caught unprepared in the summer by Michael Joseph, this time, Plymouth and Exeter were ready to defend themselves. At Plymouth watch and ward was kept for fifteen nights while the citizenry prepared to defend their town with 'Grete Gvnnes'. Twenty-five pounds of gunpowder were bought, and a variety of gunshot was cast from lead and iron bought from a local merchant. Master Pers Raynford made a handsome £1, casting ammunition for Plymouth. But the inhabitants went one step further. At the mayor's command they kitted out eight soldiers in livery of green and white – Tudor colours – and sent them to Exeter to join the army which the Earl of Devon was assembling to oppose Warbeck.[10] Their venture is indicative of how far September's events had travelled in favour of the king, and how differently the two rebellions were met at an early stage. In May the gentry of Devon had been uncoordinated and scattered over their county. Now Courtenay was mustering town and county levies at Okehampton. Then everyone had been out of touch with the king; now he addressed his gentry as his 'right welbeloued trusty noblemen'. Then they could not have paid their retinues; now the king paid for them. Then the gentry had worked in isolation from their king; now his commissioners were among them. Then the king had lacked good lines of communication; now he had a postal system stretching form Woodstock to Exeter. Then Courtenay had turned tail and run from Joseph; now he prepared to smash Warbeck. Then the king had known nothing; now he knew everything. Then the king had been powerless; now he told Courtney to

> doo the Wife of perkyn being in Sainct Buryans to be taken by see or by land out therof and to be saufly kept in ward or sent vnto vs And that also the shyppes that passed perkyn be they at Sainct Ives pensance or in othre places shulde be taken bouged orelles brent.[11]

Yet advantage is not victory. In Cornwall Warbeck had overwhelmed the king's men. The sheriff of Cornwall had been so bold as to attack Perkin's camp at Castle Kynnock, near Bodmin, but when the posse comitatus neared the camp its members deserted, *en masse*, to Warbeck.[12] The Earl of Devon was no more fortunate. Despite a firm command of his county's gentry he was forced, before 'the multitude of the enemy',[13] to retreat to Exeter. Courtenay had made his tactical withdrawal after consultation with his retinue leaders. The fragmentary evidence suggests that they tried to stop a rebel advance from Cornwall but, unable to achieve this, returned to Okehampton. At Okehampton, on Wednesday 13 September, they took stock of their situation and then advised the king of their plight. By the 16 September Henry had received their letter, and replied:

We haue wel vnderstande howe on Wednesday last ye made youre mustres besides the towne of Okehampton and there toke counseill and sad advis amonges youselfes What was best for you to doo against Perkyn and oure Rebelles his adherentes Wheupon aftre long debating and reasonyng of the matir It was thought in conclusion bettre and moore sure way for you to drawe into our Citie of Excestre for the defens and sauf keping therof to our vse than by way of bataill with the said perkyn to sette the tryall theof vpon vnliklihode

We thank you that ye of youre wisedoms haue taken soo wise a direction. ffor moore acceptable it is vnto vs to haue oure saide Citie surely kept to oure behoof than that any mysaduenture or distrusse shuylde haue happend vnto you And soo sithens ye haue taken that wey as to resort vnto oure said Citie. We praye you Cousin that for any oure former writing vnto you that ye shulde drawe you vnto oure Chambrelain notwithstanding ye kepe yourself with the othre noble men of thoes parties in oure said Citie for the suretie therof as it is abouesaid.[14]

To send the Earl of Devon reeling, was an undoubted success: but it was a false success; for, in marching to Exeter, the rebels fulfilled Henry Tudor's expectations of their behaviour. Prior to their attack on Exeter, Warbeck's commanders faced a choice: either besiege and take the city, or, following Michael Joseph's tactics, abandon it and march into southern England. In view of the potential threat from Henry they probably had no real choice. Their only hope lay in taking Exeter, and holding it against the king.

According to the Milanese, Fra Zoan Carbonariis, Henry was informed of Warbeck's arrival on 10 September, three days after the landing at Whitesand Bay.[15] Once he knew where Warbeck was, Henry set the trap to catch him. On 12 September he sent Courtenay money to pay his troops with, and he called for over 230 retinues to form a Royal Army to move against Warbeck.[16] The Royal Ward was to muster at Woodstock on 24 September and descend into the west through Oxfordshire and Wiltshire. In a letter to Sir Gilbert Talbot he explained the strategy. Giles, Lord Daubney, now restored to health, was arraying Somerset, Gloucestershire, Wiltshire and South Wales to form a van. Daubney's principal lieutenants were Lord St Amand and Sir John Cheyne, leading soldiers from Dorset and Hampshire and elsewhere in the mid-west. Where Daubney mustered his vanguard we do not know, but Bath or Bristol seem the most likely places. Well to the south of Daubney, Henry had a second army commanded by Robert, Lord Willoughby de Broke. Having returned from Scotland de Broke had arrived at Portsmouth about 12 September and resumed direct communication with Henry.[17] Henry explained to Talbot that de Broke's marines would wait at Portsmouth for use in case Warbeck slipped the net and bolted for the south coast.[18] By the time the rebels reached Exeter Henry's strategy was clear: Warbeck would be taken in the English middle and western counties, squeezed between Daubney and de Broke in front of him and the Earl of Devon behind him. On 16 September Henry wrote to Edward Courtenay:

And in caas the said perkyn comme forward and be oonys athisside our said Citie [of Exeter] and haue the same at his bak Then we praye you that leving alwayes a good company of sure folkes in that our Citie soo as it maye be allways in a good suretie ye take with you all the nobles of your said company with theire retynewes to folowe and for to be at the bakkes of our said rebelles and traitours and to sende out beforn you a certain nombre of wel horsed men to ride the said perkyn and his company for to kepe theym toguydre that they stragle not And to kepe also vitailles from theym on bothe sides theire way And over that to kepe them Watching and Waking by mean of scryes and nere approches as thoes horsemen may Wel and Wisely doo without any their great daungier in that behalue

And soo by the mean therof oure said Chambrelain bing beforn theym and ye behinde theym shal encombre the said perkyn and our traitours that they shalbe discomfited without any stoke or perill And therfor Cousin We praye you in oure affectuous Wise and all thoes noble men with you to folowe oure mynde in this behalfe And if the said traitours geve bak or flee that perkyn escape you not in any wise ffor it the chief thing We disire to haue hym broughte vnto vs a lyve.[19]

The rebels, reputedly 8,000 strong, arrived at Exeter at one o'clock in the afternoon of Sunday 17 September, and instantly laid siege. It was a mistake to besiege Exeter so strongly garrisoned. And it was a costly mistake to commit soldiers without proper armour, to attack town walls defended with gunnery. Yet such was the size of Warbeck's army, and the ferocity of its assault, that the city almost fell. The rebels took two hours to arrange themselves for battle. By three in the afternoon they were fully arrayed round Rougemont castle, covering the north and east gates, cutting Henry's line of communication with Exeter.[20] Having taken up their position they called on Courtenay to deliver them the city. This he flatly refused. Though he and his garrison were outnumbered they felt certain of relief within a week.

It was Henry's boast that Warbeck found no support for his cause among the western gentry. The defenders of Exeter were men of standing in the west: the Earl of Devon, his son William, Sir Walter Courtenay, Sir John Sapcotes, Sir Piers Edgcumbe, Sir Humphrey Fulford and many others from Devon and Cornwall.[21] The number of Cornish gentry present was probably very low and drawn from the east rather than the west of the county. Yet if the members of the garrison felt sure they would be relieved within the week they also knew that their behaviour, while the siege lasted, was a test of loyalty after the vacillations of May and June. To redeem themselves they squared up solidly behind the earl and his family. 'Beinge not longe before advertysed of the kinges dyspleasure,' says Hooker, 'they were now come to the Citie.'[22]

With little of the afternoon left, Courtenay's defiance was met with an assault on the east and north gates. As A.L. Rowse remarks, there was no point in attacking the west gate for it was easily defended. 'There was first the flat low lying [Exe] Island to cross, then the bridge over the river immediately under the ramparts and the defenders, and within the steep declivity of the High Street.'[23] On this, their first attack, they attempted to scale the city walls and storm the gates, but under fire from Courtenay's guns could not force an entry. In a letter to Henry, the earl put rebel losses in this first sortie at between three and four hundred.[24] Courtenay's garrison was a formidable one, and its morale much higher than in the summer. Courtenay had in his retinue six, possibly eight, gunners, and before Warbeck arrived he had constructed gun emplacements on the gates. He kept his thirsty gunners well provided with wine and beer during the siege. Ammunition, too, was plentiful. Almost twenty pounds was spent on gunpowder; and shot, arrows and arrowheads were bought and what could not be bought was made on the spot. John Sanyell cast gun barrels, and gun stocks were quickly cut from local timber. None the less, we should not be under the impression that Courtenay had things all his own way. The north gate bore such an attack from the rebels that it was rendered unserviceable, and a watch had to be placed overnight to guard the entrance to the city. Other citizens maintained a vigil within, and on top of, the guild hall: everyone else rested.[25]

Denied the town and with many of their fellows killed, the rebels renewed their attack on Monday morning. They must have begun shortly after dawn on Monday, for when the east gate was attacked Edward Courtenay and his son were still in their lodgings resting, or perhaps they were asleep. The first assault was made on the north gate, weakened badly on the previous day. The rebels tried to breach it with fire, but they were driven back by the gunners on the ramparts. This, however, may have been a feint, for immediately the army turned to the east gate which, says Hooker, 'they brake vpon with force and entred yn to to the Citie'; a turn of phrase which might suggest the use of some form of battering ram on the gate. The gates gave way and once inside the wall the rebels took possession of the High Street. The common alarm bell was sounded and the people of Exeter, more vigilant than their earl, began to defend themselves. By the time Courtenay and his soldiers came to their aid, Warbeck's force had fought their way into Exeter as far as Castle Lane. Now, says Hooker, the fighting became 'verie hote & fierce'. As at Deptford Strand, in June, the Cornish bow was used: Courtenay was wounded in the arm as he rushed out of his lodgings in the Blackfriars. Eventually the combined weight of citizens and soldiers drove Warbeck's men out of Exeter.

By ten in the morning Courtenay had repulsed two substantial attacks and must have been wondering whether he could hold out against a third.[26] He told Henry that for every loyalist hurt he had managed to kill twenty rebels, nevertheless, he had lost too many men and his garrison was so depleted that he could not execute all the king's orders. With so many casualties sustained on either side, without advantage, a truce was negotiated. To secure their speedy withdrawal from Exeter, Courtenay was obliged to promise the rebels that he would not come after them. The rebels too had been badly shaken and needed a breathing space. The siege of Exeter was a stalemate, but it was a stalemate in the king's favour. The town had been held and, despite his losses, Courtenay promised that he would make after the rebels as soon as he could.[27] Most heartening news of all, was that rebel troops were now beginning to desert the faux Duke of York. By eleven o'clock Warbeck was on his way toward Collumpton, on the road for Taunton, and by twelve his army was out of sight of the city. The further inland he travelled the further he entered Henry's trap.

By the time Perkin reached Taunton, on 19 September, Henry knew exactly where he was. On 16, 17 and 18 September the postal sevice to Exeter fairly hummed. Henry outlined his plan to conclude the campaign in a letter, of 20 September, to his secretary, the absentee Bishop of Bath and Wells, Oliver King. Converging from north and south, Daubney and Willoughby de Broke would block Warbeck's eastern advance. Courtenay would push from the west, and Henry himself would lead the force assembled at Woodstock to reinforce Daubney.[28] His commanders already knew their tasks: Daubney and Courtenay were to liaise with each other, and the king kept Daubney informed by a messenger, William David, of the passage of events. Five hundred pounds was sent, with Geoffrey Elice, to pay for John Cheyne's retinues.[29] Willoughby de Broke had his servants out riding to the southern coastal towns, just in case Warbeck surprised everyone by going south, and not back into Cornwall, when he was done for. And at Woodstock itself Henry called for guns and gunners to cow the west. As he told Courtenay, his was 'an armee royall of peuple soo furnisshed with artilleryes and ordinices for the felde as shalbe hable to defende any prince christian With goddes fauour'.[30]

Warbeck's rebel army had reached Taunton on 19 September. By the time they got there both the Yorkists and the Cornish knew that the game was up. There was one last card left to play. On entering Taunton Taylor and his friends claimed they were in possession of papal bulls which affirmed Richard IV to be the true son of Edward IV. When this failed to stop what was becoming mass desertion by their troops, they claimed that they were about to coin money and distribute it to all. This had been done in Dublin, for Lambert Simnel, ten years earlier; and it was a method used by conquering armies to indicate their dominance over the conquered. But those who had fought at Blackheath and Exeter drew their own conclusion. Taunton was unwalled, and its castle was being rebuilt. It was an impossible position to defend. Still they tried. On the 20 September troops were mustered in the fields adjoining Taunton and told by Warbeck's masters that they 'had a close understanding with some lords

Taunton Castle, Somerset. Taunton Castle was the Bishop of Winchester's castle. During 1497 it was being rebuilt. Warbeck came face to face with Henry VII here

of the realm'. Help was at hand. But their army had had enough. The soldiers melted away, each person 'providing theyr aune saveguard'.[31] On the previous day the king's van, under Lord Daubney, had reached Glastonbury. By the time the exiles were claiming close understanding, Daubney already had his scouts out on the roads to Taunton offering an amnesty to everyone who surrendered their arms. Unable to compete with Lord Daubney, Warbeck and his masters could do nothing, except try to save their own skins. Thus on Wednesday afternoon, 20 September, they gave out that the bridges in the direction they would take, across Sedgmoor, had been cut. In order, they said, the better to assert his right against Henry Tudor, Richard IV had decided not to advance over the moor but to take another route. Warbeck and his controllers waited for nightfall with the remains of their army. Some time after midnight they bolted from Taunton.[32]

At Taunton the remnant of his army discovered its plight on Thursday morning. Some were so amazed that they simply fled in fear. Others reacted with fury. Daubney was charged with driving the rebels back from Somerset into Cornwall, but before he arrived in Taunton a pirate, James the Rover, carried out a hideous piece of communal revenge. James had gathered togther seven or eight hundred rovers with whom he intended to serve Warbeck. But before he could put his retinue at the rebels' disposal he somehow captured John Oby, the Provost of Glasney, the tax collector who, it was held, was 'oon of the chyeff procuers & occacioners of the Rebellion of [the] Cornish men'. With Warbeck in flight and the rebels in disarray, the Rover could not serve him. Nevertheless James the Rover and his men came to Taunton with Oby. They set him in the market place and there 'tyrannously dysmembrid hym', telling Taunton's inhabitants that as a commissioner of taxes in Cornwall 'he levyed . . .

moch more money than cam unto the kyngis use, which causid grete murmer & grudge among the comons toward the kyng & lastly Rebellion . . .'.[33] Evidence of their handiwork still, presumably, littered the market place when Lord Daubney took Taunton for Henry on 22 September. Of James the Rover we hear no more. At Taunton Daubney received money for his troops and by 26 September, at the latest, he arrived in Exeter to relieve Edward Courtenay.

With Exeter secured, the roads to Woodstock were clear for a royal advance. Warbeck's flight was what Henry had been waiting for. He left Woodstock on 24 September to make a measured and well-planned advance. Even before Daubney had reached Exeter a party from its garrison had been rewarded by their king. They may have been some of that 'nombre of wel horsed men' who Henry told Courtenay to send after Warbeck, or they may have been well wishers. Howsobeit on the 25th, when Henry reached Burford, in Oxfordshire, he was met by Sir John Pecche, Sir Edward Wingfield, Sir Rowland Velville, Thomas Fogge and the Earl of Devon's son William.[34] They received their thanks, and joined the royal ward as it lumbered slowly westwards: through Cirencester, through Malmesbury, Bath, Wells and Glastonbury until it occupied the same Taunton fields that Warbeck's rebels had so recently left.

FIFTEEN

Capture and Recapture

Henry Tudor was well prepared for Warbeck's flight. All the western ports were watched, and an excellent network of posts and spies was deployed deep into Somerset and Devon. Having withstood Warbeck at Exeter, Edward Courtenay had been ordered to seize, and if necessary hole, Warbeck's vessels at St Ives or Penzance.[1] Perhaps it was while this was being done that Guy Foulcart, Warbeck's Breton captain, just escaped murder by bribing his captors with his goods. At first Warbeck and his sixty mounted supporters did as Henry anticipated: they backtracked to Minehead in order possibly to take ship for Ireland or France, or possibly in order to disguise their real intention of fleeing south and east to the coast.[2] Very soon the party split up. John Taylor got clean away. As a local man, and an ex-customs official, he would have known many good hiding places in which he could lie low and slip quietly out of England. He returned to France. A larger party escaped towards London. Led by William Lounde these men arrived in the capital at the end of September, before Warbeck himself had been captured. They took sanctuary in Westminster and St Martin le Grand and within six months they formed the nucleus of group who plotted against Henry to release Warbeck and the Earl of Warwick in 1498–9. Others were completely disillusioned by the collapse of Warbeck's campaign and his exposure as a fraud. The King's Sergeant Furrier, who had joined Warbeck in Flanders had no more heart for activism. He disguised himself as a hermit to evade capture. But after two months of wandering the English countryside he was captured and delivered to court by two yeomen who were rewarded £5 for their trouble. There remains the suspicion that he was betrayed not by these two, but by his wife, who, on Palm Sunday 1498, six months after his execution was given 10s by the king.[3]

Warbeck himself and three of his followers – John Heron, Edward Skelton and Nicholas Astley – like Lounde reversed their original direction. All Thursday 21 September he and his three companions galloped across country, between the armies of Daubney and de Broke, over the Blackmoor hills, through Cranborne Chase and the New Forest until they arrived at Beaulieu Abbey: five miles from the coast and freedom. Beaulieu had a large liberty, bordering the Solent and the channel, and Heron knew the abbot personally. Once in sanctuary Warbeck and his friends could begin to arrange transport to France. But their hopes proved false. The abbot guessed that Warbeck was one of Heron's companions and sent word to Henry.[4] It may have been this message which arrived at Woodstock on 25 September with the man that 'com from Perkyn', rewarded £1.[5] Whatever the case, Warbeck's days of freedom were numbered, for when Daubney realized what had happened he sent Sir Rice ap Thomas after Warbeck at the head of a detachment of cavalry. Two hundred, possibly as many as five hundred horsemen tracked him to Beaulieu.[6] There, surrounded by Henry's men and citizens from Southampton, Perkin's capture was imminent. Even unguarded, Perkin and his associates could not have gone very far, for when their belongings were searched they had only 10 crowns between them. None the less, Henry wanted Warbeck taken quickly. His full confession would ensure the complete collapse of the insurrection. And this it did. When the Cornish heard that Warbeck was a 'low born foreigner', not a Plantagenet it was necessary to mount a guard on Perkin to prevent them murdering him. To those who helped in the final capture the king was gracious. The mayor of Southampton personally received £40 from the 'kynges grace', though the total expense of Warbeck's capture was £482 16s 8d[7]

Once Henry had been informed of Warbeck's whereabouts he despatched a party to negotiate Warbeck's surrender. Among its members was Roger Machado, Richmond Herald, and he later told the Milanese ambassador what had transpired at Beaulieu. When they reached the abbey it was agreed that John Heron should see the king. It was agreed, before he left Beaulieu that he would either secure a pardon for all four sanctuary men, or that he would be returned to sanctuary to guard Warbeck. Having agreed these conditions he left Beaulieu for the king. In front of Henry he swore that he recognized Warbeck only as Richard IV, and that he was unaware of his imposture. By this lie Heron secured pardons for the whole group, including Perkin; the condition of his pardon being that he surrender to the king in return for his life. With his life guaranteed Perkin renounced sanctuary. He removed his sanctuary habit, and then, incredibly, as Richard IV, dressed himself in royal finery of gold cloth and set out with a small guard, among whom was Roger Machado, to meet Henry. Machado had a close look at him. He was not very handsome, indeed he had a defective left eye, but, he was well spoken and intelligent.[8]

Warbeck was brought to Henry VII at Taunton castle on 5 October. Machado was not present at the interview which followed his arrival, only the aristocracy, but he heard all about it. Warbeck knelt down in front of Henry and asked for mercy. Henry bade him rise and addressed him, 'We have heard that you call yourself Richard, son of King Edward. In this place are some', he may have indicated Thomas Howard, Earl of Surrey or perhaps the Marquess of Dorset, 'who were companions of that lord look and see if you recognise them'. This Richard, in his finery, replied that he did not know any of them, that he was not Richard, that he had never been to England before, and that he had been induced by the English and the Irish to commit the fraud and to learn English. For two years, he added, he had longed to escape from the imbroglio but fortune had been against him.[9] Do we take this for truth? Ever since he had been a child Warbeck had advanced his career by providing the answer most desired in any situation. Whatever he now felt he had enough intuition and intelligence to know that he had to make a clean breast of his imposture, or at least appear to act the part of the repentant imposter. This way might salvation lie, or at least some hope of survival. When the interview was over he was taken away to compose a full confession. Machado showed de Soncino, the Milanese ambassador to England, one of the confessions, authenticated 'per Pero Osbeck', in which he named his father, mother, grandparents, native city of Tournai, parish, schoolmasters and places he had visited.[10] Perkin's confession was intended for wide circulation and the copy which de Soncino saw was probably on its way, in the second week of October with Machado, to Charles VIII.[11] Within a week of its composition the London authorities also had their own version of Perkin's pedigree. The king had kept them well told about Warbeck's progress. On 25 September they were informed of his flight from Taunton to Minehead for example, and on 12 October the aldermen were read a number of letters from the king which established beyond all doubt Warbeck's true parentage. Already, at the beginning of October, when they heard of his capture the city authorities had ordered the singing of a solemn *Te Deum* for the deliverance of the realm.[12]

Once Warbeck was with the king he accompanied him on the rest of his progress. Henry entered Exeter on 7 October and stayed there, living in the Treasurer of Exeter Cathedral's house, until he left Exeter on 3 November. During this period he restored peace to a region which had been in political crisis for six months. Daily he enquired about rebellion, daily he had brought before him commoners of the west of England who begged for, and received, absolution for their insurrection. The men round Perkin were weeded out too. Heron's economy with the truth, that he like all the rest had believed Warbeck to be a Plantagenet, was revealed as a lie and he was imprisoned.[13] Astley and Skelton who had believed Perkin to be Richard IV were admitted to grace, and formally pardoned in December.[14] But Skelton could not keep clear of conspiracy, and within three years was back at Beaulieu Abbey plotting against Henry, this time in favour of Edmund de la Pole.[15] Recidivism of this sort is evident in the case of many of the die hards of 1497, most spectacularly in the case of John Hayes. John Taylor, it will be recalled, had involved Hayes at the beginning of the Warbeck affair, and though freed in 1493 Hayes had remained attached to the Earl of Warwick's cause. When Henry reached Exeter, Hayes was accused once again of misprision of treason and arrested. Committed to the safe keeping of the king's cofferer William Coope, he was 'in greate daunger of hys lyff for the seyd offences' and entreated William to beg the king for pardon. William managed to secure this, but the price was another huge fine. Henry obliged him to pay 500 marks for his pardon, though, since he was gaoled, William Coope had to find the money for him. Coope's reward was an outright gift from his captive of 300 marks and a repayment sum of a further £100 which Hayes had raised by selling his Somerset manor, East Ham, to Coope in order that Hayes could pay his fine. On 29 November, for the third time in fifteen years, John Hayes was pardoned for his loyalty to Edward, Earl of Warwick.[16]

The gaols at Exeter were full to bursting of men such as these, and every day captains of the rebellion of June and September were being transported across Dartmoor to join them. Guarded for his life, a week after getting to Exeter on 13 October Warbeck wrote to his mother. It is a remarkable letter, because it is the only document personal to the pretender which exists. His predicament is uppermost, even before he attempts to establish, by using family details, his veracity, 'It may please you to know that by fortune under the colour of a contrivance certain English made me believe that I was the son of the King Edward of England called his second son Richard Duke of York.' There is ambiguity here, we could read the letter, 'deceived me into believing', but the force of the deception is here, it has entered deep into Warbeck. He finds himself 'en tele perplexite', that if she is not his good mother at this hour, he will find himself in great danger thanks to the name he has assumed and because of the business in which he has become embroiled. This may be a general statement, or it may refer to the murderous intent of the Cornish. In a postscript he begs his mother to send him some money, 'so that my guards may be more amiable if I give them something'. To be well guarded was a necessity.

He recalls for his mother private details. Leaving Tournai and the state she was in, the plague deaths of his brother and sister, 'and how my father and you and I went to live in Lannoy outside the town; and you remember the beautiful Porcquiere . . .'. But the point of this letter is to achieve some salvation. 'The King of England has me in his hands. I have declared the truth of the matter to him, making humble supplication to him to pardon me for the offence I have committed, bearing in mind that I am in no way his native subject and that what I have done was in the pursuit of the wishes of his subjects. But I have not yet received any good reply from him, nor hope to have any so my heart is very sorrowful.' As bourgeois officials the Werbeques cannot have been without influence. In sending good wishes to his neighbour Guillaume Rucq and his uncle Jehan Stalyn in Tournai, Warbeck also asked to be remembered to his tutor. This appeal to his mother was that she, Nicaise Farou, should use her political influence to secure her son's release. 'I beg and request you to have pity on me and pursue my deliverance. Recommend me to my godfather Pierart Flan [his tutor] . . .'. It never bore fruit, and Perkin never returned to Flanders.[17]

Involuntary exile was also forced on Perkin's wife. Even after the affair was all over she was not allowed, and then appears not to have wanted, to return to her native Scotland. Perkin had last seen her when she had been placed in sanctuary at St Buryans. When the rebellion collapsed she was surrendered to the king's forces and brought to Bodmin. Francis Bacon maintains that the king's first concern about her was whether or not she was pregnant, because he was afraid that if she was the whole Warbeck affair would continue in the form of pretended dynasty through their children. She was not pregnant. So in mid-October, from Bodmin, where Lord Daubney, the Earl of Devon, and Lord Willoughby de Broke had a temporary headquarters, she left for Exeter.[18] Katherine Gordon was a woman renowned for her beauty as well as one of noble blood. According to Polydore Vergil, when he met her Henry VII is said to have flattered her with a typical piece of wit, saying that she was more worthy to be among the captives of a general rather than the common soldier.[19] In this manner perhaps, sleight of hand, she was denied access to her husband and prepared for life at the English court. It had been decided that she would be placed in the care of Henry's wife, Elizabeth of York. The king bought her horses and saddles for the journey from Exeter to London, and had all her food charged to his Sergeant of the Poultry. She was then placed in the hands of Windsor Herald for the journey to London. He bought her new travelling clothes: a black velvet bonnet, and a black satin gown garnished with velvet ribbons and tawny satin, and with these accoutrements she made her way to Sheen.[20]

With the immediate crisis over English political life began to reconstitute around London and the court. During September the king's mother, Henry, Duke of York, and Queen Elizabeth had been sent on progress to East Anglia. This was partly a matter of safety, partly of propaganda. Two of Warbeck's most important supporters – Debenham and Fitzwater – came from East Anglia and as we have seen Warbeck's masters had attempted to exploit the latent loyalty of the region. During Warbeck's invasion it was deemed necessary to show the royal family and the real Duke of York to the region. With the west pacified it was judged safe for the queen to return to London, and she arrived, ostensibly from pilgrimage to Walsingham, on 17 October. She was welcomed by the mayor and alderman at Bishopsgate, to a city decked for festivities. Overnight she lodged at Baynard's castle and the next day received presents, before going on to Sheen in the afternoon. Three days later, on 21 October, Katherine Gordon also reached Sheen and was presented to Edward IV's daughter Elizabeth of York, the queen.[21] This choice of household for Katherine Gordon represented propriety and security. Warbeck was a commoner, Lady Katherine Gordon was a noble woman near to the blood royal of Scotland. It was fitting that they should be placed in different, male and female, households to keep them apart socially. It was also fitting, remembering the king's earlier concerns about a possible pregnancy, that they be kept apart to prevent any such occurrence likely to lead to rumour and uncertainty in the future. Thus the king was more practical than prudish when he was reported not to allow them to sleep together. A month later, on 18 November, Henry and Warbeck arrived at Sheen.[22]

For three days the king rested at Sheen before going to Westminster. He rode on horseback to Lambeth and took the royal barge to the other side of the Thames. Assembled in Westminster Hall were representatives of the London guilds in their liveries.[23] After the king had been fulsomely praised as victor, they viewed the victor's captive. Leading a gentleman by the arm, Warbeck was paraded in front of them. Some citizens stood quizzically by, while others cursed him and swore at him. One who saw all this first hand, de Soncino, thought the king most modest in victory.[24] A few days later, as he was involved in the intensive diplomacy still unfolding, he was given an audience at Westminster. 'As I was

Elizabeth of York, Queen of England

leaving . . . they showed me Perkin . . . He did not seem to care for us to speak to him.'[25] No wonder. Everywhere the news of who he was, and what he was, was available in printed copies of his confession. Every day he was paraded through London to be spat at, sworn at, and laughed at. Throughout the city everyone discussed the lack of judgement of those who, much to their confusion, had believed him to be the second son of King Edward. On Tuesday 28 November a particularly spectacular show was put on. Perkin and a party of horsemen clattered from Westminster to the Tower, through Cheap Street and Cornhill. Following them, bound securely hand and foot, was the King's Sergeant Furrier, 'a tall and lykyly man'. The Furrier had been captured, and examined by the king. Once the king was exactly sure of his motivation he had ordered his master, Perkin, to deliver him to the Tower, 'for his ffeythfull service'. Thus derided the furrier was committed to a particularly safe part of the Tower. Warbeck, having delivered his servant to the Lieutenant of the Tower, rode back down Candlewick Street again to face jeers and curses and so to Westminster. At the end of the week, on Saturday 2 December, the Sergeant Furrier and an ex-yeoman of Elizabeth of York were tried for treason in Whitehall, Westminster. Having fled the Royal Households to join Warbeck their cases were unanswerable. They were found guilty and condemned to death. Next Monday they were brought from the Tower to Tyburn. Queen Elizabeth's yeoman, Edwards, was hanged. The Sergeant Furrier, deemed the greater rebel of the two was hanged, drawn and quartered.[26] Of Perkin, subjected to this psychological battering de Soncino wrote, two days later, 'In my opinion he bears his fortune bravely.'[27] What else could he do? For about two and a half months Maximilian I had been trying to secure his release, but could move no one.

By as early as 16 October 1497 Philip the Fair sent news to Maximilian I that 'monsieur d'York' was in the hands of the King of England. Maximilian reacted by commissioning the President of the Council of Flanders, Jehan le Sauvage, to go to England to negotiate Warbeck's surrender to Maximilian's safe keeping. The Emperor desired with all his heart the salvation and deliverance of 'our cousin the duke of York'.[28] On 8 November Sauvage was despatched to England, and Maximilian directed Philip to support him in every possible way. Sauvage was to offer up to 10,000 gold florins to anyone who could obtain Warbeck's release from Henry.[29] Perhaps he had in mind Lord Daubney who had received a pension from the Flemish after the battle of Dixmude. The pension had been suspended in the mid 1490s, but had been resumed in July 1497.[30] Sauvage was to promise also that the Duke of York and his descendants would renounce all claims to the English throne, and give an undertaking never to molest Henry again.[31] A powerful Burgundian embassy visited England during November and December of 1497. Both the President of the Council, Jehan le Sauvage, and Jehan de Courteville, Philip's principal negotiator in the ongoing trade negotiations, were received by Henry. Courteville's expenses make it clear that he was not there just about commercial relations but 'certains grandes matiers et affairs secretz'.[32] But despite the observation of such niceties as a £20 gift for Courteville, in the second week of December, no deal was done and the embassy returned on 7 January 1498.[33] How could it be? Warbeck as Richard Plantagenet was neither genuinely a prince of York nor purely the product of his own inventing. He could not be treated, as Margaret of Anjou had been by Edward IV as deserving of exile. Nor could he be treated as one so deluded that he was a diplomatic irrelevance. Those on whose behalf he had functioned were still at liberty, and the nominal master of some of these men, the Earl of Warwick, was still alive. It might be true that Richard Plantagenet was now dead. Having been reborn in Cork he had been buried at Taunton. Perkin Warbeck, however, had to disinter himself there, after almost ten years of the masquerade. This as we saw in his letter to his mother would be difficult and confusing. He could neither be rescued by Maximilian, nor could he resume the life of a citizen of

Tournai with his family. The only possibility in the present lay at the English court, as a subject of Henry VII.

Once the rebellions of 1497 were over Henry treated Warbeck well. Both the London Chronicles comment that the king extended his grace to Warbeck and that he was at liberty in the English court, so much, said the *Great Chronicle*, that it would take a great deal of space to describe it.[34] Vergil and Hall maintain that he was kept under constant surveillance to prevent his use as a figurehead in fresh trouble. Both these versions of Warbeck's fate compliment each other. Generally he was supervised by Robert Jones and William Smyth, two of Henry's household officials. Smyth was a wardrobe official of who worked his way up from Page of the Wardrobe to Groom of the Robes, while creaming off numerous grants of lands forfeited by rebels. Jones along with James Braybrook, a yeoman of the chamber, received payments on Warbeck's behalf. Nevertheless Warbeck also had two yeomen servants, Londoners – John Kebyll and John Sherwyn, to guard him at night.[35] However, while it is true that Warbeck was well guarded it is also the case that Hall and Vergil use every opportunity to increase the dramatic tension of their dynastic histories by contrasting the virtue of the Tudor dynasty with the threat from its opponents.[36] It is possible that in the spring of 1498 Warbeck was about to resume in England the career of a minor courtier he had abandoned when he left Portugal. Both he and his wife were placed at court, though the king would not allow them to sleep together. In late November 1497 Andrea Trevisano, the Venetian ambassador, saw Warbeck in a chamber at the palace of Westminster. 'He is a well

Fyfield Manor, near Oxford, home of Katherine Gordon. She was granted Fyfield and other lands in Berkshire in 1510. In 1512 she resigned the property but, with her second husband James Strangways, received it back on condition that she never went to Scotland or any other foreign country without licence of the king

favoured young man 23 years old, and his wife a very handsome woman.'[37] In December 1497 Henry personally gave Katherine Gordon a gift of £2, and in mid-March of 1498 James Braybrook laid out £2 for Perkin and another £2 for one of his wife's servants. Warbeck even had his own tailor, one Jasper.[38]

At Easter 1498 the royal entourage stayed for about two weeks at Canterbury. Here there took place the celebrated incident during which Henry VII attempted personally to disabuse a condemned Lollard of her beliefs. Here also Henry dedicated Warbeck's captured standard in the cathedral. It may well be that Warbeck and the king did this together, for he seems to have been in the party.[39] Both before and after staying in Canterbury the royal party progressed through Kent to Maidstone and Faversham to Sir John Pecche's home at Lullingstone. At Pecche's, on 18 April, Robert Jones was paid for feeding Warbeck's horse daily throughout February, March and April.[40] In May and June Henry progressed Oxfordshire, Hertfordshire and Essex, staying with Sir Thomas Lovell at least twice in May. On this progress Warbeck had a new riding gown bought for him. Despite a brief visit to the Tower on 29 May the royal party were back at Woodstock and Hertford at the end of May. But by the second week of June they had returned to the capital.[41] Six months earlier Warbeck had been publicly displayed in London. His presence on these progresses was partly a matter of security, partly to display him further, and partly to accommodate him at court. But the return to London marked the end of this attempt to integrate him at court and expunge the memory of the false Richard Plantagenet. On 9 June his yeomen warders at Westminster, Kebyll and Sherwyn, allowed him to escape.[42] From this point on he was doomed. John Ford had the right of it when in his play he had Lambert Simnel pronounce, 'Perkin, beware the rope; the hangman's coming.'[43]

Neither Warbeck nor Henry VII could outrun the shadow cast by his imposture. A month after Warbeck was introduced to the Venetian ambassador, at Christmas 1497, Henry rewarded a member of Warbeck's immediate circle, a trumpet. Trumpet players, notoriously, were used as spies.[44] Henry was right to be cautious of Warbeck, and of those who had used him previously. John Taylor was still at large. So was Atwater, and so were many involved in the 1495 plots and supporters of Warbeck in 1496 and 1497. On 6 February 1498 three such individuals met in a house in Honey Lane, in the parish of All Hallows, in Cheap Ward. Honey Lane was a poor street in a rich ward. It was narrow and dark, and had to be swept and scoured frequently to keep it clean.[45] The house belonged to one John Fynche, a London haberdasher. In the autumn and winter in which Warbeck had invaded England, 1496, a number of Yorkist supporters had been placed under bond for their future loyalty. John Fynche was one of these.[46] Met with him in his house were two gentlemen, Robert Cleymond and Thomas Astwode. Cleymond's background is unclear, though a family of that name were merchants of the Staple in Calais. At the time of the meeting he was a servant of the Earl of Warwick. Astwode, it will be recalled had been condemned to death for treason in 1495, but pardoned. His pardon, though, was dearly bought, and he had been plunged into debt and poverty. Fynche revealed to them that he knew of a prophecy which said that the bear would shortly beat his chains within the City of London. This was a clear reference to the Warwick coat of arms, the bear and the ragged staff. And thus to clarify it Fynche told Cleymond to tell his master that he hoped to hear in Cheap Street many crying 'A Warwick! A Warwick!' (as was done at the battle of Stoke) and wearing the Warwick badge of the Ragged Staff. Cheap Street was well known for its association with the rough justice of the politically disenfranchised.[47] Wat Tyler and Jack Cade had executed men there and Henry IV had burned charters issued by Richard II in Cheap Street.[48] But at this point, failing an organized rising, all Fynche could do was give Cleymond two pairs of gloves and a pot of green ginger to keep the Earl of Warwick's spirits up.

This conversation was reported in the indictment of the Earl of Warwick for treason in 1499. Of itself it is little, though treasonable, but within a year it had begotten a bizarre plot. Most comment on the plot assumes that the entire fabric was the creation of Henry VII and his agents. Yet few involved can be regarded as Henry's men, and there is no evidence in Henry VII's Chamber Issue Books that he was paying *agents provocateurs* at this time, inside the Tower or out, and no one involved in the 1498–9 plot was rewarded for information or indeed anything.[49] This is not to say that Henry did not know what was going on, nor that the plot was not allowed to run on till it had enmeshed a sufficient number of rebels for Henry to smash Plantagenet dissidence. How then did Henry destroy 'the last drop of doubtful blood in the kingdom'?

The answer lies in the behaviour of Perkin Warbeck. At midnight on the night of Trinity Sunday, 9 June 1498, Warbeck fled from his locked quarters in Westminster Palace. Henry was resident in the palace at the time.[50] Immediately it was known that Warbeck had fled a large scale operation was mounted to recover him. Stephen Bull, Henry's trusted sea captain, and William Barnefield, a yeoman of the crown with expertise in naval matters, were sent to find him. Presumably they were expected to search ships in the port of London, for fear of Warbeck's flight to Flanders, and Bull may have taken ships out into the Thames estuary and English Channel. A few days later his name is coupled with the Lord Warden of the Cinque Ports, Sir Edward Poynings, on a letter circuit to Kent. Letters were sent to every port of southern England and to principal noblemen in each region urging them in the following terms to institute a search for Perkin.[51]

> Thorowe the folly and simpleness of such as we put in truste to keepe Perkin Warbecke he is escaped from them and albeit it is noe great force where he be come yet to the intent he might be punished after his deserte we woulde gladlie have him againe. Wherfore cousyn we will and desyre you to cause good and sure serche to be made for him with all diligence along our portes creekes and passages in those partes about you that he in noe wyse passe those waies. And over this within the same portes and elsewhere that shall seem good ye make open proclamacion that whosover he be that taketh the said Perkin he shall have for his rewarde an hundred poundes with our speciall thankes.[52]

The net was cast wide: Poole, Weymouth and Lyme Regis in the west; Boston, Grimsby, King's Lynn, Ispwich and Yarmouth in the east; in the south Chichester, Southampton, Dover, Sandwich, Winchelsea, Rye and Hastings. On 10 June Bristol and Bridgwater were notified.[53] At first it may have been believed that Warbeck was going to Southampton either to take ship, or to re-enter sanctuary at Beaulieu Abbey. The king sent letters to the abbot and also to the Earl of Arundel and Lord de la Warre. The Earl of Oxford was notified and letters sent to Canterbury. But what chance did Warbeck have? And what was he trying to do? Henry had riders out around London, he set posts between Barnet and Barking Abbey, sent a group of eight yeomen north to Dunstable and had four boats crewed by yeomen of the crown watching on the Thames overnight.[54]

Perkin crossed the Thames from Westminster to the south bank. He was hemmed in and hunted. He could not reach sanctuary at Beaulieu, and did not try Westminster. There are two traditions about Warbeck's flight, an English and a Burgundian one. The English is preserved in the London Chronicles and has a desperate Warbeck throwing himself on the mercy of the Carthusian Prior of Sheen and begging him to intercede with Henry for his life.[55] The Burgundian tradition is one of Molinet's stories, in which Perkin hid himself in the reeds of the Thames for three or four days before climbing over the wall of the Carthusian house. Once he was in the charterhouse the prior refused to have anything to do with him on the grounds that the king had forbidden any help be rendered to Perkin under severe penalty. Thus the prior turned to Henry de Berghes, Bishop of Cambrai, then on embassy in England to enlist his aid. In the story de Berghes feared disgrace and would not help Warbeck, and so delivered him to Henry. In the English story de Berghes plays no part. Instead after Warbeck's arrival at Sheen, the prior first made sure that Perkin could not escape, and then went to see the king at Westminster. Knowing Henry well, belonging to a place with close ties to the king's favourite Observant Order at nearby Syon, he managed to secure a pardon for Perkin's life.[56] According to English sources this was done by refusing to leave till pardon of his life was granted. The quid pro quo here, as in similar situations, may have been a pardon for a life bought on condition of perpetual imprisonment. Which tradition is correct? Not Molinet's. De Berghes did not reach England till August. But whatever happened once the bargain was struck Warbeck was returned to Westminster, and a string of letters despatched to the places which had been placed on security alert to scale it down.[58]

The hangman had not yet arrived, but imprisonment for life had. On Friday 15 June Perkin was put on public display. He was displayed upon a carefully considered scaffold made of empty wine pipes and hogsheads of wine. On top of this sat Perkin, in the stocks, for most of the morning, while people came and looked at him as they had done six months before. Why this derisory scaffold? Was it mockery by association: empty vessels make the most noise? Or was it, for those courtiers in the know the most ironic of comments, that Warbeck had escaped in a wine pipe in 1497, but now he was imprisoned by them? Whatever the case he had to endure it only two or three hours before being taken down. Monday 18 June was the day fixed for his transfer from Westminster to the Tower. In the morning he was taken as far as the well known inn, the King's Head in Cheapside. Here again he was displayed on a scaffold of empty wine vessels, this time for about five hours, from ten in the morning till almost three in the afternoon. Crowds gathered to view the strange phenomenon.[59] Was this the second son of Edward IV or not? But at three, under a secure guard of officers of the City and the Tower he was taken out of the stocks and up Cornhill, one of the richest streets in the city, to the Tower. The next time he journeyed from the Tower was to Tyburn.

But how had Perkin managed to escape in the first place? According to the indictment of his two yeomen servants, John Kebyll and John Sherwyn, on 7 July, three weeks after his escape, Warbeck had subborned them into procuring a variety of keys and wax out of which a set of counterfeit keys were made for Warbeck to break out of prison in Westminster palace. The dismal language of the indictment, prison, excitement to treason, levying war on the king etc., is at odds with what we know of Warbeck's confinement.[60] Most literary commentators have him escaping from Westminster out of the window of the palace, and one diplomatic source goes as far as to say out of the window of the Wardrobe. But why? Warbeck's flight seems a random and directionless act. It is possible that Kebyll and Sherwyn had been subborned not by Warbeck but by the conspirators Cleymond or Astwode, they were Londoners. Men such as they and John Fynche had numerous contacts at court through their commercial transactions, but there is not a shred of evidence for this. There was a third party involved – the king. Henry's letter urging Warbeck's recapture is sanguine almost to the point of disingenuity. Warbeck had escaped, he said, 'Thorowe the folly and simpleness of suche as we put in truste to keepe' him. In Venice the diarist Sanuto reported news of the event carried by merchants, that 'the King arranged with some of Perkin's attendants that they should suggest to Perkin to escape out of his Majesty's hands; and thus did this youth do: so the King had him put in prison, where he will end his days'.[61] Such manipulation of officers and men by kings is typical of this period. It was one in which the apparently loyal (but really duplicitous) were sent on false missions, met individuals purporting to be kings, challenged them, were forgiven by the real king because they had been clever enough to see through the disguise – and then blinded years later because the king coveted the man's wife as a mistress.[62] Warbeck was what he always had been, a pawn in someone else's game, and was to remain so.

Within three weeks of Warbeck's entry to the Tower, on 10 July, one of the earl's servants, a yeoman named John Williams, introduced Thomas Astwode and Reginald Chambre to his master. The conversations were as follows. Williams to his master: 'My lord I have brought you hither this man who loves you well and he has lately escaped a great danger, for he was to have lost his head lately and yet loves you. My lord you may be sure of me and Thomas Astwode at all times.' The earl to Astwode: 'Now I have a special friend.' Astwode to the earl: 'My lord I love you and I will place myself in as great peril as I ever was in before to do you good and help to put you in your right, in which I hope once to see you.' The earl thanked him and was then introduced to Chambre. Their conversation is not recorded, but Chambre was introduced to him as a 'favourer' of his.[63] Chambre played little active part in the plot, and was pardoned in 1500. Nevertheless he remained in opposition to Henry VII as a follower of Lady Elizabeth Lucy illegitimate daughter of Edward IV. In 1503 she was described as a sympathizer of the then pretender, Edmund de la Pole, and likely to betray Calais to him. Her immediate circle, in which Chambre was counted as one, were men 'who never lovyd the kingis grace, nor never woldo'.[64]

Henry VII's aspirations in the summer of 1498 are clear in the diplomatic correspondence: to subject his people ruthlessly to arbitrary government, after the French fashion. His subjection of the people began on 13 September when he issued a commission to start punishment of the south-western rebels.[65] He had to deprive 'the people', as well as Astwode and his friends, of their *alter rex*. Thus the necessity of placing Warbeck in the Tower. This removed Warbeck from everyday political life and placed in the Tower an individual who could be manipulated if the king needed. Part of this instability sprang from the company he kept in the Tower, part from the physical conditions of imprisonment and part from the total isolation imposed on Warbeck politically as well as physically. After November 1497 he was abandoned by Maximilian I. By the time Henry began his punishment of his western shires, in September 1498 Warbeck had been given up by Margaret of Burgundy as well.

Ever since the negotiation of the Intercursus Magnus in 1496 there had been complaints from both Burgundian and English merchants about the state of English cloth trade with the Low Countries. These complaints led to prolonged ambassadorial exchanges between Philip the Fair and Henry VII, which became continuous throughout 1497, but broke down and became deadlocked in 1498. They were revived in that year because of changed circumstances in European politics; but even though there were high-level discussions at Bruges there was no proper resolution of trade difficulties till after 1500.[66] In April 1498 Henry VII was visited by Thomas Ysaac, Toison d'Or, on secret matters of the greatest importance.[67] This was probably to discuss what line England and Flanders would adopt towards the new French king, Louis XII. Such negotiations were typical of the kind of realignments which occurred on the death of any monarch, and though almost immediately Maximilian pressed for a war with France, in reality England, Spain and Flanders were renegotiating their treaties of 1493 and 1498.

For Henry VII, however, it was his relations with Flanders which more preoccupied him. At the beginning of June a spy in Brussels wrote to the Spanish ambassador informing him of a proposed Flemish embassy which aimed to resolve both commercial tensions and those surrounding continuing Flemish support for Henry's rebels.[68] Henry wanted good relations with Flanders, but was all too aware of the way Maximilian I and Philip the Fair had lent support to Warbeck, and had done nothing to fulfil the terms of the Intercursus Magnus under which the Duchess Margaret should have been deprived of her dower lands.[69] By mid-July the Flemish ambassador, Henry de Berghes, and his fellows were expected in London; though they did not actually arrive till the beginning of August. Once established in London the magnitude of their task became apparent; the negotiations in Bruges had failed and had been referred to London for further discussion. De Berghes arrived with letters from Philip and his wife Joanna only to be cold-shouldered by Henry who complained about Maximilian's recent duplicity, suggesting war against France while at the same time concluding a peace with her.[70] De Berghes wisely appealed for aid from the Spanish, and Dr de Puebla went with him to see Henry. They were greeted by a furious king but, according to de Puebla, he himself managed to calm Henry. Then, to the delight of the Flemish delegation, progress was made; but not before Henry created a savage political theatre. To ram home the point that he was not to be trifled with, he arranged a meeting between himself, de Puebla, and de Berghes and Warbeck – to humiliate the bishop who had served Warbeck in Flanders in 1495. At the beginning of August, possibly when Henry gave £100 to de Berghes, Warbeck was brought out of the tower to meet him.[71]

In July and August the court was in progress through East Anglia, from Havering to Hedingham Castle, to Lavenham, to Bury St Edmunds and on via King's Lynn to Margaret Beaufort's house at Collyweston, and so to Woodstock. Warbeck was brought to Henry and de Berghes at the Earl of Oxford's castle at Hedingham, between 6 and 11 August. (Simon Digby, Lieutenant of the Tower was paid 6s 8d on 30 July.) In a dreadful state, he was asked why he had deceived Philip. He swore to de Berghes, said de Puebla, that he had done so on Margaret's instruction, that she knew he was not Richard Plantagenet and that he had deceived every monarch in Europe except the Spanish. This was a blunt diplomatic message, not lost on de Puebla, nor on de Berghes, that foreign powers should not interfere in English affairs. They had only to look at Warbeck. ' I saw how much altered Perkin was. He is so much changed that I', said de Puebla, 'and all other persons here believe his life will be very short. He must pay for what he has done.'[72] Reports of this meeting probably persuaded Margaret of Burgundy to abandon Warbeck and the remaining rebels in Flanders. A month after de Berghes saw Warbeck, on 7 September, letters arrived in England from Margaret. The duchess asked for Henry VII's pardon and assured him of her future obedience, tantamount to recognizing him as legitimate king.[73] The diplomatic community held its breath, and rumours circulated that Henry intended secret negotiations with the archduchess, Joanna, through a chaplain. Margaret had written to Henry because he was insisting on the rigorous execution of the Intercursus Magnus to deprive her of her dower lands because she continued to harbour rebels at Malines. Philip the Fair, however, was not prepared to implement the treaty and the archduchess too rejected any implementation outright. For two-and-a-half weeks negotiations went on in secret until Henry and his council debated the subject.[74] For the trouble Margaret had caused Henry, his council loathed her. But Joanna's protection of her, and the fact that the Flemish council were unmoved by Henry's demands resulted in a compromise. Instead of demanding the full rigour of the treaty be enforced against Margaret it was decided, against the feeling of the meeting, that a courteous letter be written and conveyed to her by de Berghes.[75] In fact there is evidence that suggests Henry had already got what he wanted: the expulsion from Malines of Warbeck's supporters. John Taylor is next heard of in France. William Barley and one of the attainted of 1495,

Richard Williamson, and his servants, were already in England. Barley had received a pardon in July 1498, Williamson and his company in February. They may have been surrendered as a peace offering, or perhaps they could see what was coming; but for William Barley this meant submission to harsh fines and bonds to ensure his good behaviour in the future.[76]

By the last week in September de Berghes was on his way back to Malines. By 16 October the expenses of Jean de Lignieres, esquire, a servant of Margaret of Burgundy, were being met by Philip the Fair. De Lignieres had been in England, on embassy with Henry de Berghes.[77] De Berghes' return to Flanders signalled the end for Flemish support for Richard, Duke of York. Warbeck was alone. Deprived of the support of Margaret, isolated in the Tower, he was completely at the mercy of Henry VII and the supporters of the Earl of Warwick's lost cause.

SIXTEEN

Shaking Empty Chains

The political climate in which Warbeck now found himself could hardly have been less auspicious. Over the winter of 1498–9 Henry VII's commissioners in the west of England uncovered the extent of the rebellion of 1497. Henry had also to absorb worse news. Their work showed that much of England west of Winchester had supported rebellion, and that many in the political classes of Somerset, and some in Wiltshire and Dorset, had alienated their loyalty to him in 1497. For the moment he did nothing, because he could do nothing; to punish too severely risked creating a political backlash in a region where quiescence and consolidation were needed.[1] Yet no sooner was this enquiry over than a new pretender appeared in East Anglia. In view of the question mark hanging over some East Anglian loyalties in 1497 Henry had appointed his own men as sheriffs that year. This sensitivity to treachery explains why when Ralph Wilford, a cordwainer's son from Bishopsgate in London, declared himself to be Edward, Earl of Warwick, he was so promptly and savagely dealt with. Wilford tried unsuccessfully to raise rebellion in the region – the borders of Norfolk and Suffolk – previously dominated by the traitor Robert Chamberlain, and Gilbert Debenham and Lord Fitzwater, Warbeck's supporters. He was seized by the Earl of Oxford, forced to confess and sent to the king. Quickly tried, he was hanged on 12 February, Shrove Tuesday. Wilford was neither a Lambert Simnel, trained up for the purpose, nor a Perkin Warbeck, seized and transformed. Instead he was that not uncommon thing: an adolescent fantasist, a twenty-year-old scholar at Cambridge who had had a dream telling him could be king if he named himself Warwick.[2] Absurd he might be, but not meaningless. He had appeared in and appealed to the right place. His savage fate demonstrated the febrile state of English politics.

A month after Wilford's execution Henry VII, as was his custom, took a prognostication of the future. He was said to have asked the man who had successfully prophesied the deaths of Richard III and Edward IV how his own end would come. Diplomatically, the priest sidestepped the manner of the king's end telling him instead that his life would be in danger all year, because there were two parties of very different political creeds in his kingdom. Reportedly terrified by this prophecy Henry ordered the priest not to divulge it to anyone. He, however, did not contain himself and told a friend who told a friend. The latter was imprisoned; the prophet and the first friend absconded from court.[3] Who was the prophet? Two names are viable candidates for having committed this *faux pas* John Argentine and William Parron. Both were retained by Henry to make prognostications. Argentine was royal astrologer though he served under cover of his official capacity as king's physician, and doctor to Prince Arthur. He had cast horoscopes and nativities for Edward IV and Edward V, and had served Edward and his brother Richard in the Tower. Parron was another doctor, an Italian, who worked at court between 1490 and 1503. He blazed a trail in England by being the first of his kind to emulate continental practice. He

A fifteenth-century pharmacy. Prophecy, poison, alchemy and astrology, as well as medicine, flourished in this sort of place

cultivated a rich patron, Henry, and at the same time produced printed almanacs for the mass market. At about the time this unpalatable prophecy was reported he was rewarded by Henry for his services in astrology.[4]

Henry VII maintained a number of Italian astrologers at court. Theirs was a mischievous influence fuelling the ambitions of the political élite. Elizabeth Woodville, for example, consulted Lewis of Carleon, Margaret Beaufort's astrologer, who very nearly lost his life in 1483 because of his association with her. Edward IV's father, Richard of York, may have used a lowly London astrologer, Richard Trewythian, a man far removed from the courts who doubled as a money lender. Like many of his kind he eked out an existence providing run of the mill astrological advice.[5] Astrologers like Trewythian practised in most towns of any size. Cambridge, Bury St Edmunds, St Neots, Norwich, Nottingham and Bristol all provide examples.[6] Places where astrologers lived were well known. Bucklersbury, in Cheap Ward, where the Warbeck plot began, was famous for its apothecary shops. Could it have been from an apothecary that astrologer Fynche got the prophecy of bear and chains? In 1428 Elys Davy, a London mercer, was accused of hiring a man in a tavern in Cheap to procure a clerk who knew the art of making people waste away. It was later claimed he wanted to destroy the king.[7] Political outcasts of all types took advice from such men. William Parron boasted that he had warned Sir Edward Franke, a veteran of Stoke, to stay out of politics. Too late said Parron, it was only when he was captured for plotting against Henry VII, in 1489, that Franke remembered Parron's good advice.[8] In this *demi-monde* of fixers, medics, prophets, charlatans, merchants, suppliers of the court, and clerics who knew men in high places, the plotters moved.

In the early summer of 1499 Henry VII moved from one residence to another in the London area: first to Wanstead, then the Tower, then Greenwich then Sheen. At the end of

June Thomas Astwode was tipped off by William Walker of Wanstead, a chaplain, that the summer's progress was about to begin. He had been told by a 'certain gentleman' that Henry would leave Greenwich for Baynard's castle, and that the stopping places for progress had all been agreed. He would never return to London alive. This was probably nothing more than an echo of the prophecy which caused so much trouble. Astwode seems to have taken it as a sign for action, either because it confirmed his wishes, or, more likely, because he knew in advance the king's movements, and that the progress of this summer took him off mainland England to the Isle of Wight. Two weeks prior to his conversation with Walker, he had met a yeoman, Thomas Pounte, in All Hallows Barking, Tower ward, on 2 June. Astwode asked Pounte if he knew one or two fellows of gentle condition who could be persuaded by Astwode to help him. When Pounte asked 'For what purpose?' he was dismissed curtly with, 'You shall know hereafter.' When a month later, on 6 July, Pounte sought Astwode out again to fix the timing of their action, Astwode again dismissed him claiming that he 'could not then attend him'.[9]

All, however, was not as it seemed to Pounte. Astwode was well appraised of the king's movements and his plans were well advanced. Somehow, maybe through the earl's man, Robert Cleymond, or perhaps by his own best endeavours, Astwode had suborned several servants from within the Tower. He had also involved others: two drapers, Edmund Carre and Edward Dyxson. Dyxson was involved early, and drew Carre in. He divulged a plan to release Warbeck and the Earl of Warwick, and assured him that some of the Lieutenant of the Tower's servants were already committed to their cause. At this Carre agreed to join and, taking a book out of his purse, swore on it to be true and secret. How all the men who took the oath of secrecy joined the plot we do not know, but they shared, if not a common purpose, something of a common social background. They fell broadly into four groups: one mercantile – three drapers, a haberdasher and a merchant; one ecclesiastical – four clerks and two chaplains; one group of eight gentlemen; and one of five yeomen who straddle the ground between servant and artisan. Six conspirators can be identified as politically active long before 1499.[10] John Audley, James Audley's brother was one. He had marched with the rebel westerners to Blackheath in 1497. In the autumn before this, Thomas Warde, along with John Fynche, was placed under bond for his loyalty in 1496.[11] Warde's connections in politics go back to Richard III's reign when he was used by Richard as ambassador to France, and he continued to serve as a diplomat under Henry VII, working alongside Stephen Frion in 1488. It is possible that he defected to Warbeck in 1493, and had only just been received back into political life, being granted a general pardon on 8 February 1499, six months earlier, or may then have been suspected by the government.[12] Astwode needs no introduction, nor does William Lounde, the man who was said to have acted as Warbeck's chancellor. Less obviously political, at first sight, is Roger Ray, who may be the Long Roger the London Chronicles name as a conspirator. His career as a rebel began during Buckingham's rebellion. He was proclaimed a rebel in Kent and a reward of £100 was offered for his capture.[13] Subsequently, in 1484, he was attainted. But Henry VII's accession did not see him living out a peaceful political restoration and in 1494 he joined the major conspiracy against Henry.[14] From then till 1499 he seems to have been kept as a prisoner in the Tower. Who was Ray? Since he was named as of Southwark, in 1483, he may have been a son of William Ray, Master of the Masons of the City of London.[15] If this William is the same man William named in 1475 as the son of Sir Roger Ray, then Long Roger may have been the grandson of one of Richard, Duke of York's oldest followers. Sir Roger was a Yorkist of impeccable loyalty who had served Richard, Duke of York and been rewarded by Edward IV for his service to his father, in France, Ireland and England, with a position as senior usher of the chamber.[16] These men belonged to the same group, court and family servants, as those of the plots of 1495. Indeed they had probably escaped detection in 1495, rather than having been recruited *de novo* in 1498.

Attachment like this is known definitely for Thomas Masborough whom the chronicles correctly describe as Edward IV's bowyer. Thomas was appointed surveyor of the king's bowmakers in February 1474, and at about the same time an Edmund Masborough was a household servant of George, Duke of Clarence.[17] Others of the conspirators can by their names be identified as northern. Thomas Strangwysshe, pardoned after the 1499 plot, was from Smeeton in Yorkshire.[18] One branch of the Carre family, at Alnwick, were retainers of Richard III. Dyxson may have had a connection with the north through the Percy family of that name. The name Pynkeney, of Richard Pynkeney, is northern, associated with the Conyers family, clients of the Nevilles.[19] Thus it would seem, northern attachment to York perhaps more rightly, Neville, may have been attenuated, but it was not yet dead.

Astwode needed his men of gentle condition for one purpose, to spirit the Earl of Warwick out of England. At the beginning of August he worked hard to recruit conspirators. Dyxson, and William Proude, a haberdasher, had agreed to lade a ship with woollen cloth to smuggle the earl out of England. This was not a far-fetched suggestion. Intelligence was regularly gathered and transmitted via mercantile shipping. And All Hallows Barking, next to the Tower where most of the plot was hatched, was the first parish within the city walls with quayside access to the Thames.[20] William Basset agreed to supply the ship. Others were drawn in, either out of prior conviction or necessity. Thomas Ody at his wits ends, politically if not literally, said to Astwode on 2 August, 'Will this world not mend? By the mass I am in want of money and care not what I do, either to fight or to rob in order to have money.' Again he swore by the mass, 'I would like Peter Warbeck to be at large, because then money would be current, and it is not now.' John Walsshe, a Chantry Warden, also told Astwode that he favoured freeing Warbeck, 'If I and Peter were now in Ireland, knowing him as I now know him, we would make another kind of rumour than was lately made.' Astwode seems to have been introducing men to Warbeck on 2 August, but how is not clear. It was maintained against Ody that he met Warbeck that day and said to him, 'If you were known for such a man's son as you think yourself to be, I suppose many men in England would be glad to do. you good.' Unlike Ody, Walsshe seems to have had no doubts. When questioned by Astwode as to what he meant he said, 'I know that [Perkin Warbeck] is the second son of King Edward IV.'

One, at least, of Warbeck's long-serving supporters used secret tokens to assure Warbeck of his continued loyalty, and also probably to indicate his faith in Astwode. William Lounde asked Astwode to convey to Warbeck a gold dukket which he had, as a prearranged sign, bent with his teeth. At the same time he also used Sir Simon Digby's man, Luke Longford, as a go-between. Lounde sent Thomas Strangwysshe to Longford endowed with knowledge that when he (Lounde) had last met Warbeck he had cut his aglets, metal tags at the end of laces from his hood, and given them to Warbeck. Strangwysshe showed the aglets to Longford, and Longford passed the sign, with its attendant message of loyalty, on to Warbeck. This indicated Lounde's continuing loyalty and Longford's bona fides.[21] Such traffic moved in and out of the Tower carried by Simon Digby's servants. The maintenance of state prisoners at their own expense was an invitation to lax security, and it would appear that Digby's servants were little more than trusted prisoners, some of them presumed to be reformed rebels. With ingenuity it was possible, as it still is, to smuggle letters, and a great deal besides in and out of gaol. We must also remember that the Tower was an armoury, palace and place of business, there was much movement in and out of it each day. Cleymond was indicted for taking to Warbeck a letter of advice from a Flemish priest, one Jacques, in which Jacques advised him not to respond in any way to the promptings of Sir Simon Digby.

Tomb and effigy of Sir Simon Digby, Lieutenant of the Tower in 1498–9, Coleshill church, Warwickshire. The Digbys were devoted to Henry Tudor. By repute seven Digby brothers fought for him at Bosworth, and one, Thomas, was used to arrest plotters in 1494

According to the indictments Cleymond took the letter to Warbeck after it had been delivered to the Earl of Warwick's chamber in the Tower. First he read it, then delivered it to Warbeck and then took a reply from him for Jacques.[22]

The intentions of the conspirators gathered pace between 2 and 4 August. At this time Henry VII was almost at the furthest point in his progress away from London; at Southampton and Beaulieu, prior to a two-week visit to the Isle of Wight. At Carisbrook castle he audited the accounts of the fines taken from Warbeck's Cornish supporters.[23] But he was off the English mainland. He was out of immediate touch with London and the Tower. The plan which emerged is not clear, insomuch as it had two focuses, Warbeck as Richard IV, and the Earl of Warwick as Edward VI. According to the proof laid before his council by Henry, Warwick agreed to help Warbeck to the Crown, if he was who he said he was. But if he was not a Plantagenet, then he, Warwick, would seize the throne on his own behalf.[24] According to the indictment of the conspirators Cleymond, having received the letter from Jacques, knocked on the vault of Warbeck's chamber and told him to 'be of good cheer and comfort', promising to deliver it to him the next day. Sometime during this day Cleymond claimed he had had a conversation with Warbeck in which Warbeck advised him to seize the Tower, and between them they had devised a plan. He told this to the earl who was said to have responded, 'Why?', to which Cleymond and the others present with him said they would do it for Warbeck and him. What was proposed, between Astwode, Cleymond and Warwick, apparently at Warbeck's instigation was they seize the Tower ransack the king's treasury and take money, plate and jewels, and using gunpowder from the royal ordnance, fire the Tower. Under cover of the ensuing chaos they were to take ship to a place overseas, presumably in the vessel to be supplied by William Basset. From there they would make public proclamation against Henry inviting insurrection, paying their rebels 12*d* per day as soldiers with money from Henry's treasury. At the end of the meeting in Warwick's chamber at which the plan was discussed, Cleymond was alleged to have said, 'My Lord you are well minded in what danger, sadness, and duress you here remain: but if you will help yourself according to the form and effect of the communication and discourse had between us, you shall come out of this prison with me, I will take you out of danger, and leave you in surety.' And to indicate his deadly earnest he was said to have presented Warwick a hanger, short sword, to use in the break out. Forty-eight hours later, on 4 August, he informed his master, that their plans were known to the authorities, 'made known to the King and his Council by Peter Warbeck, and the said Peter hath accused you and me and Thomas Astwode'.[25]

Ever since Wilhelm Busch decided in 1892 that Cleymond was a double agent for Henry VII it has been customary to read this final plot as his work, the details of which were fed to him by Henry VII in order to bring down Warbeck and Warwick and provide the opportunity to execute them. Busch claimed Cleymond was guilty, and asserted that he was pardoned after the event.[26] There is no evidence for either statement, nor did Busch offer any. Reading, and re-reading, and re-reading the evidence against the conspirators it is far from easy to see who, if not Warbeck, was responsible for informing against them, or to find a motive for informing such as we might adduce for Warbeck. It is conceivable that the priest Jacques might be an *agent provocateur* since he appears only twice in the story and knew what Simon Digby was up to with Warbeck. Priests made good spies, and Henry VII used them as such. The conspirators fall into a number of different circles. Far from the centre were those mentioned only once who knew only one other person. Nearer were those involved in providing a ship, woollens or offering some specialized service. Nearer still were long-standing supporters of Warbeck, John Fynche and Thomas Warde, who still had relatively few contacts with other conspirators.

At the centre were Astwode, Cleymond and Warbeck. This plot was Astwode and Cleymond's plot. Astwode made the contacts in the London commercial world. Cleymond acted as go-between for the Earl of Warwick and certain of Warbeck's supporters. The earl himself was an innocent bystander. Of the two, Astwode and Cleymond, Astwode had by far the greatest number of direct contacts with co-conspirators: we can count over fifteen, to Cleymond's seven or eight. Cleymond therefore could have named very few conspirators. It is inconceivable, given Astwode's background as an incorrigible Yorkist that he was a double agent. At the trials he was indicted on five counts, and then executed. Of Cleymond we know nothing. He was indicted, but seemingly never tried or executed. It is thus very tempting to see this as evidence that a deal was struck with a talented double agent, and he was quietly passed over. The trouble with such a suggestion is that until Margaret Condon discovered two petitions relating to John Fynche and Thomas Warde it was unknown that Warde, though unpardoned and unexecuted, as well as untried, had died in prison.[27] We simply do not know what happened to Cleymond, and it will not do to argue, as was done in 1935, in ignorance of Warde's fate, that Cleymond, like Warde, must have done some deal with Henry VII.[28] If we have decided he was the guilty party we can read almost everything he says as implicatory of conspirators, carefully drawing them into his web until the moment they were arrested and he vanished into thin air. Nowhere is this more tempting than in his relations with Warbeck. Did Warbeck inform on the plot? Or did Cleymond skilfully shift attention away from himself and onto Warbeck.

Of the three people at the heart of this conspiracy only one person, Astwode, was cited as having carried on more treasonable conversations than Warbeck. And of the three, (himself, Cleymond and Astwode), Warbeck was cited as having contacts with the widest range of plotters. Astwode dealt with those outside the Tower. Cleymond with a few inside it but

Warbeck, cited as having had treasonable conversations with eleven men, formed a bridge between Warwick's attendants, Sir Simon Digby's servants, and Astwode's alienated world of artisans and down and outs. Given the complete lack of evidence about Cleymond we can not be sure that he did not inform to Henry, but with an unprejudiced eye it is difficult to see what his motive was. He appears at the beginning of the plot as Warwick's servant. Throughout the plot he is accepted as such, no more no less, by all the conspirators and the Earl of Warwick. There is no reward ever recorded as passing through Henry VII's Chamber Issue books to him, and he was indicted for treason. How do we read Cleymond's statement to his master? That Warbeck confessed to Henry's council? Is it simply a matter of blaming someone else to compromise their position in order to avoid discovery as a double agent? Or was it an attempt to warn the earl? The behaviour of the conspirators after the warning had may provide a clue. They continued to deal with Cleymond as one of their group. But towards Warbeck they were neither united nor sure of his integrity. One of their number refused to have anything to do with him, while another warned him not to, 'do himself any harm for anything Sir Simon Digby should say'. The inference here is that Digby was placing some form of pressure on Warbeck. To do what we do not know. For what we do not know. However, according to the indictments it was Warbeck who advised Cleymond to seize the Tower from Digby. Warbeck had been imprisoned in the Tower because Henry VII feared just such a conspiracy as Astwode's. He had been reduced by his imprisonment to near breaking point, this is clear from de Puebla's description of him. Warbeck was a broken man. Furthermore the equivocation in the conspirators's minds as they contemplated helping Warbeck must have existed in him. The extreme psychological fluctuation in identity which Warbeck had experienced in 1497 and 1498 could hardly have left him unmarked: Perkin Warbeck – Tournaisian, Richard Plantagenet – Duke of York, Perkin Warbeck – grateful subject of Henry VII, Richard Plantagenet – co-conspirator with his cousin the Earl of Warwick. By now what was he? He was all these things. And the late fiteenth century knew how to play on them all. It was an age of contrivance, irony and ambiguity. It may be that Sir Simon Digby, instructed by the king, was playing Warbeck on a line. Like Clifford in 1495 Warbeck might buy his life by supplying the council and king with information. At the same time he could goad the conspirators on to the plot the king necessarily needed to indict them and have Warwick executed. The equivocal role Warbeck had played all his life here reached its absurd logical extension. With one part of him he played Henry's loyal subject passing information to Digby, with another he was a fully committed plotter. Or did he know what he was doing? Could he divine that for him there was no way out of this hall of mirrors, and that all he could hope for was to pass on information to Henry, of a real plot against him in order to bring down with him those men who had inflicted this imposture upon him. For Warbeck this last plot may have offered the only way out, a suicidal atonement by which he regained his identity once and for all. To decide was to live, even if to live meant dying. For, as Bruno Bettelheim observes, decision making is not just an ego function; on the contrary, it is the function that creates the ego and, once created, keeps it going and growing.[29]

On 3 August 1499 someone informed Sir Simon Digby of a plot to seize the Tower, and the next day Cleymond told his master that they had been informed against. How Cleymond knew is unknown. It is possible that Cleymond was falsifying his position. It is equally possible that Cleymond had been told that Warbeck had confessed to Digby by one of Sir Simon's servants. The Tower was a very small community, and though it is said in the indictments that the king and council knew about the plot, no action was taken. Why not? If Cleymond was the guilty party it was merely a matter of rounding up the conspirators. But this does not seem to have been the intention. The intention seems to have been to flush out unknown conspirators, possibly those within the Tower. For they, Simon Digby's servants, were not fully implicated until 4 August. It was only on this date that the plan to fire the Tower, free Warbeck and snatch the earl becomes fully visible.[30]

Once the plot was discovered Cleymond immediately fled to Thomas Warde, told him of the discovery and that he intended to take sanctuary at Colchester. Warde, who probably lived in sanctuary at Westminster tried to persuade Cleymond to seek refuge there as well. But he did not entirely trust Cleymond. Cleymond asked the earl for a token which would establish his credibility as Warwick's man. The earl made Cleymond a wooden figure and sent this, via Walter Bluet, a servant of Simon Digby, with a cloak and velvet jacket to Westminster. Bluet was charged with assuring Warde that Cleymond was one of them and that he, Warde, should oversee the developing plot. In the Tower, Warbeck was the focus of attention. Warwick, who was in a chamber above his, knocked a hole in the floor of his own prison to communicate with Warbeck. 'How goes it with you? Be of good cheer,' he greeted him, and sent Walter Bluet to him with a file to break the iron bar of his window, and a hammer to break his chains. Part of the plan was that Warbeck, who was chained to his cell, would remove his shackles and wear a false shackle, easily removable. Astwode was credited with delivering this to him that day. At the same time it was asserted that Roger Ray had acted as go-between for Luke Longford and Warbeck, taking two of Longford's letters to Warbeck. One contained a long white thread so that Warbeck could communicate with the conspirators by letting down letters from his cell window. What the other was we are not told, but it may have been a code book. Warbeck was accused of giving to John Audley a book called ABC or Crosse Rowe. This was a simple substitutional code, one letter or character standing for another, so that the conspirators could send each other secret messages.[31]

Outside the Tower the men who were charged with spiriting Warwick out of the country met in St Mary Wolnoth parish. All present, five of them – Carre, Proude, Dyxson, Astwode, and Masborough – swore upon a book that they would be true and secret to their fellowship and keep and conceal their counsel. Thomas Masborough, ex-master bowyer to Edward IV, had lived between the King's Lodgings and the Round Tower, during his period of office so it may have been their intention to use Masborough as a link between the chaos they hoped to cause inside the Tower, and the ship attendant upon Warwick at the Thames wharf.[32] Less busy in a worldy fashion, John Fynche, the haberdasher, returned to his addiction in trafficking with the other world. Firstly he visited a Dr Alcok, some sort of astrologer, to find out what would become of their earl. Then he delivered to Astwode a roll of prophecy so that Astwode could study it and then show it to Warwick. We must assume that, like others circulating before and after this plot, it claimed that Henry VII's days were numbered. It seems that with these activities over, Astwode entered the Tower to see Warbeck, bearing with him not only the false shackle but also a book of prognostication, perhaps the work of Dr Alcok, or perhaps a book which was jointly a code book and a prognostication, with which he hoped to convince Warbeck to work quickly to bring off their plan.[33]

As this hole in the wall affair gathered pace, like the Cato Street conspiracy crossed with the Gunpowder Plot, Henry VII crossed the Solent from Beaulieu to the Isle of Wight. Digby knew of what was afoot, and Henry later described it as a plot 'led and made by some servants of the captain of the great Tower of London'.[34] These men, Digby's servants, seem to have played little further role, at least they are not indicted for any new treasons. Astwode continued to draw men to him. Three weeks later he received a token from a cleric, John Watson, which he passed to Cleymond to take to Warbeck. He sent a letter on from Warbeck to William Lounde, in which Warbeck asked for Lounde's aid. And he then brought Lounde into the plot to release Warbeck. By then, still at large, he and Warwick's supporters may have been so deluded by the apparent inaction of the government that they believed themselves on the brink of success. On 25 August John Fynche retired to his house in Honey Lane with a coven of astrologers, Thomas Warde, Dr Alcok and unnamed others 'professing to be versed in prophecies'. Thomas Warde had been taking soundings for them in the astrological world. He had consulted Rede of Bristol and Hurt of Nottingham and the combined conclusions of these learned men convinced him that Warwick would shortly be King of England. So excited was he that when Cleymond brought him a token from the earl, a linen cloth painted with the image of St Mary, he told Cleymond to tell the earl that Warde had revealed to him that the earl would shortly be set free.[35] The nature of this revelation, like most of these prognostications escapes us, for it was not described. It may have been 'E' prophecy, a prophecy that a deliverer named Edward, a boy king, would arise? Edward Plantagenet was hardly a boy but such notions permeated the period. 'Up Edward VI, the time has come', said one sixteenth-century prophecy, referring to Edward Tudor, but the 'E' prophecy was old by 1499. Edward could be any thus named alternative to the monarch.[36]

This was enough for the council. It had let the plot run on for three weeks after its discovery and it now moved with speed and to end the machinations of Astwode and company. On 23 August Henry was on the Isle of Wight. The next day he was on the mainland and for three weeks based himself at Winchester[37] in order to co-ordinate action against what appeared at the time a more frightful prospect than a mere plot to hold the Tower. On 1 July 1499 Edmund de la Pole, Earl of Suffolk, had fled the realm and cast himself on the mercy of the lieutenant of St Omer, in the territories of Philip the Fair. It is not completely clear why he did this. In retrospect it was represented by those concerned as flight from a monarch about to destroy de la Pole. Conventionally it is said that his flight was a guilty reaction to an act of murder, and a recent suggestion has him severely in debt as a consequence of the king's actions toward the de la Pole family after 1492.[38] What is also true is that de la Pole was fearful of his fate because the man he had murdered was the plaintiff in a case under examination by the King's Council.[39] He had placed himself thereby in contempt of the council, and opened the way to severe action against him by the king. A frightening scenario arose for Henry: Edmund de la Pole in Flanders with Philip and Margaret of Burgundy, Warbeck and Warwick attempting to take the Tower. What was to follow: the capture of the Tower, a rebellion in East Anglia led by Richard de la Pole, a landing in Kent on Warwick's behalf by his cousin, Edmund, backed by the Burgundians? Was the prognostication of March 1498 not perhaps true after all?

The way out of this maze was provided, as the way into it had been, by the French. Just as Charles VIII's ambition in Brittany had spawned the Warbeck affair, so Louis XII's anxiety to secure Henry's neutrality in Italian politics ended it. As we have seen, in the summer of 1498 England and France had renegotiated the Treaty of Étaples. The French had secured a lasting peace with England by redrawing clauses governing the expulsion of English rebels from France much more harshly, and had capped this with a commercial treaty.[40] The following year, 1499, Thomas Ruthal, later Henry VII's secretary, went to France, followed by Sir Thomas Lovell who collected part of the Étaples pension from Calais. Ruthal went to France to activate the new anti-rebel clause; for the French were now prepared to surrender the arch-rebel John Taylor to Henry VII. 'I think his majesty attaches more importance to this than to 100,000 crowns, because as the English say, quo ibo a spiritu tuo et quo a facie tua fugiam.' wrote Raimondo de Soncino to his Duke in Milan. Nothing and nobody outran Henry VII was the joke. 'Where shall I go from your spirit: or where shall I flee from your presence?' Soncino quoted Psalm 139.[41] On 2 September 1499 a French ambassador was rewarded £60. Three weeks later one Greves, who had charge of transporting him, delivered John Taylor to the king, possibly at Basingstoke.[42]

Brussels, l'Hôtel de Ville. Ultimately the kind of urban wealth seen in this building dictated that England and Flanders put Warbeck behind them, in the name of sound economy

Taylor's contact in Cork, John Atwater, with whom he had worked for many years was already in Henry's custody. In March 1498, under the terms of Poynings' Law, the Earl of Kildare was instructed to attaint Taylor's most hardened supporters, William Barry, Lord Barry and John Atwater for treason. They were accused of receiving letters from Warbeck and concealing them from the king. These attainders were not a mere matter of rubber stamping the king's intentions in Ireland, for there remained the pacification of the towns involved with Warbeck in 1497.[43] In October 1498 Kildare descended on Cork, deprived it of its charter, placed a garrison in it, and, in Ware's words, 'on the 15th day of the same month he caused the principal Citizens of Corke and the Townsmen of Kinsale to take the Oath of Allegiance to the King in his and the Councils presence, which to observe, he made them both enter into Bonds and put in Pledges. These things being done according to his mind, and Winter approaching, he went home.'[44] Having been seized by Kildare and the king's men, Atwater and his son Philip were sent to England, probably in the summer of 1499, after their attainder, for in June and July Henry gave rewards to Kildare's pursuivant and to one of his servants.[45] Only in 1500, once order had been re-established by Kildare, was Cork's charter restored to it by the king.[46]

With the begetters of the Warbeck conspiracy in his hands, and new treaty obligations in place with France, Henry was free to move against the Earl of Suffolk. In the week beginning 20 September, during which John Taylor was delivered to him, he sent his Comptroller of the Household, Sir Richard Guildford, and Master Richard Hatton, to Flanders.[47] Molinet noted that Hatton was a refined Latin orator, and he needed to be. The ambassadors tracked Philip the Fair to Brussels and delivered Henry's message to him: that while the king understood that de la Pole was not in a town under Philip's direct jurisdiction he should nevertheless remember his treaty obligations to the king. This was nothing more than a thinly veiled threat to resort to a trade embargo if he did not cooperate, and it was enough, despite the procrastination which ensued, to set in motion de la Pole's eventual expulsion from St Omer.[48] But Guildford and Hatton carried a message for Suffolk himself, and it was no gentle request. They told him bluntly that he had nowhere to run to – no place or prince to go to for succour – because Henry had extradition treaties with France, Spain, Portugal, Scotland and the archduke to ensure the return of rebels. They told him also that were he tempted to take up the life of a mercenary captain which involved fighting against Spain, Portugal, Scotland, the Archduke, Milan, Venice or anywhere in Italy, that is to become a pensioner of the King of France, he would be committing treason. If he returned and threw himself on the king's grace he would, in time, through the actions of his friends find himself restored to grace. Nothing less than submission to the king's will was acceptable. Without it 'he may never loke to recover ne comme to [England] agayn.' De la Pole returned.[49]

It was in this grim mood that, at the end of October 1499, a decision was taken regarding the whole Warbeck affair. That decision is often represented as the crowning, regrettable but necessary, act by which Henry VII achieved political pre-eminence in England and political eminence in Europe, a kind of dark jewel in the crown by which he exchanged political insecurity and the lives of Warwick and Warbeck for political security and the marriage of the Spanish Infanta to his son. It has been represented as the logical outcome of a policy which, piece by piece, secured the English throne against such as Edmund de la Pole. In this view it was the demand of Ferdinand and Isabella for stability in England that led to the executions of 1499 before they would countenance their daughter's marriage to Arthur. The whole plot then was manufactured by Henry to oblige the Spanish. There is not one shred of evidence to support anything of the above. Henry's foreign policy was not some carefully worked out plan, it was a creature of invention forced on him by the events of 1491. Real policy lay like a crashed juggernaut in the ashes of Perkin Warbeck's inventing. The years

1495–9, far from ushering in Tudor sweetness and light on the shoulders of a mighty success were but a prelude to an even darker period of politics in English history than the one just passed, until Henry VIII succeeded his father in 1509. And the decision to execute the conspirators, logical as it was, was determined by anything but logic.

The makers of political opinon at the end of 1499 were quacks, charlatans and astrologers, and on occasion that opinion veered so close to blasphemy as to be inseparable from it. Inside the Tower and in the back streets of London, Nottingham and Bristol, Warbeck and Warwick's men were assured their hour was come. At Winchester, as Henry secured his throne against them, local prophets and astrologers were arrested. At the time Henry's court astrologer William Parron was just finishing the manuscript of *De astrorum vi fatali*, his justification of astrology, and 'apologia pro vita sua', which he gave to the king; and *Anni MD Prognosticon*, his popular almanac for 1500 dedicated to Henry.[50] Henry VII's will infers that in moments of crisis the Virgin Mary was Henry's constant intercessor and deliverer. The Chamber issue books suggest that, like John Fynche, Henry was addicted to hearing prognostications. Parron told him, in *De astrorum vi fatali*, that should Warwick recover his liberty the rekindling of civil strife was the most foreseeable consequence and that, 'Unless he acts through evil intention, one prince may without sin keep prisoner another prince or lord on whose account he fears an insurrection within his own territory.' Then in a blasphemous conceit quoting St John's Gospel, he advocated Warwick's execution, 'It is expedient that one man should die for the people and the whole nation perish not, for an insurrection cannot occur in any state without the death of a great part of their people and the destruction of many great families and their property.' Then he moved on to attack the involvement of the clergy in politics.[51]

Fifteenth-century inn. Plots were hatched, contacts made and astrologers asked for in the inn

De astrorum vi fatali addressed the influence of the stars on men's fate. The most extreme example of unkind destiny Parron could find was the death of Edward IV's sons, 'What but the fate of the stars presiding at their nativity could have destroyed such innocents.' According to Parron an almanac for the year of Richard, Duke of York's birth, 1473, recorded that a white rose fell into the Thames, and that the sun and the moon were hidden while two flaming arrows fell thunderously into the river. The innocents had died as their fate determined. Their deaths had been foretold in their malign stars just as, in 1484, the benign conjunction of Saturn and Jupiter had foreshadowed Henry Tudor's victory at Bosworth. About Warbeck, Parron was sceptical. He told those who believed Warbeck to be the true Richard to purge themselves of their delusions by swallowing his (Warbeck's) confession as an emetic. Parron had been attacked for arguing that the princes were dead, so in *Anni MD Prognosticon* he lashed out. He compared his attackers, Warbeck's deluded adherents, with the Cornish, who expected Arthur's imminent return, or the Flemish, who thought that Charles the Bold was still alive. He was treading on dangerous ground. The cult of Arthur was not the property of the Cornish only. It had played a vital part in royal propaganda under Edward IV and Henry VII.[52] But the man who had cast himself as the High Priest Caiaphas (to Henry VII's Pontius Pilate?) was unlikely to blanch at this. The only way to deny the reality that Warbeck was Richard Plantagenet was to attack the hallowed belief of the returning hero. Without this legitimating belief few, or at least fewer, in England would have countenanced giving him their support to begin with.

By the time this advice was public property, in 1500, its subjects were dead. Henry VII swallowed it, if he needed to, and acted on it. It is not known how the plotters were rounded up – but the king and the lieutenant of the Tower did not have far to go to seize the majority of them. Possibly we will never know exactly how. The king's circumspection in these matters was still, twenty years later, considered admirable. On Tuesday 12 November the Chief Justice of King's Bench, John Fineux laid the evidence of the conspiracy in the Tower before the king's council. According to the record there were over sixty members in attendance, some whose loyalty had been doubted a few years before, John Kendal Prior of the hospitallers for instance. All active members of the aristocracy were present, along with Cardinal John Morton, and the most political members of the Bench of Bishops – The Lord Privy Seal, Fox, and the king's secretary, Oliver King. All the Crown's law officers attended as well as the principal officers of Prince Arthur's council. Fineux indicated the extent of the plot which the Earl of Warwick had confessed to; a conspiracy to depose the king by making Warbeck king first; and then, if he was not a Plantagenet, to have had himself made king. It was the opinion of the judiciary, said Fineux, that this amounted to a treason punishable by death. The king laid it before his council. What should be done: due process of law, or nothing? Each member was asked for his opinion in turn. If blood was to be shed, it was to be shed by all, equally responsible in open council. 'All the said Councellors and everie of theim by himself adviseth councelleth and praieth that not onlie proces but execucon of Justice be also had, of not only Perkin but also of the said Edward and other offenders.'[53] The next day, Wednesday 13 November, a commission of oyer and terminer was issued to the Mayor of London, Nicholas Alwyn, to John Fineux, seven other principal justices and a powerful group of Henry's council who had been present at the council meeting – Sir Gilbert Talbot, Sir Thomas Bourchier, Sir Richard Guildford, Sir John Risley, Sir James Tyrrell, Sir Richard Croftes, Sir John Sapcotes and Sir Robert Sheffield. The following day juries were called from the parishes of All Hallows Barking in Tower Ward, and St Mary Wolnoth in Langburne Ward to begin proceedings on 18 November.[54]

The commissioners of oyer and terminer who sat at the Guildhall on Monday 18 November processed the conspirators into two groups for their trials. The London

Chronicles noted the rumour that eight prisoners, Thomas Masborough, bowyer, John Fynche and William Proude, citizens, and five servants of Sir Simon Digby were indicted for conspiracy to murder Sir Simon Digby and free the Earl of Warwick and Perkin Warbeck.[55] The plot which emerged in indictment was the plan to seize the Tower, fire it and spirit Warwick to safety. In fact it was a larger group which included Masborough, Fynche, Proude, as well as Astwode, Walter Bluet, Roger Ray, Thomas Strangwysshe and Luke Longford – Digby's servants, and their London merchant friends Edmund Carre and Edward Dyxson as principals, and a number of less important men; John Audley, William Basset, William Lounde, Thomas Ody, Thomas Pounte, William Walker and John Walsshe.[56] Astwode was indicted on five counts, Cleymond on two counts and the earl, by implication, had committed numerous treasons. What followed this preliminary hearing was a series of show trials, one for the earl, the others (a set lasting in all for two weeks) for his supporters.

On 19 November the Earl of Oxford was commissioned as Great Chamberlain and High Admiral of England to act as High Steward in the trial of the Earl of Warwick by his peers.[57] This was a peremptory affair: the Great Chronicle noted that Warwick's fate was settled without any legal process at all.[58] On Thursday 21 November Oxford sat under a cloth of estate in the Great Hall of Westminster in the company of twenty-two peers of the realm. The commissioners of oyer and terminer then delivered the indictment to Oxford, and Sir Thomas Lovell and Sir Simon Digby appeared with the earl. Warwick was brought to the bar, confessed to the charges, pleaded guilty, and submitted to the king's grace. The King's Serjeants-at-Law and Attorney prayed for judgement and Oxford delivered it: 'That the . . . Earl of Warwick should be taken to the Tower of London, and from thence drawn through the middle of London to the gallows at Tyburn, and there hanged, cut down, disembowelled and quartered in the usual manner.'[59] The earl was then returned to the Tower and one week later, on 28 November, this most degrading sentence having been remitted, was beheaded on a small scaffold outside the Tower. The next day his head and body were taken by boat to Bisham abbey, and interred there. King Henry duly paid £12 18s 2d to meet the costs of transport and burial.[60]

The day on which Warwick was buried at Bisham, Friday 29 November, saw the beginning of the second trial determined by Henry's commissioners. According to the chronicles eight people were tried in two groups: one of five, and one of three.[61] Four were named and can be readily identified: Astwode, Bluet, Strangwysshe and Ray. The last of the five was probably John Fynche. The others were Thomas Masborough, William Proude and possibly John Williams. Astwode, Bluet, Ray and Fynche were found guilty and Strangwysshe and Proude admitted guilt. Astwode, Bluet, Ray and Strangwysshe were then sentenced to hanging, drawing and quartering at Tyburn. Their heads and quarters were then to be disposed of as the king wished. Judgement on Fynche was suspended for two days but when given, on Monday 2 December, was the same as his fellows, the death penalty. The case against John Williams was abandoned and no trial proceedings are recorded against some of those indicted: John Audley, Robert Cleymond, Thomas Ody or against those individuals named and culpable, for example, Thomas Warde, William Lounde and William Walker.[62] This lack of evidence can be considered suspicious, especially in the case of Audley and Cleymond. Yet, behind the scene, and unrecorded in chronicle or official legal record, minds were being changed and deals struck. Audley was pardoned, eventually, in 1505.[63] Strangwysshe, due to be executed in December 1499 was pardoned in July 1500.[64] One of the minor conspirators also, Reginald Chambre, was pardoned in October that year.[65] Fynche who had pleaded guilty, with Astwode et al, was not executed but remained a political prisoner in the Tower. Thomas Warde, unindicted and untried, died in the Tower.[66] William Walker probably perished also, untried in prison, for daring to speak of the king's

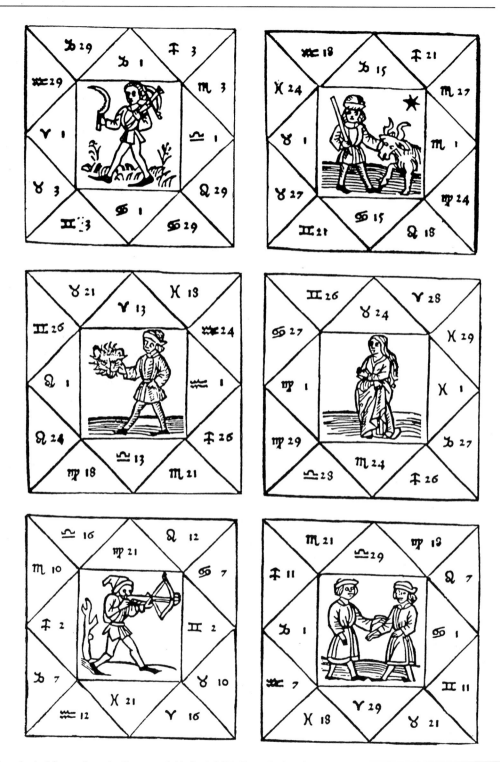

Astrological figures from the Opus astrolabi plani, 1488. Described as the most comprehensive attempt to provide an intellectual structure to understand the world, before science, astrology served everyone, conspirator and king alike

death. Thus by Wednesday 4 December when this series of executions concluded, only two conspirators were publicly executed, Walter Bluet and Thomas Astwode.[67]

Since the council meeting of 12 November the process of public destruction had taken three weeks. At the end, Astwode's and Bluet's deaths aroused little interest worthy of comment. At the beginning things had been different. When, on 21 November, John Pullan wrote to Sir Robert Plumpton, from London, about a legal action of Plumpton's, two-thirds of the letter was taken up describing the trials of Warbeck and Warwick. Warbeck's had been the first, on Saturday 16 November in the Whitehall at Westminster. Here Warbeck and his creators, Taylor and the Atwaters, father and son, were arraigned in front of Sir Simon Digby, as Knight Marshall and Sir John Turberville, Marshall of the Household. This construction, Knight Marshall and Marshall of the Household indicates the nature of their treason: treasons committed outside the realm, and treason committed attempting to escape from the king's custody. Pullan records no trial or pleading just accusation, sentence and judgement: that they should be drawn on hurdles from the Tower throughout London to Tyburn and hanged, cut down alive 'and ther bowells to be taken out and burned', and their heads and quarters to be disposed of as the king decided.[68] But as in cases such as this sentences were waived and varied. John Taylor was not executed, but imprisoned in the Tower. Here he remained after 1509, when he was denied pardon at the beginning of Henry VIII's reign.[69] How, as Warbeck's controller for nine years and a man under attainder since 1495, he escaped execution is a matter of speculation. Perhaps since he knew so much he was of more use to Henry VII alive rather than dead. He could refute any suggestion that Warbeck was other than a fake, and he knew the names of traitors as yet unreconciled to Henry. John Atwater's son, Philip, also was not executed. But his father, as a recently attainted traitor, and the man who had plucked Warbeck from Pregent Meno in 1491, was not to be spared. As for poor Perkin, Molinet says that public opinion ran against a grisly traitor's death for him, and it was decided he should be executed by simple hanging.[70]

On Saturday 23 November Warbeck and Atwater were drawn, amid huge crowds, from the Tower of London to Tyburn. Normally the London Chronicles recorded assiduously the mode of transport used by victims of public execution, but nothing is mentioned in this case.[71] So we may credit Molinet with preserving the story of Warbeck's last journey. To indicate his true status, as a condemned commoner he, and Atwater, were led through the streets of London with halters round their necks. At Tyburn a small scaffold had been erected and Warbeck was forced up onto this to face the crowd. He was surrounded by a vast sea of faces, 'an huge multitude' says the chronicler. Within minutes of his death, still he was plagued by the problem of his identity. The crowd had been drawn to the execution by the celebrity of the victim, a 'mawmet' who had invaded their realm four times in the last four years. How could a man from Tournai end up marrying the King of Scotland's cousin? How could a mere boatman's son carry off such a thing? Over and over again: was he or wasn't he Richard, Duke of York? The victim had been sent to his execution by John Taylor, John Atwater, Margaret of Burgundy, Charles VIII, James IV, Maximilian I, Philip the Fair, Edward Plantagenet and Henry Tudor. And now for Henry's sake he was about once more to forswear that false self, Richard, Duke of York. In 1491 he had tried to do this very thing upon the the Holy Evangelists at Cork. There, thanks to Taylor and Atwater he had been unable to escape. Now 'he took It there upon his deth that he never was the persoon which he was named nor anything of that blood, But a stranger born lyke wyse as beforn he had shewid'. Here was the final escape from his position as a political fly in amber.

What did he think of as he looked down on the faces upturned, looking at him, concentrating upon him? Was he thinking about leaving Tournai by the Marvis gate, with his weeping mother receding from him as he took the road to Antwerp? Or did he recall the tournaments at Tournai as a child of four or five? Or did he call to mind João II and Vaz da Cunha in Portugal, meeting Margaret Beaumont in Bruges, Katherine Gordon on the ship they took from Ayr to Cornwall, or his first sight of her at court in Scotland? Or did he think of those duplicitous Spanish diplomats? The Tyrol, Innsbruck, Beaulieu Abbey? We do not know, and we cannot ever know. What we do know is that he continued with his confession, 'that he [had] namyd him sylf to be the secund sone of kyng Edward . . . by the mean of the said John a watyr there present & othir as beffore tyme he had trwly shewyd'.

Once this story was ended, for the last time, he asked forgiveness of the king and anyone else he had offended. This is the best key to his state of mind, that impending death had effaced all memory, and action had become wholly prescribed by the reflexes of a state execution. In the days preceding execution the demeanour of victims can alter radically as the psyche distorts under the pressure of comprehending its approaching fatal wound. It can respond by a kind of growth, an upsurge of vivacity, development even. Or it can result in a somnambulistic listlessness which prefigures death. Warbeck did not respond at the scaffold with a last hysterical quip, like Anne Boleyn, or berate the headsman like the Countess of Salisbury, or adopt the futile attitude of false grandeur like Charles I. Once he had made his confession 'there upon the Galowis [he] took his deth paciently'. There was nothing else left to do.

Appendices

A. Dan William Graunte

PRO E404/81/4 – Warrant for Issue dated 12 April 1495, petition undated.

In the following petition William Graunte, Kitchener of Westminster Abbey asks Henry VII to recommence payment to him for food provided by him for Sir Humphrey Savage and Sir Gilbert Debenham.

Humbly sheweth vnto your highnes your true and daily orator dan William Graunte Kychener of your Monastery of Westmynestre/ That Wher as he by youre moost drad comaundement at your great and daily coste seeth that your Rebelles and traitors sir humfrey Savage and sir Gilbert Debenham shuld haue their daily mete and drynk and therupon diverted your gracious letters vnto the Tresourer and vndertresourer of England for to paye vnto your orator monethly for euery wek for thair said bord Wages xxs/ Notwithstanding after it pleased your grace to make restreynt of the payment therof/ soo that resteth due vnto your said Orator from the last day of Januarij vnto the xxviij day of ffevrier last past iiij li for oon hole moneth borde/ how bee it sithers it pleased your grace to directe your gracious letters to your Tresourer and vndertresourer of England for to pay and content your said Orator wekely xxs/ and bicause that the said moneth borde thus due vnto your said Orator was not expressed in your said letters they refuse to make payment therof to his coste hurt and hinderance/ Beseching your grace insomoch as your said orator hath layde oute this money vpon trust of your said commaunndemant/ to commaunde eftsones by your letters the Tresourer and vndertresourer of England that they further vpon the sight of the same paye & content vnto your said Orator the said saume of iiij ti without any obstacle dilay to the contry And he shal so pray to god for you moost noble & Royal Estate.

In the following Warrant for Issue Henry VII orders his Lord Treasurer, John Dynham and Under Treasurer Sir Robert Litton to pay for the provision of food for Savage and Debenham.

Right trusty and welbeloued and trusty and right welbeloued We grete you Wele. And late you wite that it is shewed vnto vs by supplicacion of late presented vnto vs on the behalve of Dane William Graunt kechener of our Monastery of Westminster. howe that we stande endetted vnto him in the summe of foure poundes sterlinges for mete and drinke by him deliuered for the bourde and sustenance of our two Rebelles sir humfrey Savage and sir Gilbert Debenham that is to witte from the last day of January vnto the xxiij day of ffeurier last passed after the rate of xxs by the weke as by the said supplicacion which we send vnto you herin closed ye shall perceiue more at large Whefor we willing his due contentacion in this partie wol and desire you that of our treasoure being in your keping ye furthwith content and paye vnto the said Dane William the said summe of foure poundes sterlinges And we shal see for your dishcarge in this partie at all tymes herafter Yeuen vnder our signet at our Manor of Shene the xiith day of April the tenth yere of our Reigne

B. Perkin Warbeck's Supporters on Deal Beach, 3 July 1495

PRO KB 9/52 Returned Oyer and Terminer file Kent, 1495.

On 13 July 1495 commissioners were appointed to hear the cases of the rebels captured at Deal. On 16 July at East Greenwich the commission sat and heard the case of treason against Henry Mountford and others. They were charged with levying war at Deal on 3 July 1495, and sentenced to be hanged at Tyburn. The following is a list, found both on the indictment (m 1) and enrolment (mm 9 and 10) of the trial of those accused of treason. This document doubles the names known to us of Warbeck's supporters, and is the more important because it shows the class of those who supported him, largely yeomen, and the fact that he drew support from all over England. In 1899 W.A.J. Archbold published 'Sir William Stanley and Perkin Warbeck', in *English Historical Review*, XIV. This was a transcription of a Cambridge University Library manuscript which included Mountford's indictment. However where this document provides a full list of names, places and status, the Cambridge manuscript says merely 'other false traitors and rebels'. Above each name on the indictment (m 1) is the abbreviation 'Cogn T & S' indicating a sentence of drawing and hanging.

With the exception of those places marked * modern place names have been used.

Henry Mountford	Coleshill, Warwickshire	Armiger
Richard White	Thorpe-juxta-Bellingford, Norfolk	Gentleman
Richard Malory	Monks Kirby, Warwickshire	Gentleman
John Corbet	London	Yeoman
John Belt	Guildford, Surrey	Yeoman
William Ashton	Ashton-under-Lyne, Lancashire	Gentleman
Nicholas Knollys	Sittingbourne, Kent/ Glossop, Derbyshire	Yeoman
William Edward	Droitwich, Worcester	Yeoman
William Skydmore	Hereford, Herefordshire	Yeoman
William Walgrave	Harwich, Essex	Merchant
Thomas Baryngton	Sandbach, Cheshire	Groom
Nicholas Scayff	Stamford Bridge, Yorkshire	Yeoman
Edward Lawly	Much Wenlock, Shropshire	Yeoman
Henry Parker	Norton, Derbyshire	Yeoman
Thomas Sclater	Kendal, Westmorland	Yeoman
William Scryven	Castor, Lincolnshire	Yeoman
John Cartmale	Kendal, Westmorland	Yeoman
Jordan Topnell	London	Mariner
George Style	London	Yeoman
Stephen Poteryn	Meonstoke, Hampshire	Yeoman
Walter Humfrey	Hill, Devon	Yeoman
William Vaghen	Carmarthen, Wales	Yeoman

Lawrence Clerke	Wath, Yorkshire	Yeoman
John Colyngwode	Newcastle-upon-Tyne, Northumberland	Groom
Patrick Stephens	Bristol, Gloucestershire	Yeoman
Thomas Chawey	*Gellston, Hertfordshire	Yeoman
Thomas Broun	Ripon, Yorkshire	Yeoman
Richard Cotys	*Bryfford, Shropshire	Yeoman
Robert Colclowe	Newcastle-under-Lyme, Staffordshire	Yeoman
George Softly	Bamburgh, Northumberland	Yeoman
John Virgo	Banwell, Somerset	Yeoman
Richard Pounde	London	Yeoman
Philip Crampe	Southwell, Nottinghamshire	Yeoman
John Gregory	Chipping Campden, Gloucestershire	Labourer
John Apowes	Taunton, Somerset	Yeoman
Ralph Carden	Carden, Cheshire	Yeoman
William Hunt	Hemingbrough, Yorkshire	Yeoman
John Robynson	London	Yeoman
John Somer	London	Yeoman
John Atkynson	Ripley, Yorkshire	Yeoman
John Longland	Kinlet, Shropshire	Yeoman
Thomas Morgan	London	Chaplain
John a Wode	London	Yeoman
John Hall	Sherburn-in-Elmet, Yorkshire	Labourer
Rowland Geneson	Raskelf, Yorkshire	Labourer
Henry Lount	East Sutton, Kent	Labourer
John Norrys	Little Milton, Oxfordshire	Yeoman
Edward Walton	*Alston More, Northumberland	Yeoman
Bernard Oldam	Aspenden, Hertfordshire	Chaplain
John Arter	*Blesworth, Northumberland	Yeoman
Maurice Seles	London	Goldsmith

C. Signet Letter of Henry VII, 15 February 1497

I am indebted to Professor R.L. Storey for giving me a copy of this document.

Cumbria Record Office, Carlisle 2 (City Records), no. 104.

Henry by the grace of god king of England and of ffrance and lord of Irland To the Maire and his brethren of oure Citie of Carlill that nowe be and heraftre for the tyme shalbe greting Insomoche as we knowe well that the same oure Citie is oon of the chief keyes and fortresses to the defens of this oure Reame and that the losse therof in any sodein entreprins of the scottes shulde be not oonly youre aller distruction but also a great and an vniuersal hurt to all our said Reame Whiche god defend We therfor Wol and charge you in our estraitest Wise not to suffre any maner of person or persones dwelling within our said Citie to be fromhensfurth reteyned with any man be he spiritual or temporall lord or othre by lyveree baggien clothing cognoissance or in any other Wise nor to ride or passe out of the same oure Citie in harnois to any feldes skirmysshinges affrayes or riottes with any gentilman or othre Whatsoeuer estate or degre he be of but to be abiding and attending at all seasons bothe of Warre and of peax in the same oure Citie for the defens and suretie therof ayenst the scottes if they wolde make any sodein attemptat therunto by seige or othrewise And to thentent that ye of the same oure Citie maye be of good suretie and trouthes amonges yourselfes We haue commaunded the Right Reuerend fadre in god our right trusty Counseillor the Bisshop of Carlill to take your oethes of fidelitee vnto vs Willing you therfor to be attendant vnto hym in that behalue and also to conforme you to take due obseruying of the premisses As ye tendre your owne sureties and the Weal of this Reame. And be it soo that any man disobey and be reteyned contrary to this our ordenance We than charge you straitely to certifie vs furthwith of his name by your writing And we shall soo provide for his sharpe punicon according to our lawes and statutes as othre shal therat take feer semblably toffende for tyme commyng Yeuen vndre our signet at oure Palois of Westminster the xv day of ffebruary The xiijthe yere of oure Reigne /

Abbreviations

Add. MS	Additional Manuscript, at British Library
ADN	Archives Départementales du Nord, Lille
Bacon	Francis Bacon, *The History of the Reign of King Henry the Seventh*, ed. R. Lockyer (London, 1971)
BIHR	*Bulletin of the Institute of Historical Research*
BL	British Library
CCR	*Calendar of Close Rolls*
CPR	*Calendar of Patent Rolls*
CSP Milan	*Calendar of State Papers*, Milan, Vol 1, *1385–1618*, ed. A.B. Hinds (London, 1913)
CSP Spain	*Calendar of State Papers*, Spanish, Vol 1, *Henry VII 1484–1509*, ed. G.A. Bergenroth (London, 1862)
CSP Venice 1, 4.	*Calendar of State Papers*, Venetian, Vol 1, *1202–1509*, Vol 4, *1527–33*, ed. R. Brown (London, 1864 & 1871)
Complete Peerage	*Complete Peerage of England, Scotland, Ireland and the United Kingdom*, ed. G.E. Cokayne: new edition Vicary Gibbs and others 1910–59
Emden	*A Biographical Register of the University of Oxford to AD 1500*, 3 Vols, Oxford, 1957–9) ed. A.B. Emden
Exchequer Rolls of Scotland	*Rotuli Scaccari Regum Scotorum, The Exchequer Rolls of Scotland*, ed. G. Burnett (Edinburgh, 1878–91)
Exerpta Historica	*Exerpta Historica*, ed. S. Bentley (London, 1831)
Foedera	T. Rymer, ed., *Foedera, Conventiones, Literae etc.* 20 vols (1704–35)
Great Chronicle	*The Great Chronicle of London*, ed. A.H. Thomas and I.D. Thornley, 1938
Hall	Edward Hall, *The Union of the two Noble and Illustrious Families of Lancaster and York*, ed. H. Ellis (1809)
Harley 433	The British Library Harleian Manuscript 433, ed. R.E. Horrox and P.W. Hammond, 4 Vols (Gloucester, 1979–83)
HMC	Historical Manuscripts Commission
Letters and Papers	*Letters and Papers Illustrative of the Reign of Henry VII*, ed. J. Gairdner, 2 Vols, Rolls Series, 1861–3
Molinet	*Chroniques de Jean Molinet*, ed. G. Doutrepont et O. Jodonge, Vol 2 (Brussels, 1935)
New Cambridge Modern	G.R. Potter, ed., *The New Cambridge Modern History*, Vol 1, *The Renaissance* (Cambridge, 1961)
New History of Ireland	A. Cosgrove, ed., *A New History of Ireland*, Vol 2, *Medieval Ireland, 1169–1534* (Oxford, second edition, 1993)
PRO	Public Record Office
Rot. Parlt.,	*Rotuli Parliamentorum*, Vol VI, Record Commission (1777)
Scottish Treas. Accts.	*Compotorum thesauriorum Scotorum*. Accounts of the Lord High Treasurer of Scotland, Vol 1, ed. T. Dickson (Edinburgh, 1877)
Vergil	Polydore Vergil, *Anglica Historia*, ed. D. Hay, Camden Society, New Series, Vol 74, 1950
Vitellius A XVI	C.L. Kingsford, *Chronicles of London* (Oxford, 1905)
Wedgwood, *Biographies*	J.C. Wedgwood, *History of Parliament Biographies of the members of the Commons House 1439–1509*, 1936

Notes

Preface

1. W.C. Sellar and R.J. Yeatman, *1066 and All That*, (Penguin pb., 1962), pp. 58–59.
2. G.W., 'Richard, Duke of York, and Perkin Warbeck', *Notes and Queries*, 4 May 1935, p. 310.
3. C.F. Richmond, *The Penket Papers* (Gloucester, 1986), pp. 61–75.
4. M. Bennett, *Lambert Simnel and the Battle of Stoke* (Gloucester, 1987), pp. 51, 54. C. Weightman, *Margaret of York Duchess of Burgundy* (Gloucester, 1989), pp. 158–159.
5. D. Starkey, *The English Court: from the Wars of the Roses to the Civil War* (London, 1987), pp. 75–76.
6. Mlle Carpentier, *Récits Historiques* (Paris, 1879), pp. 23–55.

Part One: To Cork

1. The Beginning and the End of the Problem

1. *Great Chronicle*, p. 291. Vitellius A XVI, pp. 227–228.
2. Warbeck's confession, see above.
3. D. Kleyn, *Richard of England* (The Kensal Press, Oxford, 1990), p. 134.
4. M. Ballard and C.S.L. Davies, 'Étienne Fryon: Burgundian Agent, English Royal Secretary and "Principal Counsellor" to Perkin Warbeck', *BIHR*, 62 (1989), pp. 246–259; esp. pp. 254–256.
5. J. Huizanga, *The Waning of the Middle Ages* (Penguin pb., 1979), pp. 20–22.
6. Vergil, p. 3. And see A. Goodman, *The Wars of the Roses* (London, 1981), p. 95.
7. Molinet, p. 436.
8. E. Herbert, *The Life and Reign of King Henry VIII* (1672), pp. 9–10.
9. S.J. Gunn, 'The Accession of Henry VIII', *BIHR*, 64 (1991), pp. 278–288.

2. A World of Displaced Men

1. M.K. Jones, 'Lady Margaret Beaufort, the Royal Council and an Early Fenland Drainage Scheme', *Lincolnshire History and Archaeology*, 21 (1986), pp. 11–18. J. Backhouse, 'Founders of the Royal Library: Edward IV and Henry VII as Collectors of Illuminated Manuscripts' in, *England in the Fifteenth Century*, ed. D. Williams (Woodbridge, 1987), pp. 23–42, esp. p. 33.
2. W.D. Phillips, Jr. and C.R. Phillips, *The Worlds of Christopher Columbus* (Cambridge, 1992), pp. 13–36 'Old Worlds in Isolation.'
3. On this and subsequent unacknowledged material on the Wars of the Roses see R.A. Griffiths, *The Reign of Henry VI* (London, 1981). R.A. Griffiths and R.S. Thomas, *The Making of the Tudor Dynasty* (Gloucester, 1985). Bennett, *Lambert Simnel and the Battle of Stoke*.
4. A. Goodman, *The Wars of the Roses*, pp. 60–63. F. Madden, 'Narratives of the arrival of Louis de Bruges, etc.', *Archaeologia*, XXVI (1835), pp. 265–286. *CSP Venice*, Vol 4, p. 461.
5. Goodman, *Wars of the Roses*, pp. 204–208.
6. Goodman, *Wars of the Roses*, pp. 89–94, 99–106.
7. Goodman, *Wars of the Roses*, pp. 163, 169–170. M. Ballard, 'An Expedition of English Archers to Liege in 1467 and the Anglo-Burgundian Marriage Alliance', *Nottingham Medieval Studies*, XXXIV (1990), pp. 152–174, esp. pp. 169–170.
8. C. Ross, *Edward IV* (London, 1974), pp. 145–160. Griffiths and Thomas, *Tudor Dynasty*, pp. 75–88, 105–108, 118–119.
9. C.S.L. Davies, 'John Morton the Holy See and the Accession of Henry VII', *English Historical Review*, CII (1987), p. 27 and also note 3.
10. C.S.L. Davies, 'Richard III, Henry VII & the Island of Jersey', *The Ricardian*, IX (1992), pp. 334–342.
11. S. O'Connor, 'Francis Lovel and the Rebels of Furness Fells', *The Ricardian*, VII (1987), pp. 366–370.
12. BL Cotton MS Titus B XI Pt 2 ff. 287r–292v.
13. C. Carpenter, *Locality and Polity* (Cambridge, 1992), p. 566.
14. R. Philpot, 'Maximilian and England 1477–1509', unpublished PhD thesis (University of London, 1975), pp. 98–100.
15. Goodman, *Wars of the Roses*, p. 108. M.A. Hicks, 'The Yorkshire Rebellion of 1489 Reconsidered', *Northern History*, XXII (1986), p. 58.
16. Scottish Treas. Accts., pp. 121, 191, 274.
17. O'Connor, *Rebels of Furness Fells*, pp. 368–369.
18. A. Conway, *Henry VII's Relations with Scotland and Ireland: 1485–1498* (Cambridge, 1932), p. 25.
19. J.M. Currin, 'Pierre Le Pennec, Henry VII of

England, and the Breton Plot of 1492', *Albion*, 23 (1991), pp. 1–22. *CPR* 1485–1494, pp. 365–366.

20. Ballard and Davies, 'Étienne Fryon', pp. 245–251.
21. M. Harsgor, *Recherches sur le Personnel du Conseil du roi sous Charles VIII et Louis XII*, 4 Vols (Lille and Paris, 1980), Vol 4, pp. 2238–2240.
22. C.A.J. Armstrong, *England, France and Burgundy in the Fifteenth Century* (London, 1983), pp. 235–236.
23. *New Cambridge Modern*, p. 242.
24. J.S.C. Bridge, *A History of France from the death of Louis XI*, 3 Vols (Oxford, 1921–29), Vol 1, pp. 112, 128, 136, 151–153, 163–168, 203–204, 209–210.
25. Currin, '1492 Plot', pp. 12–13, 15, 21.
26. Bridge, *History of France*, Vol 1, pp. 136–137, 200–202, 213–214.

3. *The Breton Wheel of Fortune*

1. *CSP* Milan, pp. 283–284.
2. *CSP* Venice, 1, p. 208.
3. Bridge, *History of France*, Vol 1, pp. 195–208.
4. *CSP* Venice, 4, pp. 455–475.
5. A. Spont, 'La Marine Française', *Revue des Questions Historiques*, 55 (1894), pp. 412–416.
6. *CSP* Venice, 4, pp. 476–479.
7. *New Cambridge Modern*, pp. 237–238.
8. *New Cambridge Modern*, pp. 224–238.
9. *New Cambridge Modern*, pp. 235–240. Harsgor, *Personnel du Conseil*, Vol 3, pp. 1711–1718.
10. *New Cambridge Modern*, p. 240.
11. Bacon, p. 108.
12. Scottish Treas. Accts., p. 175. N. Macdougall, *James IV* (Edinburgh, 1989), pp. 82–83, 91.
13. *CSP* Venice, 4, p. 481. *CSP* Milan, pp. 279–280. Macdougall, *James IV*, p. 93.
14. Spont, 'Marine Française', p. 419.
15. Macdougall, *James IV*, pp. 65–6, 87–88.
16. Conway, *Scotland and Ireland*, pp. 36–37. Macdougall, *James IV*, pp. 89–90.
17. Conway, *Scotland and Ireland*, p. 39.
18. *CPR 1485–1494*, pp. 344, 351, 352, 356, 393.
19. *CPR 1485–1494*, p. 356.
20. Spont, 'Marine Française', pp. 416–418. *CSP* Milan, pp. 278–279.
21. Bridge, *History of France*, Vol 1, pp. 66–67.
22. *Rot. Parlt.*, pp. 454–455. Spont, 'Marine Française', p. 433.
23. *Rot. Parlt.*, p. 194. *CPR 1476–1485*, pp. 129, 236, 355, 521. Ross, *Edward IV*, p. 392. *CPR 1485–1494*, p. 258. W. Campbell, ed., *Materials for a History of the Reign of Henry VII* (Rolls Series, 2 Vols 1873–1877), Vol 1, p. 201.
24. *Rot. Parlt.*, pp. 455.
25. *CCR 1485–1500*, pp. 104, 106, 129. Wedgwood, *Biographies*, pp. 170–171. P.A. Johnson, *Duke Richard of York 1411–1460* (Oxford, second edition, 1991), p. 230.
26. *Letters and Papers*, Vol 1, pp. 98–101.
27. *CPR 1485–1494*, pp. 343, 345, 396, 433.
28. *Great Chronicle*, p. 244. See Appendix B.
29. Scottish Treas. Accts., p. 176.
30. *CPR 1485–1494*, p. 357.
31. *Rot. Parlt.*, pp. 454–455.
32. Carpenter, *Locality and Polity*, pp. 576–577.

33. *Rot. Parlt.*, pp. 454–455.
34. M.A. Hicks, 'The Career of George Plantagenet, Duke of Clarence, 1449–1477', unpublished PhD thesis (University of Oxford, 1976), pp. 273, 378. *CPR 1476–1485*, pp. 128, 134, 175, 176, 183, 213, 254, 289. A.A. Mumford, *Hugh Oldham* (London, 1936), pp. 69–70. *CPR 1476–1485*, p. 545. Harley 433, Vol 2, p. 77. Davies, 'The Island of Jersey', *passim*. B.P. Wolffe, *The Royal Demesne in English History* (London, 1971), p. 182.
35. Wedgwood, *Biographies*, p. 361.
36. D. Palliser, 'Richard III and York', in R. Horrox, ed., *Richard III and the North* (Hull, 1986), pp. 64–65.
37. Mumford, *Hugh Oldham*, pp. 69–70.
38. BL Add. MS 7099, ff. 2r, 3r.
39. J.T. Rosenthal, 'Other Victims: Peeresses as War Widows, 1450–1500', *History*, 72 (1987), p. 225.
40. *Complete Peerage*, Vol 12, p. 293 and note d.
41. *Rot. Parlt.*, pp. 454–455. *CCR 1485–1500*, pp. 200–201. A. Dupuy, *Histoire de la réunion de la Bretagne a la France* (Paris, 1880), pp. 232–236.
42. Spont, 'Marine Française', pp. 418–419.
43. Spont, 'Marine Française', pp. 420–421, 433.
44. D.B. Quinn, *Analecta Historica*, 10 (Dublin, 1941), pp. 55–56. *CPR 1485–1494*, pp. 286, 455.
45. H. Touchard, *Le commerce maritime breton a la fin du moyen âge* (Nantes, 1967), pp. 273–274. S.E. Morrison, *Admiral of the Ocean Sea Christopher Columbus* (Oxford, 1942), pp. 23–25.
46. BL Add. MS 46455, f. 137 r.
47. Conway, *Scotland and Ireland*, pp. 91, 225. *New History of Ireland*, pp. 630, 672 and 677.
48. Spont, 'Marine Française', p. 418, note 6. *CPR 1485–1494*, p. 337.
49. Quinn, *Analecta Historica*, pp. 35, 54.
50. Quinn, *Analecta Historica*, pp. 34–35, 55. *CPR 1484–1494*, pp. 367, 368.
51. Currin, '1492 Plot', *passim*. I. Tanner, 'Henry VII's Expedition to France of 1492: a study of its financing, organisation and supply', unpublished MA thesis (University of Keele, 1988), pp. 48, 119.
52. Spont, 'Marine Française', pp. 425–428.
53. Spont, 'Marine Française', p. 432, note 4.

4. *But to be Young*

1. J. Gairdner, *History of the Life and Reign of Richard III* (Cambridge, 1898), pp. 334–335.
2. J. Ford, *The Chronicle History of Perkin Warbeck a Strange Truth*, ed. P. Ure (London, 1968).
3. N.J. Pryor, 'Mary Shelley's Perkin Warbeck', *The Ricardian*, IX (1991), pp. 72–73.
4. Vergil, p. 63.
5. Bacon, pp. 129–133.
6. G. Buck, *The History of the Life and Reigne of Richard III* (London, 1646, repr. 1973), pp. 74, 83–88.
7. P. Kendall, ed., *Richard III The Great Debate* (London, 1965), pp. 236–239.
8. Pryor, 'Mary Shelley', p. 73.
9. T. Gainsford, *The True and Wonderful History of Perkin Warbeck* (London, 1618). *Harleian Miscellany*, Vol 6 (1745), pp. 494–550.
10. J.D. Chastelain, *L'Imposture de Perkin Warbeck* (Brussels, 1952).

11. Kleyn, *Richard of England*, pp. 21–27.
12. Ford, *Perkin Warbeck*, Act 1, scene 1, lines 1–5, and Act 5. T.S. Eliot, *Selected Essays* (London, 1969), pp. 200–201.
13. Comte P.A. du Chastel de la Howarderie, 'Notes on the Family of the the adventurer Perkin Warbeck', *Bulletin of the Historical and Literary Society of Tournai*, XXV (1892–1894), pp. 410–414; translated copy in Barton Library of Richard III Society. Warbeck's confession, see above. Gairdner, *Richard III*, pp. 329–330.
14. Howarderie, 'Notes', *passim*. Warbeck's confession, see above.
15. D. Nicholas, *Medieval Flanders* (London, 1992), pp. 371–373. P. Rolland, *Histoire de Tournai* (Tournai & Paris, 1957), pp. 149–150.
16. Philippe de Commynes, *Memoires*, ed. M.C.E. Jones (London, 1972), pp. 15, 321–322, 338, 357. *CSP* Milan, p. 403.
17. *CSP* Milan, pp. 411–412. Nicholas, *Medieval Flanders*, pp. 254–255.
18. *CSP* Milan, p. 405.
19. Rolland, *Tournai*, pp. 161–170.
20. A. Hanham, *The Celys and their World* (Cambridge, 1985), p. 211, and refs *passim*. Nicholas, *Medieval Flanders*, pp. 286, 290–293, 377, 380.
21. Nicholas, *Medieval Flanders*, pp. 89–90, 94, 140–146, 347–348.
22. Nicholas, *Medieval Flanders*, pp. 235, 251.
23. Warbeck's confession, see above.
24. *New Cambridge Modern*, pp. 233–234.
25. Hanham, *Celys World*, pp. 293, 298.
26. *New Cambridge Modern*, pp. 233–234. Warbeck's confession, see above. J.N. Biraben, *Les Hommes et la peste en France et dans les pays européens et la mediterranées*, 2 Vols (Paris, 1975), Vol 1, pp. 380–381, 410–411, 416–417. 'Robert Favreau, Épidémies a Poitiers et dans le Centre-Ouest a la fin du Moyen Âge', *Bibliotheque de l'école des chartes*, CXXV (1968), pp. 373–379. Gairdner, *Richard III*, pp. 329–330. Hanham, *Celys' World*, p. 210.
27. F. Braudel, *The Perspective of the World* (London, 1984), p. 145. Nicholas, *Medieval Flanders*, pp. 287–307.
28. C. Roth, 'Perkin Warbeck and his Jewish Master', *Transactions of the Jewish Historical Society of England*, IX (1922), pp. 143–162.
29. Marquês De São Paio, 'A Portuguese Adventurer in the Wars of the Roses', *Anais da Academia Portuguesa da História*, 2 Séries, Vol 6 (Lisbon, 1955). Translation in Barton Library of Richard III Society. pp. 4–5, 11–12. C. Roth, 'Sir Edward Brampton, alias Duarte Brandão', *La Societé Guerneisaise* (1956), pp. 163.
30. De São Paio, 'Portuguese Adventurer', pp. 6–7. Roth, 'Sir Edward Brampton', pp. 163–164.
31. Information kindly discussed with me by Dr R. Horrox.
32. De São Paio, 'Portuguese Adventurer', pp. 12–13. Roth, 'Sir Edward Brampton', pp. 164, 165.
33. B. Williams, 'Rui de Sousa's embassy and the fate of Richard, Duke of York', *The Ricardian*, V (1981), pp. 343, and 344, note 20.
34. De São Paio, 'Portuguese Adventurer', pp. 7–8, 13–14. Roth, 'Sir Edward Brampton', p. 166. Warbeck's confession, see above.
35. *New Cambridge Modern*, p. 235. Hanham, *Celys' World*, pp. 25, 358.
36. A. Hanham, ed., 'The Cely Letters', *Early English Text Society*, Vol 273 (1975), p. 239.
37. Nicholas, *Medieval Flanders*, pp. 389–390.
38. H.V. Livermore, *Portugal a short History* (Edinburgh, 1973), pp. 77–84.
39. S.E. Morrison, *Admiral of the Ocean Sea*, p. 32.
40. B.W. Diffie and G.D. Winius, *Foundations of the Portuguese Empire 1415–1580* (Minneapolis, 1977), pp. 154–165.
41. De São Paio, 'Portuguese Adventurer', p. 8.
42. De São Paio, 'Portuguese Adventurer', p. 8. J.W. Blake, trans. and ed., *Europeans in West Africa*, 2 Vols, Hakluyt Society (London, 1942), p. 89, Brandao in 1498.
43. E.G. Ravenstein, *Martin Behaim, his life and his globe* (London, 1908), pp. 113–114.
44. Diffie and Winius, *Portuguese Empire*, pp. 157–158.
45. G.R. Crone, *Maps and their makers* (Folkestone, 1978), p. 32.
46. *CSP* Spain, p. 92. Ruy de Pina, *Cronica de el rei D. João II*, ed. A. Martins de Carvalho (Coimbra, Atlantida, 1950), p. 186.
47. C.L. Scofield, *The Life and Reign of Edward IV*, 2 Vols (London, 1923), Vol 2, pp. 351–352.
48. J. Gairdner, ed., *Memorials of King Henry VII*, Rolls Series (1858), pp. 360, 364. Livermore, *Portugal* p. 76.
49. Pina, *Cronica*, pp. 102, 156. Diffie & Winius, p. 165.
50. F. Gayo, *Nobiliário de Famílias de Portugal* (no date), pp. 147, 151.
51. G.R. Crone, trans. and ed., *The Voyages of Cadamosto*, Hakluyt Society (London, 1937), pp. 128–133.
52. Crone, *Cadamosto*, pp. 134, 140–141.
53. W.B. Greenlee, trans. and ed., *The Voyages of Pedro Álvares Cabral to Brazil and India*, Hakluyt Scociety (London, 1938), pp. xlviii, l–li, lx, 34–40, esp. 38.
54. Antonio Caetano de Sousa, *História Genealógica da Casa Real Portugueza*, Vol III (Lisbon, 1737), pp. 172–173. Gayo, *Nobiliario*, p. 151.
55. Warbeck's confession, see above. H. Touchard, *Le commerce maritime breton* (1967) pp. 223, 273–274.
56. F.F. Armesto, *The Canary Islands after the Conquest* (Oxford, 1982), p. 158. I owe this reference to Prof. M.C.E. Jones.
57. Touchard, *Commerce maritime breton*, p. 274 and note 367. Braudel, *Perspective of the World*, p. 148.
58. Touchard, *Commerce maritime breton*, p. 241.
59. Touchard, *Commerce maritime breton*, pp. 222–223. *New History of Ireland*, pp. 493, 494.
60. Touchard, *Commerce maritime breton*, p. 238. *New History of Ireland*, p. 517.
61. Touchard, *Commerce maritime breton*, pp. 181–182, 237. *New History of Ireland*, pp. 498–508.
62. Touchard, *Commerce maritime breton*, p. 238.

5. The Resurrection of Richard Plantagenet

1. B. de Breffny and R. ffoliot, *The Houses of Ireland* (London, 1975), p. 17. *New History of Ireland*, pp. 516–517.
2. Breffny and ffoliot, *Houses of Ireland*, pp. 17–23.
3. Warbeck's confession, see above.
4. D. Bryan, *Gerald FitzGerald the Great Earl of Kildare (1456–1513)* (Dublin and Cork, 1933), pp. 17, 33, 40, 51–53, 104, 141.
5. Gairdner, *Richard III*, pp. 329–330.
6. J.A.C. Brown, *Techniques of Persuasion*, (Penguin pb., 1963), pp. 278–279, and following.
7. Dr Desmons, 'Un tournaisien prétendant au trône d'Angleterre', *Revue Tournaisienne*, 4–5 (1901), pp. 1–2. Translation in Barton library of Richard III Society.
8. K. Thomas, *Religion and the Decline of Magic* (Penguin pb., 1978), p. 506.
9. D.B. Quinn, *England and the Discovery of America, 1481–1620* (London, 1974), pp. 169–170.
10. Warbeck's confession, see above.
11. W. Busch, *England under the Tudors*, Vol 1, *King Henry VII* (London, 1895), p. 86.
12. Gairdner, *Richard III*, pp. 329–330.
13. *CPR 1485–1494*, p. 423.
14. *New History of Ireland*, pp. 625–626.
15. Warbeck's confession, see above. And see Appendix B.
16. Harley 433, Vol 3, p. 109, 108–111.
17. *New History of Ireland*, p. 613–615.
18. *New History of Ireland*, p. 615. Scottish Treas. Accts., pp. 181, 182, 183.
19. *Letters and Papers*, Vol 2, p. 55.
20. Conway, *Scotland and Ireland*, p. 52.
21. BL Cotton MS Titus B XI Part 2, ff. 291r, 294r–v, 295v, 296r–v, 297r.
22. W.M. Hennessy and B. MacCarthy, ed., *Annals of Ulster*, 4 Vols, Rolls Series (Dublin, 1888–1901) Vol 3, *1379–1541*, p. 365.
23. *Annals of Ulster*, Vol 3, p. 357.
24. ADN B 2144, f. 89v, 91r–v, 92v, 95v, 150r–v.
25. A. Morel-Fatio, 'Marguerite D'York et Perkin Warbeck', in *Mélanges D'Histoire offert a M. Charles Bémont* (Paris, 1913), pp. 411–416, esp. p. 415.
26. Scottish Treas. Accts., pp. 181, 183, 184, 199.
27. Scottish Treas. Accts., p. 199.
28. Morel-Fatio, 'Marguerite D'York', p. 414–415.
29. F. Madden, 'Documents relating to Perkin Warbeck, with Remarks on his History', *Archaeologia*, XXVII (1838), pp. 156–158, 199–200.
30. Gairdner, *Memorials*, pp. 65–66.
31. Ballard and Davies, 'Étienne Fryon', p. 255.
32. Spont, 'Marine Française', p. 418.
33. Spont, 'Marine Française', p. 431.
34. Ballard and Davies, 'Étienne Fryon', pp. 245–246, 248–251, 257–259.
35. Morel-Fatio, 'Marguerite D'York', p. 415.
36. Spont, 'Marine Française', p. 418, note 6, p. 433.
37. Madden, 'Documents', p. 157.

Part Two: At Large

6. The Dreadful Deadman

1. Scottish Treas. Accts., pp. 120, 191, 199–200, 274 and following. Rot. Parlt., p. 239. *CPR 1485–1494*, pp. 39, 112, 341. Harley 433, Vol 2, p. 198.
2. Scottish Treas. Accts., p. 199.
3. Morel-Fatio, 'Marguerite D'York', p. 415.
4. ADN B 2144, ff. 110v, 155r–157r, 159r.
5. Morel-Fatio, 'Marguerite D'York', p. 415.
6. Hall, p. 463.
7. Desmons, 'Un tournaisian prétendant', pp. 1–2.
8. *CSP* Milan, p. 380.
9. Bacon, p. 135.
10. Hall, p. 463. *Foedera*, XII, p. 508. And Treaty, pp. 497–505. Subsidiary agreements, pp. 505–513.
11. *CSP* Milan, p. 291.
12. *CSP* Milan, p. 291.
13. Vergil, p. 65.
14. Morel-Fatio, 'Marguerite D'York', p. 415.
15. W. Blockmans, 'The Devotions of a Lonely Duchess', in *Margaret of York, Simon Marmion and the Visions of Tondal*, ed., T. Kren (Malibu, California, 1992), pp. 29–46.
16. Hall, p. 463.
17. Gairdner, *Memorials*, pp. 65–66.
18. ADN B 2146, ff. 83r–v. Weightman, *Margaret of York*, p. 172.
19. Bacon, p. 137.
20. L. Gilliodts-Van Severn, *Inventaire des archives de la ville de Bruges* (Bruges, 1876), Vol 6, pp. 369–370.
21. Madden, 'Documents', p. 177. Wedgwood, *Biographies*, pp. 892–893.
22. Thomas, *Religion and Magic*, pp. 493–501. W.M. Ormrod, *The Reign of Edward III* (Yale, 1990), p. 5.
23. *Rot. Parlt.*, p. 194.
24. Thomas, *Religion and Magic*, pp. 498–501.
25. E. Strachey, *Caxton's Text of Le Morte d'Arthur* (London, 1898), p. 481.
26. Thomas, *Religion and Magic*, pp. 461–469.
27. C.W. Previté-Orton, 'An Elizabethan Prophecy', *History*, 2 (1918) pp. 207–218. Alison Allan, 'Yorkist Propaganda: Pedigree, prophecy and the "British History" in the Reign of Edward IV', in C. Ross, *Patronage, Pedigree and Power* (Gloucester, 1979), pp. 171–192.
28. J. Leland, *Itineraries*, 5 Vols., ed. L.T. Smith, (Centaur pb., London, 1964), Vol 1, p. 307–308.
29. Previté-Orton, 'An Elizabethan Prophecy', pp. 209–210, Gairdner, *Memorials*, p. 66. *CSP* Milan, p. 326.
30. PRO KB9/934/5. I am indebted to Mr Alan Cameron for providing me with this reference.
31. W.E. Hampton, 'The White Rose under the First Tudors', Part 1, *The Ricardian*, VII (1987), p. 416. J. Bruce, ed., 'Historie of the Arrival of Edward IV in England, etc.', *Camden Society*, Old Series, 1 (1838), p. 5. Scofield, *Edward IV*, Vol 2, p. 205. Horrox, *Richard III*, p. 80. A. Crawford, *The Household Books of John Howard, Duke of Norfolk, 1462–1471, 1481–1483* (Stroud, 1992), pp. II, 244–246.
32. PRO KB9/934/5. *Foedera*, XII, pp. 526–527.

33. W.G. Davis, 'Whetehill of Calais', *New England Historical and Genealogical Register*, 102–103 (1948), pp. 241–254, esp. pp. 252–253 and (1949), pp. 5–19. *Foedera*, XII, pp. 526–527. *CCR 1485–1500*, p. 201. Madden, 'Documents', pp. 175–177, 207–209.

34. W.A.J. Archbold, 'Sir William Stanley and Perkin Warbeck', *English Historical Review*, XIV (1899), pp. 530–533. Wedgwood, *Biographies*, pp. 265–266, 742.

35. *New History of Ireland*, pp. 615–616. Conway, Scotland and Ireland, pp. 49–55.

36. Conway, *Scotland and Ireland*, pp. 53–54 and notes 1–4. Quinn, *Analecta Historica*, pp. 35–37, 57.

37. Conway, *Scotland and Ireland*, p. 55. *CPR 1485–1494*, pp. 423, 424.

38. *CPR 1485–1494*, pp. 429–430. And see *CCR 1485–1500*, pp. 200–201.

39. Conway, *Scotland and Ireland*, pp. 55–60. *New History of Ireland*, pp. 616–618.

40. ADN B 2144, ff. 89v–141r (Jan–Nov 1492), 135r–141r, 161r–162v (Nov 1492). B 2146, ff. 97r–98r, 101r, 121r–122r (Thomelin Hazart's expenses). *Exerpta Historica*, p. 94.

41. G. Temperley, *Henry VII* (London, 1917), p. 414. Conway, *Scotland and Ireland*, p. 56. *Exerpta Historica*, p. 95.

42. Vergil, p. 69. Hall, p. 465.

43. Gainsford, *Perkin Warbeck*, p. 518.

44. H. Ellis, *Original Letters Illustrative of English History*, 1st Series, Vol 1 (1824) pp. 19–21.

45. Vergil, p. 69.

46. *CPR 1485–1509*, pp. 441, 442, 481–508. R.L. Storey, *The Reign of Henry VII* (London, 1968), p. 82.

47. *Great Chronicle*, p. 248.

48. *Exerpta Historica*, p. 94. Archbold, 'Stanley and Warbeck', p. 531. Vergil, p. 69.

49. Conway, *Scotland and Ireland*, pp. 148–149.

50. *CPR 1485–1494*, p. 451.

51. Ellis, *Letters Illustrative*, 1st Ser, Vol 1, p. 21. HMC *Various Collections*, Vol IV (1907), p. 211.

52. PRO KB9/51, returned Oyer and Terminer file. KB9/404 m.16r Indictment.

53. *Rot. Parlt.*, p. 461. Wedgwood, *Biographies*, pp. 470–471. Horrox, *Richard III*, p. 305.

54. Madden, 'Documents', p. 175. *New Cambridge Modern*, pp. 200, 240–241, 398–399. ADN Quittance dated 24 April 1493 Carton B 2129. ADN B 2146, ff. 101r–v, 115r.

55. Ellis, *Letters Illustrative*, 1st Ser, Vol 1, p. 20.

56. ADN B 2146, f. 108r.

57. A.F. Pollard, *The Reign of Henry VII from Contemporary Sources*, 3 Vols (London, 1913), Vol 3, pp. 25–26. ADN B 2146, f. 113v.

58. *New Cambridge Modern*, p. 242. ADN B ff. 104r, 114r, 119r. Vergil, pp. 69, 71. Hall, p. 466.

59. ADN B 2146, f. 118r.

60. Vergil, p. 71.

61. *New Cambridge Modern*, pp. 243–244, 246–7.

62. Northampton Record Office, FitzWilliam Roll 370. I am most grateful to Colin Richmond for drawing my attention to the existence of this manuscript.

63. P.L. Hughes and J.F. Larkin, *Tudor Royal Proclamations*, Vol 1 (New Haven and London, 1964), p. 35.

7. A Wood of Suspicion

1. M. Génard, 'Marguerite d'Yorck, duchesse de Bourgogne, et la Rose blanche (1495)', *Bulletins de la Commission Royale d'Histoire*, 4th Series, Vol 2 (Brussels, 1887), pp. 9–22, esp. pp. 11, 15.

2. Morel-Fatio, 'Marguerite D'York', p. 415.

3. Gairdner, *Memorials*, p. 66.

4. Hall, p. 465.

5. Morel-Fatio, 'Marguerite D'York', pp. 415–416.

6. Madden, 'Documents', pp. 156–158, 199–200.

7. ADN B 2146, f. 123r–v.

8. E.M. Lichnowsky, *Geschichte des Hauses Hapsburg*, Vol 8 (Vienna, 1844) p. 724. I owe a copy of this to Dr R. Philpot.

9. Molinet, pp. 376–385.

10. Tiroler Landesarchiv, Innsbruck, Urkunden, Allgemeine Reihe I, 8226.

11. G. Benecke, *Maximilian I* (London, 1982) pp. 8–10, 120–123.

12. Philpot, 'Maximilian and England', p. 165.

13. Philpot, 'Maximilian and England', p. 166.

14. R. De Roover, *Money, Banking and Credit in Medieval Bruges* (Cambridge, Mass., 1948), pp. 21, 23, 87, 88.

15. Philpot, 'Maximilian and England', p. 166.

16. T.H. Lloyd, *The English Wool Trade in the Middle Ages* (Cambridge, 1977), p. 283.

17. *Great Chronicle*, pp. 248–249.

18. G. Schanz, *Englische Handelspolitik Gegen ende des Mittelalters*, 2 Vols (Leipzig, 1881), Vol 2, pp. 407–408.

19. Schanz, *Handelspolitik*, pp. 191–193.

20. PRO E 101/517/11 ff. 4v–6r.

21. Schanz, *Handelspolitik* p. 193–194.

22. I. Arthurson, 'Espionage and Intelligence from the Wars of the Roses to the Reformation Nottingham' *Medieval Studies*, XXXV (1991), pp. 144–148. Weightman, *Margaret of York*, p. 74. L. Stark, 'Anglo Burgundian Diplomacy 1467–1485', unpublished M.Phil. thesis (University of London, 1977), p. 140.

23. *Letters and Papers*, Vol 1, p. 235.

24. *Rot. Parlt.*, p. 503.

25. Madden, 'Documents', pp. 165–166, 202. Vergil, p. 79.

26. Archbold, 'Stanley and Warbeck', pp. 532–533.

27. Great Chronicle, p. 250.

28. Archbold, 'Stanley and Warbeck', pp. 532–533. *CPR 1485–1494*, p. 461. Rot. Parlt., pp. 503–504. *CPR 1494–1509*, pp. 175, 190. *Exerpta Historica*, p. 124.

29. Gairdner, *Richard III*, pp. 287–288.

30. *Great Chronicle*, pp. 283–284.

31. Armstrong, *England, France and Burgundy*, pp. 154, 156.

32. Génard, 'La Rose blanche', pp. 14, 19. *CPR 1485–1494*, p. 27.

33. *CPR 1494–1509*, p. 214. *Great Chronicle*, pp. 282–283. *CCR 1485–1500*, p. 214.

34. PRO C1/199/83. I owe this reference to Lesley Stark. *CPR 1494–1509*, pp. 338, 497, 575.

35. *Great Chronicle*, pp. 256–257.

36. Ravenstein, *Martin Behaim*, pp. 43–45, 113–114.

37. Vergil, p. 67.

38. Madden, 'Documents', pp. 172–177, 205–209. B. Newns, 'The Hospice of St. Thomas and the English Crown 1474–1538', *The Venerabile*, XXI

(1962), p. 190. I owe this reference to Dr. S.J. Gunn.

39. Madden, 'Documents', p. 176.
40. I. Arthurson, 'A Question of Loyalty', *The Ricardian*, VII (1987), p. 405.
41. *Letters and Papers*, Vol 1, p. 235.
42. PRO DL 28/2/2 unfoliated. Payment of money by treasurer of Calais by virtue of letters from King dated 22 October 1495.
43. Arthurson, 'Espionage and Intelligence', p. 140.
44. Bacon, p. 140.
45. J. Gairdner, *The Paston Letters* (London, 1900) Vol III, pp. 5–6.
46. Bacon, p. 140. Vergil, pp. 71, 75.
47. Molinet, p. 420.
48. Gairdner, *Memorials*, p. 70.
49. See Appendix B.
50. Benecke, *Maximilian I*, pp. 130–131.
51. Conway, *Scotland and Ireland*, p. 60.
52. *CPR 1494–1509*, p. 12.
53. See Appendix A. PRO E101/517/11 f. 9v.
54. HMC *Fourteenth Report*, Appendix Part VIII (1895), pp. 245–246.
55. HMC *Fourteenth Report*, etc., pp. 245–246.
56. Madden, 'Documents', pp. 165, 201.
57. *Exerpta Historica*, pp. 95–96. Madden, 'Documents', pp. 165, 201.
58. ADN B 2148, ff. 102r, 105v.
59. Madden, 'Documents', pp. 164–170, 200–204. Scottish Treas. Accts., p. 233.
60. Molinet, pp. 395–399.
61. *CPR 1494–1509*, p. 12.
62. Temperley, *Henry VII*, pp. 414–415.
63. *Letters and Papers*, Vol 1, pp. 388–404.
64. *Letters and Papers*, Vol 1, pp. 388, 389, 392–393, 394. *Rot. Parlt.*, p. 489.
65. PRO E101/517/11ff. 2v, 3r, 7v.
66. *CPR 1494–1509*, p. 27.
67. *Exerpta Historica*, p. 99. Harley 433, Vol 2, p. 48.
68. *CPR 1494–1509*, p. 7.
69. *Letters and Papers*, Vol 1, pp. 389, 392, 403–404.
70. Madden, 'Documents', pp. 167–168, and notes g and h, p. 167.
71. ADN B 2148, f. 118v. Molinet, p. 419.

8. *True Men*

1. C.G. Bayne and W.H. Dunham, 'Select Cases in the Council of Henry VII', *Selden Society*, 75 (London, 1956) pp. 28–29.
2. *Great Chronicle*, p. 256.
3. Crawford, *The Household Books of John Howard*, pp. II, 244–246.
4. *CSP* Milan, p. 292.
5. G.M. Coles, 'The Lordship of Middleham especially in Yorkist and Tudor Times', unpublished MA thesis (University of Liverpool, 1961), Appendix B, p. 18. Horrox, *Richard III*, pp. 56, 278–279 and note 33. Carpenter, *Locality and Polity*, p. 585, n. 113. *CPR 1476–1485*, pp. 47, 274, 354, 533, 561.
6. *CPR 1485–1494*, pp. 85, 134, 279, 353, 488, 506. Gairdner, *Memorials*, pp. 369–389. *Letters and Papers*, Vol 2, p. 291.
7. Vergil, p. 75.
8. *Great Chronicle*, p. 256.
9. *CPR 1494–1509*, p. 13. *Great Chronicle*, p. 256.
10. Génard, 'La Rose blanche', pp. 14, 19, 22.
11. Molinet, p. 420.
12. *Great Chronicle*, p. 256.
13. *Exerpta Historica*, p. 101.
14. Vergil, pp. 73, 75.
15. *Exerpta Historica*, pp. 99, 100, 101.
16. Hall, p. 469.
17. Vergil, pp. 75, 77. Hall, p. 469.
18. Vergil, pp. 75, 77. Hall, pp. 469–470. *Exerpta Historica*, p. 101.
19. *CPR 1494–1509*, pp. 29–30.
20. *Great Chronicle*, pp. 256–258. Vitellius A XVI, p. 204. *CCR 1485–1500*, pp. 236, 253, 268, 339.
21. Archbold, 'Stanley and Warbeck', pp. 530–531.
22. *Great Chronicle*, p. 258.
23. *Exerpta Historica*, p. 100. BL Add. MS 7099, f. 24r. *Great Chronicle*, p. 258.
24. *CPR 1494–1509*, pp. 30–31. PRO KB9/934/5.
25. *Great Chronicle*, p. 275.
26. PRO KB9/404/16. KB9/51/7. D.M. Loades, *Politics and the Nation 1450–1660* (Fontana pb., 1974), p. 109. Starkey, *The English Court*, pp. 75–76. S.J. Gunn, 'The Courtiers of Henry VII', *English Historical Review*, CVIII (1993), pp. 46–47. Carpenter, *Locality and Polity*, p. 587. PRO E101/414/6 f. 225r. PRO E101/517/11 f. 9r.
27. J.G. Nicols and J. Bruce, 'Wills from Doctors Commons, etc.', *Camden Society* (1863), pp. 1–9, esp 3–4. Armstrong, *England, France and Burgundy*, pp. 154, 156.
28. Emden, Vol 2, p. 1136. *CCR 1485–1500*, p. 232.
29. Wills from Doctors Commons, p. 8. Emden, Vol 2, p. 1136.
30. Emden, Vol 2, pp. 1101–1102. Madden, 'Documents', pp. 173, 205. Newns, 'The Hospice of St. Thomas', p. 190.
31. *Dictionary of National Biography*, sub Harliston, article by C.L. Kingsford.
32. Wills from Doctors Commons, pp. 5–6. Armstrong, *England, France and Burgundy*, p. 156. *CPR 1477–1485*, p. 217. Weightman, Margaret of York, p. 168.
33. Stark, 'Anglo-Burgundian Diplomacy', pp. 127–129, 148, 150–151. Wedgwood, *Biographies*, p. 855.
34. ADN B 2225/29541. Dated 18 July 1479.
35. Davis, 'Whetehill of Calais', (1948), pp. 243–252, (1949), p. 5. Stark, 'Anglo-Burgundian Diplomacy', pp. 127, 140. Horrox, *Richard III*, pp. 172, 240.
36. *Arrival Chronicle*, p. 2.
37. Horrox, *Richard III*, pp. 205–212. Harley 433, Vol 2, pp. 95, 96, 104, 138. T.B. Pugh, 'Henry VII and the English Nobility', in G.W. Bernard, ed., *The Tudor Nobility* (Manchester, 1992), pp. 50, 91 note 5.
38. Hampton, 'The White Rose under the First Tudors', Part 1, p. 416.
39. Horrox, *Richard III*, p. 80.
40. *CPR 1461–1467*, p. 47. *Calendar of Fine Rolls 1468–1476*, p. 305. *CPR 1467–1477*, pp. 15, 216, 268, 352, 491, 619, 620, 621. *CPR 1476–1498*, pp. 91, 99, 108, 276–277. *CPR 1476–1485*, pp. 307, 528. Stark, 'Anglo-Burgundian Diplomacy', pp. 146, 194. Wedgwood, *Biographies*, pp. 145–146.
41. N.F. Blake, *Caxton and his World* (London, 1969), pp. 40–45, 52–53, 83–86, 95–96, 232. W. Blades, *The Biography and Typography of William Caxton* (London, 1877, repr., 1971), p. 22.

42. Armstrong, *England, France and Burgundy*, p. 170. Weightman, *Margaret of York*, pp. 156, 157, 168. Scofield, Edward IV, Vol 2, pp. 99, 254, 265. Madden, 'Documents', pp. 177, 208. Emden, Vol 2, pp. 1101–1102.
43. Blades, William Caxton, pp. 220–221.
44. C.F. Richmond, 'After McFarlane', *History*, 66 (1983), p. 60, note 25. Horrox, *Richard III*, pp. 76–81. HMC *Various*, Vol II (1903), pp. 330–332.
45. Horrox, *Richard III*, pp. 278–282. Crawford, *The Household Books of John Howard*, p. x.
46. Horrox, *Richard III*, pp. 278–282.
47. *CCR 1476–1485*, pp. 345, 401.
48. R. Virgoe, 'The Recovery of the Howards in East Anglia, 1484 to 1529' in E.W. Ives, R.J. Knecht & J.J. Scarisbrick, eds., *Wealth and Power in Tudor England* (London, 1978) pp. 6, 8–10. *CPR 1485–1494*, pp. 101, 127.
49. Gairdner, *Paston Letters*, Vol 3, pp. 322–323, 334. Horrox, *Richard III*, p. 78.
50. Campbell, *Materials*, Vol 2, pp. 472–473. Virgoe, 'Recovery of Howards', pp. 10–19.
51. Bayne and Dunham, 'Select Cases in the Council of Henry VII', pp. 23, 25.
52. Horrox, *Richard III*, pp. 14, 285, 287.
53. *CPR 1485–1494*, pp. 42, 112.
54. J.P. Collier, ed., *Household Books of John Duke of Norfolk*, Roxburghe Club (London, 1844), p. 496.
55. M.J. Bennett, 'Henry VII and the Northern Rising of 1489', *English Historical Review*, CV (1990), p. 54, note 2.
56. *CPR 1485–1494*, pp. 334, 341.
57. Hall, p. 469. Carpenter, *Locality and Polity*, p. 585.
58. M.K. Jones, 'Sir William Stanley of Holt: politics and family allegiance in the late fifteenth century', *Welsh History Review*, 14 (1988), pp. 1–22.
59. D.J. Clayton, 'The Administation of the County Palatine of Chester 1442–1485', *Chetham Society*, 3rd ser, Vol 35 (Manchester, 1990), pp. 79–81, 108–110.
60. Jones, 'Sir William Stanley of Holt', p. 18.
61. PRO E154/2/5 f. 13v.
62. Vergil, p. 75.
63. *Great Chronicle*, p. 250. Jones, 'Sir William Stanley of Holt', pp. 16, 21, note 93.
64. *CPR 1494–1509*, p. 24. *CCR 1485–1500*, p. 240.
65. Clayton, 'County Palatine of Chester', p. 59.
66. Wedgwood, *Biographies*, p. 742.
67. Molinet, p. 420.
68. See Appendix B.
69. Horrox, *Richard III*, pp. 41–43, 47, 142, 175, 191, 199, 286. PRO DL 29/119/1964. I owe this latter reference to the kindness of Dr R. Horrox. *Victoria County History of Lancashire*, Vol IV, pp. 342, 347. F.R. Raines, ed., 'Visitation of Lancashire by William Flower, 1567', *Chetham Society*, LXXXI (1870), pp. 63–64.
70. Carpenter, *Locality and Polity*, pp. 560–587.
71. *CCR 1485–1500*, p. 35.
72. W. Dugdale, *Antiquities of Warwickshire* (London, 1656) p. 732.
73. See Appendix B. *Victoria County History of Warwickshire*, Vol IV, p. 175.
74. Carpenter, *Locality and Polity*, p. 551, note 119.
75. Wedgwood, *Biographies*, p. 706.
76. Wedgwood, *Biographies*, p. 603. *CPR 1461–1467*,

p. 574. *CPR 1467–1477*, p. 634. *Victoria County History of Warwickshire*, Vol IV, p. 51. *Calendar of Fine Rolls, 1471–1485*, pp. 18–19. Carpenter, *Locality and Polity*, p. 695.
77. Virgoe, 'Recovery of Howards', pp. 3–6.
78. *Great Chronicle*, p. 258.
79. PRO KB9/51/7. *Exerpta Historica*, p. 95.
80. Carpenter, *Locality and Polity*, p. 588. PRO PSO 2/3.
81. Madden, 'Documents', pp. 174–175, 206–207.
82. Madden, 'Documents', pp. 171–173, esp. 173, note x. 'Calendar of Entries in the Papal Registers relating to Great Britain and Ireland', *Papal Letters 1484–1492* (London, 1960), p. 275.
83. S.B. Chrimes, *Henry VII* (London, 1977), p. 327.
84. Bacon, p. 149.

9. *The Red Rose and the White*

1. De Roover, Money, Banking and Credit, p. 21. Madden, 'Documents', pp. 175, 208.
2. Génard, 'La Rose blanche', pp. 9–22.
3. Rigsarkivet, Copenhagen, TKUA. Alm. Del 1, 5. Kong Hans Brevbog 1506–1512. J.G. Kam, *Waar was dat huis in de Warmoesstraat* (Amsterdam, 1968), p. 51. Gemeentelijke Archiefdienst, Amsterdam, Archeif 5004 Weeskamer (Court of Chancery) Inbrengregister, deel 8 f. 296v. Communication of 8 August 1992 from P.H.J. van der Laan, Gemeentearchief, Amsterdam.
4. *Letters and Papers*, Vol 1, p. 264–265.
5. Exchequer Rolls of Scotland, Vol X, p. 614. Rigsarkivet, Copenhagen, TKUA. Alm. Del 1, 5. Kong Hans Brevbog 1506–1512.
6. ADN B 164. Translated Kleyn, *Richard of England*, pp. 193–195. Original is in Vienna. Philpot, 'Maximilian and England', 167, note 1.
7. Philpot, 'Maximilian and England', p. 167.
8. ADN B 2153/ 70610, 70620, 70622, 70623. Code found on 70621, 70619. ADN B 2151, ff. 284r, 286r–289v.
9. H. Ulmann, *Maximilian Kaiser Maximilian I*, Vol 1 (Stuttgart, 1884) p. 264, esp. note 1.
10. ADN B 2151, f. 215r.
11. Madden, 'Documents', pp. 175–176, 208.
12. *CPR 1494–1509*, p. 32.
13. Conway, *Scotland and Ireland*, p. 83.
14. Conway, *Scotland and Ireland*, pp. 60–62, 78–79. *New History of Ireland*, pp. 638–9.
15. *New History of Ireland*, pp. 639–640.
16. *New History of Ireland*, p. 640.
17. Conway, *Scotland and Ireland*, pp. 79, 216–217. *New History of Ireland*, p. 640.
18. Bryan, *The Great Earl of Kildare*, pp. 198–199. *New History of Ireland*, pp. 621, 632–633. Conway, *Scotland and Ireland*, pp81, 89–90. Macdougall, *James IV*, pp. 117, 267.
19. Conway, *Scotland and Ireland*, p. 233. *New History of Ireland*, pp. 621–627, 812. Macdougall, *James IV*, pp. 115–120.
20. Bryan, *The Great Earl of Kildare*, pp. 197–198.
21. *CPR 1494–1509*, p. 129.
22. *CPR 1494–1509*, p. 76. Bryan, *The Great Earl of Kildare*, p. 197.
23. Conway, *Scotland and Ireland*, pp. 71, 83.
24. *CSP Venice*, 1, p. 219.

25. Scottish Treas. Accts., p. 233.
26. Macdougall, *James IV*, pp. 112–120. *CSP* Venice, 1, pp. 219–220.
27. Macdougall, *James IV*, pp. 119–120.
28. Macdougall, *James IV*, p. 99.
29. BL Cotton MS Titus B XI Pt 2, f. 284r–v.
30. City of Canterbury Corporation Archives, F/A2 f. 238v.
31. *CSP* Venice, 1, p. 219.
32. Gairdner, *Memorials*, pp. 393–399 ADN B 458/17919. Weightman, *Margaret of York*, pp. 121, 125, 134, 194, 198, 200, 201, 203, 216.
33. Gairdner, *Memorials*, pp. 393–399.
34. ADN B 2151, f. 127r, 131v, 135v.
35. Gairdner, *Paston Letters*, Vol III, pp. 387–388.
36. *Letters and Papers*, Vol 2, pp. 299, 300, 308. L. Visser-Fuchs, 'English Events in Caspar Weinrich's Danzig Chronicle 1461–1495', *The Ricardian*, VII (1986), pp. 310–320. esp. pp. 317–318.
37. F. Brassart, 'Le Blason de Lalaing, etc.', *Souvenirs de la Flandre Wallonne*, Tome 18 (Douai, 1878) pp. 44–46.
38. Weightman, *Margaret of York*, pp. 174, 175. ADN B 2151, f. 215r, B 2152/70534, B 2153/70642, B 3512/70669, B 2183/73104, 74898, 75063. Brassart, 'Le Blason de Lalaing', p. 45.
39. Molinet, p. 421.
40. J. Zurita, *Annales de la Corona de Aragon*, Vol 3, 1610, p. 134. *CSP* Spain, p. 59. *Great Chronicle*, p. 259.
41. Davies, 'The Island of Jersey', p. 335. *CPR 1476–1485*, p. 545.
42. See Appendix B. *Great Chronicle*, p. 260. Vitellius A XVI, p. 207. Gairdner, *Paston Letters*, Vol III, pp. 386–387.
43. Vergil, p. 81. See Appendix B.
44. *Rot. Parlt.*, pp. 503–504. L.C. Atreed, ed., *York House Books 1461–1490*, 2 Vols (Stroud, 1991), Vol 2, p. 421.
45. *Rot Parlt.*, pp. 503–504. *CPR 1485–1494*, p. 306. *CPR 1494–1509*, pp. 142, 333. Harley 433, Vol 1, p. 278.
46. *Exerpta Historica*, p. 101. BL Add. MS 7099 f. 22r.
47. ADN B 2151, ff. 121v, 122r.
48. Molinet, pp. 420–421.
49. Madden, 'Documents', pp. 176, 208.
50. Gairdner, *Paston Letters*, Vol III, p. 386. PRO KB9/51/7.
51. *CPR 1494–1509*, p. 37.
52. *Arrival Chronicle*, p. 2.
53. Kleyn, *Richard of England*, p. 201.
54. *Arrival Chronicle*, pp. 2–3.
55. Gairdner, *Memorials*, p. 67. Gairdner, *Paston Letters*, Vol III, pp. 387–388.
56. Temperley, *Henry VII*, p. 415. City of Canterbury Corporation Archives, F/A 2 f. 258v.
57. Gairdner, *Paston Letters*, Vol III, p. 388.
58. BL Add. MS 29617, f. 128r–v. BL Egerton MS 2107 f. 47v. *Exerpta Historica*, p. 103.
59. Kent Archives Office, Sandwich Year Book, called the White Book; S/AC 2 f. 41r. PRO E36/8 f. 102v.
60. City of Canterbury Corporation Archives, F/A 2 f. 265v. Molinet, p. 421.
61. Molinet, pp. 421–422. Gairdner, *Paston Letters*, Vol III, p. 386.
62. PRO E404/82 unnumbered, dated 28 October 1496.
63. *Great Chronicle*, pp. 259–260.
64. Gairdner, *Paston Letters*, Vol III, p. 388. Vergil, p. 83.
65. BL Add. MS 7099, f. 26r. Temperley, *Henry VII*, p. 415.
66. Kent Archive Office, S/AC f. 41r. *Letters and Papers*, Vol 2, pp. 298, 299. Conway, *Scotland and Ireland*, pp. 84–86.
67. BL Add. MS 7099, f. 28r. *CPR 1494–1509*, pp. 34, 41, 42, 44.
68. Bryan, *The Great Earl of Kildare*, pp. 197–198. Lambeth Palace Library MS 632, ff. 255v–256r.
69. Bryan, *The Great Earl of Kildare*, pp. 197–198. Lambeth Palace Library MS 632, ff. 255v–256r.
70. Bryan, *The Great Earl of Kildare*, pp. 198–199. Lambeth Palace Library MS 632, ff. 255v–256r. See Conway, *Scotland and Ireland*, p. 167.
71. Bryan, *The Great Earl of Kildare*, pp. 197–198. Lambeth Palace Library MS 632, ff. 255v–256r. Conway, *Scotland and Ireland*, pp. 86, 87, 182, note 5, 183. *Letters and Papers*, Vol 2, p. 302. *New History of Ireland*, p. 643.
72. *New History of Ireland*, pp. 621–625. Macdougall, *James IV*, pp. 116–117, 119, 120, 134, 198, 200, 266–267.
73. Macdougall, *James IV*, pp. 116–197. Conway, *Scotland and Ireland*, p. 233–234.
74. Conway, *Scotland and Ireland*, pp. 86, note 5, 175.
75. *CSP* Venice, 1, pp. 223–224.
76. *CSP* Venice, 4, pp. 482–483. Philpot, 'Maximilian and England', p. 168 and note 3.
77. ADN B 2155, ff. 159r–160v, 162r–164v.
78. Macdougall, *James IV*, pp. 120–121.
79. Macdougall, *James IV*, pp. 120–122. Scottish Treas. Accts., pp. 242, 267.
80. Macdougall, *James IV*, p. 122. Scottish Treas. Accts., p. 267.
81. Scottish Treas. Accts., p. 267.
82. *Great Chronicle*, p. 260.
83. *CPR 1494–1509*, p. 52.
84. W.H. Stevenson, ed., *Records of the Borough of Nottingham*, 8 Vols (Nottingham, 1882–1900), Vol III, p. 401.
85. Kent Archives Office, S/AC 2 f. 41r.
86. City of Canterbury Corporation Archives, F/A 2 f. 258v.
87. Haus-, Hof-, und Staatsarchiv, Vienna, Maximiliana 4 f. 267r–v. I am most grateful to Dr R. Philpot for allowing me to use her copy of this document.
88. *CSP* Spain, p. 59. Zurita, *Annales*, Vol 3, p. 134.
89. *CSP* Spain, p. 59. *Great Chronicle*, p. 259. Vitellius A XVI, pp. 205–206. Gairdner, *Paston Letters*, Vol III, p. 386.
90. PRO E404/82 unnumbered, dated 14 November 1495. *Great Chronicle*, p. 259. Vitellius A XVI, p. 205–206.
91. Molinet, p. 422. PRO KB9/52.
92. *Great Chronicle*, p. 259.
93. BL Add. MS 7099, f. 26r. And those returned from the King to London, *Great Chronicle*, p. 260.
94. Quinn, *Analecta Historica*, p. 61. *CPR 1495–1509*, p. 37.
95. *Great Chronicle*, p. 260. BL Add. MS 29617, ff. 128v, 129r.
96. BL Add. MS 7099, f. 26r. *Great Chronicle*, p. 260.

Vitellius A XVI, p. 207. Carpenter, *Locality and Polity*, p. 587, note 120.

97. *Great Chronicle*, p. 260. C.L. Kingsford, ed., *A Survey of London by John Stow*, 2 Vols (Oxford, 1908), Vol 2, pp. 70–71, 376.

10. A War of Nerves

1. *Exchequer Rolls of Scotland*, Vol X, p. 614.
2. Scottish Treas. Accts., pp. 262–264. *Exchequer Rolls of Scotland*, Vol X, pp. 567–577.
3. Vergil, pp. 85–87.
4. *CSP Spain*, pp. 185–186.
5. Gairdner, *Memorials*, p. 70.
6. Macdougall, *James IV*, p. 122.
7. Scottish Record Office, Edinburgh, GD 279/9. Dated 30 December 1495.
8. *CSP Spain*, pp. 78–79.
9. Macdougall, *James IV*, pp. 122–123. Molinet, p. 422.
10. Scottish Treas. Accts., p. 268. *Exchequer Rolls of Scotland*, Vol X, pp. 588–589.
11. Scottish Treas. Accts., p. 269. *Exchequer Rolls of Scotland*, Vol X, p. 580.
12. Macdougall, *James IV*, pp. 123–125.
13. PRO E101/414/16 ff. 4r, 6r, 10v, 12r, 22r, 22v, 23r–v. *Letters and Papers*, Vol 2, p. 306.
14. Haus-, Hof-, und Staatsarchiv, Vienna, Maximiliana 4 f. 267r–v. *Exerpta Historica*, p. 103.
15. ADN B 2155, ff. 81v, 159r–163v, 165r. PRO E101/414/6 ff. 3r, 8r, 20r.
16. *CSP Venice*, 1, pp. 225–228.
17. *CSP Venice*, 1, pp. 228–229, 236.
18. *CSP Venice*, 1, p. 232.
19. Philpot, 'Maximilian and England', p. 169 and note 3.
20. *Foedera*, XII, pp. 578–591, esp. pp. 579–580.
21. *Exerpta Historica*, p. 104.
22. Madden, 'Documents', pp. 179–181.
23. *CSP Venice*, 1, p. 236. *CSP Spain*, p. 111. Madden, 'Documents', pp. 179–181. Conway, *Scotland and Ireland*, pp. 82–83.
24. *CSP Venice*, 1, pp. 228, 237–244. *CSP Spain*, p. 110.
25. G. Mattingley, *Renaissance Diplomacy* (Penguin pb., 1973), pp. 133–135, 139, 142–145.
26. *CSP Spain*, pp. 92, 93.
27. *CSP Spain*, p. 98. Macdougall, *James IV*, pp. 123–125.
28. *CSP Spain*, pp. 103–104.
29. *CSP Spain*, p. 111.
30. *CSP Spain*, pp. 104, 106.
31. *CSP Spain*, pp. 108–110, 113–114, 116, 124–128.
32. *CPR 1494–1509*, pp. 67–68.
33. PRO E101/414/6 f. 23v.
34. D. Macpherson, ed., *Rotuli Scotiae 1291–1516*, Vol 2 (1819), p. 520.
35. Macdougall, *James IV*, p. 127.
36. Macpherson, *Rotuli Scotiae*, Vol 2, p. 522. PRO E101/414/6 f. 38r. Scottish Treas. Accts., p. 278.
37. Scottish Treas. Accts., pp. 280–287.
38. PRO E101/414/6 ff. 27r, 29r, 29v, 30r, 34r, 37r.
39. Scottish Treas. Accts., p. 274.
40. Scottish Treas. Accts., p. 277.
41. Scottish Treas. Accts., p. 274.
42. Scottish Treas. Accts., pp. 274, 276.
43. Conway, *Scotland and Ireland*, pp. 236–239.
44. Ellis, *Letters Illustrative*, 1st ser, Vol 1, pp. 23–24.

Bennett, *Lambert Simnel and the Battle of Stoke*, pp. 74, 125. *Rot. Parlt.*, p. 545. PRO E101/517/11 f. 7v. Horrox, *Richard III*, pp. 14, 41, 51, 191, 193, 194, 266.

45. See Appendix B.
46. Horrox, *Richard III*, pp. 79, 194. A.J. Pollard, *North Eastern England during the Wars of the Roses* (Oxford, 1990), p. 359. *CPR 1485–1494*, pp. 171, 191. *CPR 1494–1509*, p. 47.
47. See Appendix B.
48. Ellis, *Letters Illustrative*, 1st ser, Vol 1, p. 24.
49. Madden, 'Documents', pp. 175, 207.
50. *Letters and Papers*, Vol 2, pp. 323–326.
51. *Letters and Papers*, Vol 2, pp. 324–325.
52. J. Petre, ed., *Richard III, Crown and People* (Gloucester, 1985), p. 227.
53. *CPR 1494–1509*, p. 49.
54. John Water, despite repeated assertions (Madden, 'Documents', p. 178. and Kleyn, *Richard of England*, p. 86) is not to be confused with John Atwater of Cork. John Water is identified as member of the Hospice of St Thomas in Rome, admitted 3 May 1493. Lilly was an executor of Peter Husee's will (PRO Prob 11/11/39), one of his servants, and admitted to the hospice 3 May 1490. Kendal was Chamberlain of the Hospice 1486–1491. I owe all the foregoing to Dr S.J. Gunn, to whom I am most indebted.
55. *CCR 1485–1500*, p. 276.
56. *CSP Spain*, pp. 103, 111, 112.
57. *CSP Venice*, 1, p. 247. *CSP Milan*, p. 299.
58. C. Ross, *Wars of the Roses* (London, 1976), p. 43.
59. *CCR 1485–1500*, p. 289. J.R. Lander, *Crown and Nobility 1450–1509* (London, 1976), pp. 286–288.
60. *Complete Peerage*, Vol 12, p. 395.
61. Bryan, *The Great Earl of Kildare*, pp. 198–199.
62. *CPR 1485–1494*, p. 232. Quinn, *Analecta Historica*, p. 64.
63. Conway, *Scotland and Ireland*, pp. 221–225.
64. Ellis, *Letters Illustrative*, 1st ser, Vol 1, p. 24.
65. Conway, *Scotland and Ireland*, pp. 89–90.
66. Pollard, *Reign of Henry VII from Contemporary Sources*, Vol 3, p. 285.
67. PRO E101/414/6 ff. 38v, 41r, 42r, 43r. Conway, *Scotland and Ireland*, pp. 226–232. *New History of Ireland*, pp. 645–648.
68. Conway, *Scotland and Ireland*, pp. 93–95. PRO E101/414/6 f. 42r–v. PRO C82/151.
69. Conway, *Scotland and Ireland*, p. 94. *CPR 1494–1509*, p. 76.
70. *CPR 1494–1509*, p. 158.
71. Scottish Treas. Accts., pp. 289–292.
72. Gairdner, *Richard III*, p. 302. Ellis, *Letters Illustrative*, 1st ser, Vol 1, pp. 23–24.
73. Ellis, *Letters Illustrative*, 1st ser, Vol 1, p. 23.
74. Ellis, *Letters Illustrative*, 1st ser, Vol 1, pp. 25, 29. Macdougall, *James IV*, pp. 128–130.
75. Ellis, *Letters Illustrative*, 1st ser, Vol 1, pp. 25, 26, 28, 30. Macdougall. *James IV*, pp. 128–130.
76. ADN B 2155, f. 129v.
77. Macdougall, *James IV*, pp. 123–124. *CSP Spain*, p. 120.
78. *CSP Spain*, p. 127.
79. *CSP Spain*, pp. 88, 111. PRO E101/414/6 f. 48r–v; rewards to the French ambassadors, 28–30 September 1496.

80. Ellis, *Letters Illustrative*, 1st ser, Vol 1, pp. 26–28.
81. Scottish Treas. Accts., pp. 292–296.

11. Failure

1. Nat. Lib. Wales, Carreg-lwyd series I, 695.
2. *CCR 1485–1500*, pp. 363–364. T.B. Macaulay, *The History of England from the Accession of James II*, Vol 1 (London, 1849), pp. 524–525.
3. Vergil, pp. 89–91.
4. A. Raine, *York Civic Records*, Vol 2, Yorkshire Archaeological Society Record Series, No 103 (1941), p. 128. PRO E101/414/6 ff. 46r, 47r, 48r–v
.5. Macdougall, *James IV*, pp. 130–132.
6. Vergil, p. 89.
7. Scottish Treas. Accts., pp. 299–301. Macdougall, *James IV*, pp. 132–133. *Great Chronicle*, p. 264. Vitellius A XVI, p. 210.
8. Macdougall, *James IV*, p. 134. *Exchequer Rolls of Scotland*, Vol XI, p. 22. P. Gouldesborough, ed., 'The Accounts of Sir Duncan Forester of Skipinch Comptroller 1495–1499', *Scottish History Society*, 3rd Series, Vol 50 (Edinburgh, 1958) p. 65.
9. *Bibliotek des Literarischen Vereins in Stuttgart*, Vol X (Stuttgart, 1845), pp. 147–149.
10. Scottish Treas. Accts., p. 303.
11. Scottish Treas. Accts., pp. 301–304. Gouldesborough, 'Accounts of Duncan Forester', pp. 80–81. *Exchequer Rolls of Scotland*, Vol XI, p. 43.
12. Madden, 'Documents', pp. 182–184.
13. Scofield, *Edward IV*, Vol 1, p. 260. H. Talbot, *The English Achilles* (London, 1981), pp. 157, 159.
14. Scofield, *Edward IV*, Vol 1, pp. 386–387, 408, 508; Vol 2, pp. 108, 253, 329.
15. Harley 433, Vol 1, p. 209; Vol 3, pp. 24–26, 35, 40–46. *CSP Spain*, p. 32. Campbell, *Materials*, Vol 2, p. 563.
16. Vitellius A XVI, p. 212. *Great Chronicle*, p. 260. Wedgwood, *Biographies*, p. 706.
17. See Appendix A.
18. PRO E101/517/11 f. 9v.
19. *Letters and Papers*, Vol 1, p. 181. PRO E101/414/6 ff. 60v, 63v, 12 March 1497 payment to Lady Fitzwater of £33 6s 8d; Lovell, f. 64v.
20. Scottish Treas. Accts., p. 303.
21. *Letters and Papers*, Vol 1, p. lxiii, note 1.
22. Conway, *Scotland and Ireland*, pp. 95–98, 232–235. *Letters and Papers*, Vol 2, p. 326. *New History of Ireland*, pp. 645–647.
23. *New History of Ireland*, p. 646.
24. Conway, *Scotland and Ireland*, p. 233. Macdougall, *James IV*, pp. 103–105, 116, 178.
25. Conway, *Scotland and Ireland*, p. 233.
26. PRO E101/414/6 ff. 55v, 60r. E405/79 m. 15v.
27. *CSP Spain*, p. 104.
28. Hughes and Larkin, *Tudor Proclamations*, p. 58.
29. Corporation of London Record Office, Repertory, Vol 1, ff. 6v, 7r. *Great Chronicle*, p. 262. J. Scattergood, *John Skelton: The Complete English Poems* (Penguin pb., 1983), p. 37.
30. PRO E404/82. Unnumbered warrant with date partially destroyed; October 1496. E.C. Batten, 'A Letter Missive to John Calycote of Shepton Mallet', *Proceedings of the Somerset Archaeological and Natural History Society*, Vol XXX (1894), pp. 159–165, esp. p. 159. Raine, *York Civic Records*, Vol 2, pp. 131–132.
31. *Great Chronicle*, pp. 274–275, Vitellius A XVI, pp. 211, 213. Macdougall, *James IV*, p. 133.
32. *Rot. Parlt.*, p. 509.
33. Macpherson, *Rotuli Scotiae*, Vol 2, p. 522.
34. PRO E 101/414/6 ff. 40r–49v, 55r, v, E 405/79 mm. 15r–17v 23r, E 36/8 ff. 23r–25r, 28, 35. J. Hunter, *South Yorkshire*, 2 Vols (London, 1828–1831) Vol 2, p. 313. *CPR 1494–1509*, pp. 87, 89–92.
35. Macdougall, *James IV*, pp. 134–135.
36. Hunter, *South Yorkshire*, Vol 2, p. 313. J. Weever, *Ancient Funeral Monuments* (1767), p. 836.
37. BL Cotton MS Caligula B III f. 13r. *Exchequer Rolls of Scotland*, Vol XI, pp. 29, 214. Scottish Treas. Accts., pp. 309–310.
38. Macdougall, *James IV*, p. 135.
39. Macdougall, *James IV*, p. 135.
40. Emden, Vol 3, p. 1669. See Appendix C.
41. See Appendix C.
42. *CCR 1485–1500*, p. 298.
43. *CCR 1485–1500*, p. 291. Horrox, *Richard III*, pp. 129, 217, 267.
44. *CCR 1485–1500*, p. 289. *CPR 1494–1509*, p. 333.
45. *CCR 1485–1500*, pp. 289, 298–299.
46. PRO E101/414/6 f. 61r.
47. ADN B 2159, ff. 104r, 109v, 114r, 116v, 163v, 166v.
48. *CSP* Spain, p. 140.
49. *Letters and Papers*, Vol 1, pp. 104–107.
50. This paragraph and all the following on military preparations against Scotland are drawn from I. Arthurson, 'The King's Voyage into Scotland: The War that Never Was', in D. Williams ed., *England in the Fifteenth Century* (Woodbridge, 1987), pp. 1–23.
51. Scottish Treas. Accts., pp. 324–332. *Exchequer Rolls of Scotland*, Vol XI, pp. 39, 87.
52. Scottish Treas. Accts., pp. 335–340. Macdougall, *James IV*, pp. 135–136.
53. Scottish Treas. Accts., pp. 358, 365, 371.
54. Scottish Record Office, Edinburgh, RH9/1/1 f. 125r–v.
55. Scottish Treas. Accts., pp. 333, 339.
56. The previous two paragraphs are drawn from Arthurson, 'The War that Never Was'.

12. Success

1. Horrox, *Richard III*, p. 324. *Great Chronicle*, p. 278.
2. M.L. Bush, 'Tax Reform and Rebellion in Early Tudor England', *History*, 76 (1991), pp. 395–396.
3. Bush, 'Tax Reform and Rebellion', p. 388.
4. PRO E36/14 pp. 225–373.
5. 'The Rising of 1497 – A Revolt of the Peasantry', in J. Rosenthal and C. Richmond, *People, Politics and Community in the Later Middle Ages* (Gloucester, 1987), pp. 1–18.
6. Vergil, p. 93.
7. I. Arthurson, '1497 and the Western Rising', unpublished PhD thesis (University of Keele, 1981), pp. 182–195.
8. Arthurson, '1497', p. 194.
9. Arthurson, '1497', map 6 opposite p. 487.
10. PRO SC11/828.

11. Wedgwood, *Biographies*, pp. 29–30.
12. Ross, *Edward IV*, p. 130.
13. W. Sterry, *The Eton College Register 1441–1698* (1943), p. 14.
14. Horrox, *Richard III*, pp. 31, 104 note 36, 160, 183, 203.
15. Arthurson, '1497', pp. 541–542.
16. *Great Chronicle*, p. 278.
17. Arthurson, '1497', pp. 520–528. Harley 433, Vol 1, pp. 73, 277.
18. Zurita, *Annales*, Vol 3, pp. 133.
19. Gairdner, *Richard III*, p. 320.
20. *Rot. Parlt.*, p. 545.
21. E. Curtis, ed., *Calendar of Ormond Deeds*, 6 Vols (Dublin, 1932–1943), Vol 4, p. 332.
22. L.T. Smith, ed., *The Maire of Bristowe is Kalendar by Robert Ricart*, Camden Society, New Series, Vol 5 (1872), p. 48–49. *CSP Venice*, 1, p. 256. *Great Chronicle*, p. 276.
23. *Great Chronicle*, p. 276.
24. PRO KB9/441/6.
25. PRO E101/414/6 f. 76r.
26. PRO KB9/441/6.
27. *Great Chronicle*, p. 276. *Letters and Papers*, Vol 1, p. 232.
28. Arthurson, '1497', pp. 222–225.
29. Arthurson, '1497', pp. 682–706. Hunter, *South Yorkshire*, Vol 2, p. 313.
30. Hughes and Larkin, *Tudor Proclamations*, pp. 39–40.
31. Kleyn, *Richard of England*, pp. 122–123.
32. Vergil, p. 127. Westminster Abbey Muniment 12245. Dr M.K. Jones kindly suggested to me that Sir Robert may be Robert Southwell.
33. *CCR 1485–1500*, pp. 306.
34. Arthurson, '1497', p. 603.
35. Carpenter, *Locality and Polity*, p. 551.
36. M.M. Condon, 'Ruling Elites in the Reign of Henry VII', in C. Ross, *Patronage Pedigree and Power*, pp. 125–126, 140, note 84. *CCR 1485–1500*, p. 290.
37. Arthurson, '1497', pp. 688, 700. PRO PSO 2/3. *Letters and Papers*, Vol 1, 180.
38. *Great Chronicle*, p. 276.
39. PRO SC8/345/C2.

13. Cat and Mouse

1. Macdougall, *James IV*, p. 137.
2. Scottish Treas. Accts., pp. 340–342.
3. Scottish Treas. Accts., pp. 343–344.
4. Macdougall, *James IV*, pp. 137–138.
5. Zurita, *Annales*, Vol 5, pp. 133–134.
6. Vergil, pp. 101–103.
7. Zurita, *Annales*, Vol 3, p. 133. Scottish Treas. Accts., pp. 340–342.
8. Scottish Treas. Accts., pp. 343–345.
9. R.K. Hannay, ed., R.L. Mackie and A. Spilman, *The Letters of James IV 1505–1513*, Scottish History Society, 3rd Series, Vol 45 (1953), pp. 7, 9, 99. *Registrum Secreti Sigili Regum Scotorum, Register of Privy Seal of Scotland*, Vol 1, AD 1488–1529, ed., M. Livingstone (1908), p. 13, no. 99. *Exchequer Rolls of Scotland*, Vol XI, p. 372.
10. Scottish Treas. Accts., pp. 343–345.
11. Zurita, *Annales*, Vol 3, p. 134. Scottish Treas. Accts., pp. 358–365.

12. M. Oppenheim, *Naval Accounts and Inventories of the Reign of Henry VII*, Navy Records Society (1886), p. 240.
13. J. Stuart, *Extracts from the Council Register of the Burgh of Aberdeen 1398–1570*, Spalding Club (Aberdeen, 1844), pp. 62–63. Scottish Treas. Accts., pp. 344–348.
14. Scottish Treas. Accts., pp. 344–345.
15. PRO C82/164. Macpherson, *Rotuli Scotiae*, Vol 2, p. 530. *Letters and Papers*, Vol 1, pp. 104–111. P.S. and H.M. Allen, *The Letters of Richard Fox 1486–1527* (Oxford, 1929), p. 136.
16. *Great Chronicle*, p. 279. Hunter, *South Yorkshire* Vol 2, p. 313.
17. *CSP* Milan, p. 319.
18. Scottish Treas Accts., pp. 345–351, and pp. cliv, clv, 313, 314 for compositions. Macdougall, *James IV*, pp. 139–139. *Great Chronicle*, p. 279.
19. Scottish Treas. Accts., pp. 347, 350, clvi. PRO Durham 3/61 mm. 5r, 12, 13r, 15r.
20. Macdougall, *James IV*, p. 139. *Great Chronicle*, p. 280. J.D. Marwick, ed., *Extracts from the Records of the Burgh of Edinburgh 1403–1528*, Scottish Burgh Records Society (Edinburgh, 1869), pp. 71–72. Scottish Treas. Accts., pp. 351–352.
21. Macdougall, *James IV*, p. 139. Scottish Treas. Accts., pp. 351–352.
22. PRO E405/79 mm. 34r, 39v, E36/8 f. 17r–v. *Great Chronicle*, pp. 279–280. Weever, *Funeral Monuments*, p. 386.
23. *Great Chronicle*, p. 277. PRO E405/79 m. 34r. Oppenheim, *Naval Accounts*, p. 126.
24. *Great Chronicle*, pp. 277, 280–281. Oppenheim, *Naval Accounts*, pp. liii, 129–130. PRO E405/79 m. 34r–v.
25. *Great Chronicle*, p. 280. Weever, *Funeral Monuments*, p. 836. PRO E36/8 ff. 10r, 100r.
26. *CSP* Spain, p. 190. Scottish Treas. Accts., p. 353. *Great Chronicle*, pp. 280–281. W.A. Shaw, *Knights of England*, 2 Vols (London, 1906), Vol 2, p. 31. Scottish Treas Accts., p. 353.
27. Oppenheim, *Naval Accounts*, p. 240.
28. Zurita, *Annales*, Vol 3, pp. 133–134. Curtis. *Ormond Deeds*, Vol 4, p. 332.
29. Gairdner, *Richard III*, pp. 321–325. *Letters and Papers*, Vol 2, pp. 258–261.
30. *Frasers' Magazine for Town and Country*, Vol 32, (September 1843) no. 189, pp. 282–300. Ellis, *Letters Illustrative*, 1st ser, Vol 1, 1824, p. 32r. Lambeth Palace Library MS 632, f. 251r.
31. *New History of Ireland*, pp. 647–649.
32. Curtis, *Ormond Deeds*, Vol 4, p. 332.
33. Lambeth Palace Library MS 632, f. 256r.
34. *CSP* Spain, p. 186.
35. Zurita, *Annales*, Vol 3, pp. 133–134.

Part Three: In England

14. In the Time of Perkin

1. *Rot. Parlt.*, p. 545. These two paragraphs are taken from unpublished work on the geography of the 1497 rebellion. A good impression of western Cornwall is got from L.T. Smith, *Leland's*

Itinerary, Vol 1, pp. 317–21. On the Earl of Oxford: Ross, *Edward IV*, pp. 176, 191–192.

2. *3rd Annual Report of the Deputy Keeper of the Public Records*, (1842), Appendix II, p. 42.

3. This information and all subsequent quotations relating to Warbeck are from a signet letter of 16 September 1497 from Henry VII to Edward Courtenay, Earl of Devon. The letter is used by kind permission of its owners Mr and Mrs H. Spiro of New York.

4. F.E. Halliday, ed., R. Carew, *Survey of Cornwall* (London, 1953), p. 233.

5. *Rot Parlt.*, p. 545. PRO SC8/345/C2.

6. Bayne and Dunham, 'Select Cases in the Council of Henry VII', pp. cxxxii–cxxxiii.

7. *CSP* Milan, p. 325. *3rd Annual Report of the Deputy Keeper of the Public Records*, Appendix II, p. 42.

8. *CSP* Milan, p. 325.

9. *CSP* Milan, pp. 325, 327. *Great Chronicle*, p. 281. Vitellius A XVI, p. 217.

10. Devon Record Office (Plymouth) W130 ff. 38v–40r.

11. Spiro letter, 16 September 1497.

12. R. Polwhele, *The History of Cornwall*, 4 Vols (1803–1808, repr. 1978), Vol 4, p. 54.

13. *CSP* Milan, p. 327.

14. Spiro letter, 16 September 1497.

15. *CSP* Milan, p. 327.

16. PRO E101/414/6 f. 87r. PRO E36/126 f. 22v.

17. Arthurson, '1497', pp. 590–631. Ellis, *Letters Illustrative*, 1st ser, Vol 1, p. 33. Oppenheim, *Naval Accounts*, p. 241. Spiro letter, 16 September 1497.

18. Ellis, *Letters Illustrative*, 1st ser, Vol 1, pp. 34, 36–37. PRO E101/414/6 f. 87r.

19. Spiro letter, 16 September 1497.

20. Ellis, *Letters Illustrative*, 1st ser, Vol 1, p. 34.

21. Devon Record Office (Exeter) ECR Book 51 (John Hooker's Commonplace Book) f. 328r–v.

22. Devon Record Office (Exeter) ECR Book 51 f. 328v.

23. A.L. Rowse, *Tudor Cornwall* (London, 1969), p. 131.

24. Ellis, *Letters Illustrative*, 1st ser, Vol 1, p. 34.

25. Devon Record Office (Exeter) ECR Receivers' Accounts Years 12–13 Henry VII, m. 3v.

26. Devon Record Office (Exeter) ECR Book 51 f. 328v. Ellis, *Letters Illustrative*, 1st ser, Vol 1, pp. 36–37. *Great Chronicle*, p. 281. Vitellius A XVI, p. 217.

27. Ellis, *Letters Illustrative*, 1st ser, Vol 1, pp. 36–37.

28. PRO E101/414/6 ff. 87r–88r. Ellis, *Letters Illustrative*, 1st ser, Vol 1, p. 35.

29. PRO E101/414/6 f. 88r. PRO E36/126 f. 22v.

30. Southampton City Record Office, SC5/1/24A f. 1v. Spiro letter, 16 September 1497.

31. *Great Chronicle*, p. 282. Vitellius A XVI p. 217.

32. *CSP* Milan, pp. 327–328. *Great Chronicle*, p. 282. Vitellius A XVI, p. 217.

33. Vitellius A XVI, p. 218. *Great Chronicle*, p. 282. *CSP* Milan, p. 328.

34. PRO E404/82 unnumbered warrant for issue, dated Woodstock 25 September 1497. See also PRO E101/414/6 f.

15. *Capture and Recapture*

1. Spiro letter, 16 September 1497.

2. Corporation of London Record Office, Journal 10 f. 103r. PRO E101/414/6 ff. 88r–v, 89r. Ellis, *Letters Illustrative*, 1st ser, Vol 1, pp. 37–38.

3. Vitellius A XVI, pp. 218, 221. *Great Chronicle*, pp. 282–284. PRO E101/414/16 ff. 6v, 22v.

4. *CSP* Milan, pp. 329–330.

5. PRO E101/414/6 f. 90v.

6. *CSP* Milan, p. 329. PRO E 101/414/6/ f. 89v. *Great Chronicle*, p. 282. Vitellius A XVI, p. 217. Southampton City Record Office, SC 5/1/24A f. 1v. *The Cambrian Register* (1795), p. 123 and note.

7. *CSP* Milan, p. 328. Southampton City Record Office, SC 5/31 f. 19v. PRO E36/126 f. 22v. PRO E 101/414/6 ff. 88v, 90r–v.

8. *CSP* Milan, pp. 329–330.

9. PRO E101/414/16 f. 1r. *CSP* Milan, p. 330.

10. *CSP* Milan, p. 330.

11. PRO E101/414/16 f. 2r.

12. *Great Chronicle*, pp. 282–283, 286. Vitellius A XVI, pp. 217, 218. Corporation of London Record Office, Journal 10, f. 103r.

13. *CSP* Milan, p. 331.

14. *CPR 1494–1509*, pp. 122, 123.

15. J.A. Robinson, 'Correspondence of the Bishop Oliver King and Sir Reginald Bray', *Proceedings of the Somerset Archaeological and Natural History Society*, LX (1915), pp. 9–10.

16. PRO C1/279/47 & 48. I owe these references to the kindness of Miss Margaret Condon. *CPR 1494–1509*, p. 122.

17. Gairdner, *Richard III*, pp. 329–330.

18. Bacon, p. 186.

19. Bacon, p. 186. Vergil, p. 109.

20. PRO E36/126 f. 37v. PRO E101/517/21 24th document. *Letters and Papers*, Vol 2, pp. 73–74.

21. PRO E101/414/14 f. 5r. *Great Chronicle*, p. 283.

22. PRO E101/414/16 f. 5r. *Great Chronicle*, p. 283. Vitellius A XVI, p. 219.

23. *Great Chronicle*, p. 283. Vitellius A XVI, p. 219.

24. *CSP* Milan, p. 332.

25. *CSP* Milan, p. 333.

26. *CSP* Milan, p. 335. *Great Chronicle*, pp. 283–284. Vitellius A XVI, p. 221.

27. *CSP* Milan, p. 335.

28. Philpot, 'Maximilian and England', p. 170.

29. Philpot, 'Maximilian and England', p. 170.

30. ADN B 20135/155656.

31. Philpot, 'Maximilian and England', p. 170.

32. ADN B 2159, ff. 161v, 172r.

33. PRO E101/414/16 ff. 7r, 8r.

34. *Great Chronicle*, p. 287. Vitellius A XVI, p. 223.

35. *CPR 1494–1509*, (Smyth) pp. 8, 16, 142, 156–157; (Braybrook), pp. 38, 83, 142, 267. PRO KB9/416/22. I owe this reference to the kindness of Mr Alan Cameron.

36. Vergil, p. 111. Hall, p. 486.

37. *CSP* Venice, 1, p. 266.

38. PRO E101/414/16 ff. 6v, 9r, 19r, 24r. *Exerpta Historica*, p. 121.

39. Temperley, *Henry VII*, p. 416. *Great Chronicle*, p. 286. PRO E101/414/16 f. 24r–v.

40. Temperley, *Henry VII*, p. 416. PRO E101/414/16 ff. 24r.

41. PRO E101/414/16 ff. 27r, 29r. Temperley, *Henry VII*, p. 416.

42. PRO KB9/416/22.

43. Ford, *Perkin Warbeck*, Act V, scene III, line 78.

44. PRO E101/414/16 f. 9r. On trumpets as spies:

Arthurson, 'Espionage and Intelligence', pp. 144–145.
45. Stow, *Survey of London*, Vol 1, p. 271.
46. M.M. Condon, 'The Kaleidoscope of Treason: Fragments of the Bosworth Story', *The Ricardian*, VII (1986), pp. 208–212.
47. *53rd Report of the Deputy Keeper of the Public Records* (1892), Appendix II, pp. 32–33.
48. Stow, *Survey of London*, Vol 1, p. 265.
49. PRO E101/414/16 (1497–1498), E101/415/3 (1499–1502). Spies and 'appeachers' are otherwise regularly noted.
50. PRO KB9/416/22.
51. PRO E101/414/16 f. 30r.
52. HMC 10th Report, Appendix VI (1887), p. 2.
53. PRO E101/414/16 f. 30r-v.
54. PRO E101/414/16 f. 30r-v.
55. *Great Chronicle*, p. 287. Vitellius A XVI, p. 223.
56. Molinet, pp. 466–467.
57. *Exerpta Historica*, p. 119.
58. PRO E101/414/16 f. 30v.
59. *Great Chronicle*, p. 287. Vitellius A XVI, p. 223.
60. PRO KB9/416/22.
61. *CSP* Venice, 1, p. 269.
62. Arthurson, 'Espionage and Intelligence', p. 154.
63. *53rd Report of Deputy Keeper*, p. 33.
64. *CPR 1494–1509*, p. 215. *Letters and Papers*, Vol 1, p. 237.
65. *CPR 1494–1509*, p. 159.
66. ADN B 2162, f. 166r-v.
67. ADN B 2162, f. 164v.
68. *CSP* Spain, p. 150.
69. *CSP* Spain, p. 161.
70. *CSP* Spain, pp. 163, 188, 189.
71. *CSP* Spain, pp. 189, 195–196. *Exerpta Historica*, p. 119.
72. Temperley, *Henry VII*, p. 416. *CSP* Spain, pp. 185–186. PRO E101/414/16 f. 36r.
73. *CSP* Spain, p. 196.
74. *CSP* Spain, p. 196.
75. *CSP* Spain, p. 198.
76. *CPR 1494–1509*, pp. 124, 134. *CCR 1485–1500*, p. 313. *CCR 1500–1509*, p. 182, see p. 192 also.
77. ADN B 2163/71335.

16. *Shaking Empty Chains*

1. Arthurson, '1497', pp. 11–15.
2. *Great Chronicle*, p. 289. Vitellius A XVI, p. 225.
3. *CSP* Spain, p. 206.
4. Armstrong, *England, France and Burgundy*, pp. 157–178. J. North, *Horoscopes and History*, Warburg Institute Surveys and Texts XIII (London, 1986), pp. 142, 157–161.
5. North, *Horoscopes and History*, pp. 141–149, 156.
6. North, *Horoscopes and History*, p. 155. Bayne and Dunham, 'Select Cases in the Council of Henry VII', pp. 154–156, 158, 165, 167–8. *53rd Report of Deputy Keeper*, p. 32.
7. Stow, *Survey of London*, Vol 1, pp. 258–261. S. Thrupp, *The Merchant Class of Medieval London* (Michigan, repr 1992), p. 273.
8. Armstrong, *England, France, and Burgundy*, pp. 158, 167–171.
9. Temperley, *Henry VII*, pp. 416–417. *53rd Report of the Deputy Keeper*, pp. 31–32, 35.
10. *53rd Report of the Deputy Keeper*, p. 31.
11. *Rot. Parlt.*, p. 544. *CCR 1485–1500*, pp. 282–283. Condon, 'Kaleidoscope of Treason', pp. 209–211 and note 3.
12. Harley 433, Vol 3, p. 1. Campbell, *Materials*, Vol 2, pp. 85, 128, 377, *CPR 1494–1500*, p. 156. Note (p. 20) pardon of 20 March 1495.
13. Harley 433, Vol 2, p. 48.
14. *Exerpta Historica*, p. 99.
15. Wedgwood, *Biographies*, p. 711. P.E. Jones, ed. *Calendar of the Plea and Memoranda Rolls of the City of London 1458–1482* (Cambridge, 1961), pp. 117, 119, 145.
16. Wedgwood, *Biographies*, p. 711. *CPR 1461–1467*, p. 139. *CPR 1467–1477*, pp. 530, 531.
17. PRO E404/76/1/80 and 76/4/102. *Great Chronicle*, p. 291.
18. *CPR 1494–1509*, p. 205.
19. Horrox, *Richard III*, pp. 79, 194. Jones, *City of London Plea Rolls* etc., p. 148. Pollard, *North Eastern England*, pp. 113, 183, 194–195, 347, 353. A.F. Sutton & P.W. Hammond, *The Coronation of Richard III the Extant Documents* (Gloucester, 1983), p. 336.
20. G.H. Gater and W.H. Godfrey, 'All Hallows Barking by the Tower', *Survey of London*, XV Part II (London, 1954), pp. 1–2.
21. *53rd Report of the Deputy Keeper*, p. 31.
22. *53rd Report of the Deputy Keeper*, p. 34.
23. PRO E101/415/3 f. 161v. Temperley, *Henry VII*, pp. 416–417.
24. Bayne and Dunham, 'Select Cases in the Council of Henry VII', p. 32.
25. *53rd Report of the Deputy Keeper*, pp. 34–35. *3rd Report of the Deputy Keeper*, pp. 216–217.
26. Busch, *Henry VII*, p. 120. Busch's notes pp. 349–350 are silent about the supposed pardon.
27. *53rd Report of the Deputy Keeper*, pp. 30–36. *3rd Report of the Deputy Keeper*, pp. 216–217. Condon, 'Kaleidoscope of Treason', pp. 208–212.
28. G.W., 'Richard, Duke of York, and Perkin Warbeck', p. 310.
29. *53rd Report of the Deputy Keeper*, p. 34. Bruno Bettelheim, *The Informed Heart* (New York, Avon pb.), 1971), p. 73.
30. *3rd Report of the Deputy Keeper*, pp. 216–217.
31. *3rd Report of the Deputy Keeper*, p. 217. *53rd Report of the Deputy Keeper*, p. 34. Arthurson, 'Espionage and Intelligence', pp. 149–151 for types of codes.
32. *53rd Report of the Deputy Keeper*, pp. 34–35. *CPR 1461–1467*, p. 538. *CPR 1467–1477*, p. 420.
33. *53rd Report of the Deputy Keeper*, pp. 34–35.
34. BL Add. MS 46455, f. 136r.
35. *53rd Report of the Deputy Keeper*, pp. 32–33.
36. Thomas, *Religion and Magic*, pp. 500–501.
37. PRO E101/415/3 f. 161v. Temperley, *Henry VII*, pp. 416–417.
38. T.B. Pugh, 'Henry VII and the English Nobility', in Bernard, ed., *Tudor Nobility*, pp. 64–65, 94 note 41. Molinet, pp. 465–466.
39. Bayne and Dunham, 'Select Cases in the Council of Henry VII', p. 30. H.A. Napier, *Historical Notices of Swyncombe and Ewelme* (Oxford, 1858), pp. 168–172. *CPR 1494–1509*, p. 58.

40. Bridge, *History of France*, Vol 3, pp. 44–46.
41. *CSP* Milan, pp. 379–380. *CSP* Venice, 1, pp. 284–285.
42. PRO E101/414/16 f. 77v.
43. *CPR 1494–1509*, p. 129.
44. Bryan, *The Great Earl of Kildare*, p. 226.
45. Quinn, *Analecta Historica*, 10, p. 67.
46. *New History of Ireland*, p. 650.
47. *Letters and Papers*, Vol 1, p. 129.
48. Molinet, pp. 465–466.
49. *Letters and Papers*, Vol 1, pp. 131–134.
50. Armstrong, *England, France and Burgundy*, pp. 161–163, 175. *Exerpta Historica*, pp. 122–123.
51. Armstrong, *England, France and Burgundy*, pp. 165–166.
52. Armstrong, *England, France and Burgundy*, pp. 172 and notes 3 and 4, pp. 173–175.
53. Bayne and Dunham, 'Select Cases in the Council of Henry VII', p. 32.
54. *53rd Report of the Deputy Keeper*, pp. 30–31.
55. *Great Chronicle*, p. 291. Vitellius A XVI, p. 227.
56. *53rd Report of the Deputy Keeper*, p. 34. *3rd Report of the Deputy Keeper*, pp. 216–217.
57. *3rd Report of the Deputy Keeper*, p. 218.
58. *Great Chronicle*, p. 291.
59. *3rd Report of the Deputy Keeper*, p. 218.
60. *Great Chronicle*, pp. 291–292. *Exerpta Historica*, p. 123.
61. *Great Chronicle*, p. 291. Vitellius A XVI, p. 227.
62. *53rd Report of the Deputy Keeper*, p. 33 and footnote *.
63. *CPR 1494–1509*, p. 392.
64. *CPR 1494–1509*, p. 205.
65. *CPR 1494–1509*, p. 215.
66. Condon, 'Kaleidoscope of Treason', pp. 209–211.
67. *Great Chronicle*, p. 291. Vitellius A XVI, p. 227.
68. T. Stapleton, ed., 'The Plumpton Correspondence', *Camden Society*, Old Series 4 (1839), pp. 141–143.
69. J.S. Brewer and R.H. Brodie, *Letters Foreign and Domestic of the Reign of Henry VIII*, Vol 1, Part 1 (London, 1920), p. 8.
70. Molinet, p. 467.
71. *Great Chronicle*, p. 291. Vitellius A XVI, p. 227.
72. Molinet, p. 467.
73. *Great Chronicle*, p. 291.

Further Reading

Further reading on any subject of the English 1490s cannot claim to be comprehensive. Unlike the Yorkist period which precedes it, and Henry VIII's reign which follows it, Henry VII's reign has not been well served by narrative historians. There are only three narratives all written over 70 years ago: Gladys Temperley's 1917 biography *Henry VII*, James Gairdner's *Henry the Seventh* of 1906, and Wilhelm Busch's *England under the Tudors*, 1, *King Henry VII*, published in English in 1895.

The Wars of the Roses

The background to the events of this book is the Wars of the Roses. They may best be followed in survey form in Charles Ross's *Wars of the Roses* (London, 1976) or Anthony Goodman's *The Wars of the Roses. Military Activity and English Society, 1452–1490* (London, 1981). R.A. Griffiths, *The Reign of Henry VI* (London, 1981), Charles Ross's *Edward IV* (London, 1974) and *Richard III* (London, 1981) form a solid core of political biographies. In the last few years historians' concerns have turned to some of the themes touched on in the opening chapters of this book. Loyalty, a subject in the recent past dismissed as of little importance, is now being re-examined. The most profound study of loyalty and loyalties is Rosemary Horrox's 1989 book *Richard III. A Study in Service*; and my great debt to her is obvious. In 1987 I published, 'A Question of Loyalty', *The Ricardian*, VII, and in 1989 M.A. Hicks published a second paper on the subject which can be found in that author's *Richard III and his Rivals* (London, 1991). Honour is examined in M.E. James's *Past and Present Supplement*, 3, 'English Politics and the Concept of Honour 1485–1642'. The subject of exiles has not attracted a great deal of attention. R.A. Griffiths and R.S. Thomas, *The Making of the Tudor Dynasty* (Gloucester, 1985) perforce has exile as one of its studies, and W.E. Hampton's two articles 'The White Rose under the First Tudors' Parts 2 and 3, *The Ricardian*, VII (1987) track Edmund and Richard de la Pole across late medieval Europe.

Prophecy, Astrology, Espionage

Much of the writing about late fifteenth-century politicians has its objects of study rationally calculating chances: militarily, politically or tenurially. It is clear, however, that chances were taken irrationally and intuitively. The mental world of the late fifteenth century can be entered in Johan Huizinga's classic *The Waning of the Middle Ages*. The background to the prophetic utterances which buoyed up the spirits of high and low alike is investigated by Keith Thomas's *Religion and the Decline of Magic* (Penguin books). Here are sleeping heroes and returning princes. The propaganda value of such ideas is explored by Alison Allan in 'Yorkist Propaganda: Pedigree, Prophecy and the "British History" in the Reign of Edward IV', in *Patronage, Pedigree and Power*, edited by Charles Ross (Gloucester, 1979). Texts of prophecies, many of which circulated during the Wars of the Roses and were then adapted in the sixteenth century, can be read first-hand in S.L. Jansen, *Political Protest and Prophecy under Henry VIII* (Woodbridge, 1991). The essential early modern overview of astrology and its connections with prophecy is found in Keith Thomas's book. But the seminal article as far as this study is concerned is C.A.J. Armstrong's 1960 paper 'An Italian Astrologer at the Court of Henry VII'; republished in *England, France and Burgundy* (London, 1983). Hilary Carey's 1992 *Courting Disaster* surveys the subject. Espionage, as dingy a subject as astrology, is investigated by M. Ballard and C.S.L. Davies in 'Étienne Fryon: Burgundian Agent, English Royal Secretary and "Principal Counsellor" to Perkin Warbeck', *Bulletin of the Institute of Historical Research*, 62 (1989) and in my 'Espionage and Intelligence from the Wars of the Roses to the Reformation', *Nottingham Medieval Studies*, XXXV (1991).

Perkin Warbeck

Perkin Warbeck has been the subject of a number of treatments, dramatic, historical and fictional. Essential reading would pass by all the heavy-handed seventeenth-century studies of Warbeck – Buck and Gainsford, and even the accessible Bacon – in favour of John Ford's 1634 play, *The Chronicle History of Perkin Warbeck A Strange Truth*. Act V gets closer to the strangeness of Warbeck than anything else we have. A collection of documents in print since 1838, Frederic Madden's 'Documents relating to the History of Perkin Warbeck', *Archaeologia*, XXVII, prints letters, ambassadorial instructions and Bernard de Vignolles' deposition about John Kendal. More documents can be found in Diana Kleyn's *Richard of England* (Kensal Press, Oxford, 1990) which reprints Chastel de la

Howarderie's information about the Warbeck family. For those convinced that Warbeck was the Duke of York, and therefore unconvinced by this work, Kleyn's is the Yorkist apologia and has a comprehensive bibliography of works of a similar conviction. A.J. Pollard, *Richard III and the Princes in the Tower* (Stroud, 1991), concludes that the real Richard Duke of York was dead probably by September 1483. Those who want their documents without a gloss are referred to the observation of Warbeck and his patrons recorded in the *Calendars of State Papers* relating to England and Milan, Venice and Spain. All the diplomacy is here, as are a number of first-hand descriptions of Warbeck between 1497 and 1499. Less easily read are the London chronicles, *The Great Chronicle*, privately printed in 1938 and the Vitellius A XVI Chronicle published in C.L. Kingsford's *Chronicles of London* (Oxford, 1905, reprinted Dursley, 1977), but they provide memorable stories about Perkin, as does the Burgundian historiographer Jean Molinet in his *Chroniques*, ed. G. Doutrepont and O. Jodogne, 3 vols (Brussels, 1935). Extracts from many of these sources, but not Molinet, can be found in A.F. Pollard, *The Reign of Henry VII from Contemporary Sources*, 3 vols (London, 1913–1914). Volume 1 contains material on Warbeck, Volume 3, Irish Material.

Places, Commerce, Exploration

To follow Warbeck before his fall, in Cork, is to discover the individuality of places in late medieval Europe. Still a good starting place is the *New Cambridge Modern History*, Volume 1, *The Renaissance 1493–1520* (Cambridge, 1961). This contains an excellent chapter on The Burgundian Netherlands, 1477–1521 by C.A.J. Armstrong, and much more besides. The full Flemish social background is available for the first time in English in David Nicholas's *Medieval Flanders* (London, 1992). The brilliance of that culture can be seen in print in W. Prevenier and W. Blockmans, *The Burgundian Netherlands* (Cambridge, 1986). A series of pioneering studies of England and Burgundy in the Wars of the Roses is found in C.A.J. Armstrong's *England, France and Burgundy in the Fifteenth Century*. The best introduction to medieval Ireland is now Art Cosgrove, ed., *A New History of Ireland*, Volume 2, *Medieval Ireland 1169–1534* (Oxford, 2nd ed. 1993). All aspects of Irish life, literature, architecture and trade are here. So much of Warbeck's story is bound up with commerce that the reader should look at Fernand Braudel's massive 3-volume work on *Civilization and Capitalism 15th–18th Century* (London, 1982–1984): *The Structures of Everyday Life, The Wheels of Commerce, The Perspective of the World*. Its maps and pictures alone make it worth dipping in to. Exploration can be followed in the most up-to-date study, W.D. Phillips, Jr. and C.R. Phillips, *The Worlds of Christopher Columbus* (Cambridge, 1992) and in the volumes of the Hakluyt Society. This provides a wonderful repository of extracts of Portuguese chronicles in translation. Portugal itself has been well served by H.V. Livermore who has provided a number of studies of Portuguese history, popular and academic, over a period of thirty years. The English dimension to maritime history, with connections military, political and cutural, is to be found in D.B. Quinn, *England and the Discovery of America, 1481–1620* (London, 1974).

People

After the fall, Warbeck's story is less of place and more of people. His and his masters' advancement depended on their ruthless exploitation of personal contacts. Political France is still well served by John S.C. Bridge's 3-volume, 1921-9 study, *A History of France from the Death of Louis XI*. Christine Weightman's 1989 biography of Margaret of York, Duchess of Burgundy, is an all-round picture. But for our purposes Wim Blockmans, 'The Devotions of a Lonely Duchess', is the single most penetrating modern study, in T. Kren, ed., *Margaret of York, Simon Marmion and the Visions of Tondal* (Malibu, California, 1992). Margaret's great ally, Maximilian I, is the subject of two German works, the older H. Ulmann, *Kaiser Maximilian I*, 2 vols (Stuttgart, 1884, 1891) and the modern H. Weisflecker, *Kaiser Maximilian I*, 5 vols (Munich, 1971–1986). C.A.J. Armstrong has much to say on Maximilian in the *New Cambridge Modern*, as does Bridge in his *History of France*. The irrational, quirky, nature of the man is explored in Gerhard Benecke's *Maximilian I (1459–1519): an analytical biography* (London, 1982). Maximilian also figures in Norman Macdougall's recent biography of his ally of the 1490s, *James IV* (Edinburgh, 1989). Irish personalities of the late Middle Ages have few biographers, the notable exception being Donough Bryan's *Gerald Fitzgerald the Great Earl of Kildare, 1456–1513*, (Dublin and Cork, 1933). However, in *A New History of Ireland* D.B. Quinn provides numerous lightning sketches of Gaelic chieftains and Anglo-Irish lords. Agnes Conway's *Henry VII's Relations with Scotland and Ireland, 1485–1498* (Cambridge, 1932) places Anglo-Irish families and members of the English administration in Ireland. She provided the basic understanding of her subject and prints a substantial number of important letters and official documents. The easiest way into the biographical thickets of the English ruling class is through the twelve volumes of the *Complete Peerage* and Josiah Wedgwood's *Biographies of the Members of the House of Commons, 1439–1509* (London, 1936). A superb guide to the careers of Richard III's retinue and affinity is Rosemary Horrox's, *Richard III*. This volume combines both a structural and a functional approach to politics. But in the case of William Stanley we are, unfortunately, obliged to choose between the structural and the functional. Christine Carpenter's *Locality and Polity* (Cambridge, 1992), in which Stanley figures, is largely structural, as also is M.K. Jones, 'Sir William Stanley of Holt: politics and family allegiance in the late fifteenth century', *Welsh History Review*, 14 (1988). Less concerned with structures of patronage or violence is D. Clayton's *The Administration of the County Palatine of Chester 1442–1485*, Chetham Society, 3rd ser, Vol 35 (Manchester, 1990), which, as its title suggests, emphasizes the workings of government as well as its structure. This book describes Sir William Stanley's repeated support of York and his behaviour in political crises. Henry VII as man is still well served by the final chapter of S.B. Chrimes, *Henry VII* (London, 1977), 'The King's Grace'.

Index of Principal Names

In view of the nature of this work and the ambiguity attending the persons of Richard Plantagenet, Duke of York (born 1473) and Perkin Warbeck of Tournai neither has an entry in this index.